Essays Toward a Symbolic of Motives, 1950–1955

Parlor Press books by Kenneth Burke

Letters from Kenneth Burke to William H. Rueckert,
1959–1987, edited by William H. Rueckert (2003)

Kenneth Burke on Shakespeare, edited by Scott L. Newstok (2006)

Essays Toward a Symbolic of Motives, 1950–1955,
edited by William H. Rueckert (2007)

Equipment for Living: The Literary Reviews of Kenneth Burke,
edited by Nathaniel Rivers and Ryan Weber (2007)

Parlor Press books authored by William H. Rueckert

Faulkner from Within: Destructive and Generative
Being in the Novels of William Faulkner (2004)

Essays Toward a Symbolic of Motives, 1950–1955

Kenneth Burke

Selected, Arranged, and Edited by

William H. Rueckert

Parlor Press
West Lafayette, Indiana
www.parlorpress.com

Parlor Press LLC, 816 Robinson Street, West Lafayette, Indiana 47906

Permission to reprint selections in this volume are acknowledged in the chapters themselves. For their support of this project, we are grateful to The Kenneth Burke Literary Trust, the *Chicago Review*, the *Hudson Review*, the National Society for the Study of Education, the *Sewanee Review*, and Mrs. Eva Hindus.

S A N: 2 5 4 – 8 8 7 9

Library of Congress Cataloging-in-Publication Data

Burke, Kenneth, 1897–1993.
  Essays toward a symbolic of motives, 1950–1955 / Kenneth Burke ; selected, arranged and edited by William H. Rueckert.
    p. cm.
  Includes bibliographical references and index.
  ISBN 1–932559–34–5 (pbk. : alk. paper) -- ISBN 1–932559–35–3 (hardcover : alk. paper) -- ISBN 1–932559–36–1 (adobe ebk.)
  1. Symbolism in literature. 2. Literary form. I. Rueckert, William H. (William Howe), 1926– II. Title.

PN56.S9B87 2006
809'.912--dc22

2006034891

Cover and book design by David Blakesley
Printed on acid-free paper.

Parlor Press, LLC is an independent publisher of scholarly and trade titles in print and multimedia formats. This book is available in paperback, cloth, and Adobe eBook formats from Parlor Press on the Internet at http://www.parlorpress.com or through online and brick-and-mortar bookstores. For submission information or to find out about Parlor Press publications, write to Parlor Press, 816 Robinson St., West Lafayette, Indiana, 47906, or e-mail editor@parlorpress.com.

For David Blakesley and Barbara Rueckert,
Dedicated Burkeans
—WHR

Contents

Preface

The purpose of this collection is to finally make available in a single volume the essential texts, some long out of print and hard to come by, some never published, from Burke's earliest version of *A Symbolic of Motives*. Some of the texts included here have been readily available in *Language as Symbolic Action*—such as the "Goethe's *Faust*, Part I" essay—but others have not, and they include most of the rest of the material in this collection. I have briefly discussed all of these selections in the Introduction, "Versions of *A Symbolic of Motives*."

I am a big believer in the power of books, of having things readily available in a single volume one can take off the shelf and study over and over again. I have known most of the essays for a long time, but it has always been my ambition to have them in a single book on the shelf next to Burke's other books. Thanks to David Blakesley, Parlor Press, and my wife Barbara, I have finally realized that ambition in this, my last, Burke project.

William H. Rueckert
Fairport, NY
January, 2003

Introduction

WE KNOW OF AT LEAST THREE VERSIONS OF *A SYMBOLIC OF MOTIVES:* there is the one that I have assembled here, which is now called *Essays Toward A Symbolic of Motives, 1950–1955*. It consists of selected essays from among those Burke wrote and published between 1950 and 1955, which he clearly indicated were to be part of *A Symbolic of Motives,* as he originally conceived it. He has left us various lists indicating which of these essays were to be part of *A Symbolic of Motives*. The most complete list[1] can be found at the end of his essay, "Linguistic Approach to Problems of Education" (1955). I have included selections from that essay in this collection, as well as the list of items Burke added in a footnote at the end of the essay. The second version of *A Symbolic of Motives* is called *Poetics, Dramatistically Considered,* which

---

[1] At the end of "Linguistic Approach to Problems of Education" (1955), Burke writes:

A work now in preparation, *A Symbolic of Motives,* will deal with poetics and the technique of "indexing" literary works. Meanwhile, among articles by the present author already published on this subject are: "The Vegetal Radicalism of Theodore Roethke" (*Sewanee Review,* Winter 1950); "Three Definitions" (*Kenyon Review,* Spring, 1951); "*Othello:* An Essay to Illustrate a Method" (*Hudson Review,* Summer, 1951); "Form and Persecution in the *Oresteia*" (*Sewanee Review,* Summer, 1952); "Imitation" (*Accent,* Autumn, 1952); "*Ethan Brand:* A Preparatory Investigation" (*Hopkins Review,* Winter, 1952); "Mysticism as a Solution to the Poet's Dilemma" (in collaboration with Stanley Romaine Hopper (*Spiritual Problems in Contemporary Literature,* edited by Stanley Romaine Hopper, published by Institute for Religious and Social Studies, distributed by Harper & Bros., 1952); "Fact, Inference, and Proof in the Analysis of Literary Symbolism" (paper presented at Thirteen Conference on Science, Philosophy, and Religion, and published in a volume distributed by Harper & Bros., 1954).

Burke wrote and assembled from published and unpublished material from 1957 to 1958, during the year he spent as a Fellow at the Center for Advanced Study in the Behavioral Sciences at Stanford University. Burke sent me a copy of this manuscript in 1959, after I first wrote to him. He also sent it to others and distributed it in multi-lithographed form to his classes at the Indiana School of Letters. Many Burke scholars are familiar with this manuscript. David Cratis Williams has written a long, comprehensive essay on this manuscript, which he included in *Unending Conversations,* the volume of Burke studies and writings that he edited with Greig Henderson in 2001. The third version of *A Symbolic of Motives* is actually called *A Symbolic of Motives.* I first saw this manuscript when Anthony Burke sent me a copy after he discovered it among Burke's papers in the house at Andover after Burke's death in 1993. As far as we can now tell from Burke's letters to me and others, Burke put this version of *A Symbolic of Motives* together from published and unpublished material around 1963. We know that Burke gave copies of it to others, like Trevor Melia when he was at Pittsburgh, long before I ever saw it, but that nobody ever did anything with it until I sent a copy to David Cratis Williams while he and Greig Henderson were choosing the material that would go into *Unending Conversations.* This was Burke's last serious attempt to prepare a coherent, sustained version of *A Symbolic of Motives.* He abandoned this manuscript midway through Part 2 while he was revising and shortening his long essay entitled "The Thinking of the Body." This essay must have been written sometime after 1955. Burke included a long version of it in *Poetics, Dramatistically Considered,* published it separately in *The Psychoanalytic Review* in 1963, and included a shortened version of it in *Language as Symbolic Action.* Although there are references to a Part 3 in this third version of *A Symbolic of Motives,* there is no indication anywhere of what Burke intended to include in Part 3. We know from his letters that Burke was still struggling with *A Symbolic of Motives* in 1969 after Libbie died when he spent some time at Yaddo in Saratoga Springs. Burke finally abandoned his attempts to put any kind of version of *A Symbolic of Motives* together in the late 1970s.

What we have, then, are three versions of *A Symbolic of Motives* and more than twenty years of struggle on Burke's part while whatever *A Symbolic of Motives* was to be underwent a whole series of transformations in his mind and in his published and unpublished work.

Burke began work on *A Symbolic of Motives* as soon as he finished *A Rhetoric of Motives* in 1950. His intention from the very beginning was to write a dramatistic poetics to go with his dramatistic *A Grammar of Motives* and *A Rhetoric of Motives*. By 1955, he clearly had enough written and published on this project to make a book called *A Symbolic of Motives*. But there were some problems that must have stopped him. He did not like Prentice-Hall and did not want to go on with them as his publisher. He had begun his relationship with Hermes in 1951 and was engaged, with them, in reissuing all of his books from the 1930s, plus his first book of poetry, *A Book of Moments*. His work on the poetics also was bogged down in his attempt to work out the physiological counterparts of his theory of catharsis—the central concept in his poetics. He began to do this in an essay called "The Thinking of the Body" in which he tries to show that the pity, fear, and pride that were purged in tragedy, according to Aristotle, had their physiological counterparts in the sexual, urinal, and fecal purges of the body, which Burke had identified as the "demonic trinity" in his *A Grammar of Motives*. Burke began to insist that no catharsis was complete until these bodily purges had been expressed in the imagery of a given work. Burke's long essay "The Thinking of the Body" is an attempt to prove this thesis and involves him in some of the most tortured and absurd analyses he ever wrote, most of which are dependent upon the analysis of what he takes to be puns and hidden references to what he liked to call the no-no realm of the three bodily functions mentioned above. The absurdities to which proving this thesis led Burke can be clearly seen in the final pages of the third version of *A Symbolic of Motives* in which he revises and shortens "The Thinking of the Body" essay and offers us long lists of the many kinds of references that could be functioning as puns and hidden references to various kinds of bodily purgative functions.

Burke was very busy with a variety of projects between 1950 and 1961 when *The Rhetoric of Religion* was published and then again in the early and mid-1960s when he resolved his problems about a publisher and began his happy relationship with the University of California Press—thanks largely to the work of Bob Zachary. *A Symbolic of Motives* got lost in all of this because Burke still could not decide what to do with it or how to put together what he had written to make a book. The closest he came to presenting us with a coherent version of his dramatistic poetics was in *Poetics, Dramatistically Considered* which, although it seems complete as it stands, Burke never seemed inclined to have published as a book but let circulate as a manuscript for all of those years. Burke did include material that was clearly part of all three versions of *A Symbolic of Motives* in *Language as Symbolic Action,* and although he did occasionally try to work on *A Symbolic of Motives* after that, he had really abandoned the project because in most ways, his dramatistic poetics was all written in one form or another and complete for anyone who wanted to take the trouble to assemble the different essays and manuscripts and work the theory and methodology out. As usual, Burke was ready to move on to new projects, and did, after *Language as Symbolic Action.* Libbie Burke's death in 1969, after her long terminal illness, was a devastation to Burke. Libbie Burke was always a great champion of *A Symbolic of Motives.* We know that she typed the third version and that she kept at Burke to finish this grand project. Had she stayed well and lived, he might have brought it to closure. As it was, Burke lost his drive to make books, although he never lost his drive to keep writing, to keep working out his latest project, which was logology. He worked on with great energy and intellectual vigor until 1984 when he finally completed the two new afterwords for *Permanence and Change* and *Attitudes toward History.* But he never resumed work on his *Symbolic of Motives* after 1969, even though he refers to it in notes for some of his essays in the 1970s.

If we want to know what Burke's never-published *A Symbolic of Motives* is all about, what his dramatistic poetics consisted of, we have to work our way through all three of his versions of it and sort them out to try to determine the transformations that the original conception of it went through and why, as David Cratis Williams has argued, Burke was never able to settle on any single conception of what *A Symbolic of Motives* was to be. Here, then, is a brief summary of what we have in the three versions that Burke left us between 1950, when he first began writing the essays that were to go into *A Symbolic of Motives* and what he took out of these different versions to include in *Language as Symbolic Action* in 1966. The three versions have the following titles in what follows: *Essays Toward A Symbolic of Motives, 1950–1955, Poetics, Dramatistically Considered* (1957–1958), and *A Symbolic of Motives* (1963–1964), and, finally, *Language as Symbolic Action* (1966). All of these versions of what might have been in *A Symbolic of Motives* had Burke ever decided to make a book or books of it have been discussed at some length in my book, *Kenneth Burke and the Drama of Human*

Relations, 2nd edition, and by David Cratis Williams and I in our essays in *Unending Conversations.* Other Burke scholars, such as Robert
Wess, have also discussed them. Hopefully, at some future point, all
three versions will be published and we will have all the necessary texts
readily available to us for study and analysis.

In *Essays Toward A Symbolic of Motives, 1950–1955,* I have selected only some of the major essays Burke wrote and published in this
time period while he was still working from his original conception
of what *A Symbolic of Motives* should be, as he defined it in *A Rhetoric of Motives.* Burke's grand plan for his dramatistic project was to
follow Aristotle and write a modern grammar, rhetoric, poetics, and
ethics. Working with a five-year schedule, Burke published *A Grammar of Motives* in 1945, *A Rhetoric of Motives* in 1950 and was ready, it
seems, to publish *A Symbolic of Motives* in 1955, and, presumably, his
Ethics of Motives by 1960, at the end of a twenty-year period of prodigious work and thought. But Burke became a victim of his own genius and his tendency to succumb to what he has called the "counter-
gridlock motive." In the twenty years after *A Rhetoric of Motives* was
published, which were certainly among the most productive years of
Burke's long and productive life, he pursued one project after another:
he finished up his work on Dramatism with his omnibus *Language as
Symbolic Action* collection of essays; he began work on Logology with
The Rhetoric of Religion; he had his books from the 1930s reissued by
Hermes, he found a new publisher for *The Rhetoric of Religion* in The
Beacon Press, and began his relationship with the University of California Press which, at one time in the 1970s had all of Burke's books
in print at the same time; he traveled and taught and lectured all over
the United States; he became famous both here and abroad. It is no
wonder, then, that *A Symbolic of Motives* never got assembled and published as a book, though it certainly got finished—that is, thoroughly
worked out—as Burke's dramatistic poetics. What we lack is not the
dramatistic poetics, but a definitive version of it as selected and arranged by Burke. Burke was a great reviser and a careful arranger of
the material that was included in his published books. But he did not
leave any instructions as to how he would have put *A Symbolic of Motives* together in one or, probably, two volumes, and although he left
us lists of essays written between 1950 and 1955 that were to be part
of his *Symbolic of Motives,* he did not indicate how to arrange them or

even which ones would have survived and been included when final decisions had to be made.

I have arranged the material included in *Essays Toward A Symbolic of Motives, 1950–1955* in a logical rather than a chronological way. The essays in Part I are methodological in the sense that they represent points of departure for a dramatistic analysis. The essay on "Imitation" is common to all versions of *A Symbolic of Motives* in one form or another because Burke kept revising it when he did later versions. It is essential to Burke's dramatistic analysis because it redefines imitation to include the essential Burkean conception of entelechy—or the drive toward perfection intrinsic to language and to all forms of imitation and to literature in general. Burke loved definitions, as we can see in "Three Definitions," and always preferred to work from them, as is obvious in the individual analyses in Part II or in Burke's "Definition of Man" in *Language as Symbolic Action*. In "The Language of Poetry 'Dramatistically' Considered, Part 1," Burke uses the classic definitions for the three main functions of language (to teach, to please, to persuade) and adds a fourth, to portray, as a way of understanding what it is poetry (literature in general) does. The final methodological essays, "Fact, Inference, and Proof" defines and illustrates two of Burke's most basic analytic approaches to a text, Indexing and Joycing (pun analysis) and uses Joyce's *Portrait of the Artist As a Young Man* to illustrate the application of these analytic techniques. Both are featured in all of Burke's dramatistic analyses of individual texts. Properly understood, Indexing is the key to Burke's theory of what a literary text is and how it works, and Joycing is one of the keys to Burke's theory that words contain multiple meanings.

Part 2 contains five essays that show Burke at work on individual texts and the work of individual authors—Roethke ("The Vegetal Radicalism of Theodore Roethke," 1950) and Whitman ("Policy Made Personal: Whitman's Verse and Prose-Salient Traits," 1955). Two of these essays—"The *Oresteia*," 1952, and "*Othello*: an Essay to Illustrate a Method," 1951—work out Burke's theory of tragedy as an imitation of a tension, and the other, "*Ethan Brand*: A Preparatory Investigation," 1952, is one of the best examples we have of how Burke sets up a text in order to go to work on it. All of Burke's literary criticism is characterized by an emphasis on individual texts and what he liked to call their labyrinthine internal consistency.

The two selections in Part 3 are intended to explain, in different ways, what Burke means by "socioanagogic" and why he selected whole texts as his representative anecdotes. The selections from "Linguistic Approach to Problems of Education," 1955, is probably Burke's most concise and articulate discursive explanation of why he analyzes texts the way he does; and the analysis of "Goethe's *Faust*, Part 1," 1955, is probably Burke's most brilliant and comprehensive dramatistic analysis of a single text we have. Only his analysis of "*Othello:* an Essay to Illustrate a Method" can really be compared to it for what it tells us about Burke's dramatistic poetics and what it reveals to us about Burke as a literary critic.

I have deliberately minimized my commentary on these selections because, for one thing, I have discussed this material before in *Kenneth Burke and the Drama of Human Relations* and because I want readers to encounter Burke's analyses directly and experience the full force of his encounters with these great texts and, to use his own terminology, to "earn" them for themselves. These early essays that Burke wrote for *A Symbolic of Motives* are among the most concentrated and most detailed analyses of individual texts that Burke ever wrote in his long involvement with literature. They reveal Burke at the height of his powers as a reader (analyzer and interpreter) of texts, fulfilling his own definition that the original *A Symbolic of Motives* should be devoted to the study of individual, self-contained symbolic actions and structures.

If we take the list of essays that I have included in *Essays Toward A Symbolic of Motives, 1950–1955*, all of which are on Burke's 1955 list of what was to be included in *A Symbolic of Motives*, and compare it to the contents of *Poetics, Dramatistically Considered*, his second version of *A Symbolic of Motives*, which he wrote and assembled in 1957 and 1958, we have a ready way to see what transformations occurred in Burke's conception of *A Symbolic of Motives* between the first and second versions. It is easy to do this by noting, what, based on version one, has been included, excluded, and added in version two.

Poetics, Dramatistically Considered

Table of Contents
1. Poetics," "Aesthetic," and Artistic
2. Logic of the Terms
3. Imitation (Mimesis)

Still to come, Burke says in a note, are a section on comic catharsis, further references to individual works, footnotes indicating other developments, and an appendix reprinting various related essays.

First of all, note that the only individual text left for analysis in this list is the *Orestes* trilogy and that all of the other individual texts and individual author analysis have been excluded. What has been added is all of the new material on catharsis: "Catharsis, First View," "Pity, Fear and Pride," "The Thinking of the Body," "Beyond Catharsis" and "Catharsis, Second View." It is true that there are many references to individual texts in all this new material on catharsis, but there are no sustained analyses like the one of "*Ethan Brand:* A Preparatory Investigation," "*Othello:* An Essay to Illustrate a Method," and "Goethe's *Faust,* Part I" nor any analyses like those of Roethke and Whitman. Also gone is most of the material I included in *Essays Toward A Symbolic of Motives, 1950–1955*, Part 1, especially items 2, 3, and 4. What is left or still included is the essay on "A 'Dramatistic' View of Imitation" and multiple references to Aristotle, drama, and tragedy. Most of *Poetics, Dramatistically Considered* works out a theory of drama, tragedy, and literature in general as symbolic action. The major emphasis in *Poetics, Dramatistically Considered* is on catharsis, both as Aristotle defines it and as Burke redefines it, adding pride to pity and fear, and adding the whole concept of body thinking (the demonic trinity, the physiological counterparts of pity, fear and pride—the sexual, urinal, and fecal—to the cathartic process. Catharsis—the purgative redemptive motive—has been at the center of Burke's thinking about literature since *The Philosophy of Literary Form*, but what is added in *Poetics, Dramatistically Considered* is what Burke describes as his great "breakthrough" in his thinking about his dramatistic poetics, which is "The Thinking of the Body" essay, and Burke's insistence in that essay that, to be complete, all cathartic experiences must also express the three major bodily motives, or Freud's cloacal motive, the whole realm of privacy. As Burke says in his note on this essay, once this idea occurred to him about the thinking of the body, it ran away with him and he used his considerable intellectual powers and ingenuity to work the idea out and to apply it, with his usual thoroughness, to a great variety of most unlikely texts. The original version of this essay in *Poetics, Dramatistically Considered* is 104 typescript pages. All the later, revised versions are much shorter.

After *Poetics, Dramatistically Considered* in 1957 and 1958, Burke was preoccupied with other matters than *A Symbolic of Motives*—chiefly with logology and *The Rhetoric of Religion,* which he had begun writing, and with the Hermes editions of his works of the 1930s. Burke did not go back to his *A Symbolic of Motives* until the early 1960s after *The Rhetoric of Religion* was published in 1961 and he had written the final chapter for it, his masterful dialogue between TL (The Lord) and S (Satan), "Epilogue: Prologue in Heaven." When he did go back to *A Symbolic of Motives,* probably in 1963, he wrote and assembled what I have called the third version of *A Symbolic of Motives,* the manuscript that was actually called *A Symbolic of Motives* and was more about 270 pages long and clearly a sustained and coherent effort to rethink his *A Symbolic of Motives* by choosing a different point of departure (*A Symbolic of Motives,* third version, begins where *Poetics, Dramatistically Considered* ends, with an essay called "The Poetic Motive" (see the table of contents for this manuscript in *Unending Conversations*) and proceeding in a very orderly fashion in Part 1 from language in general, to poetry in particular, and then to imitation, catharsis, examples from many different kinds of literary works, tragedy, and finally his breakthrough in the much-revised "Thinking of the Body" material in Part 2, where the manuscript abruptly ends.

The history of *A Symbolic of Motives* after this point gets very complicated because of the essays Burke decided to write in the 1960s and because of what he decided to include in *Language as Symbolic Action* in 1966 from his earlier versions of *A Symbolic of Motives* and from the many essays he wrote in the early 1960s. From the earlier version of *A Symbolic of Motives,* Burke included the Roethke essay (1950), a revised and shortened version of his *Oresteia* essay (1952), the whole of the

"Goethe's *Faust,* Part I" essay (1955) which was originally published as parts 2 and 3 of "The Language of Poetry Dramatistically Considered," "The Poetic Motive" (1958), "The Thinking of the Body" (1957–1958) in a shortened, revised version, which first appeared in full in *Poetics, Dramatistically Considered,* various versions of essays on language in general and poetry in particular that were part of *A Symbolic of Motives,* version three, and *Poetics, Dramatistically Considered.* Burke also included all of the literary essays he wrote in the early 1960s in Part 2 of *Language as Symbolic Action,* which really completed work on his dramatistic poetics when combined or added to what we have in the three earlier versions of *A Symbolic of Motives* and the long essay on St. Augustine's *Confessions* that he included in *The Rhetoric of Religion.* Burke seldom wrote about literary texts after 1966, one of the few exceptions being his 1969 essay on *King Lear* ("Form and Psychosis in *King Lear*"). He was done with his dramatistic poetics and focused his mind and energy on logology, which was his successor to dramatism. *Language as Symbolic Action* is really the culmination of Burke's long involvement with dramatism, which began after *The Philosophy of Literary Form* (1941) and lasted for the next twenty-five years.

Burke maybe showed more sense than most of the critics who kept asking him when he was going to finish his Symbolic—or, as he referred to it in his years with one of his wonderful puns, his Sin Ballix. He kept insisting that it was done and that all of it had been published or was available in manuscripts so why make a fuss about getting it out in a single book. Yes and no to that. Much of it had been published, but going back over the documents as I have done here, one realizes that by 1993 when Burke died, much of what had been published was out-of-print or that Burke had revised and shortened many of the original essays so that it was not really possible to get a sense of the nature of Burke's achievement in his mature years as a literary critic. In fact, Burke has sort of been forgotten as a literary critic as scholars have become absorbed in working out dramatism or logology or Burke's comic perspective or his rhetoric and his language theory and the place of all this in the whole movement toward explaining everything in terms of language that has prevailed in recent years. Burke, of course, encouraged this because of the centrality of language in both dramatism and logology and the emphasis on rhetoric throughout his work and his insistence that his work is really primarily about the drama of human relations (*On Human Nature*) rather than literature.

My purpose here in collecting some of the early essays Burke wrote for his *A Symbolic of Motives* is to reclaim a little of Burke for literary criticism. I first encountered Burke in his capacity as a literary critic and it was with his literary criticism that I did my first serious work on him way back when. I have been down a lot of different roads with Burke since then, so I suppose it is most appropriate that I end up where I began in this attempt to reclaim some of him for literature and literary criticism, which after all were my own fields for all my years of teaching and writing. It seems ironic to me now that when I began writing on Burke in the late 1950s, all of the essays that I have collected here were available for study, but what eventually happened to his *A Symbolic of Motives* over the years through 1966 was not, and it is only after Burke died and finally let go of all this material (because he would not agree to any arrangement of it while he was alive), that it became possible to finally study the unpublished manuscripts as well as all of the published material and begin to make sense out of it and see it for what it is and rediscover the power and resourcefulness of Burke's dramatistic poetics.

Hopefully, another scholar will do for the third version of *A Symbolic of Motives* what David Cratis Williams has done for *Poetics, Dramatistically Considered"* and then someone will come along and put all these dramatistic poetics texts into their appropriate place in relation to Burke's other books and dramatism as a whole and establish or re-establish Burke's proper place in the history of modern American literary criticism.

—William H. Rueckert

Essays Toward a Symbolic of Motives, 1950–1955

Part 1

Some Basic Requirements for a Dramatistic Poetic

1

A "Dramatistic" View
of "Imitation"[1]

[This is an excerpt from a much longer essay concerned with the "carving out" of a Poetics, and taking Aristotle's treatise as its point of departure. Its stress upon "Dramatism," as contrasted with "scientism," is in no way meant to imply a derogation of science as such. The "Dramatistic" perspective approaches the poem in terms of *action,* whereas "scientism" approaches the poem in terms of *knowledge.* And the author would contend that, though poems, and even works of sheer persuasion, may have value as information, or "news," the direct approach to their nature as forms is not through such a route.

Any scientific work can be studied purely for its persuasiveness or beauty (i.e., as rhetoric or poetic); any rhetorical work can be studied purely for its beauty or truth (i.e., as pure poetry or as scientific information); and any poem can be studied either as a piece of rhetorical exhortation or as a means of purveying information (news, knowledge, science). But *essentially, culminatively,* it is only *scientific* works that should be approached *directly* in terms of truth, knowledge, perception, and the like. (Unless we have overlooked it, the word "truth" does not appear in the *Poetics.* It does, however, appear in many scientistically tinged translations.)

In the present pages, we consider Aristotle's key term, *mimesis,* from this point of view, as we try to show how the *culminative* emphasis in his notion of the "entelechy" was obscured by a notion of representa-

---

¹ *Accent* 12.4 (August 1952): 229–41. © The Kenneth Burke Literary Trust. Used by permission.

tion that is nearer to the stress upon the average or "statistical" as a test of the representative. Othello, for instance, would be a "culminative" or "entelechial" depiction of a jealous husband. He is not the statistical average (though some people seem to think they have reclaimed him for science by discovering that there actually was one notorious case of a Moor who strangled his wife in Shakespeare's time).]

"DRAMATISTICALLY," WE WOULD ADMONISH that "imitation" and "representation" are not wholly adequate translations of *mimesis.* These words are slightly too "scientist" in their connotations. There is no reason to replace them, particularly since the usage has been established by so many centuries of tradition—and there are no handier equivalents anyhow. We need merely to point out the respects in which, unless we deliberately make allowance for differences between the original word and its translations, the translations can mislead.

First, when you are told that drama is "the imitation of an action" (sometimes also phrased as "imitation of life" or "imitation of nature") you might get around the overly photographic or "documentary" suggestions in such expressions by recalling that Aristotle also lists flute-playing and lyre-playing as "imitations." The overly scientist emphasis may also arise in this way: Where the original says merely *mimesis,* translators often add words, making the statement read "imitations (or representations) of life (or of nature)."

Greek tragedy being much nearer to grand opera than to the style of modern naturalism, its "imitations" included many ritualistic elements (as with the masks of the actors and the traditional dance movements of the chorus) that could only be interpreted as *interferences* with imitation, if the term had merely some such meaning as the faithful depicting of the "lifelike."

For a beginning, let us consider a scattering of terms that might help us loosen up our notion of "imitation." To an extent, we might substitute: "the *miming* of an action." (Recall where Chaplin, for instance, "imitates" a dancer by taking two forks, sticking a roll on the end of each, and acting "life-like" *in terms of this* greatly disparate medium.) Or: "the ritual figuring of an action" (since Greek tragedy was built about "quantitative" parts that, whatever their origin in nature, were as ceremonious as the processional and recessional of the Episcopalian service). Or: "the stylizing of an action." (The characters in Greek tragedy stood for certain civic functions somewhat as with

the heroic posturing of an equestrian statue in a public park.) Or:
"the symbolizing of an action." (Hence, we would hold that our term,
"symbolic action," aids greatly in the reclaiming of lost connotations
here.)

"Nature" or "life" is the world of *history*. And history in Aristotle's
scheme is the realm of *particulars*, whereas he tells us that "imitations"
are concerned with *universals*. What does he mean by this distinction?
(The distinction would allow us to add, among our scattered correctives, "the universalizing of an action.")

The difficulty seems to involve the fact that many critics who have
directly or roundabout adored Aristotle's stress upon "imitation" do
not at all share the particular "philosophy of the act" implicit in his use
of the term. Such short-cutting makes for what we call the "scientist"
fallacy, a materialist stress upon the scenic document, "truth to life"
in an "informational" sense, whereas Aristotle rated Spectacle (that is,
scene) as the lowest among the six parts of Tragedy. An obscuring of
the distinction (Coleridge's) between "imitation" and "copy" results,
we believe, from the use of Aristotle's term without reference to the
theory of the "entelechy" that was an integral part of it.

The world of modern technology is so thoroughly built in accordance with concepts of place and motion developed from Galileo and
similar experimental geniuses, that if we approach the whole subject
of motivation from this point of view, not only shall we not believe in
the notion of the "entelechy," we shall have trouble in understanding
it, and even more trouble in understanding how anybody ever could
have believed in it.

In Sir Philip Sidney's *Apology for Poetry*, there is a passage admirably designed to show how the notion of the "entelechy" gradually
ceased to be applied in the Western critics' use of the term, "imitation." (And since the "entelechy" is essentially Dramatistic, a term for
action, in contrast with the great Renaissance inquiries into *motion*, it
would be fitting to recall that Sidney was a contemporary of Galileo's,
though Galileo survived him by more than half a century.) Sidney is
discussing the "Heroical" (that is, Epic poetry):

> But if anything be already said in the defense of
> sweet Poetry, all concurreth to the maintaining the
> Heroical, which is not only a kind, but the best, and
> most accomplished kind of Poetry. For as the image
> of each action stirreth and instructeth the mind, so

the lofty images of the Worthies most inflameth the
mind with desire to be worthy [let us at this point interrupt to recall the almost psychotic emphasis upon
the *digne* and *indigne* in Corneille's tragedies, the test
of worthiness being, of course, such as fits the ideals
of the French court, or more specifically, submission
to the French monarch, whose rule was by Corneille
identified with both the will of God and the love of
country] and informs with counsel how to be worthy. Only let *Aeneas* be worn in the tablet of your
memory, how he governeth himself in the ruin of his
Country, in the preserving his old Father, and carrying away his religious ceremonies: in obeying the
God's commandment to leave *Dido,* though not only
all passionate kindness, but even the humane consideration of virtuous gratefulness, would have craved
other of him. How in storms, how in sports, how in
war, how in peace, how a fugitive, how victorious,
how besieged, how besieging, how to strangers, how
to allies, how to enemies, how to his own: lastly, how
in his inward self, and how in his outward government. . . .

Now, in the "entelechy" is the idea that a given kind of being fully
"actualizes" itself by living up to the potentialities natural to its kind.
(Man is not wholly complete as man, for instance, unless he has completely attained the rational maturity possible to man as a species. A
tree's actualization requires not only not rationality, but not even loco-
motion for its completeness of being, though of course its actualization
requires the kinds of motion needed for its growth.) We can see the
strong vestiges of "entelechial" thinking in Sidney's statement; for he
would have us note how Aeneas imitates kinds of perfection (finishedness, completeness, in the sense of "the compleat angler"). According
to this interpretation, by "how in storms" Sidney means that Virgil
shows Aeneas perfectly *storm-tossed;* "how a fugitive" would mean, the
sum-total of fugitive, the very essence of the fugitive, the embodiment
of the exact traits, in the exact proportions, that would best imitate
the fugitive's role.

No, we would modify our account here somewhat. Pure entelechial imitation would obviously have a less moralistically didactic slant

than we find in Sidney's formula. Already, the entelechy is on the way out. Insofar as foul-mouthed Thersites, in the *Iliad,* is the "perfect" exemplar of what Hegel calls "Thersitism," he too would be an entelechial imitation. A playwright entelechially motivated might thus look not just for perfect heroes; he would also seek for the exact situation, the exact expressions, the exact relationships, the exact thoughts and choices, that would constitute the perfect coward, the perfect hypocrite, the perfect traitor, and so on.

We do not say that the actual concept of the entelechy is needed for literary criticism. We are saying that the full significance of "imitation" has been lost to us—and by thinking of the "entelechial principle" we can better discount the scientist meanings that have engrafted themselves upon the strongly Dramatistic term. Philip Wheelwright's thoughtful translation of selections from Aristotle variously renders the term as: "actuality," "fulfilment," "state of perfect fulfilment," "realization," "full actual character." W. R. Ross, for the *Metaphysics,* uses "complete reality." In his introduction to an edition of Leibnitz's *Monadology,* Robert Latta defines entelechy as "the principle of a thing in the sense of its implicit perfect realization." And in another passage he says: "*Entelecheia* in Aristotle is the state of perfection or realization in which *energeia* [actualization] as a process, ends." Windelband gives his definition a somewhat idealistic twist: "self-realization of the essence in the phenomena." *Encyclopaedia Britannica,* Eleventh Edition: "The perfection of the form of a thing is its entelechy, in virtue of which it attains its fullest realization of function." Zeller points to the etymology: "Entelecheia means that which has its perfection, its end *(telos)* in itself."

In the *De Anima,* Aristotle calls the soul an entelechy. In the *Metaphysics* the term is applied to God, the "first essence," which "has no matter because it is complete reality."

Leibnitz borrowed the word to describe his monads, each of whom is said to be an entelechy. The word here means *tendency* of a thing to unfold its nature. But the application is atomistic, and incipiently scientist (since each monad is said to be a unit of innate *perception,* a notion that fits well with the epistemological turn from act to cognition as generating principle of the terminology).

However, Leibnitz's notion of his sensitive monads, each partially reflecting the nature of the entire universe, is useful for our purposes. He says: "The world is entirely in each of its parts, but more distinctly in some than in others." This may or may not be true of the particles that compose the material universe, but it is certainly true of the various terms that cluster together in a single universe of discourse. Hence our belief that *entelecheia* is present, though not "distinctly," in Aristotle's use of *mimesis* with regard to the symbolic action of poetry.

We might put it thus: Given the full range of human characters and situations there would not merely be the entelechial imitating of man's noblest potentialities *qua* man; there would also be the actualizing of human types within the species. For though man, in his perfection, would be essentially rational, according to the Aristotelian scheme, there will also be characteristic ways of departing from this rationality. And the entelechial principle would prevail insofar as you "imitate" any such departure, or imitate different situations. Thus the ruler's typical ways of being to perfection "himself" as ruler would differ from those in which the poet might "be himself," etc.

We deliberately use here the expression "be oneself" to give a glimpse of entelechial thinking behind the formula, though the notion of "kind" has been individualized. One is exhorted to be a kind all by oneself, in accordance with idealistic emphases that transform the realistic concern with role or act into a cult of "pure" personality.

This is not the place to consider at length the many ways in which the *entelechial* principle was later lost in the idea of "imitation," or warped into a different shape by the increasingly "scientist" connotations that obscured the original implications of the term. But a few of the main ones are obvious, since they can be seen in Sidney's statement.

The didactic emphasis (the Renaissance stress upon "instruction" as an important element of poetry) is the first great deviation. The how's of Sidney's statement were given a moralistically pragmatic slant, with the hierarchal motive in art conceived too narrowly. Thus when discussing "the utility of tragedy" (*Reflections on the Poetic Art*, Section XLV) Fontenelle says that he does not understand Aristotle's formula for "the purgation of the passions by means of the passions"; then he continues:

> It seems to me that the greatest utility of the theatre is to render virtue amiable to men, to accustom them to interest themselves in virtue, to touch their hearts, to put before them great examples of resoluteness and courage in their misfortunes, and by that

means to fortify and elevate their sentiments. From
that it follows that not only must characters be virtuous but also that they must be virtuous in the proud
and elevated manner of Corneille, so that they will
strengthen the heart and give lessons in courage.

There are endless variants on this notion, of tragedy as a set of models for noble action (though the connotations of nobility gradually shift from the gestures
of the Court to the bourgeois virtues of sentiment, a
shift discernible in the Fontenelle quotation).

By the same token, comedy is praised for producing the same effect
by opposite means, since it uses ridicule to deter men from temptations
that would threaten the social order. One sample of this endlessly varied theme should be enough for our purposes. (René Rapin, *The Poetics of Aristotle*, section XXV):

> Comedy is an image of common life; its end is to
> show on the stage the faults of particulars, in order
> to amend the faults of the public, and to correct the
> people through a fear of being rendered ridiculous.
> So that which is most proper to excite laughter is that
> which is most essential to comedy.[2]

Another mode of departure was, of course, through the use of
stock characters and stock situations, a burlesque of "universality" got
through sheer lack of invention. Such procedure did not need to be
asked for; low canons of rhetoric would spontaneously lead merce-
nary playwrights into this path, since one must appeal through an
audience's sense of the "natural," and a convention can become "natural" in this sense (as with superficial "typing," the "typical" Irishman,
"typical" Jew, "typical" Englishman, etc.). Such canons of "naturalness" now help protect a great deal of Hollywooden art against the
encroachments of serious foreign films. Largely, of course, such protection is contrived by an extra-artistic device: control over the system
of distribution. But it can also rely on a low form of aesthetic conserva-
tism (there are admirable kinds of such) in the movie audiences.

---

[2] Both of these citations are from *Dramatic Essays of the Neoclassic Age*,
edited by Henry Hitch Adams and Baxter Hathaway.

Our movie-goers are supposed to be in search of "entertainment." But actually, they will pay good money *to be bored.* We do not mean that they are cheated, in being led to expect more than they get. We mean that they *positively demand boredom.* For in such boredom there is solace, there is the implied assurance that all is as was. It is the modern equivalent, in "movie temples" (when witnessing a murder mystery, for instance) to the almost irresistibly sleep-producing intonations of a hell-fire sermon in the earlier dispensation.

Be that as it may, once "typicality" (in the sense of stock characters and stock plots) has come to be deemed "natural," a scientist test can raise good aesthetic questions. (Above all, for instance, it questions the habit of assigning to each nationality a single role, like the animals in Aesop's Fables.) There is thus a positive reason for becoming insensitive to the entelechial aspect of imitation: insofar as universality has thus degenerated into the use of conventional signs for recalling conventional attitudes, art can reinvigorate itself only "scientistically," by fresh "observation," by checking its utterances against the many *particulars* of life.

But while realism, in this "naturalistic" sense, is necessary, the very zeal of critics in expounding it can take us too far from a concern with the range of major motives that figure in aesthetic appeal. And if you read a novel, say, about nondescript, Bohemian, cosmopolite, and perverted characters roaming through the bars and brothels of pre-war or post-war or between-wars Europe, we would propose that you'd come nearer to explaining its nature if you adapted Sidney's formula than if you heralded it as a purely "naturalistic" emancipation from "moralistic" and "didactic" bias. That is, you should say: The author is showing us *how to be the perfect,* "compleat," nondescript, Bohemian, cosmopolite, perverted wanderer in the bars and brothels, etc. In this sense, his imitations would have the kind of *fulfilment* that we would associate with the entelechial aspect of imitation, in contrast with a purely naturalistic kind *(reportage).*

Here would be the bond between "imitation" and the "universal." After the German romantic philosophers, perhaps the notion is often contained in the term "idealization." (It is a useful term for the purpose, if you remember its range: at one end, the questionably eulogistic attributing of excellencies to someone or something; at the other, the attaining of the purposive simplicity we get in such ironic expressions as "the ideal liar," "the ideal thief.")

One imitates entelechially, thereby attaining a universal, insofar as the individual is shown living up to the potentialities of its genus. There is such entelechial thought in Shakespeare's phrase, "every inch a king." (One also glimpses the hierarchal motive in the notion of the entelechy.)

And so, in sum, were the poem (for instance) to imitate a sailor universally, entelechially, it would have him represent to the full the potentialities of sailor as such: speaking nautical terms (even perhaps to the extent of applying nautical analogies to non-nautical matters), scrupulous in the performing of his duties at sea (yet revealing exactly the most relevant temptations to the dereliction of such duties), looking perhaps with a carnival eye upon his times in port, etc. He would not be merely "typed," though typing would be the corresponding corruption of such a norm. And insofar as the feeling for this norm began to weaken, the same insight might be preserved somewhat in canons of "instruction" (which would involve the corresponding antithesis, canons of "amusement"). "Instruction" could then become conceived in hierarchal terms overly narrow: hence would result a kind of moral pragmatism, instructions how to be the ideal sailor for the greater glory of such-and-such an empire-builder. And whether we end with merely the stock character of a sailor, or with a falsely heroicized figure, "naturalism" would be our corrective. However, though its "scientist" emphasis might help refresh art, it would in turn lead to a faulty analysis of poetic excellence. Critics would suggest that the writer appealed by purely naturalistic imitation of particular sailors. At this point, we would attempt to recover the entelechial ingredient in imitation. Or at the very least, even if you would ban the entelechy as a bit of outmoded nonsense, we would reaffirm our contention that you must at least take it into account when asking what *Aristotle* meant by *mimesis* (in contrast with what the term can seem to mean, when translated as "imitation" or "representation," and thus used after several centuries during which "nature" came progressively to be equated with the processes of technology).

And when thus summing up, we might note how the "fourfold method" of mediaeval criticism in its way also departed somewhat from the entelechy even while partially preserving its genius. In effect, it broke the entelechy-universal into four pieces, each of which thereafter could be featured, or even proclaimed exclusively. From the stressing of the literal could come the "documentary" school ("naturalism," the "scientist" bias). From the stressing of the moralistic or "tropologi-cal" could come "instruction" (hence, tragedy as a book; of etiquette for the heroics of empire; comedy as a book of etiquette in reverse, the use of ridicule to deter deviations). From the stressing of the "alle-gorical" would come the featuring of temporal or local allusiveness as the be-all and end-all of poetry. (One can see how both "allusiveness" and "instruction" could be telescoped eventually into aspects of the "documentary.") And from the "anagogic" could come "amusement." (Once the concerns with grace, power, felicity, perfection, and the like have been secularized for use as terms to describe purely *aesthetic* ul-timates—in accord with the translating of the religious passion into the romantic passion—then the "radiance" of an aesthetic object can be said to reside in its sheer delight as a pleasurable sensuous thing existing here and now, obviously another emphasis that has been tele-scoped into the scientist-literal.) In our *Rhetoric,* we have sought to show how such "grace" (of the *ars gratia artis* sort*)* is emblematic of a *social* anagoge, as the objects of "natural" experience (in the empiricist sense) can secretly represent social judgments related to the real but somewhat confused hierarchy of social classes. "Amusement" thus now covers the use of art to ends implicitly "propagandistic." For the "natu-ralness" of such art derives from its conformity with conventions that would uphold the status quo (even though, inexorably, by the ironies of history, they are making for exactly the contrary outcome: general inaccuracy, when coached and perfected with systematic efficiency, *must* become a Pandora's box that opens itself).

The present cult of the "myth" can also be fitted into these thoughts on entelechy. For the "mythic" now is usually proposed in opposition to overly scientific, naturalistic, "documentary" or materialistic crite-ria in art. In part, the controversy is rooted in extra-aesthetic consid-erations. The myth can serve as "idealization" in the merely eulogistic sense; or, when not downright eulogistic, it can at least be *deflective,* as were some immediately present and materialistically explainable po-litico-economic conflict to be viewed exclusively in the "higher" terms of some mythic or prehistoric struggle, fall, or curse. In this respect, the market for a myth may be explained by critics on purely aesthetic grounds, whereas the supposed "universality" of the supposedly "aes-thetic" can be a temporary way of using art to avoid the accurate con-templation of non-aesthetic elements.

But there is one good argument in behalf of myth, as we realize when we consider, for instance, the various ways in which the three great Greek tragic playwrights used myth. If you relate characters to one another after the analogy of some myth, you automatically acquire an underlying simplicity of structure that almost requires you to make the various roles "universal." You can get the point by thinking, in contrast, of some complicated modern novel or drama of intrigue (a feeble variant of the "scientist psychosis"), in which you are dragged through a "mysterious" muddle of false leads and loose ends, to end on some hastily contrived gadget of explanation (or rather, an anti-climax disguised as an explanation). Contrast such an unprincipled contraption with the stark lines of a Greek tragedy, which possesses in its way the same simplicity as one finds in Greek architecture and Greek statuary of the classic period. Even much of the best Elizabethan tragedy suffers by comparison. The outraged lover, the unjust king, the avenging son, the suppliant fugitive, the blind seer, the tortured god—the myths "naturally" led the playwright to cast his perception of particulars into such universal molds, giving his "imitations" the *summarizing* quality that adds up to the notion of the "entelechy."

Thus, even though Sartre uses myth perversely, he does contrive to exploit it for its formal, simplifying function. And a play of intrigue can be improved formally by even an artificial imposing of mythic lines upon it. In *The American Scholar*, Winter 1950–51, Malcolm Cowley touches upon this point somewhat when, discussing the possible effect of the "New Criticism" on creative writers, he says:

> It may terrify them; it may stop them from writing at all, or, if they do write, it may cause them to write according to one of the formulas advanced by whichever New Critic is teaching that year at Princeton or wherever it may be—according to a number of formulas, like a beautiful one followed by Frederick Buechner in his first novel, *A Long Day's Dying.* The formula is simply to find classical myth, tell the myth in the shape of a lecture delivered to Princeton boys, and then restate the myth in contemporary terms, always stepping down the intensity of the myth into mild contemporary equivalents.

The observation suggests that the mythic frame might even become a mechanical subterfuge, a device of play-doctoring. But we are suggesting that a formal virtue, however perverted, rests at the roots of such a possible vice.

As we tried to show elsewhere, in our analysis of *Othello*, the concept of "tensions" can also be applied, as a way of re-introducing an equivalent of the entelechy in imitation. For if there is a certain tension in human relations, the artist may exploit it dramatically by analyzing it into parts, "breaking it down" into a set of interrelated roles (a device that permits the tension to be "processed"; for whereas in human relations it just is, the breaking of it into parts permits these parts to act upon one another, in a series of operations that, when followed in exactly the order they have in their particular whole, lead to a "catharsis"). Roles chosen by such a test are likely to be "entelechial" imitations, since they will imitate not particular individuals, but basic human situations and strategies, translated into equivalent terms of personality.

When the "tensions" are too local (as with the tensions of temporary factional disputes), often a sheerly rhetorical motive can be misinterpreted "scientistically." Thus, when looking for evidence that a certain social situation prevails, sociological critics will sometimes cite the prevalence of such a topic in popular literature of the times. But often a rhetorical discount is necessary. For instance, a speaker held that, in his opinion, life in the United States was much more "matriarchal" than "patriarchal." And as proof, he cited the fact that so many motion pictures play up the type of the put-upon husband and father, whose frustrations about the house are humorously amplified, while he mumbles to himself ineffectually, being treated patronizingly by wife, children, servants, tradesmen, and even the family dog, but masochistically and without fail paying the bills with which all the other members of the family blithely saddle him. Maybe yes, maybe no. But before taking this stock character at face value, as evidence of a correspondingly prevalent social type, one should certainly consider the possibility that the role is the sentimentalizing of a situation quite different.

Imagine, for instance, a husband who is unquestionably the head of the family. Each day he goes off to work as to a "mystery," so far as his family at home is concerned. They know only what he chooses to tell them. Everything necessarily centers about him, since he is the wage-earner. Things must be so arranged that he catches exactly the right train, gets exactly the right food at exactly the right time, sleeps for exactly the right interval [. . .] and insofar as such requirements are not met, he must grumble mightily for his rights. Each day he goes into a world of "adventure," his absence being in essence as unaccountable as the daily disappearance of Cupid was to Psyche. Under such conditions, might not the wife feel herself inferior? Then if, of an afternoon, she goes to a movie temple for her meditations and devotions, would there not be "medicine" for her in the picture of a husband thus lovingly put upon, a lovable old bear essentially as timid as the lion in the *Wizard of Oz?* And so on. In brief, might the part be featured in this popular art precisely because it did not directly reflect the motives in the social situation itself, but was an "idealization" of them? There would, of course, be certain superficial signs about, to give the character plausibility. But the main function of the character would derive not from a corresponding "documentary" reality, but rather from the ingratiating triviality of the distortion.

In the *Poetics* there are several passing references to the appeal of "wonder" in the imitations of tragedy, and we shall revert to the theme when we come to that term. Meanwhile, we should note this "complicating factor": Once the resources of imitation have been systematically exploited by a priesthood, imitations can be endowed with a magical power not present in the things imitated. Hofmannsthal tells of a tribe that fears neither man nor tiger, but the tribesmen are paralyzed with terror when a priest dances before them wearing a tiger pelt. And we know of a child who awoke in the night, shrieking, from the dream of a snake. Yet the next day he placidly bathed in a pool while a water snake lay on a branch nearby. His mother asked him: "Why aren't you worried about this snake, when you were so afraid of the snake you dreamed about last night?" And he answered: "This one is real." There is a magic in imitations, that probably draws in part upon the magic of dreams (which a priesthood can interweave with the magic of class). Such considerations lead us to the "hierarchal" motives that lurk in the entelechy (touching upon it as "enigmatic," containing the mystery and magic, the "wonder," of class relationships).

From our point of view, however, the *Poetics,* beneath its essayistic facade, would in this regard be itself a kind of "dramatic analysis," with the terms of a single tension being so broken apart that they can curatively or cathartically operate upon one another like characters in

a play. Thus the wonder in entelechial imitation is not explicitly said
to be a part of it, but is broken off, treated as an independent term,
existing in its own right, its secret relation to its partner-term being revealed not by explicit tracing of the relationship between them, but by
the fact that they appear in the same context (*apparently* related only
by "and": there is imitation *and* there is wonder).

But, just as previously our doubts about the "scientist" grounding
of a character led us into rhetoric in the superficial sense, here we touch
upon rhetoric in the profoundest sense. Or rather, we come upon the
centre, where rhetoric and poetic coalesce, where the *intrinsic radiance*
of an aesthetic object has social implications in its very essence. And
as we have said before, we are unable to maintain our vision steadily,
where this moment is concerned. Here is the point where the divinity
of the ultimate ground merges deceptively with the pseudo-divinity of
class relationships. We have claimed that "naturalism" but reproduces,
more self-protectively (from the standpoint of "scientist" norms), the
deceptions of "supernaturalism" (insofar as "supernaturalism" can be
a disguise for temporal interests in terms of the eternal, a shift that
Hobbes would call "making men see double"). If we are right, then
Aristotle's stress upon "nature" as the grounding for men's delight
in imitation should secretly contain such a "drama" as we have here
caught glimpses of.

Conversely, we can catch glimpses of an entelechial grammar behind the pathos of John, XIX, 30: "When Jesus therefore had received
the vinegar, he said, It is finished"; *consummatum est; es ist vollbracht;*
the Greek text has *Tetelestai,* a verb perfect passive in form, that contains the *telos* of "entelechy," to designate an "end," not just as a dying
or desisting, but rather as a purpose, now at last fulfilled.

2

Three Definitions[1]

THE FIRST OF THE DEFINITIONS TO BE OFFERED HERE is the broadest. It concerns "the lyric" in general. The second will deal with "the Platonic dialogue," considered as a literary species. It is built around the examination of Plato's dialogues alone: but because the form has been so often followed to varying degrees by other writers, the definition bears upon a field much wider than the works of Plato on which it was based. The third will be the narrowest. It was designed solely to provide a formula for Joyce's *Portrait of the Artist as a Young Man.* This single work was considered somewhat "angelically," as a kind all by itself. (We say "angelically," thinking of Aquinas's doctrine that each individual angel is a distinct species, and the only member of its kind.) But though we treat the work as *sui generis,* we necessarily define it in terms of some classification. Tentatively, we propose "lyric novel" as the generic name for this work, considered as a species. The prototype of such definition is Aristotle's formula for tragedy, in the *Poetics* (Bywater translation).

A tragedy, then is the imitation of an action that is serious and also, as having magnitude, complete in itself; in language with pleasurable accessories, each kind brought in separately in the parts of the work; in a dramatic, not in a narrative form; with incidents arousing pity and fear, wherewith to accomplish its catharsis of such emotions. Here by "language with pleasurable accessories" I mean that with rhythm and harmony or song superadded; and by "the kinds separately" I mean

---

[1] *The Kenyon Review* 12.2 (Spring 1951): 173–92. © The Kenneth Burke Literary Trust. Used by permission.

that some portions are worked out with verse only, and others in turn with song.

I. The "Lyric"

Definition:

> A short complete poem, elevated or intense in thought and sentiment, expressing and evoking a unified attitude towards a momentous situation more or less explicitly implied—in diction harmonious and rhythmical, often but not necessarily rhymed—the structure lending itself readily to a musical accompaniment strongly repetitive in quality; the gratification of the whole residing in the nature of the work as an ordered summation of emotional experience otherwise fragmentary, inarticulate, and unsimplified.

Comments:

"A short, complete poem." Insofar as a fragment of a larger work can be excerpted and offered as a lyric, it must meet these tests of brevity and completeness, to be a *perfect* lyric. Lyrics can, however, have a function over and above their completeness. Thus, recall Aristotle's observation that the earlier writers of tragedy used choral songs as integral parts of the action, whereas later these became merely intercalary pieces, having no more to do with the plot of one play than of another.

"Elevated or intense." "Intense" because even a mood of sullenness or vindictiveness would be a fit subject for a lyric. Sometimes maybe even "dense" would be the word, or "condensed." Maybe "dense" would serve to cover both "elevated" and "intense."

"Thought and sentiment." The contemporary stress upon the purely sensory nature of the lyric image makes this part of the formula look a bit quaint? But let's recover the whole process here by disclosing the "sentiments" implicit in the "sensations," and the "thoughts" implicit in the "sentiments." True, in one poet's poem of a few lines, such a search may be tenuous, or the findings hard to establish beyond question. But if the critic can gauge the particular poet's language by the study of other poems by the same poet using the same terms, an entire "philosophy" can be evolved.

"Expressing and evoking." We might bring the two steps together in the one word "communicating." But the lyric, at least the subjective lyric, in contrast with the drama, tends to be first an outcry, and second a persuasion. Hence, our preference for splitting into two aspects the single use of a communicative medium.

"A unified attitude." The "lyric attitude," as vs. the "dramatic act." Attitude as gesture, as posture. Think of it in the most plastic sense. As with the statue of a man on horseback, being heroic, in a public park (the scene integral to the gesture and posture not being there at all). Strictly speaking, an attitude is by its very nature "unified." Even an attitude of hesitancy or internal division is "unified" in the formal sense, if the work in its entirety rounds out precisely that.

Attitude "towards a momentous situation." Are we being too tricky here, in this word "momentous"? We wanted a word that connoted the significant, outstanding, distinct, or distinguished. "Momentous" would seem to do this, in meaning "of moment." But there are also suggestions of the "momentary" in the word (hence involving us by another route in the lyric "arrest"). We could think here also of the ways in which Hegel might divide an idea into "moments," and thereby we also verge upon the "motivational."

Situation "more or less explicitly implied." That is, the lyric attitude implies some kind of situation. The situation may be the vaguest sort: The poet stands alone by the seashore while the waves are rolling in; or, the poet is separated from his beloved; or, the poet is old, remembering his youth—etc. Or the situation may be given in great detail. Indeed, a lyric may be, on its face, but a listing of descriptive details specifying a scene but these images are all manifestations of a single *attitude* (attitude being incipient act, and image implying attitude towards the thing imaged).

"In diction harmonious and rhythmical, often but not necessarily rhymed." The formula would accommodate both strict and free verse, as it should.

"The structure lending itself readily to a musical accompaniment strongly repetitive in nature." This part of the definition involves ultimately something so idealistic (rather than realistic) as "tendencies" or "trends." Hence, maybe this should be out. It implies definition in terms of "ideal paradigm," as with our account of the five acts in

Shakespearean tragedy. Might put the case thus: Recall, for instance, Lord Raglan's book on *The Hero*. His recipe of 22 points for distinguishing such a mythic figure. But he does not attempt to find all 22 points for characterizing every such hero. Here is the list in its ideal perfection. But any given mythic hero may fail to qualify in some or other of the particulars.

Raglan's pattern in toto: (1) Hero's mother a royal virgin; (2) father a king and (3) often a near relative of mother; (4) circumstances of hero's conception unusual; (5) reputed to be son of a god; (6) at birth, attempt is made, usually by father or grand-father, to kill him; (7) he is spirited away and (8) reared by foster parents in far country; (9) childhood vague; (10) at manhood he returns or goes to his future kingdom; (11) after victory over king and/or giant, dragon, or wild beast, (12) he marries princess, often daughter of predecessor; (13) becomes king; (14) for a time reigns uneventfully; (15) prescribes laws; (16) later loses favor with gods and/or his subjects; (17) is driven from throne and city; (18) meets with mysterious death, (19) often at top of hill; (20) his children, if any, do not succeed him; (21) his body is not buried; (22) nevertheless he has one or more holy sepulchres.

In accordance with this formula, Oedipus scores 22, Theseus 20, Romulus 18, Hercules 17, Jason 15, Dionysus 19, Joseph 12, Moses 20, Robin Hood 13, etc.

Similarly, could we legitimately be to this extent "idealistic" in our definition: Could we say that the lyric "tends ideally" to be of such a nature as would adapt it to rondo-like musical forms; hence, it would have stanzas varying in sense though metrically similar, and built about a recurrent refrain. It could be studied as a departure from this "*Urform,*" or archetype. But it need not preserve such a structure explicitly, to qualify as a lyric.

"The gratification of the whole residing in the nature of the work as an ordered summation of emotional experience otherwise fragmentary, inarticulate, and unsimplified." This "gratification" (or "lyric pleasure") would correspond to the "catharsis" of "pity, fear, and like emotions" (named by Aristotle as the tragic pleasure). An attitude is a summing-up (as were all the details of an actual experience to terminate in an attitude of cheerfulness or gloom on our part). But, as compared with the order in the poem, wherein things fall together felicitously, the experiences reflected there are "fragmentary, inarticulate, and unsimplified."

One colleague, erroneously hearing the last word as "simplified," gave us a further insight into the problems of definition at this point. Presumably he was thinking of the experience in art as more complex than the experiences in life. There is certainly a sense in which this can be so: The reader of the poem must "make allowances" for the fact that the poem is an artifact, its moods artificial—and in this respect the poem could be called less "simple" than the actual attitudes it imitates. But when calling the poem a simplification and life outside the poem unsimplified, we have in mind the sense of unity (order) supplied by the poem. Croce would give the name of "catharsis" to such transcending of emotional matter by artistic form, or "expression."

II. Platonic Dialogue

Definition:

> A methodic inquiry into first principles, as they are related to the principles of particular subject-matters. The method is by question and answer, engaging at least two persons directly, and others indirectly. The persons are differentiated as to both thought and character. The dialogue is explicitly organized in accordance with the dialectics of definition (generalization, division, successive sub-division, and a ladder of terms graded as regards relative distance from some norm). "Myths" are introduced sometimes as illustration, sometimes as the basis of a new motive that will pervade the disparate matter and infuse it with a common spirit. A kind of catharsis is got, by refutation of error, and by transcendence.

Comments:

"First principles, as they are related to the principles of particular subject-matters." We have in mind here the distinction between Platonist and Aristotelian method (the distinction that Richard McKeon has called "holoscopic" and "meroscopic" respectively). That is, when Plato discusses some particular field, he does so by asking how it is related to "the Good" universally.

"The method is by question and answer." Thus consider, in Demetrius's *On Style,* this passage showing how different writers would develop the same idea:

In fine, it is with language as with a lump of wax, out of which one man will mould a dog, another an ox, another a horse. One will deal with his subject in the way of exposition and asseveration, saying (for example) that "men leave property to their children, but they do not therewith leave the knowledge which will rightly use the legacy": a way of putting it which is called "Aristippean." Another will (as Xenophon commonly does) express the same thought in the way of precept, as "men ought to leave not only money to their children, but also the knowledge which will use the money rightly."

What is specifically called the "Socratic" manner (*eidos Sokratikon*)—one which seems to have excited the emulation of Aeschines and Plato in no common degree—would recast the foregoing proposition in an interrogative form, somewhat as follows. "My dear lad, how much property has your father left you? Is it considerable and not easily assessed? It is considerable, Socrates. Well now, has he also left you the knowledge which will use it rightly?" In this way Socrates insensibly drives the lad into a corner; he reminds him that he is ignorant; he urges him to get instruction.

Socrates breaks the maxim into a statement gradually unfolded through a succession of stages, alternate questions and answers, the questions being designed to call forth answers all leading in the direction of the final statement, which thereby is pointed up as discovery, something suddenly pounced upon.

"Engaging at least two persons directly and others indirectly." The *Republic* threatens to break the frame here, as it is narrated by Socrates throughout. But the assertions are developed in the usual manner: Socrates tells of questions he put to others, and of questions and assertions made by him atop their replies.

"The persons are differentiated as to both thought and character." Since the dialogue is essentially a "drama of ideas," the appeal of character might be classed as Aristotle classed rhythm, harmony, and song in tragedy: among the "sweeteners" (*hedusmata;* in the Bywater translation, "pleasurable accessories").

"Terms graded as regards relative distance from some norm." In the *Phaedrus,* for instance, all leads up to, and away from, the sentence: "There abides the very being with which true knowledge is concerned;

the colorless, formless, intangible essence, visible only to mind, the pilot of the soul." This is the point of withinness-of-withinness, there just having been a reference to the "heaven above the heavens" (*hyperouranion*). Or, otherwise put: Here is talk of a "return home" to "the interior of the heavens"; the imagery concerns an ultimate feasting (ambrosia and nectar), which equals "knowledge absolute in existence absolute" ("the knowledge being in that which is beingly being"). And a few lines further on: Plato proposes his hierarchy of nine degrees, from the highest, the soul born in philosopher, artist, musician, lover, down to the lowest, the tyrant. The form thus aims not only to infuse the many with a principle of oneness, but to specify conditions that correspond to different stages of remoteness from the one (absolute being).

"Myths [. . .] introduced as illustrations" are merely "rational" aids to vivid exposition, like anecdotes. "Myths [. . .] as the basis of a new motive that will pervade the disparate matter and infuse it with a common spirit" are of a different sort. They serve to introduce an ironic image that lifts the dialogue into a higher dimension—and thereafter, things in the lower dimensions are seen in the light of this new vision. We might add here: The vision is wondrous, and designed to evoke by wonder the assent of reverence. (In the *Theaetetus,* several new starts are contrived, not by the introduction of a full-fledged myth, but by a new metaphor or analogy, that sets up a new perspective, or angle of vision, a series of *veerings,* with an effect of high comedy inasmuch as Socrates gets complete assent at each stage, before professing himself dissatisfied, stirring things up again, and dragging us away to a new search.)

"A kind of catharsis is got, by refutation of error, and by transcendence." They are not quite the same. The constant refuting of errors (and its corresponding method: the clarifying of ambiguities) provides the same formal satisfaction as one might get by removing rubbish or by putting scattered papers in order. But the "transcendence" is more positive, involving a kind of "Kierkegaardian leap," as with the new motive introduced by a mythic image, and the subsequent perceiving of this motive, however faintly, in all things that were, prior to its introduction, viewed without reference to it. (In its way the form fulfills the Gide-Stein ideal of a form that reveals the stages of its development into a form.)

Perhaps we should distinguish introduction, transitions, epilogue and "stages." Perhaps these would correspond to the "quantitative parts" of tragedy, discussed in Chapter XII of the *Poetics*. By the "stages" we mean the successive levels of the dialogue, treated as stations of a journey, or as steps in an initiation. On that, more later.

III. The Joyce Portrait

Definition:

> A serious prose narrative, imitating an agent's spiritual, adventures, in the development of a new attitude, with its corresponding doctrine; it employs an intense, elevated, or otherwise exceptional diction (involving a principle of selectivity that makes it representative in the *culminative* sense rather than as tested by *statistical averages*); the unity of action centers in the unity of the main character, whose transformations coincide with the stages of the plot; like the lyric proper, it places great reliance upon sensory images, not merely for purposes of vividness (*enargeia*) but to serve structural ends (the images thus taking on "mythic" dimensions that transcend their specifically sensory significance); the seriousness of the agent and the magnitude of his trials serve to dignify the development towards which the work is directed.

Comments:

"A serious prose narrative." Some readers have shown an inclination to overrate the possibility that Joyce would have us "discount" Stephen. The work as a whole is complexly motivated; for instance, Lynch's "sulphuryellow" remarks to Stephen, while Stephen is explaining his *ars poetica,* should be taken as an integral part of the motivation, not merely as an irrelevant heckling. But we would not thereby conclude that the reader similarly is to "heckle" Stephen. Stephen is naive and excessive, but his trials are to be viewed sympathetically. Even though we are not intended to take the hell-fire sermon as seriously as he did, we are intended to feel that Stephen's agitation was quite "proper" to his condition. Even though we may partly smile, we take each stage of his development "seriously."

"Imitating an agent's spiritual adventures." Not the adventures of a Jason or an Odysseus—but in the order of meditation, scruples, "change of heart." (Nor is Joyce's *Ulysses* the adventures of an Odysseus.)

"In the development of a new attitude." Perhaps most would prefer "vision" to "attitude." (Should we also seek to include here the fact that the work as a whole gains unity in terms of the central agent's sensibility and development?)

"With its corresponding doctrine." It is surprising how many analysts, even when asked to discuss the over-all stages in the development of this work, will omit the "catechism," the *doctrinal* equivalent of Stephen's shift from religious to aesthetic vocation. (Here is the respect in which this "lyric novel" overlaps upon another species, an *Erziehungsroman* like Goethe's *Wilhelm Meister*. Ironically, though Joyce became a symbol of pure aestheticism, his novel is a *plea* for certain artistic policies.)

"Involving a principle of selectivity that makes it 'representative' in the *culminative* sense rather than as tested by statistical averages." Stephen is not "representative" in the "statistical" sense. He is a rarity. But many modern writers have in one way or another adapted religious coordinates to aesthetic ends. And Joyce imagines such a course "to perfection." This is what we mean by its "culminative" nature.

"The images may accordingly take on 'mythic' dimensions that transcend their specifically sensory significance." We have in mind here the development that Joyce called an "epiphany." Our remarks on the Platonic dialogue would indicate respects in which the Joycean form paralleled Plato's use of the "mythic image" for the figuring of a new motivational dimension. Insofar as the bathing girl stands for Stephen's new vocation, she is a "mythic" image, as distinct from a purely "sensory" image. She is "enigmatic," or "emblematic" of the motives that transcend her meaning as a "natural object."

"The seriousness of the agent and the magnitude of his trials serve to dignify the development towards which the work is directed." Elsewhere we have offered four ways of subdividing the idea of tragedy: (1) Tragedy as a species (as with Aristotle's definition of one particular kind of tragedy; a different kind of definition would be needed for, say, Cornelian tragedy); (2) the "tragic rhythm" (the progression from action, through passion, to learning); (3) the "tragic spirit" (the general cult of "mortification" or "resignation"; an ultimate or "cumulative" expression of social repressions voluntarily enacted by the self upon the self, in response to problems of private property in the social order); (4) "tragedy as a rhetorical device, as a means of dignification" (arguing for a cause by depicting a serious person who is willing to sacrifice himself in its behalf; the device has somewhat Satanistic aspects here, as with the heroics of Stephen's willingness to consider the possibility that eternal damnation might result from his aesthetic "pride").

IV "Stages"

Consider Chapter XII in the *Poetics,* the listing of a tragedy's "quantitative" parts (Prologue, Episode, Exode, Parode, Stasimon, Commos). Here we touch upon the dialectic of "stages." But Aristotle was so eager to disassociate himself from the Platonist dialectic in general, and to establish a purely secular analysis of tragic "pleasure" (despite its vestiges of ritual "cure") his treatment here is quite perfunctory. The feeling for the "stages" of a development is slighted.

Our biggest loss here is unquestionably in Aristotle's unconcern with the trilogy as a form. His analysis of tragedy centers about individual works considered as separate units. Yet what of trilogies like Aeschylus's *Oresteia,* where each play carries the over-all development one step farther? (And, of course, if we had the material, we might further extend our theories of form until we also treated the contrasted fourth drama, the final burlesque or "satyr-play," as an integral part of the playwright's statement in its entirety.)

Modern anthropologists have supplied information and speculations that enable us to bring Chapter XII to life. (See George Thomson's *Aeschylus and Athens,* p. 192, for a chart suggesting how the "quantitative parts" of tragedy developed from patterns of religious ritual. Similarly, this Marxist-tempered variant of the Hegelian dialectic serves well for throwing light upon the trilogy as a form. Such considerations are directed two ways. First, the three stages of the only surviving trilogy are analyzed; next, a similar logic of the parts is assumed, in reasoned guesses as to the likely developments in the *Prometheus* trilogy, of which only the first play survives, though fragments of the others are extant.)

Often, however, anthropology has fed the present fad for "myth" in ways that mislead. For instance, many purely dialectical considerations are stated in an insufficiently generalized form; as a result, a term local to the study of ritual will be used to designate a process that is not necessarily ritualistic at all.

Thus, consider the most highly generalized resources of discursive reason: "composition and division." Because such resources are universal to human thinking, they will also be found exemplified in primitive rituals. The principle of "division," for instance, is present in *sparagmos,* the rending of the god's flesh in primitive religious practices. Or the principle of "composition" is present here, inasmuch as the members of the group are thought to be made consubstantial by thus ceremoniously eating of the same magical substance. Suppose, then, for "division" in general, we used the word *sparagmos,* or rending and tearing of the divine sacrifice, and for "composition" in general we used some term for the tribal love-feast. The most rational processes of science or everyday life would thus be expressed in terms that referred merely to the application of them in one specific subject matter. Scientific *analysis* might thus be treated as a vestigial survival of *sparagmos.* The current over-use of terms for the processes of ritual and myth has two had effects: first, it can make even realistic common sense look like an attenuated survival of primitive magic; second, by thus misdirecting our attention, it can keep us from perceiving the mythic elements that really do infuse our culture (mythic elements rooted in the magic of property, with its avowed and unavowed, spontaneous and deliberate, forms of priestcraft).

While it is our job to brood over man's dismal bondage to the magic of social relations as rooted in property, and thus to mention this topic in a hit-and-run sort of way whenever the given subject offers such an inkling, for the moment we are trying to suggest that the dialectic of "stages" (sometimes called "levels") was not adequately considered in the case of the definition which we have taken as our model. So we suggested a possible corrective, plus a corrective to the possible misuse of that.

In the *Portrait,* considered from the standpoint of "stages," the first three chapters would be like courses "prerequisite" to the choice Stephen makes in Chapter IV, where he turns from priestly to artistic vocation. However, we should not overlook an intermediate stage here. After thought of *"ordination"* [. . .] of "a grave and ordered and passionless life that awaited him, a life without material cares" [. . .], of himself as "a being apart in every *order*" [. . .], of the window that might be his "if he ever joined the *order*" [. . .], of his destiny "to be elusive of social or religious *orders*," there is talk of himself as "about to fall," then "he crossed the bridge over the stream of the Tolka," whereat he contemplates the opposite of order: "Then, bending to the left, he followed the lane which led up to his house. The faint sour stink of rotted cabbages came towards him from the kitchen gardens on the rising ground above the river. He smiled to think that it was this *disorder,* [throughout, italics ours] the misrule and confusion of his father's house and the stagnation of vegetable life, which was to win the day in his soul." Not quite. For the next episode will detail the vision of the hawklike man and the bird-girl (flight away, flight up, a *transcending* of the rotted cabbages). Hence, all told: from the priestly calling, *through* the dismal alternative, *to* the new exaltation, the aesthetic jesuitry that will be his purging of the alternative disorder, that will fly above it. And since the disorder had been "to the left," and since Part I should "implicitly contain" what eventuates, we might appropriately recall young Stephen's first triumph, as regards the pandybat episode, when he had gone "not to the corridor but up the staircase on the right that led up to the castle." Here is accurate writing.

We could continue with further "stages." Does not Stephen's statement of his *ars poetica,* in a concerto-like relation with Lynch, correspond to the doctrinal stage in the Phaedrus, following the myth in Socrates' second speech (which was itself the third stage of the dialogue as a whole)?

Joyce's story, "The Dead" (in *Dubliners),* seems particularly to profit by a close attention to "stages."

In the first of its three parts, the keynote is expectancy, which is amplified by many appropriate details: talk of preparations, arrivals, introductions, apprehensions, while fittingly the section ends on an unfinished story. All these details are in terms of everyday sociality, to do with the warming-up of the party, stressing an avid engrossment in such an order of motives, as though they were the very essence of reality. There are a few superficial references to the theme of death (the passing mention of two dead relatives who are never mentioned again, and Gabriel's remark that he had been delayed because it had taken his wife "three mortal hours" to dress). And there is one enigmatic detail, though at this stage of the story it looks wholly realistic: the reference to the snow on Gabriel's galoshes and overcoat as he enters, bringing in a "cold fragrant air from out-of-doors."

The second stage, dealing with the party at its height, could be analyzed almost as a catalogue of superficial socialities, each in its way slightly false or misfit. The mood was set incipiently in the first part, when Gabriel offers the servant a tip. He had known her before she became a servant, hence his act (involving sociality of a sort) is not quite right. In the second stage, there is a welter of such intangible infelicities, as with the fact that Mary Jane's singing received the most vigorous applause from "four young men in the doorway who had gone away to the refreshment-room at the beginning of the piece but had come back when the piano had stopped." This section is a thesaurus of what we might call "halfway" socialities, such as Miss Ivor's "propagandism" for the Irish movement (in leaving early, she cries, "*Bean-nacht libh*"), Freddy's drunken amiability, Gabriel's dutiful conversation with Freddy's mother, the parlor talk about music, the conviviality through common participation in the materials of the feast, Gabriel's slightly hollow after-dinner speech that was noisily acclaimed, Gabriel's distant relationship to two of the women who are giving the party, the few words with his wife indicating familiarity without intimacy, the somewhat gingerly treatment of the one Protestant among Catholics.

Such is the theme amplified, with apparent realistic engrossment, in this section. There are also a few explicit but glancing references to death. One threatens to be serious, when some of the Catholics try to tell the Protestant why certain monks sleep in their coffins; but "as the subject had grown lugubrious it was buried in a silence of the table," etc. And twice there is the enigmatic antithesis, the theme of the snow in the night, still wholly realistic in guise: "Gabriel's warm trembling fingers tapped the cold pane of the window. How cool it must be outside! How pleasant it would be to walk out alone, first along by the river and then through the park! The snow would be lying on the branches of the trees and forming a bright cap on the top of the Wellington Monument." In the other passage, there is likewise a reference to the "gleaming cap of snow" that Gabriel associated with the Monument. (One never knows how exacting to be, when comparing such passages; yet, as regards these references to the "cap" of snow, looking back we note that, when Gabriel first entered, the light fringe of snow lay "like a cape" on his shoulders. Cap—cape. Where secret identifi-

cations are taking form, since we are in time to learn that this snow
stands for some essence beyond the appearances of halfway sociality,
might not the signatures mark their secret relationship thus punwise?

In any case, the third section deals with events following the party.
The cycle of realistic expectations and eventualities is drawing to a
close. The party breaks up. We are now free to penetrate the implications of the antithetical moment. ("How much more pleasant it would
be there than at the supper table!" Gabriel had thought, in one of
those two outlaw flashes when he had imagined the snow outside in
the night.)

The first two sections were best described, we think, by a block-
like method. Thus, for the first, we simply noted how the theme of
expectancy could be stated in variation; and for the second, we broke
the analysis into a list of variations on the theme of halfway sociality.
For the point we were trying to make, it didn't matter in what order
we listed these details. But the third section concerns initiation into a
mystery. It is to take us beyond the realm of realism, as so conceived,
into the realm of ideality. Hence, there is a strict succession of stages,
in the development towards a more exacting kind of vision. Each stage
is the way-in to the next, as the narrow-visioned expectations of the
party had been the way-in to the disclosures following the party.

The party is over. Where will we go? Is there not a symbolism
emerging in the realism, when Gabriel tells the anecdote of the old
horse that went round and round the monument? Next, the topic becomes that of every-which-way (we are still undecided), as the cabman is given conflicting directions by different members of the party.
"The confusion grew greater and the cabman was directed differently by Freddy Malins and Mr. Browne, each of whom had his head
out through a window of the cab. The difficulty was to know where
to drop Mr. Browne along the route, and Aunt Kate, Aunt Julia and
Mary Jane helped the discussion from the doorstep with cross-direc-
tions and contradictions and abundance of laughter." Finally, "the
horse was whipped up and the cab rattled off along the quay amid
a chorus of laughter and adieus." We are en route, so far as realistic
topics are concerned. But Gabriel and his wife have not yet left. And
the development from now on is to concern them. Tableau: A man is
singing; Gabriel's wife, Gretta, is listening attentively, standing on the
staircase, "near the top of the first flight"; Gabriel, below, is looking up

admiringly. And "he asked himself what is a woman standing on the stairs in the shadows, listening to distant music, a symbol of."

Previously we mentioned the form of the *Theaetetus:* how, every time Socrates had brought things to an apparently satisfactory close, each such landing-place was found to be but the occasion for a new flight, a new search, that first seemed like an arrival, then opened up a new disclosure in turn. We believe that the remainder of this story possesses "dialectical form" in much that same sense. You might even call it the narrative equivalent of a Platonic dialogue. For from now on, Gabriel goes through a series of disclosures. Each time, he thinks he is really close to the essence; then another consideration emerges, that requires him to move on again. Let's be as bluntly schematic as possible. It is not our job to regive the quality of the story; for that, one should go to the story itself. The stages, schematized, are these:

(1) As against the familiar but not intimate relations we have already seen, between Gabriel and his wife, here is a new motive; Gabriel sees "grace and mystery in her attitude as if she were a symbol of something." And later, just before she asks the name of the song, at the sight of her flushed cheeks and shining eyes "a sudden tide of joy went leaping out of his heart."

(2) They had arranged to spend the night in a nearby hotel. Hence, passages to suggest that he is recovering some of the emotions he had felt at the time of their honeymoon. ("Their children, his writing, her household cares had not quenched all their souls' tender fire," a reflection growing out of realistic reference to a literal fire.)

(3) Crossing a bridge, amid talk of the snow on the statue, while "Gabriel was again in a cab with her, galloping to catch the boat, galloping to their honeymoon."

(4) Building up the sense of Gabriel's possessiveness ("happy that she was his, proud of her grace and wifely carriage [. . .] a keen pang of lust [. . .] a new adventure," etc.).

(5) But, after the porter has assigned them to their room and left, the moment does not seem right. Gabriel's irritation.

(6) She kisses him, calls him "a generous person." His self-satisfaction. "Now that she had fallen to him so easily, he wondered why he had been so diffident."

(7) Then the disclosures begin. He finds that he has misgauged everything. She has been thinking of that song. (Gabriel sees himself in the mirror) .

(8) At first taken aback, he next recovers his gentleness, then makes further inquiries. Angry, he learns that the song reminds her of a boy, Michael Furey, who used to sing the song. His jealousy. (Thus, up to now, each step nearer to her had been but the preparation for a more accurate sense of their separation.)

(9) On further inquiry, he learns of the boy's frail love for her. "I think he died for me," Gretta said, whereat "A vague terror seized Gabriel at this answer, as if, at that hour when he had hoped to triumph, some impalpable and vindictive being was coming against him, gathering forces against him in its vague world." [2] He died for her? Died that something might live? It is an arresting possibility.

(10) After telling of this adolescent attachment, she cries herself to sleep.

So, we have narrowed things down, from all the party, to Gabriel and Gretta, and now to Gabriel alone. The next two pages or so involve a silent discipline, while he brings himself to relinquish his last claims upon her, as specifically his. The world of *conditions* is now to be transcended. Gretta had called him "generous," in a passage that Gabriel had misgauged. Now we learn that "generous tears filled Gabriel's eyes." The transcending of conditions, the ideal abandoning of property, is stated in Joyce's own words, thus: "His own identity was falling

---

[2] One observer analyzing the *Portrait,* noted that among the body-spirit equations were grease and gas, grease being to body as gas is to spirit. Hence, on learning that Michael Furey "was in the gasworks," we assume that his spirituality is thus signalized roundabout, too. But we don't quite know what to make of the possible relation between "Gretta" and "great" in these lines:

> "I suppose you were in love with this Michael Furey, Gretta," he said.
> "I was great with him at that time," she said.

Probably nothing should be made of it. But we do believe that such correlations should be noted tentatively. For we would ask ourselves how methodic a terminology is. Correspondences should be noted. But they should be left at loose ends, except when there are good reasons for tying such ends together.

out into a grey impalpable world: the solid world itself, which these dead had one time reared and lived in, dissolving and dwindling." For "his soul had approached that region where dwell the vast hosts of the dead."

Understandably, for if the world of conditions is the world of the living, then the transcending of conditions will, by the logic of such terms, equal the world of the dead. (Or, Kant-wise, we contemplate the divine; for if God transcends nature, and nature is the world of conditions, then God is the unconditioned.)

Psychologically, there are other likely interpretations here. Gabriel, finally, loves his wife, not even in terms of his honeymoon (with its strong connotations of ownership), but through the medium of an adolescent, dead at seventeen. With this dead boy he identifies himself. Perhaps because here likewise was a kind of unconditionedness, in the Gidean sense, that all was still largely in the realm of unfulfilled possibilities, inclinations or dispositions not yet rigidified into channels? There is even the chance that, in his final yielding, his identification with the dead boy, he is meeting again his own past adolescent self, with all its range of susceptibilities, surviving now only like a shade in his memory.

In any case, once we have been brought to this stage of "generosity," where Gabriel can at last arrive at the order of ideal sociality, seeing all living things in terms of it, we return to the topic of snow, which becomes the mythic image, in the world of conditions, standing for the transcendence above the conditioned.

It was falling on every part of the dark central plain, on the treeless hills, falling softly upon the Bog of Allen and, farther westward, softly falling into the dark mutinous Shannon waves. It was falling, too, upon every part of the lonely churchyard on the hill where Michael Furey lay buried. It lay thickly drifted on the crooked crosses and headstones, on the spears of the little gate, on the barren thorns. His soul swooned slowly as he heard the snow falling faintly through the universe and faintly falling, like the descent of their last end, upon the living and the dead.

"Upon the living and the dead." That is, upon the two as merged. That is, upon the world of conditions as seen through the spirit of conditions transcended, of ideal sociality beyond material divisiveness.

3

The Language of Poetry, "Dramatistically" Considered[1]

IN THE FIRST SECTION OF THIS PAPER, partially following and partially departing from Cicero's "three offices of the orator," we propose that four "offices" be considered as essential to the analysis of poetic symbolism. Since our discussion in this first part is in general terms, we alter the procedure in the second section by using Goethe's *Faust* as text and making specific observations about it, along the lines previously indicated. As regards the relation between individual texts and social motives in general (poetic "beauty" as seen in terms of social tensions), we aim to indicate how the work reflects, and "cathartically" transforms for aesthetic purposes, the "pyramidal" motives of the social order, by the tragic symbolizing of a "perfect" victimage. We lay special stress upon the Negative here, because of its relation to the ethical (which characteristically heads in such negatives as the Decalogue). In the third section we seek to round out our concerns by indicating how the symbolizing of perfect victimage relates to a purely technical kind of perfection (the "entelechial" principle that we consider natural to the genius of language).

---

[1] This essay first appeared in *Chicago Review*. "The Language of Poetry, 'Dramatistically Considered.'" *Chicago Review* 8.4 (Fall 1954): 88–102. Reprinted by permission. The essay was originally written for a symbolism seminar conducted in 1952–1953 by The Institute for Religious and Social Studies, New York.

I

We would spin this discussion from Cicero's terms for the "three offices of the orator." (See *Orator, De Oratore,* and St. Augustine's use of this alignment for his analysis of Christian persuasion in his *De Doctrina Christiana.)*

First office: to teach or inform (*docere*). Second office: to please (*delectare*). Third office: to move, or "bend" (*movere, flectare*).

Thus instead of beginning with a theory of "signs," and looking for ways to "expand" it into a theory of "symbols," we begin with terms that assume the full "emotionality" of speech. [2]

The first office (*docere*) would be the indicative or scientific function of speech, its relation to matters of *knowledge.* The third office (*movere*) would be the persuasive or rhetorical function of speech, its use to arouse in an auditor some attitude that implies a desired kind of *act* or acquiescence in a desired kind of *policy.* The second office, to please or entertain (*delectare*), must, for our purposes, be redefined.

---

[2] If we did begin with a theory of signs in the narrower sense, we should begin realistically rather than epistemologically: that is, our basic proposition would be, "Each thing is the sign of something else" (Not the sign of everything else!). For instance, the symptoms of a disease would be considered as "natural signs" of that disease, regardless of whether they were properly interpreted. And the disease in turn would be the sign of conditions varying in scope. These conditions may, for instance, be the sign of a deficiency in diet, which in turn may in one case be the sign of dietary ignorance, in another case the sign of poverty. And the ignorance or poverty would be signs of still other conditions, our belief in their reality as signs of other things justifying us in our attempt to find out what they may be signs of (as cryptologists seek to interpret the signs of a lost language, the records of which have their particular structure precisely because they are signs, though the analyst when he begins his study has very little idea what they may be signs of). (In this way, to be sure, the quest for signs may expand to the point where the discussion of some one thing leads us into the discussion of almost everything. In this sense, by telescoping all the steps, one might say that each thing is the sign of "everything else," somewhat as the detective may spin his whole detection from some crucial bit of evidence which could be said to "sum up" the entire chain of his evidence. But insofar as all the intermediate steps of induction and deduction are supplied, the broad interpretation of a tiny detail is not essentially "mystical" or "unscientific." At the worst it is the inaccurate use of a sound principle.)

In its simplest guise, the "entertainment" aspect of an orator's speech corresponds to the fiction in a popular commercial magazine. The fiction is nominally of the "art for art's sake" sort. But it functions rhetorically to assemble an audience which the rhetorical advertisements can then address as prospective customers. Similarly, an orator who is trying to persuade an audience to some decision or attitude must find ways of keeping his audience sufficiently amused so that they will continue to be an audience (though the purpose of his address is not to amuse them, but to enlist them in some "cause"). For the purposes of this paper, however, the "second office" must be greatly expanded beyond so rudimentary a notion of the pleasurable.

The first and third offices concern elements *outside* the address. (The first is, at least ostensibly, concerned with information about nonverbal "reality"; and the third is directed toward the moving of the auditor to attitudes with practical consequences which, it is hoped, will prevail after the speech is over.) But we would expand the second office in keeping with a principle of *internality*.

Insofar as a work is appealing *through the laws of its resources as a medium,* we would treat such appeal as a function of the second office.

Man being the typically language-using species, there is for him an intrinsic delight in the *sheer exercising* of his distinctive characteristic (language, or symbol-using in general). This delight in itself is not addressed either to "reality" or to "the auditor." It is a delight in the internal consistency of a symbolic structure as such (in such a spinning-out-of-itself as Santayana calls the distinguishing mark of dialectics).

Aristotle, it will be recalled, had divided up the field of rhetoric somewhat differently. He distinguished not three offices of the orator but three kinds of oratory: the deliberative (as with debates on public policy); the forensic (as with pleas in the law courts); and the epideictic or demonstrative (concerned with matters of praise and blame). The third would probably have included such modern variants as a publicity man's attempt to "build up" his client in the public imagination. A patriotic oration delivered at a celebration of Independence Day would be a closer approximation.

The nearest overlap between Aristotle's way of carving up the field and Cicero's is the area where Aristotle's category of the "epideictic" or "demonstrative" overlaps upon Cicero's *second* office. The overlap becomes more obvious when we think of oratory in decay. The decadent

Athenian orator, for instance, might deliver an oration in praise of his beloved's cosmetics; or the decadent Roman orator might delight his audience by improvising a trick-laden oration on a topic called out to him from the audience. And you could, as you prefer, class such toying with the medium for its own sake either as an instance of the second Ciceronian office or as an instance of Aristotelian epideictic.

(Indeed, precisely when such oratory is in decay its condition may best reveal the delight in the linguistic forms as such. Whereas the formal devices were invented for the purposes of intense persuasion, a weakening of moral urgency brought strongly to the fore the cult of sheer formality. When men had nothing much to say they could still enjoy the purely internal exercise of the saying.)

Over and beyond the profound significance of the reference in Spinoza's *Ethics,* the work has appealed to men because it "dramatizes" the principle of internal development. Spinoza's proposal to spin his demonstrations *more geometrico* from a limited number of definitions and axioms was a very entertaining gesture. All cogent argument has an appeal of this sort, the appeal of symbolic structure developing from its own internal resources, in accordance with its own principles. But in Spinoza's case the principle of internality was more than merely *formal,* it was challengingly *formalistic.* Considered as rhetoric, it was a kind of stylistic "conceit"; and in this sense it meets the requirements of Cicero's second office (though, of course, only for readers who can find such a difficult device of exposition "entertaining").

The often-heard statements that mathematics is "elegant," or that the solving of problems in physics can be "beautiful," or that there can be something "aesthetic" in "science," would seem to involve our proposal for widening the scope of Cicero's second office to include this sheer delight in symbolic unfolding for its own sake (a delight one could expect of an animal species whose every attainment and every misfortune strikingly shows the results of its symbol-using fury).

Science, as knowledge or information, would obviously belong with the first office. But in its nature as expression for its own sake a scientific exposition would be like a "poem." Indeed, though scientific utterance is primarily indicative, "descriptive," it can also be analyzed secondarily as either poetically expressive or rhetorically hortatory; similarly, even "pure" poetry can be analyzed secondarily as "scientific information" or as "rhetorical propaganda"; and rhetoric has both its measure of "truth" and its measure of "poetry." (In his treatise *On the*

Sublime Longinus shows us how, once the urgency of the occasion is past, an orator's attempts to move an audience to practical decisions involve formal devices that can be enjoyed for themselves, as pure appeals to the "imagination.")

In sum, arbitrarily assigning to the letters *svid* the meaning "a loathsome person," if one says, "Mr. Q is a svid" not just because he is but because one wants the auditor to loathe him, one is using the term rhetorically. If one says "Mr. Q is a svid" not because he is, or because one wants people to loathe him, but just because one takes delight in vituperation as such, then one is using the term poetically (as sheer exercising of the linguistic medium). If one says "Mr. Q is a svid" purely because Mr. Q is actually deemed loathsome, one is using the term scientifically, indicatively. And the test of this usage would be in the fact that one could accomplish one's purpose as well, if not better, by a "neutral" paraphrase, as were one to add, "And by a 'svid' I mean a person deemed loathsome by persons who may or may not be justified in their judgment." Though a complete absence of attitude is probably impossible, a typical scientific expression can at least point in that direction, whereas rhetorical expression will seek to make the attitude as intense as is deemed proper to the desired practical ("external") result, while poetry will seek to make the attitude as intense as is deemed proper to the desired "aesthetic" ("internal") result.

Such a purely "aesthetic" aim can greatly contribute to "science" (or perhaps, more properly, to "philosophy," science in the sense of "wisdom" rather than "knowledge"): for, by sheerly internal spinning, it may seek complications of itself, as were the poet at one point to have his "hero" admired for doing much the same thing as his "villain" was loathed for doing at another point; and out of such sheer "exercising" of the medium's resources there can unfold, at least in glimpses, deftly "perverse" moments that lead toward a profoundly humane pity.

Doctor Nagel's essay on "Symbolism and Science" divides his terms into three classes: "descriptive symbols," "auxiliary symbols," and "maxims." Do we not here find the three "offices," but transformed to fit the specific needs of his field? The "descriptive" symbols would correspond to the external or scenic reference of the first office. Since he defines an "auxiliary symbol" as one "whose primary function is to serve as a connection between other symbols," he would here seem to be discussing the sheerly internal aspect of a symbolism, the interconnective devices whereby it can be spun out of itself. This would fit perfectly with the second office, once its scope had been expanded to include the appeal of symbolic internality as such (an "aesthetic" appeal that Doctor Nagel has also mentioned, though in a somewhat different placement). And since "maxims" are said to "formulate instructions or resolutions as to how to employ symbols," here would be the *hortatory* function of the third office.

All three, we repeat, have been transformed to meet the specific requirements of the subject-matter. Thus we are most decidedly not saying that a scientific "maxim" would be "nothing but" what Cicero meant by devices for "moving" an audience. On the contrary! But it seems that, *mutatis mutandis,* the *principles* of the three "offices" still figure here. (Logic, as the orderly generalizing of observed "facts," would lean toward the office of *docere;* insofar as logic appeals by reason of our delight in the sheer exercising of its own internal resources, it would lean toward the office of *delectare;* and the office of *movere,* of persuasion, would be provided by the "cogency" of the maxims in guiding the reader to the desired conclusions.)

But though we have considered an utterance in terms of external reference ("objective reality"), internal development (consistency), and effect upon the auditor (persuasion), there is a fourth "office" still to be taken care of. We refer to the utterance as "portraiture," as the "self-expression" of an agent, as an act characteristic of the poet's "personality" whether or not he so wills it. Aristotle deals with this problem from the purely rhetorical point of view when discussing devices whereby the speaker can deliberately promote an audience's confidence in him simply as a person, regardless of the cause that is being advocated or of the speaker's true nature. And Cicero impinges upon this fourth consideration in the very *form* of his formula, which concerns the three offices of the *orator.*

A poetic symbolism, when appreciated in its internality, is received as a kind of *symbolic action undertaken in and for itself,* a "free exercise" implicitly guided by the developmental principles which it embodies. In this respect it differs from the "reconnaissance," or *preparation for action,* which is the indicative function of scientific utterance, and from the *inducement to action* which is the persuasive function of rhetorical utterance. But in its role as *self-portraiture,* poetic symbolism obligates us to a different kind of search.

The "weighting" of words arises from extra-poetic situations in the social order. A relative fixity of conditions in the social order (what

Malinowski would have called the "context of situation") makes it possible for a person to learn what Bentham would call the "censorial" nature of terms ("appellatives"). One learns it by hearing the terms used in contexts that imply moral judgments. However, one may next "play with" such terms, experimentally giving them a range of meanings that do not fit their orthodox use as sheer instruments of "social control." That is, *by setting up special conditions within a given work of art* one might, without "demoralization," even bring things to a point where, in effect, terms for the loathsome could be applied to a most admirable person and vice versa.

Some critics might grow morally indignant. In effect, they would be saying that the simple rhetorical usefulness of the term was being endangered by such "free" poetic exercising. If the term was weighted for practical ends, and if such orthodox rhetorical weighting is poetically undone, then a tiny verbal revolution has taken place. And a vigilant orthodoxy might choose to be outraged at this implied threat to the given social order. [3]

---

[3] Since writing the first draft of these pages I have seen the report of the seminar meeting for February 5th, where Doctor MacIver's distinction between sign and symbol is well summed up thus: "The sign is a pointer or indicator, the symbol an evoker." This distinction is unquestionably sufficient for many purposes. But we believe that, where poetry is concerned, the concept of "evocation" must be subdivided. For there is a notable difference between poetic expression and rhetorical persuasion, though both would be aspects of "evocation."

It is notable that whereas Ogden and Richards in *The Meaning of Meaning* favor a dichotomy much like the one Doctor MacIver opts for, Richards in his *Principles of Literary Criticism* attributes to poetry a kind of attitudinizing that is qualified differently from the attitudes evoked by rhetoric. Whereas rhetorical evocation should make us want to "go out and do something about it," poetic evocation should be a closed system of gratifications. Rhetoric is a stimulus to some subsequent act; but the kind of action proper to the reading of poetry is an end product in itself.

True, there is a sense in which everything has implications beyond itself; even a rock lying inertly by the roadside may have, as part of its "future," the possibility of being picked up and thrown. Similarly, poetic symbolism may have effects upon our future conduct, in the most practical sense of the term. But, *as poetry,* its appeal is in its state of *completion,* not its *futurity.* It leads into the future only incidentally, or because the future is implicitly in it. It appeals, that is, by its *finishedness,* or "perfection."

There are other possibilities, of course. For instance, a more liberal-minded critic might hold that, even as a means of social control, the weighting of words in poetry should not be too strict, too much like the manifestation of a sheerly mechanical conditioning. Such a critic might hold that in the long run art better serves even a purely *pragmatic* function, as an instrument of social cohesion, when it can admit to contemplation a very wide range of meanings.

The liberal critic might also point to the fact that, in the given work, *a special set of conditions* was more or less clearly posited. In this respect he might point out that the transformations of the terms were *controlled,* as in the dialectic of a properly controlled dialogue. (If they really were!) In any case, here would seem to be the situation, as regards the "portraiture" (be it voluntary or involuntary) in a work of art:

Human personality is not just "pure." It is formed with reference to social roles. Accordingly, the "personality" in a work of art impinges upon the social situation in general. Intrinsic analysis leads us to study the work of art as a kind of act in and for itself. But a concern with the "personality" of a work involves us in the study of the work as the act of an agent in a scene.

Of what sort, then, is the agent? And of what sort is his scene? Otherwise put: What is his biography? And where is it placed in history?

Obviously, there is a great range of answers possible to such questions. We can conceive of biography in the most minute sense: detailed information regarding some particular taxpayer at some particular time and place. Or, at the other extreme, we can think of the given work's "personality" as the snapshot of some one posture that is at least momentarily typical of "mankind" in general. And the intermediate

---

We believe that such is the case even with so-called "propaganda" art. Imagine a work, for instance, designed to arouse in the audience an attitude of great sympathy or animosity with regard to some contemporary faction or cause. Even so clearly tendentious or didactic a work appeals *poetically* by the satisfactory exercising of such emotions in the immediate present. Even the sense of "futurity" that might be aroused by such a work appeals by its nature as an attitude summed up, or completed, *now.* (We shall consider later a notable respect in which a distinction between "sign" and "symbol" necessarily becomes confused, so far as the analysis of poetic expression is concerned; for a poetic expression may in part owe its evocative function to its function as indicative.)

views are many, if not infinite. Is there, then, a special argument for a single emphasis among the lot?

Probably not, "in general." As many angles as there are, or can be, are "right." For there is a sense in which every perspective upon existence, as viewed from some individual existing spot, is "justified" by being what it is. And there might properly be even more biographies than there were people. *But when we narrow our considerations to the special terms of a symbolism seminar, do not the conditions of our inquiry itself point toward the criterion we are looking for?* That is: Should we not consider the "personality" of a poem in terms of the *symbolic* ingredients in personality?

Personality so viewed is a kind of "congealed conduct." Insofar as an act is representative (or "symbolic") of an agent, that act is the manifestation of some underlying "moral principle" in the agent. Insofar as the act does not represent some underlying principle of the agent's character, some fixed trait of his personality, then it is not truly characteristic of him. Then it is not so much an act as an accident (so far as its relation to the *agent* is concerned, though it may be consistent with some motive supplied by the *scene*).

But surely poetic structures that are developed as the distillations, or summings-up, of long or intense personal experience and of exceptional technical concentration should be studied as "acts," not as "accidents." And, symbol-wise, our *general* approach to the "personality" of any particular symbolic structure would be through considerations of the fact that man is an essentially symbol-using species.

Thus as regards the "personality" of an art work, its "fourth office," we in a symbolism seminar should approach our problems through a central concern with the characteristics of a society of typically *symbol-using* organisms (their typical resources and embarrassments). [4]

The writer of this paper believes that such an approach centers in the symbolizing of guilt, redemption, hierarchy, mortification, victimage, "catharsis." And for reasons discussed elsewhere (notably in an essay, "A Dramatistic View of the Origins of Language," now appearing serially in *The Quarterly Journal of Speech*), he would lay special stress upon the role of negativity in language. For he believes

---

[4] In its function as characteristic perhaps it might as well be considered as but a variant of the "first" office? For it is as much a "natural sign" as are the symptoms of an ailment, though there can be much controversy as to exactly what it may be a sign of.

that negativity is a peculiarly linguistic invention; and that "Personality" or "Character," considered as an overriding or underlying motivational principle in the work of art, profoundly involves the principle of negativity (which takes surprisingly many forms, including many quasi-positive ones).

Though we do not believe that "poetic exercising" as such involves the settling of scores outside the work of art (since the work of art, in its internality, is as extrinsic to the world's problems as are the purely internal relations of a crossword puzzle), such an admission by no means ties us to the notion that poetry, in its bountiful verbal materiality, is to be considered as thus confined. The work of art is produced by a constant succession of new decisions on the part of the author. Even when a work reaches the fatal point at which it "begins to write itself," spinning from what has gone before, and perhaps actually *forcing* the writer to change his original plans (in case he has laid down co-ordinates which, he finds in the course of writing, don't have the implications he originally imputed to them)—even then, if the agent were not constantly goaded anew, the project would lapse.

And what goads him, over and beyond the "logic" of his premises? Or what goaded him to hit upon such implied premises in the first place? We take it that the goad arises from extra-aesthetic tensions in the social order. At this point the artist's individual personality dissolves into the "personality" of the given social order, while that in turn dissolves into principles of "sociality" in general. The negative genius of language, or symbol-using, heads in the thou-shalt-not's of the ethical, proscriptions shaped with regard to the given social order and its corresponding kinds of ownership, expectancy, and obligation. All such "values" provide material for "free" use in a work of art.

In the *Poetics* Aristotle gives a perfect instance of such use when, having said that a tragedy is more effective if the action is made to seem marvelous, he remarks that accidental occurrences are most likely to arouse a sense of wonder if they are made to seem providential, as when the statue of Mitys fell and killed the man who had killed Mitys. The feeling of fatality is here considered purely as a resource to be exploited for a poetic effect. This is what we would call a "free" use of a religious propensity.

André Gide, as a master of perversity, clearly illustrates such "free" poetic use of a general human propensity by his treatment of the *acte gratuit,* the pragmatically motiveless crime, done for sheer love of the art, as pure gesture. This conceit, setting up an "aesthetic" of crime, troubles and outrages the reader in a way that even the cruelest of offences cannot do when motivated by no matter how abominable a purpose. About the edges of our consciousness we feel the whole logic of worldly conspiracy being dissolved by this parody of divine freedom, a parody because God's act of creation was gratuitous. Thus as a poetic device it gives the reader a new "thrill," getting (in a wholly non-Aristotelian way) the appeal of the "marvelous" in the forming of the plot. It may be studied specifically in terms of Gide's character (in which connection it seems related to the motives of his work that are manifested in its homosexual motifs). It may be studied more generally in terms of its relation to the contemporary social order, which, for one reason or another, has called forth many excellent works of perverse cast. Or it may be studied more generally still, as one way, among many possible ones, in which the principle of negativity can be "personalized," in terms of human character. (Gide summed it up formally in connection with his character Lafcadio, to whom "thou shalt not [. . .] " invariably suggested "what would happen if [. . .] ?")

The principle of negativity is personalized differently (becomes a different kind of "strategy") in Hemingway's short story, "A Clean, Well-Lighted Place," which comes to a focus in the parody of the Lord's Prayer as the word "nothing" is substituted for nearly all the substantival words in the text, thus: "our nada who art in nada, nada be thy name thy kingdom nada thy will be nada in nada as it is in nada," etc.

But the principle of negativity by no means always takes perverse forms. Here, for instance, is a passage in Emerson where it is quite edifying:

> Sensible objects conform to the premonitions of Reason and reflect the conscience. All things are moral; and in their boundless changes have an unceasing reference to spiritual nature. Therefore is nature glorious with form, color, and motion; that every globe in the remotest heaven, every chemical change from the rudest crystal up to the laws of life, every change of vegetation from the first principle of growth in the eye of a leaf, to the tropical forest and antediluvian coal-mine, every animal function from the sponge up to Hercules, shall hint or thunder to man the laws of right and wrong, and echo the Ten Commandments.

For present purposes, we shall survey (far too briefly, so far as justice to the text is concerned) the first part of Goethe's *Faust*. The negative guidance of the work is clear enough, as regards the role of Mephistopheles. Also, we can observe with relative ease the relations between the "character" of the work and the "magic" of the social order (brought together through the personal medium of an author who was both romantic poet and court minister). And by taking a specific case as our text we might be able to discover what kinds of distinctions are necessary or possible for the analysis of poetic symbolism.

A purely indicative function, for instance, may be clearly demarcated from an evocative one where such things as labels on bottles in a laboratory are concerned. But though the name of a character in a fiction is indicative, serving with perfect accuracy to differentiate a reference to this character from a reference to any other ideal entity in the book, there is also a respect in which the name may come to have a kind of "summational" nature, even in its purely indicative functions. That is, the name comes to *be a sign* for certain kinds of expectancies on the part of the reader, so that, when the character appears, certain kinds of development rather than other kinds are anticipated (or "predicted"). The name here becomes, we might say, the sign not of an entity but of a *principle*. And though such a principle is a necessary condition for the evoking of emotional attitudes in the reader, it is on the signalizing side of the name's functioning.

One might state the problem thus: We come to expect of a certain character a certain quality of action. Depending upon our sympathies, we may or may not "want" such action to prevail at a given time in the plot. Or, more accurately, supposing that we don't want it to prevail, we nonetheless "hope against hope" that, if it does prevail, *it will prevail* under conditions that will somehow make it acceptable. The "evocative" ingredient in the name depends upon our *attitude* toward the quality of action expected, as being deemed "natural" to the given character. But regardless of how our sympathies might line up, the name must first of all be purely and simply a true sign for the given quality of action anticipated in connection with it. If it is not, the work is inferior as a fiction. The tendency to equate science with the signatory or indicative and art with the evocative can conceal the exceptional degree to which the "first office" figures in the arousing of poetic expectancies (the proper poetic equivalent of "prediction").

Conversely, the distinction conceals from us the intense "pageantry" of science, its nature as a social "magic," as a discipline infused, or made radiant by motives extrinsic to its specialties as such, but intrinsic to it as a mode of action evolved by the symbol-using species of organism. The bottles in the laboratory are not just "labeled." There is a sense in which they are not merely "perceived," but evoke "emotions." Furtively, they become "home," or "second nature."

The "personality" of symbols, which they necessarily possess by reason of the fact that they are used by persons, involves ultimately their place in human pageantry generically. And we contend that a study of symbolism should aim to penetrate ultimately into the magic of this hierarchal realm. "Local" problems in the theory of signs, we hold, should be treated in ways that fit well with the analysis of all social pageantry, as determined by the inclusion of linguistic elements.

Let us now turn to *Faust,* not in the hopes of making an adequate analysis in so brief a space, but by way of illustrating what we consider typical concerns in the "dramatistic" analysis of poetic symbolism.[5]

[To be concluded]

---

[5] Incidentally, since we have referred to Doctor Nagel's paper, we might close this section by saluting what we consider to be a perfectly "dramatistic" moment in it. We refer to his remarks on the principle of causality: "The principle states no 'law of nature' and has no identifiable descriptive content. On the contrary, the principle functions as a maxim, as a somewhat vague rule for directing the course of inquiry, as an injunction to interpret and organize our experience in a certain manner. For what the principle says in effect is this: When some occurrence takes place, look for the circumstances which are necessary and sufficient conditions for that occurrence! Do not cease your quest until such circumstances have been discovered, and count no analysis as adequate or complete which does not terminate in the construction of a theory that conforms to the pattern of a deterministic schema of interpretation! [. . .] It is perhaps a debatable question whether the total rejection of the principle does not entail the complete abandonment of the scientific enterprise." One should also note the strongly negative cast of this statement, first in the explicit negatives, next in the implied negativity of words like "rejection" and "abandonment," and finally in the fact that Doctor Nagel explicitly points out the negative implications of his words "maxim," "rule," and "injunction." Here is an area where "pragmatism" and "dramatism" *quite happily* overlap.

4

Fact, Inference, and Proof in the Analysis of Literary Symbolism[1]

I

THIS ESSAY IS PART OF A PROJECT called "Theory of the Index," concerned with the taking of preparatory notes for purposes of critical analysis. The hope is to make the analysis of literary symbolism as systematic as possible, while allowing for an experimental range required by the subtle and complex nature of the subject matter.

Fundamentally, the essay is built about the "principle of the concordance." But whereas concordances, listing all passages where a given word appears in a text, have been compiled for a few major works, obviously criticism cannot have the advantage of such scholarship when studying the terminology of most literary texts. And even where concordances are available, there must be grounds for paying more attention to some terms than to others.

Here, treating the individual words of a work as the basic "facts" of that work, and using for test case some problems in the "indexing" of James Joyce's *A Portrait of the Artist as a Young Man*,[2] the essay asks

---

[1] *Perspectives by Incongruity/Terms for Order*, Kenneth Burke, ed. Stanley Edgar Hyman, Indiana University Press, 1964. 145–72. © The Kenneth Burke Literary Trust. Used by permission.

[2] For purposes of ready reference, where illustration seems necessary, the rules and principles discussed here will be illustrated by reference to a single text, James Joyce's *A Portrait of the Artist as a Young Man*. The essay stresses methodological considerations that the critic encounters in attempt-

49

how to operate with these "facts," how to use them as a means of keeping one's inferences under control, yet how to go beyond them, for purposes of inference, when seeking to characterize the motives and "salient traits" of the work, in its nature as a total symbolic structure.

Insofar as possible, we confine the realm of the "factual" to a low but necessary and unquestioned order of observations. Thus, it is a "fact" that the book proper begins, "Once upon a time and a very good time it was [. . .]" etc., and ends: "old father, old artificer, stand me now and ever in good stead." We say it is a fact that the "book proper" so begins and so ends. But it is also a "fact" that the text begins with a prior quotation from Ovid's *Metamorphoses* and ends on a reference to duality of scene: "Dublin, 1904/Trieste, 1914." We might get different results, depending upon which of these "facts" we worked from. But in either case, the existence of such "facts" is literally verifiable. "Facts" are what was said or done, as interpreted in the strictest possible sense.

The ideal "atomic fact" in literary symbolism is probably the individual word. We do not say that the literary work is "nothing but" words. We do say that it is "at least" words. True, a word is further reducible to smaller oral and visual particles (letters and phonemes); and such reducibility allows for special cases of "alchemic" transformation whereby the accident of a word's structure may surreptitiously relate it (punwise) to other words that happen to be similar in structure though "semantically" quite distinct from it. But the word is the first full "perfection" of a term. And we move from it either way as our base, either "back" to the dissolution of meaning that threatens it by reason of its accidental punwise associates, or "forward" to its dissolution through inclusion in a "higher meaning," which attains *its* perfection in the sentence.

Surprisingly enough, such a terministic approach to symbolism can be much more "factual" than is the case with reports about actual conditions or happenings in the extrasymbolic realm. In the extrasymbolic realm, there is usually a higher necessary percentage of "interpretation" or "inference" in a statement we call "factual." We can but infer what the diplomat did. But we can cite "factually" some report that

---

ing to characterize the "salient traits" of this work in its nature as a symbolic structure. Page numbers refer to the cheapest edition (the Signet paper edition); it is chosen because such indexing usually requires that the book be defaced by indicative markings.

says what he did. People usually think that the nonsymbolic realm is the clear one, while the symbolic realm is hazy. But if you agree that the words, or terms, in a book are its "facts," then by the same token you see there is a sense in which we get our view of *deeds* as facts from our sense of *words* as facts, rather than *vice versa*.

In this strict usage, many observations that might ordinarily be treated under the headings of "fact" fall on the side of "inference." For instance, when referring to the formula, "Dublin, 1904/Trieste, 1914," we described it as "a duality of scene." There is a slight tendentiousness here; for our characterization leans to the side of "Dublin *versus* Trieste" rather than to the side of "Dublin equals Trieste" (toward opposition rather than apposition). And when referring to the quotation from Ovid, we might rather have referred to the quoted words themselves, stressing perhaps the *original context* from which they were lifted. Thus quickly and spontaneously we smuggle inferences, or interpretations, into our report of the "factual." Yet, insofar as there is a record, there is an underlying structure of "factuality" to which we can repeatedly repair, in the hopes of hermeneutic improvement.

"Proof," then, would be of two sorts. While grounding itself in reference to the textual "facts," it must seek to make clear all elements of inference or interpretation it adds to these facts; and it must offer a rationale for its selections and interpretations. Ideally, it might even begin from different orders of "facts," and show how they led in the end to the same interpretation. We should not have much difficulty, for instance, in showing how "Dublin *versus* Trieste" could still allow for "Dublin equals Trieste," for there are respects in which Joyce's (or Stephen's!) original motives are transformed, and there are respects in which they were continued.

At the point of greatest ideal distance, an attempt to ground the analysis of literary symbolism in "terministic factuality" is to be contrasted with the analysis of symbols in terms of "analogy." If, for instance, the *word*, "tree," appears in two contexts, we would not begin by asking ourselves what rare "symbolic" meaning a tree might have, in either religious or psychoanalytic allegory. We would begin rather with the literal fact that this term bridges the two contexts.

Or let us go a step further. Suppose that you *did* begin with some pat meaning for tree, over and above its meaning as a positive concept. (In our hypothetical case, we are assuming that, whatever else "tree" may stand for, in these two contexts it at least refers to a tree in the primary dictionary sense, as it might not if one reference was to a "family tree.") Suppose you were prepared to say *in advance* exactly what recondite meaning the "image" of a tree might have, in its nature as a "symbol" enigmatically "emblematic" of esoteric meanings. (For instance, we could imagine a psychologist saying, "It's not just a 'tree'; it's a father-symbol, or a mother-symbol, or in general a parent-symbol.") Even if we granted that your "symbolic" or "analogical" meaning for "tree" was correct, *the fact would still remain* that the term had one particular set of associates in some particular work. This is the kind of interconnectedness we would watch, when studying the "facts" of an identical word that recurs in changing *contexts.* Such an investigation would be in contrast with the confining of one's interpretation to equivalences—"analogies"—already established even before one looks at the given text.

The "analogical" method is alluring, because by it you get these things settled once and for all. A good literature student, trained in the ways of indexing of "contexts" requires that each work be studied anew, "from scratch." Night, bird, sun, blood, tree, mountain, death? No matter, once the topic is introduced, analogy has the answer, without ever looking further.

Part of the trouble, to be sure, comes from the fact that often brief poems are the texts used. And the short lyric is the most *difficult* form to explain, as its transformations are necessarily quick, while being concealed beneath the lyric's urgent need to establish intense unity of mood (a need so urgent that in most lyrics the transformations are negligible, though such is not the case with great lyrists like Keats). Long forms (epics, dramas, novels, or poetic *sequences*) afford the most viable material for the study of terms in changing contexts. And the principles we learn through this better documented analysis can then be applied, *mutatis mutandis,* to the study of lyric "naturalness."

Three illustrations, before proceeding:

On p. 36, in connection with the episode of Stephen's unjust punishment, we read: " [. . .] the swish of the sleeve of the soutane as the pandybat was lifted to strike [. . .]" and "the soutane sleeve swished again as the pandybat was lifted [. . .] " On p. 119: "Then, just as he was wishing that some unforeseen cause might prevent the director from coming, he had heard the handle of the door turning and the swish of a soutane." Here the recurrence of the swish establishes a purely "factual" bond between the two passages; and this factual bond is to be noted first as such, in its sheer terminal identity, without reference to "symbolic" or "analogical" meanings. More remotely, the "swish" might be said to *subsist* punwise in "was wishing." Hence, if this iterative verb-form were noted elsewhere in the work, one might tentatively include its context, too, as part of this grouping (made by leaps and zigzags through the narrative).

Or one may isolate this concordance: p. 73 top, citing Shelley's "Art thou pale for weariness"; p. 136, Ben Jonson's, "I was not wearier where I lay"; p. 174, in Stephen's villanelle, "Are you not weary of ardent ways?"; and on p. 175, when Stephen is watching the birds as an augury, "leaning wearily on his ashplant [. . .] the ashplant on which he leaned wearily [. . .] a sense of fear of the unknown moved in the heart of his weariness." (Ordinarily, we take it that the various grammatical forms of a word can be treated as identical. But one must always be prepared for a case where this will not be so. One could imagine a work, for instance, in which "fly" and "flight" were so used that "fly" was found to appear only in contexts meaning "soar above" or "transcend," whereas "flight" was only in contexts meaning "flee." Ordinarily, "flight" would cover both meanings, as we believe the symbol of flight does in Joyce. Or should we say that in Stephens ecstatic vision of artistic flight the "negative" sense of *fleeing* attains rather the "positive" sense of *flying?*)

Or again: on p. 168 top, Stephen's esthetic is stated doctrinally thus: "The artist, like the god of the creation, remains within or behind or beyond or above his handiwork, invisible, refined out of existence, indifferent, paring his fingernails." Without yet asking ourselves what such paring of the nails may "symbolize," we "factually" unite this passage with "[. . .] some fellows called him Lady Boyle because he was always at his nails, paring them" (p. 30 top); and (p. 32): "Mr. Gleason had round shiny cuffs and clean white wrists and fattish white hands and the nails of them were long and pointed. Perhaps he pared them too like Lady Boyle."

Such concordances are initially noted without inference or interpretation. For whereas purely terministic correlation can serve the ends of "analogical" or "symbolic" exegesis, it is far more tentative and empirical, with a constant demand for fresh inquiry. In fact, one may experimentally note many correlations of this sort without being able to fit them into an over-all scheme of interpretation.

But a grounding in the concordances of "terminal factuality" is by no means a solution to our problems.

2

If we are to begin with a "factual" index, what do we feature? Obviously, we cannot make a concordance of every book we read. And besides, even if we had a concordance before we began, we must find some principle of selection, since some terms are much more likely than others to yield good hermeneutical results. If a researcher is looking for *some particular topic,* of course, there is no problem of selection. But if the critic is attempting to characterize, in as well rounded a way as he can, the salient traits of the given work, trying to give an over-all interpretation of it as a unified symbolic act, he has a lot more to do than merely look for terminal correlations.

Almost without thinking, he will select certain key terms. For instance, every reader would spontaneously agree that "Stephen Dedalus" is a term to be featured. And at the very least, he would expand the name in the directions explicitly indicated by Joyce: Daedalus, Stephanoumenos, Stephaneforos.

Also, the title suggests that the critic might ask himself: "What will be the *operational* definition of 'artist' in this work?" One must be wary of titles, however. For often they were assigned or altered to meet real or imagined conditions of the market; and sometimes a work may be given a title purely for its sales value as a title, which was invented without reference to the work so entitled. In the case of the *Portrait,* of course, it would be generally agreed that the work is depicting the growth of an artist (*as so defined*) not only emotionally but in terms of a doctrine explicitly stated. For, ironically, although Stephen's doctrine denounces the "didactic" in art, it is itself as "didactic" as the Gospel; in fact it is an esthetic gospel.

But whereas the primary terms of a work operate by secondary connections, we can never be quite sure what secondary terms are likely to produce the best results. For instance, the first few lines of the book refer twice to "baby tuckoo." In a sense, this is Stephen's "real" name; for by the resources natural to narrative, an *essence* is stated in terms of temporal priority. Tentatively, then, we note it. And having done so, we find these possibly related entries: (p. 10 foot) "tucking the end of the nightshirt"; (p. 13) "little feet tucked up"; (p. 183) "a leather portfolio tucked under his armpit." What, then, of "Tusker Boyle" (p. 30), the unsavory fellow whom we have already mentioned in connection with the paring of his fingernails, a reference also connected with reference to the artist's "handiwork" (p. 168 top)? But the reference to hands also radiates in another direction, including both the priest's painful paddling of Stephen's hands in the pandybat episode, and the episode at the top of p. 124, where Stephen withdraws his hand from the priest as a sign that he is not to choose the religious vocation, but to become instead a "priest of the imagination." (The scene was introduced by the already cited reference to the "swish of the soutane.") This and the four references in sixteen lines to the "pain" suffered in the pandybat episode have as counterpart in the later passage an assurance that the music which had distracted him from the priest's promises dissolved his thoughts "painlessly and "noiselessly."

We could radiate in many other directions. On p. 30, for instance, the reference to Tusker (or Lady) Boyle had led immediately into talk of Eileen's hands, with the memory of the time when this Protestant girl had put her hand into his pocket. Her hands "were like ivory; only soft. That was the meaning of *Tower of Ivory*," etc., whereat we can radiate to "yellow ivory" and "mottled tusks of elephants," on p. 138.

We could go on. But already we glimpse how, without our asking ourselves just what any of our bridging terms may mean "analogically" or "symbolically," a circle of terminal interrelationships is beginning to build up. And even though we might abandon some positions under pressure (as for instance the series "tuckoo-tucking-Tusker-tusks"), we find connections of similar import being established by many other routes, most of them not requiring us to do any punwise "joycing" of terms (though we might at least be justified in applying such tentatives to even early work by Joyce, in the likelihood that his later typical susceptibilities were already emerging).

But let us get back to our more immediate problem. What *should* have been indexed in the opening pages? There was a "moocow" ("symbolically" maternal?), there was a father with a "hairy face," there is a progression from "baby tuckoo" to "moocow" to "Betty Byrne" (beddy burn?!) to "lemon platt" (which puzzles us, except insofar as it may be yellow, anent which more anon). There are some *childishly* distorted jingles. And these may so set the rules of this *adult* work that we can look tentatively for such distortion *as a principle,* operating perhaps over and above the examples explicitly given in the text. (Otherwise put: if these paragraphs are *under the sign of* such punwise distortion, might we not be justified in asking whether there could also be *displaced* distortion, such as would be there if *particular* distortions were taken to stand for more than themselves, indicating that a *principle* of distortion was operating *at this point?* We bring up the possibility, to suggest *methodological* reasons why we might experimentally so pun on "Betty Byrne" as we did. We would remind our reader, however, that *we are as yet committed to nothing,* so far as this text goes. *In advance,* we make allowance for a latitudinarian range—as contrasted with those who, in advance, have it all sewed up. But we need not yet make decisions.)

Should we have noted that "His mother had a nicer smell than his father"? In any case, there are many other references to smell (pp. 10, 12, and 14, for instance); and the passage becomes doubly interesting when, in his stage of contrition (p. 116) Stephen has trouble mortifying his sense of smell: "To mortify his smell was more difficult as he found in himself no instinctive repugnance to bad odors," etc.

Where do we start? Where do we stop?

Let us admit: there must be a certain amount of waste motion here, particularly if one undertakes an index before having a fairly clear idea of a book's developments. One is threatened with a kind of methodic demoralization—for anything might pay off. Yet by an "index" we most decidedly do not mean such lists (by author or topic) as one finds in the back of a book. In fact, whereas an index is normally made by entries on a set of cards which are then rearranged alphabetically, we must allow our entries to remain "in the order of their appearance." For a purely alphabetical reordering makes it almost impossible to inspect a work in its *unfoldings.* And we must keep on the move, watching both for static interrelationships and for *principles of transformation* whereby a motive may progress from one combination through another to a third, etc.

Over and above whatever we may enter in our index, there will be the search for "stages." Methodologically, such a search implies a theory of "substance." That is, in contrast with those "semantic" theories which would banish from their vocabulary any term for "substance," we must believe above all in the reasonableness of "entitling." Confronting a complexity of details, we do not confine ourselves merely to the detailed tracing of interrelationships among them, or among the ones that we consider outstanding. We must also keep prodding ourselves to attempt answering this question: "Suppose you were required to find an over-all title for this entire batch of particulars. What would that be?"

The *Portrait* is in five parts, which are merely numbered. What, then, should their titles be, if they had titles? We say that such a question implies a grounding in the term, "substance," or in the *furtive* function indicated by that term, because it implies that all the disparate details included under one head are infused with a common spirit, or purpose, *i.e.,* are *consubstantial.* We may be in varying degrees right or wrong, as regards the substance that we impute to a given set of details. But they are ultimately organized with relation to one another by their joint participation in a unitary purpose, or "idea." In brief, we must keep hypothetically shifting between the particular and the general.

True: you can take it for granted that, once such a range is available, you can always attain *some* level of generalization in terms of which disparate details might be substantially related. Ideally, one seeks for terms that account for kinship not only with regard to tests of consistency; one also wants to place *sequences, developments,* showing why the parts are *in precisely that order and no other;* and if one seeks to be overthorough here, the excess should be revealed by trouble in finding cogent rationalizations.

Often, for instance, the critic may be overzealous in trying to show how a whole plot may unfold from some original situation, somewhat like an artificial Japanese flower unfolding in water. But an accurate analysis would have to show how a series of new steps was needed, to carry the work from its opening "germ" to its final "growth." Thus, some opening imagery might be said to contain the later plot "in germ." (We have seen this very *Portrait* so analyzed.) But on closer analysis you will find that the opening imagery "pointed to" the ultimate destination of the plot only in the sense that, if one makes a sweep of the hand from south-southwest to north-northwest, one has thereby "implicitly" pointed due west. Critics who would analyze a book as an unfolding from an all-inclusive implication will need to use a different kind of dialectic as well. They will need to show by what successive stages a work is "narrowed down"; for its "unfolding" will be rather like a definition that begins with too broad a category, and gradually imposes strictures until the subject is "pinpointed" (as with the game of Twenty Questions).

In the case of the *Portrait,* whatever difficulties we might have in deciding how we would specifically treat any of the details in Part I, we could "idealize" the problem in general terms thus: we note that this work leads up to the explicit propounding of an Esthetic (a doctrine, catechism, or "philosophy" of art). Then we ask how each of the parts might look, as seen from this point of view. The first part deals with rudimentary sensory perception, primary sensations of smell, touch, sight, sound, taste (basic bodily feelings that, at a later stage in the story, will be methodically "mortified"). And there is our answer. Lo! the *Esthetic* begins in simple *aisthesis.* So, in this sense, the entire first chapter could be entitled "Childhood Sensibility." It will "render" the basic requirement for the artist, as defined by the terms (and their transformations) in this particular work. It depicts the kind of personality, or temperament, required of one who would take this course that leads to the Joycean diploma (to a chair spiritually endowed by Joycean Foundations). Family relations, religion, and even politics are thus "esthetically" experienced in this opening part—experienced not as mature "ideas," or even as adolescent "passions," but as "sensations," or "images."

But whereas we would thus entitle the first section of the *Portrait,* we do not want our whole argument to depend upon this one particular choice. We are here interested mainly in the attempt to illustrate the *principle* we are discussing. We might further note that, though "Childhood Sensibility" as a title fits *developmentally* into the story as a whole, it does not suggest a logic of development *within* the single chapter it is intended to sum up. It merely provides a term for describing *self-consistency* among the details of the chapter. It names them solely in terms of "repetitive" form, so far as their relation to one another is concerned. And only when treating them *en bloc,* with relation to the entire five chapters, do we suggest a measure of "progressive" form here. Ideally, therefore, we should also ask ourselves into what substages (with appropriate titles) this chapter on "Childhood Sensibility" should in turn be divided. At least, when indexing, we keep thus resurveying, in quest of developments. (The thought also suggests why an index arranged alphabetically would conceal too much for our purposes.)

The very rigors of our stress upon "terminal factuality" as the ideal beginning quickly force us to become aware of this step from particulars to generalizings (a step the exact nature of which is often concealed beneath terms like "symbol" and "analogy"). Hypothetically, even in a long work there might be no significant literal repeating of key terms. (We have heard tell of some ancient Chinese *tour de force* in which, though it is a work of considerable length, no single character is repeated. And one would usually be hard-pressed for a wide range of literal repetitions in individual lyrics, though the quest of "factually" joined contexts usually yields good results where we have an opportunity to study a poet's terminology as maintained through several poems.) And even with the Joyce *Portrait*, which abounds in factually related contexts, we confront a notable place where we would obviously accept suicidal restrictions if we refused to take the generalizing or idealizing step from particulars to principles (or, in this case, from particular words to the more general *themes* or *topics* that these words signify).

We have in mind Stephen's formula for his artistic jesuitry, "silence, exile, and cunning." "Silence" yields good results, even factually. It is a word that appears at all notable moments along the road of Stephen's development up to the pronouncing of his esthetic creed. There are a few references to cunning, the most pointed being this passage on p. 144 (all italics ours, to indicate terms we consider focal here):

> Stephen saw the *silent* soul of a jesuit look out at him from the pale loveless eyes. Like Ignatius he was lame lout in his eyes burned no spark of Ignatius's enthusiasm. Even the legendary *craft* of the company, a *craft;* subtler and more *secret* than its fabled books of *secret* subtle wisdom, had not fired his soul with the energy of apostleship. It seemed as if he used the shifts and lore and *cunning* of the world, as bidden to do, for the greater glory of God, without *joy* in their handling or hatred of that in them which was evil but turning them, with a firm gesture of obedience, back upon themselves; and for all this *silent service* it seemed as if he loved not at all the master and little if at all, the ends he served.

The references to "service" touch upon the *non serviam* theme that emerged so startlingly in the sermon. And the silence-exile-cunning formula (p. 194) had been immediately preceded by Stephen's challenge, "I will not serve," etc. We here see "cunning" and "silence" interwoven quite "factually." Also, we see the references to "craft" that could lead us into the final theme (patronymically punning) of the labyrinthine "artificer."

Yet "artificer" is not literally (thus not "factually") identical with "craft." And as for "exile": unless we missed some entries (and we may have!) the particular word does not appear elsewhere in this text. However, even assuming that we are correct, a punctiliousness bordering on "methodological suicide" would be required to keep us from including, under the *principle* of "exile," Stephen's question, "Symbol of departure or loneliness?" (p. 176), when he is considering the augury of the birds that stand for his new vocation. And once we can equate "exile" with *aloneness* (and *its* kinds of secrecy, either guilty or gestatory) we open our inquiry almost to a frenzy of entries: For "alone," in this story of a renegade Catholic boy who "forges"[3] a vocation somehow also under the aegis of a Protestant girl's hands, is as typical as any adjective in the book. Whereupon we find reasons to question whether the *apparent* disjunction (departure or loneliness) is really a disjunction at all. Far from their being antitheses in this work, the difference between them is hardly that between a bursting bud and a newly opened blossom.

In sum, once you go from "factual" word to a theme or topic that would include *synonyms* of this word, you are on the way to including also what we might call "operational synonyms," words which are synonyms in this particular text though they would not be so listed in a dictionary. That is, not only would a word like "stillness" be included under the same head as "silence," but you might also include here a silent *gesture* that was called "the vehicle of a vague speech," particularly as it is a scene in which we are explicitly told that he "stood silent" (pp. 76–77). Or, otherwise put: similarly, variants of "loneliness" *and* "departure" (hence even the theme of the flying bird) might be classed with "exile." And "cunning" in being extended to cover the artistic "craft," might thus expand not only into Daedalian, laby-

---

[3] (p. 199) "To forge in the smithy of my soul the uncreated conscience of my race"; (p. 131) "A hawklike man flying sunward above the sea, a prophecy of the end he had been born to serve . [. . .] a symbol of the artist forging anew in his workshop out of the sluggish matter of the earth a new soaring impalpable imperishable being"; (p. 139) "The monkish learning, in terms of which he was trying to forge out an esthetic philosophy." (Incidentally, we would watch a word like "force," on the chance that it may turn out to be a punwise, furtive variant of "forge.")

rinthine artifice, "maze," etc., but also into that doctrinal circle the center of which is the term, "imagination." We would then need some summarizing term, such as "the Joycean artist," or "the hawkman motive," to include under one head the "fact" that "silence," "exile," and "cunning" are *trinitarian* terms, which in turn are themselves linked sometimes dictionarywise (as synonyms), and sometimes "operationally" (in terms of contexts interconnected roundabout).[4]

Clearly, in the analysis of short lyrics where terms cannot be repeated in many contexts, one spontaneously looks for what the old rhetoric called "amplification," some theme or topic that is restated in many ways, no single one of which could be taken as a sufficient summing up. (Here again, ideally, we might try to find working subtitles for each stanza, as a way of aggressively asking ourselves whether we can honestly say that the lyric really does get ahead, even while pausing to summarize attitudinally.)

In essentializing by entitlement, one again confronts the usual range of choices between some particular of plot or situation and some wide generalization. Specifically, for instance, we might have chosen to call the first chapter "The Pandybat," since the artist's sensitivity is built plotwise about this as its crowning incident. The second stage (marking the turn from childhood sensibility to youthful passion) is built about the logic of "The Fall," the incident in which the chapter

---

[4] Any connection by synonyms should always be watched for the possibility of a lurking antithesis. That is, words on their face synonymous may really *function* as antitheses in a given symbol-system. Conversely, words *apparently* "as different as day and night" may be but operational concealments of a single motive. The apparent contrast between "male" and "female," for instance, is often better analyzable as "active" and "passive" aspects of a single motive operating reflexively. And words that are synonyms on their face may be found to conceal a distinction of *attitude* that is not "natural" to a language generally. For instance, "realm" and "region" might be so distinguished that "realm" was on the "heavenly" side while "region" inclined towards the "hellish." We believe that all writers have idiosyncratic usages of this sort, their works having a greater *poetic* consistency than is *rhetorically* apparent. Indeed, we incline to suspect that all good works have "consistency to spare," so far as purely rhetorical reception is concerned, at least when one is asked about the possible rhetorical appeal of some particular internal relationship that was not noted until lengthy critical analysis had disclosed it. But only through an "excess" of such consistency (we suspect) can a work hope to have "consistency enough" for the job of wholly establishing the desired attitude in the reader.

terminates. With this title, it so happens, there is no need to decide whether we are being particular or general, or even whether we are discussing content or form. (Ideally, working titles are best when they simultaneously suggest both the gist of the story as such and the developmental stage in the purely formal sense.) We say the "logic" of the fall, as in this work the fall is a *necessary* stage in the development of the esthetic. Thus, later, p. 158, Stephen says, "The soul is born [. . .] first in those moments I told you of." And we shall later try to indicate, indexwise, with what thoroughness the work interweaves its terms to this end.

Surely, the third chapter should be called "The Sermon." For that ironic masterpiece of rhetorical amplification is clearly the turning point of the chapter. To say as much, however, is to make a discovery about the form of this novel. For though the culmination of the sermon is close even to the mathematical center of the book (on p. 101 of a 199 page text we come to the "last and crowning torture of all tortures [. . .] the eternity of hell"), there is a very important sense in which the peripety is reserved for Chapter IV, which we might call "The New Vocation." We shall later try to show how thorough a crisis there may have been in Chapter III, in Stephen's emotions following the sermon, as revealed in the study of the Joycean esthetic. Meanwhile, we may recall that, when the choice between religion and art is finally made, it is a qualified choice, as art will be conceived in terms of theology secularized. Following Joycean theories of the emblematic image, we might also have called Chapter IV "Epiphany"; for in Stephen's vision of the bird-girl the symbol of his new vocation is made manifest. Chapter V might then be called "The New Doctrine," for we here get the catechistic equivalent of the revelation that forms the ecstatic end of Chapter IV.

When an author himself provides subtitles (and thus threatens to deprive the critic of certain delightful exercisings) at least the critic can experimentally shuttle, in looking for particular equivalents where the titles are general, and *vice versa*. But though all such essentializing by entitlement helps force us to decide what terms we should especially feature in our index, there are other procedures available.

3

First, let us consider a somewhat nondescript procedure. Some notations seem more likely than others to keep critical observation centrally directed. We list these at random:

Note all striking terms for acts, attitudes, ideas, images, relationships.

Note oppositions. In the *Portrait*, of course, we watch particularly anything bearing upon the distinction between art and religion. And as usual with such a dialectic, we watch for shifts whereby the oppositions become appositions. Stephen's secularizing of theology, for instance, could not be adequately interpreted either as a flat rejection of theological thought or as a continuation of it. Stephen has what Buck Mulligan in *Ulysses* calls "the cursed jesuit strain [. . .] only it's injected the wrong way." And it could be classed as another variant of the many literary tactics reflecting a shift from the religious passion to the romantic (or sexual) passion (the extremes being perhaps the varied imagery of self-crucifixion that characterizes much nineteenth-century literary Satanism).

Pay particular attention to beginnings and endings of sections or subsections. Note characteristics defining transitional moments. Note *breaks* (a point to which we shall return later, as we believe that, following the sermon, there is a notable stylistic break, a notable interruption of the continuity, even though Joyce's artistry keeps it from being felt as an outright violation of the reader's expectations already formed).

Watch names, as indicative of essence. (Cf. *numen, nomen, omen*.) In one's preparatory index, it is permissible to "joyce" them, for heuristic purposes, by even extreme punwise transformations. Not just from "dedalus" to "daedalus," for instance. But, why not even "dead louse," in view of the important part that the catching and rolling of the louse played (pp. 182–183) in Stephen's correcting of a misremembered quotation that contained the strategic word, "fall"? (The context has, besides "falls" twice in the quoted line, "falling" twice, "dying falling" once, "fall" once, and "fell" twice. But though Stephen likens himself to a louse, it is the louse that falls this time. He himself is already imbued with the spirit of Daedalian flight, whereby his fall has become transformed into a rise.)

Experimental tinkering with names does not in itself provide *proof* of anything. (So keep it a secret between us and the index). But it does suggest lines of inquiry, by bringing up new possibilities of internal relationship. On p. 167, for instance, when explaining his esthetic doctrine, Stephen says: "If a man hacking in fury at a block of wood [. . .] make there an image of a cow, is that cow a work of art?" Whereat we might recall not only the reference to cow with which this work began, but also the figure of the dead adolescent lover of Gabriel's wife in Joyce's story, "The Dead." Even the hint of "ivory" is found there (the step from Tusker-Lady Boyle to Tower-of-Ivory Eileen) in Gabriel's suspicion that his wife had had a clandestine meeting with Furey when ostensibly she "wanted to go to Galway with that Ivors girl." We should also recall that the story ends on a paragraph in which the word, "falling," appears no less than seven times, in the final ecstatic "epiphany" of the snow "falling softly [. . .] softly falling [. . .] falling faintly [. . .] faintly falling." (There was another notable reference to "falling" in this story. When Gabriel and his wife are about to enter the hotel room where he hopes to enjoy a kind of second honeymoon, the narrative states: "In the silence Gabriel could hear the falling of the molten wax into the tray," etc. The reference is to a "guttering" and "unstable" candle.) The possible fury-Furey tie-up is thus seen to have brought us by another route to the "logic of the fall" that is so important an aspect of Stephen's esthetic.[5]

While watching for the expressions that best name a given character's number, watch also for incidental properties of one character that are present in another. Such properties in common may provide

---

[5] In an essay, "Three Definitions" (*The Kenyon Review*, Spring, 1951) we suggest the possibility that "Michael Furey" stands for a "dead" adolescent self that was an aspect of the same motives as Gabriel represented in a much later stage of development. Thus, in a sense, it would be *his own rivalry* that Gabriel was jealous of. We went on to indicate how the final imaginal merging of "living" and "dead" resolved this conflict. We also proceeded to indicate how such psychologistic interpretations would not be "ultimate" or "prior." And we suggested *formal* considerations whereby the story might even be considered as solving in *narrative* terms much the same problem that Kant solves philosophically in his distinction between the "conditioned" and the "unconditioned." Note, however, that just as we would break "analogy" and "symbolism" into such piecemeal problems, and would not offer "myth" as a solution here (that is, would not reduce this work simply to the "myth of Daedalus" or the "Faustian myth" or even the "Christian myth"), so we do not reduce the work to purely "philosophic" terms (as though narrative were but a way of saying roundabout what philosophy can say directly).

insight into the ways whereby figures on their face disparate are to be treated as different manifestations of a common motive.

Note internal forms. While noting them in their particularity, try also to conceptualize them. For instance, here's a neat job for someone who believes as much in the discipline of literary analysis as a mathematician believes in his mathematics: on pp. 182–183, conceptualize the steps from the misremembered line, "Darkness falls from the air," to the correction, "Brightness falls from the air." Of course, there are good memorizers who could reproduce the stages for you word for word. But there is a sense in which such accurate memory is itself "unprincipled," being not much more rational than a mechanical recording of the passage.

Watch for a point of *farthest internality*. We believe that in the *Portrait* this point occurs just after the sermon, most notably in the circular passage (p. 105 top) beginning, "We knew perfectly well of course," [. . .] and ending "We of course knew perfectly well," with its center in the expression, "endeavouring to try to induce himself to try to endeavour."

Note details of *scene* that may stand "astrologically" for motivations affecting character, or for some eventual act in which that character will complete himself. When such correspondences eventualize, they afford us sharper insight into the *steps* of a work, on its road from emergence to fulfillment. The best illustration we have for this rule is in the first chapter of Conrad's *Victory*. There has been talk of Heyst living on an island "as if he were perched on the highest peak of the Himalayas," for "an island is but the top of a mountain" (an expression which we indexed, as the author himself so pointedly made the "equation" for us); then the description proceeds thus:

> His nearest neighbour—I am speaking now of things showing some sort of animation—was an indolent volcano which smoked faintly all day with its head just above the northern horizon, and at night levelled at him, from among the clear stars, a dull red glow, expanding and collapsing spasmodically like the end of a gigantic cigar puffed at intermittently in the dark. Axel Heyst was also a smoker. And when he lounged out on his verandah with his cheroot, the last thing before going to bed, he made in the night the same

> sort of glow and of the same size as that other one so
> many miles away.

We could hardly fail to note so "empathic" an image, whereby an object far distant was enigmatically "equated" with a near personal property of an agent (the construct giving us a particularly ingenious kind of scene-agent ratio). And this entry later "pays off" handsomely, of course, as this same volcano breaks into agitation coincidentally with the plot's eruption into crisis. (This conformity between act and scene is not explained "rationally," as were the plot to have been shaped directly by the condition of the volcano. Rather, it serves the function of "rhetorical amplification," by restating in scenic terms the quality of the action that takes place with that scene as characteristic background. It is like an interpretative comment upon the action, almost a kind of "natural chorus.")

Another instance of the same sort occurs shortly after the beginning of Part II, with the description of the scene in which Heyst has his first fatal meeting with Lena:

> The Zangiacomo hand was not making music; it was
> simply murdering silence with a vulgar, ferocious en-
> ergy. One felt as if witnessing a deed of violence; and
> that impression was so strong that it seemed marvel-
> lous to see the people sitting so quietly on their chairs,
> drinking so calmly out of their glasses, and giving no
> signs of distress, anger or fear.

Particularly we note such a moment because it characterizes a "first," the time when Heyst and Lena first meet. And we later see that it "astrologically" foretold the quality of the action that would eventuate from this meeting. Such "foreshadowing" is standard. But when we extend the same principle for subtler inquiry, we are admonished to make a special noting of all first appearances (if only noting no more than the page number, on the possibility that a later survey of all these moments might reveal internal terministic consistencies not originally perceived).

In particular, one should note expressions marking secrecy, privacy, mystery, marvel, power, silence, guilt. Such terms are likely to point in the direction of central concerns in all cultures. Here also we might include terms for order, since the pyramidal nature of order brings us close to relations of "superiority" and "inferiority," with the many kinds of tension "natural" to social inequality. Such observations lead us in turn to watch for the particular devices whereby the given work "states a policy" with regard to a society's typical "problems." Here we seek hints for characterizing the work as a "strategy."

In general, we proceed by having in mind four "pyramids" or "hierarchies": (1) the pyramid of language, which allows for a Platonist climb from particulars toward "higher orders of generalization"; (2) the social pyramid, with its more or less clearly defined ladder of classes and distinctions; (3) the "natural" or "physical" pyramid (headed in such perspectives as the Darwinian genealogy); (4) the "spiritual" pyramid ("celestial" or "supernatural"). The social and linguistic pyramids are "naturally" interwoven, we take it, as language is a social product. And since the empirically linguistic is properly our center of reference when analyzing secular literary texts, we watch for ways whereby the "natural" and "supernatural" pyramids more or less clearly reflect the structure of the sociolinguistic pair.

In so doing, we do not necessarily deny that there are "natural" or "supernatural" orders, existing in their own right. We merely note that both, the one "beneath" *ideas,* the other "above" *ideas,* will necessarily be expressed in terms that reflect the *ideological* structures indigenous to the social and linguistic orders. In this sense, both "natural" and "supernatural" may be analyzable as sociolinguistic "pageantry" (by which we refer to the communicative ways, the cults of parade, exhibition, or appeal, that typify man as the typically symbol-using animal).

As all this adds up to what we might call the "hierarchal psychosis," we ask how such a psychosis might be undergoing a "cure," or "purge," within the terms of the given work, considered as a terminology. We can expect many variants of such symbolic cure; for man, as the typically symbol-using species, is naturally rich in such resources. So our thoughts about hierarchal tension lead us to watch for modes of *catharsis,* or of *transcendence,* that may offer a symbolic solution within the *given symbol-system of the particular work we are analyzing.*

We are even willing to look for ways whereby the artistic strategy that is a "solution" may serve to reestablish the very tension it is resolving. Or, if that way of stating the case seems too ironic, let us watch at least for cathartic devices whereby a rising (as seen from one angle) is a fall (as seen from another), whereby, lo! a "fall" can be a "rise." The possibility is of great importance in the case of the *Portrait,* the "factual" analysis of which *explicitly* depicts a *fall* in terms of a *soaring above*. Note, in particular, this passage (p. 125):

> He would fall. He had not yet fallen but he would
> fall silently, in an instant. Not to fall was too hard,
> too hard; and he felt the silent lapse of his soul, as it
> would be at some instant to come, falling, falling, but
> not yet fallen, still unfallen, but about to fall.

Recall that this passage marks, almost "sloganistically," the step intermediate between Stephen's rejection of the religious vocation and his ecstatic vision of the bird-girl who stands imaginally for his artistic vocation.

We could here add other such rules of thumb, involving questions that require us to write over again, in this one essay, the *Motivorum* books on which we have been for some time engaged. But we finally hit upon one basic principle that might cut across all such a *gatherum omnium,* and might be argued for even if the reader did not agree with anything we have said up to this point. It is based upon an "entelechial" mode of thought. And we consider it in our next section.

4

By the "entelechial" test, we have in mind this principle: look for *moments* at which, in your opinion, the work comes to *fruition.* Imbue yourself with the terminology of these moments. And spin from them. Thus, at the very least, you would have the "epiphany" near the end of Chapter IV to guide you:

> A girl stood before him in midstream; alone and still,
> gazing out to sea. She seemed like one whom magic
> had changed into the likeness of a strange and beau-
> tiful seabird. Her long slender bare legs were delicate
> as a crane's and pure save where an emerald trail of
> seaweed had fashioned itself as a sign upon the flesh.
> Her thighs, fuller and softhued as ivory, were bared
> almost to the hips where the white fringes of her
> drawers were like feathering of soft white down. Her
> slate-blue skirts were kilted boldly about her waist
> and dovetailed behind her. Her bosom was a bird's,
> soft and slight, slight and soft as the breast of some

darkplumaged dove. But her long fair hair was girlish: and girlish, and touched with the wonder of mortal beauty, her face.

[. . .]

—Heavenly God! cried Stephen's soul, in an out-
burst of profane joy.—

He turned away from her suddenly and set off
across the strand. His cheeks were aflame; his body
was aglow; his limbs were trembling. On and on and
on he strode, far out over the sands, singing wildly to
the sea, crying to greet the advent of the life that had
cried to him.

Her image had passed into his soul for ever and
no word had broken the holy silence of his ecstasy.
Her eyes had called him and his soul had leaped at
the call. To live, to err, to fall, to triumph, to recre-
ate life out of life! A wild angel had appeared to him,
the angel of mortal youth and beauty, an envoy from
the fair courts of life, to throw open before him in an
instant of ecstasy the gates of all the ways of error and
glory. On and on and on and on!

We could continue through the next half-page that concludes the
chapter. But we might better make our point by selections:

"Heard his heart in the silence [. . .] the tide was near
the turn [. . .] the silence of the evening [. . .] closed
his eyes in a languor of sleep (we forgot to list the
moments of sleep and the occasions and contents
of dream, among the major things to watch) [. . .]
swooning into some new world, fantastic, dim, uncertain as under sea [. . .] trembling and unfolding, a
breaking light, an opening flower [. . .] evening had
fallen [. . .] a rim of the young moon [. . .] and the tide
was flowing in fast to the land [. . .] islanding [. . .]"

Here, you might say, there would be many things to watch, including the word, "the," if you were argumentative enough. (And we must
admit: we would not by any means say categorically that, in some

structure, you could not learn more by indexing the "the's" than by any other term.)

Basically, though, you have seen the bird-girl, who is to stand for motives far beyond her nature as sheer image. So, *at the very least,* with this obvious fulfillment to guide you, you would put in your index the first implicit announcements of the bird theme, on p 2: "the eagles will come and pull out his eyes"; "the greasy leather orb flew like a heavy bird through the grey light." You do not know just how you will use these entries. You are not even sure that you will use them at all. But you note them. You would note them because of the fact that they are classed among things to do with birdness, a category experimentally broad enough to include Stephen's roommate Heron, the final reference to "old father, old artificer," the vision of the "hawklike man," and (pp. 175–176) the augury of the birds circling "from left to right," their emblematic nature defined by questionable disjunction as "symbol of departure or of loneliness." Also, as we are trying ever to see *beyond* the symbolizings in the given work even while trying to see as far as we can into that work's purely internal consistency, we *especially* note all *eye* terms with regard to Joyce, even beyond the eye-I pun natural to the accidents of English. And having in mind the step from "dying fallings of sweet airs" to "sucking mouths" on p. 182, we dare think also of the "blind mouths" in Milton's "Lycidas," while the reference to "scum" here throws us back to Stephen's childhood baptism in rat-infested scum (p. 7), and other incidences of this term (pp. 49, 52, 85). One should remember, for later use, that on p. 49 this scum is called "yellow": yellow turns out to be a particularly notable color, because of its specific relation to Stephen's esthetic, as we shall explain later.

If (in this same passage of "epiphany") you have noted "soft," which appears six times in six lines (p. 132–133), surely a sufficient incidence to make it experimentally notable, then you would certainly note (p. 106) the "soft language" twice so called, and equated with "stale shite" and the horrors that were "circling closer and closer to enclose." Or you would note the words linking "sin" and softness that terminate Chapter II, the chapter we have entitled "The Fall." [6]

---

[6] The partially involuntary fall through sexual passion at the end of Chapter II might be distinguished from the deliberate fall of Chapter IV (the choice of a new vocation) somewhat as "passive" is distinguished from "active." It is the latter that Stephen equates with Luciferian pride, epitomized

If you asked what the young moon meant, and took notes to find out, you would get the answer doubly, though ambiguously, on p. 176 top: "Thoth, the god of writers [. . .] bearing on his narrow ibis head the cusped moon. .. . He would not have remembered the god's name but that it was like an Irish oath." The reference to "profane joy" might admonish us to note the "tears of joy" and the "tremor of fear and joy" in the brothel scene (pp. 66–76). "Silence" we have already discussed. Meanwhile, beyond the sheer pattern of the turning tide (transitional scene for transitional act) we would note the further pattern in the fact that, upon seeing the girl who is henceforth to stand for his vocation, Stephen exaltedly turns *from her,* going "on and on and on."

Since the bird-girl is a "wild angel," whose presence sanctions his resolve "to live, to err, to fall" (p. 133), and since the word, "wild," appears several times in this passage of "fulfillment" which we have been experimentally examining for cues as to the terms that we might favor in our index, we watch "wild." It occurs in many notable contexts, including (p. 106) the passage where, in his terror, Stephen undergoes a purgation in the most literal, physical sense: "clasping his cold forehead wildly, he vomited profusely in agony."

---

in his many variants of the formula, "I will not serve." All told, the accountancy is somewhat like this: The earlier passionate fall prepared for the later vocational choice; the two were thus related as different species of a common genus (a genus also marked by such "operational synonyms" as "soft," "circling," "yellow," and "scum"). By the time the book is finished, the theme of falling has become translated into the theme of ecstatic elevation, even while retaining signs of its beginnings.

We might also note how music figures in this psychic bookkeeping. Music stands for the new motive. When turning from the Bible as doctrine, Stephen still loved it as music (p. 79). When the jesuit was proposing that he become a priest, the sound of distant music snapped the continuity (p. 124). The themes of rising and falling are interwoven with the music theme and the bird theme as the music theme itself has this design: "It seemed to him that he heard notes of fitful music leaping upwards a tone and downwards a diminishing fourth, upwards a tone and downwards a major third" (p. 127); "But the notes were long and shrill and whirring, unlike the cry of vermin, falling a third or a fourth and trilled as the flying beaks clove the air. Their cry was shrill and clear and fine and falling like threads of silken light unwound from whirring spools" (p. 175). (And, of course, when considering this purely grammatical disjunction between vermin and the new vocation, we would note rather how, so far as sheer imagery is concerned, the two themes are *brought together,* being as it were "said in the same breath.")

But with that reference to Stephen's physical purgation, following the sermon and his almost cataleptic response to it (pp. 104–105) as he pauses in terror outside the door of his room, our inquiry could well take another turn. For immediately after the physical cleansing, a new life begins. We read that "the city was spinning about herself a soft cocoon of yellowish haze" (p. 106 foot). Yet on both pp. 76 and 77, the flames of the brothels were called "yellow." Later, when the esthetic doctrine is being spelled out, one of Stephen's companions who participates in the definition of the doctrine is Lynch, with his "excrementitious intellect" and his resolve "to swear in yellow" (pp. 159, 165, etc.) Yellow is the first color we encounter (line two) in *Ulysses.* The passage somewhat sacrilegiously equates shaving with the ministry of the Mass. In the *Portrait,* we note how we again circle back to the theme of Lady Boyle, since Stephen at one point (as we already noted) ponders on "yellow ivory" and the "mottled tusks of elephants" (p. 138). Nor should we forget that the bird-girl (p. 132 foot) had thighs "softhued as ivory." And we can now discern how the *principle* of yellow, though not the *literal* term, is lurking (p. 30) in the turn from Lady Boyle paring his nails to the memory of Eileen, whose hands were " like ivory; only soft."

Admittedly, our work has hardly more than begun, so far as the study of this particular text is concerned. In particular, for instance, we would like to have talked at some length about the passage which we take to be the moment of farthest internality, the "circular" paragraph at the top of p. 105. We have tried elsewhere to show that this "break" in the structure of the work (the sudden brief irruption of Joyce's later manner into a narrative style otherwise traditionally realistic) can be related to the principle of "arrest" that characterizes Stephen's esthetic, as proclaimed in Part V. For it is precisely here that Stephen, terrified by the sermon, pauses, unable to cross a threshold: precisely at this moment of arrest, there leaps forth the passage cryptically prophetic of the later manner:

> —We knew perfectly well of course that although it was bound to come to the light he would find considerable difficulty in endeavouring to try to induce himself to try to endeavour to ascertain the spiritual plenipotentiary and so we knew of course perfectly well—

We believe that much can be done with this "break," even beyond the confines of the one hook. But in any case, for the time being we can note that it is another of those places where the book comes to a kind of *ad interim* fulfillment; hence it would be another place from which our search could radiate. On the next page, for instance, it leads "factually" into talk of "circling. Stephen's doctrine itself, of course, would be another "entelechial moment" to work from, particularly if one remembered that Stephen's interlocutors in the discussion are to be taken as part of the definition. We could add a few other spots (for instance, the formula, "Silence, exile, and cunning," is a splendid fulfillment, or culminating moment). There are eight or nine such in all.

Similarly, there are places where some one word flares up like a *nova,* as we saw with regard to the word, "fall." These, too, would be watched as "fulfillments."

All told, one proceeds from such places, where the work comes to a temporary head. One radiates in search of labyrinthine internal consistency, while at the same time watching for progressions. One tries to be aware of one's shifts between "factuality" and "thematic" generalizing. One watches for over-al social tensions, and for the varying tactics of "purification" with regard to them. And one is thereby talking about "symbolism," willy-nilly.[7]

---

[7] We have omitted mention of one area that we tentatively call "channels of affinity." They would be to the study of Poetics what "topics" are to the study of rhetoric. But whereas the traditional "topics" were static ("places"), channels of affinity would be developmental. It is our notion that certain progressions are more "natural" than others. Thus with the progression "from Venus to Mars" or *vice versa.* Or the progression from awe to liquid light. Or from sex to food (as two basic orders of appetition). Such "naturalness" may be primarily due to the nature of the body. But it can also be a part of "second nature." For instance, one finds in our society many progressions from thought of woman to thought of the hunt, but such a double-meaning for venery is socially conditioned. We have been taking notes of this sort on a purely empirical basis. And we are still quite uncertain as to how they should be classified. Certain ones however, recur so often, with effective results (in both serious and comic works), we do think there is something real to work on here despite the shiftiness of the material.

Part 2

Dramatistic Analyses of Individual Texts and Authors

5

Ethan Brand: A Preparatory Investigation[1,2]

FIRST, JOYCING THE TITLE: "HEATHEN FIRE"? "Brand" also has possible connotations of "branding" (the guilty sign, as in *The Scarlet*

---

[1] *The Hopkins Review* 5.2 (Winter 1952): 45–65. © The Kenneth Burke Literary Trust. Used by permission.

[2] An author seldom has a good excuse for offering a first draft in preference to a finished article. But in this case we might have. For these pages (part of a work in progress, *A Symbolic of Motives*) belong in a section called "Theory of the Index, that deals with the pragmatics of note-taking. And the more informal the observations are, the better they illustrate our point. So, except for the change of a few glaring mistakes in grammar and of a few inversions that too greatly obscured the sense, these notes are submitted exactly as first written.

The rules of procedure at this stage of critical preparation allow one to admit "hunches" that might later be discarded because: (1) they are proved wrong; (2) they led into a blind alley; (3) they led to a later statement that seemed better guarded; (4) they could not be backed by sufficient evidence (though the critic still clung to them in secret, hoping that he might later find a way of redeeming them).

The stress here is mainly upon internalities of the writer's terminology. A fuller analysis of linguistic action would lead to personal and environmental elements. Such ranging might begin with Hawthorne's American Notebooks. In connection with "little Joe," for instance, the editor notes details that correspond to observations Hawthorne made about his own son. And there is an entry describing a little boy (of the same name) in a bar-room. Among other things, he was plagued by the older men who put quids of

Letter, or "The Birthmark"). The nature of the plot also amplifies the meaning in the sense of "firebrand." Consider also the analogy with the lime-out-of-marble development (the purification process); for instance, among the dictionary meanings for "brand" we find: "A stick or piece of wood partly burnt, whether burning or after the fire is extinct."

What of "Bartram, the lime-burner?" He is tending the same kiln that Brand tended years before. Hence, we may look for some essential relation between Bartram and Brand. Even tonally, the relation is quite marked:

> B r a n d
> B a r t (ram).

Both begin with the same letter. The next two letters are merely transposed (the Hercules-Heracles kind of structure). *N-d-t* are cognates, *d* being a voiced *t* (as the simplest way to discern the relation between *n* and *d* or *n* and *t* is to pronounce n while holding the nostrils shut). What of "ram"?

And with the many references to "kiln" (as in "sat watching his kiln at nightfall"): the word joyces itself, "kill."

---

tobacco into his mouth, "under pretence of giving him a fig." Similarly, the various run-down bar-room "worthies" appear in the Notebooks, sketched from real life. Or words like "singular" and "pry" gain new dimensions from their appearance in such other contexts.

> But to illustrate such ranging, we plan to take another work as text, Coleridge's "Ancient Mariner," for which we have specified three orders of analysis (1) The sort of observations one might make if one had only the single poem, in isolation, and did not even know its author; (3) the sort of observations that would be in order if one knew the author, and could treat the poem in a context with Coleridge's other poetry. (3) the sort of observations one might make if he could also consider Coleridge's essay-istic writings, notes, letters, biographical data, and the like. This is part of a project for "The Carving-out Of a Poetics," that aims to meet the canons of Poetics as a special field, while at the same time considering the wider realm of linguistic action generally. (K. B.)

"While his little son played at building houses with the scattered fragments of marble." Here we would consider the possibility that this child, who is frightened by Brand, represents the *early stage* of a development fulfilled in Brand. Does he stand for a period prior to an awakening into guilt? Yet this playing with the fragments of marble should be watched as an incipient manifestation of the outcome. (Thus, the boy would represent not just "innocence," but innocence as modified by fright for the future guilt into which he would develop. The guilt in "playing" as so conceived seems likely to include such connotations as you can glimpse in an adolescent hokku we once saw: "The gorgeous vase is shattered? I shall make pretty playthings of the bits." There are many ways in which to symbolize guilt; but with Hawthorne, who loved the "singular," we may properly look always for reflexive imagery.)

This first paragraph also contains the theme of the mirthless laughter. (The Hawthorne outward sign of the inward guilt is here auditory. It is usually visual.) It is "like a wind shaking the boughs of the forest." The theme of "shaking" is repeated a few lines further on, when Bartram tells his son that the sound is of "some merry fellow from the bar-room in the village [. . .] shaking his jolly sides at the foot of Graylock." When the child, ("more sensitive than the obtuse, middle-aged clown") complains of fright, saying "he does not laugh like a man that is glad," the father answers gruffly: "You will never make a man, I do believe; there is too much of your mother in you."

Next comes a long paragraph important for the characterization of Ethan Brand's motives. First: We have to do with a *return to origins*. This is "the same lime-kiln that had been the scene of Ethan Brand's solitary and meditative life, before he began his search for the Unpardonable Sin." Here had occurred "that portentous night when the IDEA was first developed." What kind of act belonged here? Answer: Here he "had thrown his dark thoughts into the intense glow of its furnace, and melted them, as it were, into the one thought that took possession of his life." We heard talk of a *shaking*, to do with Ethan's solitary ways. We now add an imagery of *projection*. (Could that mirthless cry, out into nowhere, be in the order of an "ejaculation"? We recall no such word to do with it.) In any case, we note that the tossing-into-the-furnace is related to the *ideal*, as regards both "the IDEA," the "dark thoughts," and the typical idealist merger, since this "kiln" had "melted" the many thoughts "into the one thought that

took possession of his life." Later it will be called the "Master Sin." In
any case, the author's own explicit acknowledgment that we here have
to do with some unitary essence pervading a multiplicity of details
gives us further authority to look for such [. . .] In the rest of the paragraph, the quality of the act is conveyed by a discussion of scene. This
kiln is "a rude, round, tower-like structure." Psychoanalytically, towers
have phallic connotations; and particularly where we are concerned
with "Sin," we might expect to find such possibilities in the offing.
What to do with this detail: "There was an opening at the bottom of
the tower, like an over-mouth, but large enough to admit a man in a
stooping posture, and provided with a massive iron door." What's an
"over-mouth"? In any case, the expression *brings us into the category of
the bodily.* And at least as a possibility we should recall that "mouth"
can be ambiguous. ("An opening affording entrance or exit," says the
dictionary.) This much, in any case, is certain: this door "seemed to
give admittance into the hillside," and "resembled nothing so much as
the private entrance to the infernal regions." So, it has to do with internality, the private, such inward-going as is associated with the infernal
(as per the Unpardonable Sin).

The reference to "admittance into the hillside" is further developed
in the next paragraph. Such lime-kilns are "for the purpose of burning the white marble which composes a large part of the substance of
the hills." This is a "lonesome" occupation, and in the case of Brand a
"thoughtful" one—as he "had mused to such strange purpose, in days
gone by, while the fire in this very kiln was burning." The "purpose"
of the burning is here clearly identified with the "purpose" of the musing (the *ideal* motive).

We are next told that "the man who now watched the fire was
of a different order, and troubled himself with no thoughts save the
very few that were requisite to his business." Alike to an extent, we
should say, but quite different too. Considerations of "analogy" might
be enough for the moment. That is: The motive will be broken into
a spectrum. The uneasy child is one such fragment; a corresponding
insensitive adult would be another. (Similarly, in *The Scarlet Letter,*
the range of guilt is extended even to include, among its variants, the
witch-nature of Mistress Hibbens, the Governor's sister.)

A few paragraphs further on, Brand arrives on the scene. What is
to be made of his illumination? That is, Bartram opens the door of
the kiln, "whence immediately issued a gush of fierce light, that smote

full upon the stranger's face and figure." Because of Young Goodman Brown, we note that his clothes are described as brown. And the theme returns elsewhere in the story.

Next page or so, deals with such details as: the boy's fear; Ethan's "grizzled" appearance (the fire theme figuring also in reference to "those deeply sunken eyes, which gleamed like fires within the entrance of a mysterious cavern"); Ethan's professional prophesying ("a few hours more will convert the stone to lime, and his identifying of his former skill as a limeburner with his search for the Unpardonable Sin (which he situated as did Dimsdale: "Ethan Brand laid his finger on his own heart").

Talk of the Unpardonable Sin leads into talk of its corresponding sign, the mirthless laughter, the "laugh of scorn," (Hester Prynne, near the end of Chapter II of *The Scarlet Letter,* had found the solemn gaze of the throng "intolerable," and "longed rather to behold all those rigid countenances contorted with scornful merriment, and herself the object." Here Brand laughs thus scornfully at himself, for having looked "into every heart, save his own, for what was hidden in no other breast.") This laughter is discussed in terms of the "laughter of one asleep, even if be a little child,—the madman's laugh,—the wild, screaming laugh of a born idiot," the "utterance of fiends or hobgoblins."

Bartram sends his son to fetch the "jolly fellows" from the tavern with the news that Ethan has returned with knowledge of the Unpardonable Sin. During the interim between the boy's departure and his return with the rundown drunkards, we read analyses that reveal something of the underlying kinship between Brand and Bart(ram). Bartram regrets that the child has gone. "He felt that the little fellow's presence had been a barrier between his guest and himself." The "indistinct blackness" of Ethan's crime "made his memory riotous with a throng of evil shapes that asserted their kindred with the Master Sin, whatever it might be." For "they were all of one family; they went to and fro between his breast and Ethan Brand's and carried dark greetings from one to the other." The talk of "man's corrupted nature" here seems close to notions of universal depravity. Bartram, presumably, is in his individual character thoughtless, and free of the sin mainly by reason of his bluntness—but his embarrassment on being alone with Ethan forces him to get inklings of an essential nature, involving mankind generically?

The next paragraph deals with the Sin in terms of a Satanic in-
tercourse. "Brand, it was said, had conversed with Satan himself in
the lurid blaze of this very kiln." He "had been accustomed to evoke
a fiend from the hot furnace of the lime-kiln, night after night, in
order to confer with him about the Unpardonable Sin." This fiend
had "crept in at the iron door," to "abide" in the heat until again summoned. This was the "hollow prison-house of the fire." Yet Ethan
tells Bartram that he has not found the Unpardonable Sin in "many
a human heart that was seven times hotter with sinful passions than
yonder furnace is with fire." Hence, its relation to fire is certainly to
fire-with-a-difference. Then, as regards purely *doctrinal* statement, the
motive is described thus:

> "It is a sin that grew within my own breast," replied
> Ethan Brand, standing erect with a pride that distin-
> guishes all enthusiasts of his stamp. "A sin that grew
> nowhere else! The sin of an intellect that triumphed
> over the sense of brotherhood with man and rever-
> ence for God, and sacrificed everything to its own
> mighty claims! The only sin that deserves a recom-
> pense of immortal agony! Freely, were it to do again,
> would I incur the guilt. Unshrinkingly I accept the
> retribution!"

In its doctrinal aspect, the "Sin" here seems to be the dyslogistic
term for the principle of "singularity" that can also on many occasions
be presented eulogistically. Indeed, the theme of the witches' sabbath
in Hawthorne seems to involve a paradox of this sort: the bewitched
wretches who thus resort to black magic are all wholly separate from
one another, and their sinister revels are a communing of the essentially separated. Or, stated in terms, of dialectical resources: once you have
words for persons who are cursed by separation from one another, you
can next so manipulate the terminology that you can depict a *meeting*
of such; but be admonished that, even in their communal rites, they
remain in essence apart from one another In any case, we must ask
ourselves what *non-doctrinal* strands are implicit in the motive here
doctrinally enunciated.

What is the purpose of the "three worthies" who now appear, summoned from the tavern to greet their former acquaintance, Ethan?
That is, what is *developed* by their appearance, considered as a step in

the total unfolding? Is it merely a variation on the theme? Or does it move things forward?

As regards "analogy": like Bartram, they seem to stress one strand of the motivation. Bartram evidently stood for the kind of bluntness that could protect one from Ethan's scruples (though the protection would be of a kind that Ethan despised). Do not the run-down "worthies" represent another aspect of this same motive? But just as Bartram was momentarily capable of concerns that went beyond his usual bluntness, so these rum-soaked degenerates share, by their very degeneracy, in the motivation as a whole? Symbolically at least, when they arrive they are illuminated by the flood of light from the lime-kiln, just as Ethan had been. And they presumably represent a phase of Ethan's development, since they are his former cronies (even though, in keeping with his New Loneliness, he now so harshly rejects them).

The first of them is doubly decayed. A "stage-agent," he represents a trade "now almost extinct," while he personally is "wilted," "smoke-dried," "wrinkled," famous as a "dry joker" (variant of the ungodly laugh?), while "a certain flavor of brandy-toddy and tobacco-smoke [. . .] impregnated all his ideas and expressions." He is not named, but it may be worth noting that he wears a brown coat. The second is Lawyer Giles, "an elderly ragamuffin" who "in his better days" had been a "sharp practitioner," but had now succumbed to "flip, and sling, and toddy, and cocktails," whereat he finally slid "from intellectual to various kinds and degrees of bodily labor till at last, to adopt his own phrase, he slid into a soap-vat." Since soap, as a cleanser, implies guilt (or at least, since there is always that *possibility*), let us look at the details by which this second representative of a past period (hence *necessary* period) in Ethan's life is characterized: "In other words, Giles was now a soap-boiler [. . .] He had come to be but the fragment of a human being, a part of one foot having been chopped off by an axe, and an entire hand torn away by the devilish grip of a steam-engine." (See elsewhere, our notes on the *guilty hand* in Hawthorne, even to Hester's "needlework," and to the shape of the branding on the woman's face in "A Birthmark.") Yet, "though the corporeal hand was gone, a spiritual member remained; for, stretching forth the stump, Giles steadily averred that he felt an invisible thumb and fingers with as vivid a sensation as before the real ones were amputated." Henceforth, he had to fight "with his one hand." (As per our many observations on narrative terms for essence, we would interpret "he had come to be" as synonymous with "he was in essence" or "he stood for." And, prophesying after the event, we would note the significance of this "stump," as adumbration of an "elderly dog" which, later in the story, will at a crucial moment begin chasing a tail "a great deal shorter than it should have been." And as regards the relations between "corporeal" and "spiritual," we should certainly also note that, even though the author is telling us how run-down this fellow is, we are also informed that "he had still kept up the courage and spirit of a man," as he "fought" even though having this one hand.

The third was a "village doctor," nameless like the first of these three. Or was he wholly nameless? At least, we are told that "Brand[y] possessed this man like an evil spirit." So far as design goes, he overlaps upon Lawyer Giles to the extent that he was a "half-gentlemanly figure." And he overlaps upon the stage-agent as regards tobacco, for he "had an everlasting pipe in his mouth, and, as somebody said, in allusion to his habit of swearing, it was always alight with hell-fire." Overlaps upon the stage-agent only? Why not also upon Brand, as regards the hell-fire? And could swearing be a variant of that universally directed kind of putting-forth we find in Ethan's demonic laughter? In any case, all three of these figures (who are obviously restatements of a single motivational step) are summed up by Ethan when he tells them to begone: "Leave me . . . ye brute beasts, that have made yourselves so, shrivelling up your souls with fiery liquors!" (Even a variant of the *fire* here.)

Then, clearly, there is a shift: to talk of old Humphrey and his daughter. The old man would have news of his daughter. She had left home and become a circus-performer. Why circus-performer? The artist? But in a not quite reputable guise? In any case, we learn that Ethan had in some ambiguous way wooed her:

> Ethan Brand's eye quailed beneath the old man's. That daughter, from whom he so earnestly desired a word of greeting, was the Esther of our tale, the very girl whom, with such cold and remorseless purpose, Ethan Brand had made the subject of a psychological experiment, and wasted, absorbed, and perhaps annihilated her soul, in the process.
>
> "Yes," he murmured, turning away from the hoary wanderer, "it is no delusion. There is an Unpardonable Sin."

A new step is now taken. Was it in answer to the talk of the "psychological experiment," which perhaps attained its fullest description
in "The Birthmark," where the "mad scientist" theme (as antithetical to love of woman) is put into symbolic operation, plus the twist
that the *man's* guilt is signalized in the sign of the red hand on the
woman's face? (As for the Great Stone Face: Here is the Great Frigid-
ity. Here the stones are made transcendent. Here is the essence of the
snow—but don't look too ardently at Hawthorne's snow, lest it melt
into a dream of sorts.)

Anyhow, we now get children again. And "an old German Jew
travelling with a diorama on his back." He overlaps upon our hero
via the fact that our hero had been a traveller, since he had been a
wanderer-in-search? "Jew" for the guilt theme (in the sense that being-
discriminated-against-socially could stand for being-guilty-morally)?
What of the diorama, the lewd internality of the peering it afforded?

In any case, we are now even more clearly on the theme of the-
making-manifest. This Jew called everyone "Captain." I don't know
what to make of that. But I do know that, in "The May-Pole [equals
tower?] of Merry Mount," it is a word used by the Puritan killjoy, En-
dicott. And, perhaps more relevantly, I consider that, in the present
story, the little nameless boy towards the end gets a name, and it is
"little Joe"—and he it is who is summoned by Bart(ram) to see Brand's
remains after the self-killing (such remains being another narrative
device for the figuring of essence). And the diorama, however dingy it
may be, is explicitly called an exhibit (hence our justification for noting its development via stages from the topic of the circus-performer.)

The pictures of this diorama recover likewise a prior station in the
development. "The pictures were worn out, moreover, tattered, full of
cracks and wrinkles, dingy with tobacco-smoke." (Might not this give
us some equations for tobacco-smoke, that burlesque of the "spiritual,"
that exhalation into nowhere, hence also in its way a scattering-abroad?)
"And these pictures were otherwise in a most pitiable condition." Not
so good an exhibit, this. Yet idealism is nothing if not the being-made-
manifest. What, then, should we make of the fact that, as the exhibit
proceeds, it is obscenely sullied by "a gigantic, brown [there it comes
to fruition] hairy hand [hand? the guilty hand]—which might have
been mistaken for the Hand of Destiny, though, in truth, it was only
the showman's." Now, is not this the point of the within-the-within?
Is not this a show-within-a-show? Hence, have we not *by progression*

arrived at essence now? (If we are correct in our notion that one is at rock bottom when one has got to the withinness-of-withinness, as per the heaven-above-the-heavens, or *hyperouranion,* at the peripety-moment in the Phaedrus.)

Yet we missed the point slightly. We should have seen. *Here* the "little boy" is specified: he becomes "little Joe." And lo! here is the most internal, and internally reflexive, moment of all:

> When, with much merriment at its abominable deficiency of merit, the exhibition was concluded, the German bade little Joe [and this whole incident of the diorama had been introduced in terms of an "amusement at hand"] put his head into the box. Viewed through the magnifying-glasses, the boy's round, rosy [might we legitimately recall the equating of rose with guilt in *The Scarlet Letter?*] visage assumed the strangest imaginable aspect of an immense Titanic child, the mouth grinning broadly, and the eyes and every other feature overflowing [overflowing?] with fun at the joke. [Joke? what kind of play is this?] Suddenly, however, that merry face turned pale, and its expression changed to horror, for this easily impressed and excitable child had become sensible that the eye of Ethan Brand was fixed upon him through the glass.

What is this back-and-forth? When Ethan-at-his-beginnings (as the sensitive child foreboding) meets Ethan-at-his-endings. What kind of fixation is this? Do not the immediately subsequent events make it clear? First, after talk of the child's fear, we are told that there was something by way of the Unpardonable Sin in that show-box ("I find it to be a heavy matter in my show-box,—this Unpardonable Sin! By my faith, Captain, it has wearied my shoulders, this long day, to carry it over the mountain"—and I wonder whether, at this point, when the "Captain" says "by my faith," we could legitimately recall that Young Goodman Brown's wife was called Faith, and he was all set to leave her for the black isolation of the witches' sabbath, though alas! via the lex talionis, the reflexive design of justice, he came upon her too, in that dismal communion of the disparate.) Also, to what extent might we equate this magnification with the cosmologizing of the guilt in Chapter XII of *The Scarlet Letter,* when the A is seen even like a meteor in heaven, and a black glove is found afterwards on the scaffold. (It is our hero's glove, though the sexton says, "A pure hand needs no glove to cover it!")

In any case, we maintain, this *mutuality* (i.e., reflexive relation) is made clear (expatiated upon) in the next episode (the equivalent, in this idiom, of an Aesop fable). "The Jew's exhibition had scarcely been concluded, when a great elderly dog (this is, indeed, a story of the "elderly")—who seemed to be his own master (a variant of the isolation-separation-singularity theme?) [. . .]—saw fit to render himself the object of public notice. (Variant of the transgression made manifest, as in *The Scarlet Letter?* Here approached via the circus-performer and the internality of the diorama, with its obscene brown hand, the equivalent of which apparently was the mutual eyeing of Ethan and little Joe-Jew?) [. . .] Now, all of a sudden, this grave and venerable quadruped, of his own mere motion, and without the slightest suggestion from anybody else, (again his motives are out of himself, as with the soul self-moving, proclaimed at the moment of ultimate internality in the *Phaedrus?*) began to run around after his tail, which, to heighten the absurdity of the proceeding, was a great deal shorter than it should have been." (Was it a tail at all, so far as the parable is concerned?)

However, merely to translate "tail" into "phallus" and stop at that would be to be deceived indeed. Might this circling quest (in design like Ethan's return to his point of departure) represent something of both? Or rather, might the action be *generalized* (with phallus for "beginning," tail for "end")? Whereupon, in burlesque, is enacted the search for efficient cause and final cause, in one? Hence, the metaphysical quest, caricatured in terms of ambiguities to do with a dog's body (and in the spirit of the theme announced in reference to an "over-mouth")? Hence, so far as ultimates are concerned, there was necessarily the unattainable to be figured in this fierce race

> [. . .] until, utterly exhausted, and as far from the goal as ever, the foolish old dog ceased his performance as suddenly as he had begun it. The next moment he was as mild, quiet, sensible, and respectable in his deportment, as when he first scraped acquaintance with the company. (To the shaking, the ejaculatory, and the self-involved, are now added the connotations of friction.)

The incident is now, in sum, called an "exhibition" by a "canine performer" who, though he had been applauded, "appeared totally unable to repeat his very successful effort to amuse the spectators." So there had been success of a sort, after which some urgency, or purpose, seems to have abated. In any case, the author is prompt to make clear the nature of this episode as a reflection upon his hero:

> Meanwhile, Ethan Brand had resumed his seat upon
> the log, and moved, as it might be, by a perception
> of some remote analogy between his own case and
> that of this self-pursuing cur, he broke into the awful
> laugh, which, more than any other token, expressed
> the condition of his inward being.

The passage clearly gives us authority for saying that, each time Brand laughed, he was in the act of chasing his own tail, while "louder and fiercer grew his yells of rage and animosity." And this design is of his very essence ("expressed the condition of his inward being").

This laugh chills the merriment of the men from the tavern, who now hurry home, leaving Ethan, Bartram, and little Joe, in "a solitude, set in a vast gloom of forest." Had the dog's act also *foretold?* Since it stood for Ethan's essence, was that essence now to receive a corresponding *manifestation?* "It seemed to little Joe—a timorous and imaginative child—that the silent forest was holding its breath until some fearful thing should happen." The story is on the verge of some culmination. (Incidentally, "imagination" being as high a word with Hawthorne as with Coleridge, the designation of little Joe as "imaginative child" is almost enough, once you add little-child-shall-lead-them connotations, to assure you that the premonition is as trustworthy as Bard Bracy's dream in "Christabel," the dream of the snake coiled with the dove: "And with the dove it heaves and stirs,/ Swelling its neck as she swelled hers!"). Father and son retire, leaving Ethan to tend the furnace alone, and perhaps (Bartram suggests) to commune with the "Devil" that is in it. The boy has tears in his eyes, "for his tender spirit had an intuition of the bleak and terrible loneliness in which this man had enveloped himself."

The story now has a kind of ultimate stock-taking, prior to the final act that will manifest the nature of the agent. Alone before the fire, he reviews "the gradual but marvellous change that had been wrought upon him by the search to which he had devoted himself." First had

been a period of "tenderness" [. . .] "love and sympathy for mankind" [.
. .] "pity for human guilt and woe." (This is figured in the sympathetic
child. And in *The Scarlet Letter,* we might recall, the sense of her own
guilt helps Hester to become sympathetic towards the guilt and suffering of others.) At this stage, he had viewed "the heart of man" as "a
temple, originally divine, and, however desecrated, still to be held sacred by a brother." Then "he deprecated the success of his pursuit, and
prayed that the Unpardonable Sin might never be revealed to him."

Do we make too much of the next step? For it is scarcely noticeable,
yet we would dwell upon it as of major importance:

> Then ensued that vast intellectual development,
> which, in its progress, disturbed the counterpoise be-
> tween his mind and heart. The Idea that possessed
> his life had operated as a means of education; it had
> gone on cultivating his powers to the highest point of
> which they were susceptible; it had raised him from
> the level of an unlettered laborer to stand on a star-
> lit eminence, [in the second chapter of *The Scarlet
> Letter,* the scaffold from which Hester Prynne looks
> down is called a "miserable eminence"] whither the
> philosophers of the earth, laden with the lore of uni-
> versities, might vainly strive to clamber after him. But
> where was the heart? That, indeed, had withered,—
> had contracted,—had hardened,—had perished! It
> had ceased to partake of the universal throb. He had
> lost his hold of the magnetic chain of humanity. [In
> Chapter XII, "The Minister's Vigil," where the guilt
> is cosmologized, as the A is seen like a meteor in the
> sky, at one point when Hester is holding Pearl by the
> hand, "The minister felt for the child's other hand,
> and took it. The moment that he did so, there came
> what seemed a tumultuous rush of new life, other life
> than his own, pouring like a torrent into his heart,
> and hurrying through all his veins, as if the mother
> and the child were communicating their vital warmth
> to his half-torpid system. The three formed an elec-
> tric circle."]

Ethan clearly equates the Unpardonable Sin with intellect, as contrasted with the heart. But intellect also means climbing in the specifically careerist sense, from "unlettered laborer" to "star-lit eminence." It was such "progress" that "disturbed the counterpoise between his mind and heart." The reflexive element figures, in that such separation from the "universal throb" equals the "self-pursuing." In sum: "Ethan Brand became a fiend." And all is set for the culminating reflexive act, dialectically the reflexive-to-end-reflexives, when the fiend outside the furnace attains total communion with his other, the fiend inside the furnace.

Earlier Ethan had bitterly dismissed his former cronies of the tavern: "Ye brute beasts, that have made yourselves so, shrivelling up your souls with fiery liquors!" And now we are told: "As the lonely man bent forward over this terrible body of fire, the blasting heat smote up against his person with a breath that, it might be supposed, would have scorched and shrivelled him up in a moment." His expression becomes "that of a fiend on the verge of plunging into his gulf of intensest torment." He calls: "O star of heaven, that shone on me of old, as if to light me onward and upward!—farewell all, and forever. Come, deadly element of Fire,—henceforth my familiar friend! Embrace me as I do thee!"

Here many things occur to us. First, note this talk of *ascent* just before he is to make his last *descent*. Note also the variant of the formula in the *Poetics,* which states that the most effective conflicts of tragedy involve familiars. Note that the reflexive nature of the laugh here attains its finality, since Ethan lets it peal forth one last time before he leaps. Note the passion in this "intellect."

And perhaps we should also note: Though this is the point at which he falls into the flames, fiend embracing fiend to the death, this eventuality is not yet made wholly explicit. *There are still* developments to take place, even after Heathen Fire has merged with Fire.

We are now *outside* his internality, as we began: back with crude Bartram and little Joe. And in the early morning sunshine, after the suicide in the solitary night. There is the vision of the village in the valley. The spires of two churches are mentioned (a duality of motives perhaps still to be delved into?). "The old, smoke-dried stage-agent" is already up. He is the only person individually mentioned (except, of course, the father and son by the lime-kiln). Why he? Might it be because, as "stage-agent," he is here, to represent the principle of *trans-*

formation (travel by stages) that is still with us? There is mist, scattered "over the breasts of the surrounding mountains." Why "*breasts*"? We might recall that the lime-kiln into which Ethan had plunged, like Matthew Arnold's Empedocles into Mount Aetna, had "seemed to give admittance into the hill-side," and was like "the private entrance into the infernal regions, which the shepherds of the Delectable Mountains were accustomed to show the pilgrims." Yet, we must admit, just before he leapt, our hero had disclaimed a mother, thus: "O Mother Earth [. . .] who are no more my Mother, and into whose bosom this frame shall never be resolved! O mankind whose brotherhood I have cast off, and trampled thy great heart beneath my feet!"

There are resources here. We don't like to fall back on "ambivalence," feeling that it is less the word for a solution than for a to-be-solved. Yet, given the incest-awe, we might be entitled to interpret this ejaculation loosely, thus: Here being motivated by the search for origins, the author must at some point conceive of such a start in terms of a return to the mother; but, once the stage of "childish innocence" is past, such an *agape*-love necessarily lies beyond the mists of *eros*-love; hence, the *agape* motive (as an ultimate experiential motive for essence, as stated in narrative terms of origin) calls forth the *topic* of the maternal (regardless of how this topic will be treated); and the *eros*-motive, with its corresponding tabus making for incest-awe, calls forth the *negative,* a purely Grammatical resource, to be discounted in accordance with our principle: In imagery there is no negative.

Other resources, short-cuts: We already noted, even in dictionaries, the ambivalence of "mouth," as per bodily entrance but fluminous exit. Correspondingly, we noted the ambiguities of tail and phallus. And, still on the subject of ultimates, after the ambiguous self-slaying, there stand the *two* spires (their churchly-celestial-essential nature obvious enough, but their corresponding distinction in the realm of empirical motives not yet having been wholly accounted for—which reminds us that we might note a kind of Catholic Mariolatry lurking in the background of *The Scarlet Letter,* Hester once being likened to Madonna with child, once to a nun, while her good offices by way of nursing the unfortunate might roundabout equal maternal care for infant). See Chapter II in which, immediately after Hester has ascended the scaffold as an exhibit of shame to the multitude, Hawthorne writes:

> Had there been a Papist among the crowd of Puritans,
> he might have seen in this beautiful woman, so pic-

> turesque in her attire and mien, and with the infant
> at her bosom, an object to remind him of the image
> of Divine Maternity, [. . .] something which should
> remind him, indeed, but only by contrast, of that
> sacred image of sinless motherhood, whose infant
> was to redeem the world. Here, there was the taint
> of deepest sin in the most sacred quality of human
> life, working such effect, that the world was only the
> darker for this woman's beauty, and the more lost for
> the infant she had borne.

Add also, that Dimsdale and Hester meet in the "mother-forest" (Hawthorne's term for the scene that sums up the quality of their relationship).

Returning, now, to the scene in early morning, after Brand's death (could we say) by his own hand: We submit that this moment is similar in quality to the one that Wordsworth fixes in the sonnet "On Westminster Bridge" (the perfect lyric, by our formula, since it so obviously figures a *crossing*, but at the moment of *arrest*). Here the mood is got less beautifully, but it is established. And at the very least it is *stated* (that is, the sensory image is said to represent a transcendent condition, as a mythic image):

> Stepping from one to another of the clouds that rest-
> ed on the hills, and hence to the loftier brotherhood
> that sailed in air, it seemed almost as if a mortal man
> might thus ascend into the heavenly regions. Earth
> was so mingled with sky that it was a day-dream to
> look at it.

Has not Idealism (the IDEA) triumphed after all? Should we think that this *development* is over, simply because *Brand* has died? No, as readers we are still being "processed." Implications go on moving towards explication, somewhat as the cells of a body live on, even after the centers of consciousness are killed.

Dialectically, we might say that there has been a *separating out.* After the enigmatic suicide, something "ascended," and something was "left behind." This design is stated almost explicitly.

We have already cited the passage signalizing the ascent. (To hell with Brand; at least, *we* have been purified.) We shall later discuss what was "left behind" (in Hawthorne's terms, "the relics of Ethan

Brand"). In between, note, there is a transition (and quite in terms of the stage-agent):

> To supply that charm of the familiar and homely, which Nature so readily adopts into a scene like this, the stage-coach was rattling down the mountain-road, and the driver sounded his horn, while Echo caught up the notes, and intertwined them into a rich and varied and elaborate harmony, of which the original performer could lay claim to little share. The great hills played a concert among themselves, each contributing a strain of airy sweetness.

What goes on here? We have risen. Now, via the movement of the stage-coach, we descend again. But, so far, we have kept the spirit of the ascension with us. These sounds are like a god coming down to earth, like spirit materialized. Whatever the problems of "the IDEA" (equals Unpardonable Sin) might have been, by this ultimate self-pursuit (self-sacrifice) they are resolved. Hence, though the reflexive survives in Echo, it now involves a kind of mutuality that is a happy communing of the "great hills." Has the *person* been purified by merging into *Nature* (the principle of the *person purified* thus remaining there enigmatically, as it will be disclosed by almost doctrinaire devices, in "The Great Stone Face"?) In any case, look quizzically at that "airy sweetness," and you'll see lurking, in the design of "Echo," the ancient curse, but now transformed. That is, as regards human relations: the "star-lit eminence" (thumbs down) has become the equivalent thumbs-up. Idealism, as compensation for the divisions of property (and of class formed by property) has come into its own. The Unpardonable Sin has been forgiven. But we spoke of a separating-out. And on that, the story ends:

> "Come up here, Joe!" said he.
> So little Joe ran up the hillock, and stood by his father's side. The marble was all burnt into perfect, snow-white lime. But on its surface, in the midst of the circle,—[previously, the flames had been said to dance "madly, as within a magic circle"] snow-white, too, and thoroughly converted into lime,—[a kind of purified dregs, or offal?] lay a human skeleton, in the attitude of a person who, after long toil, lies down to

long repose. Within the ribs—strange to say was the
shape of a human heart.

"Was the fellow's heart made of marble?" cried
Bartram, in some perplexity at this phenomenon. "At
any rate, it is burnt into what looks like special good
lime; and, taking all the bones together, my kiln is
half a bushel the richer for him."

So saying, the rude lime-burner lifted his pole,
and letting it fall upon the skeleton, the relics of
Ethan Brand were crumbled into fragments.

We end, then, on this residue, rudely treated. (We might almost say
pragmatically transformed, since it is considered in terms of utility.)
We should also note that, Grammatically, there is a slight irresolution
in the closing sentence. For, after the "and," the participle "letting"
would require that not "relics" but "lime-burner" be the subject of this
final statement. So, at the very end, there is a slight deflection, or eva-
sion, though we don't know exactly what to make of it.

So much for the sheer indexing of the story, by way of preparation.

Speculations on "Fire"

First, the body-spirit pair playing so explicit a role in Hawthorne, we
should begin by asking about the possibilities of fire, from the standpoint of the "demonic trinity" (the privy functions). The guilt theme,
made specific in terms of the lime-kiln as "private entrance to the
infernal," would admonish us to this end (though, by our way of sub-
scribing to the Freudian "cloacal theory" in general, we would always
be on the look-out for the expression of "fleshly depravity"—and its
transcending—in terms of "corruption" and "pollution" as explicitly
or implicity equated with the *pudenda*).

Hence, "this terrible body of fire" (we cite from the story) might
relate to the "demonic trinity" thus:

Fire sexual (as per sexual burning; cf. St. Paul);

Fire diuretic (arrived at roundabout? via "water" to "put out" the
fire; recall Gulliver's putting out of the fire in the palace of
Lilliputian king; recall childhood lore: if you have seen a fire
that day, you wet the bed that night).

Fire fecal (the extracting through fire, the lime as the residue from the burning of the marble).

(Should we make it "fire urinal," so that they all end in "al"?)

We shall develop later the refinements on the relation between the "body" and the "spirit" (relations that involve transcendentalism generally, as a brand of idealism, and as complicated by the possibility that flatulency too can be a "curlike" kind of *pneuma*).

In our "Preparatory Analysis" (or "Index") we have indicated how the parental-personal motive might figure here. For the *eros*-fire surrounds the *agape*-fire like a "protecting circle," as incest-tabus stand between the offspring-fragment and its return to the uterine-unitary source. (Recall that this is a story of return: that is, it expresses "essence" in narrative terms, of beginning and ending.) It would, of course, follow that Siegfried's going through the fire to Brunnhilde was such a crossing. What, then, of the fire that danced here, "madly, as within a magic circle"? Has something become displaced? Perhaps, for a wholly orthodox bookkeeping, the central fire should not be exactly "fire" at all, but "light," a *transcendent* fire? There was such radiance. Recall the blasts, almost throwings-forth, of illumination when the lime-kiln door was thrown open, at strategic points. But apparently, a *division of species* had become a merger, had been generalized. (Watch the unification via "the IDEA" for exactly that.) Hence, what should have been steps, was one. However, recall that there is a distinct consciousness of steps. (Recall the stage-agent.) "Misplaced steps," then? (By contract we should be through improvising now, but we find tentatives encroaching upon us, regardless of intent.)

Meantime, we should have said enough to indicate how "fire" (considered now as an idealistic fusion-equals-confusion, or merger-equals-muddle) could include a personal dimension not quite the same as a bodily dimension. Or, if you will, it can figure a motive, or complex of motives, *beginning* in the sheerly bodily, but subsequently modified by semi-political motives, in the sense of the familial.

But we should not stop at that. Where is the "stately" motive? ("Stately" is a word we got from *The Scarlet Letter,* to name the peculiarly hierarchal or socio-anagogic motive, the civic.) How could fire be "stately"?

Now: the "stately" involves "order" (unequal social "kinds" included within a single "universe of discourse"). Hence, our dwelling upon the passage, however brief, in which the "Unpardonable Sin" (which is so intimately involved with "fire") is shown explicitly to be connected with the "careerist climb" (one way of signalizing, with attitude, the social pyramid).

Our problem, then: to inquire into the paths whereby the "stately" motive might be implicit in the fire symbol. Relevantly to our present speculations, a friend said:

"I was working in the cellar, which had become a fantastic clutter. I had had a carpenter build several shelves, on which I was rearranging things. And I was scraping into one pile the refuse-laden surface of earth, mixed with small stones, bits of broken glass, and the like. Presumably the procedure was too symbolic to go unregistered. That night I dreamed of shovelling dirt on to that same pile—and of a sudden, there was a spurt of flames, rising from the dirt on the point of the shovel."

An accurate dream-conceit. "Dirt," as so conceived, can "burn." Such ordering can involve imagery of fire as its "logical conclusion" (even where the materials, literally, precluded combustion) because it equals a *cleansing* and the *purgatory* connotations of fire are clearly established. [3]

To recapitulate: In thoughts of *order* (when translated into narrative terms) there are thoughts of *ordering;* in thoughts of ordering there are thoughts of *cleansing;* and thoughts of cleansing can well attain their ultimate representation in imagery of the *purgatorial fire.* (And here, in turn, would be the unburdenings seminal, urinal, fecal—for the bodily ambiguities of the dream are obvious.)

So might there be a rising too, in Ethan's descent into the flames? Not just in the sense of an ascent, but in the sense of a wider generalization: in the sense that rising-falling *specifically* involves the up-down mode of thought generically?

_____

[3] It seems obvious that purgatorial fire, like cleansing soap, can thereby be "dirty." But if you want an explicit example of polluted fire, see Plutarch on Aristides: "On their consulting the oracle about offering sacrifice, Apollo answered that they should dedicate an altar to Jupiter of freedom, but should not sacrifice until they had extinguished the fires throughout the country, as having been defiled by the barbarians, and had kindled unpolluted fire at the common altar of Delphi." [. . .] Similarly, the Apocalypse-like view of the world itself as ultimately engulfed in flame is presumably the cosmologizing (the "perfection") of such a motive. Here is "dirt" transcended totally, by conversion into its purgatorial other.

Otherwise put: Socio-anagogically, the concern with fire can figure a concern with Authority (hence, with the politics of Justice). Here we are thinking in terms of the gerundive: Order as the to-be-ordered (as grass can equal duty if it means the "to be cut"; and the totality of duty-laden things in the material realm can add up to the manifestation of "God," the over-all generalization of command, the "Categorical Imperative"). And since the to-be-ordered equals the to-be-cleansed, order can be figured in the image of the purgatorial fire (cf. Dante).

Materialists explain Prometheus's rebellious stealing of the fire for man too mechanically, by a shortcut. That is, noting the role of fire in invention, they take fire-making to stand for invention generally. It is true that Prometheus was often credited with having taught invention generally. And one certainly could not rule this out as a possible derivation among many. Indeed, it is clearly a major strand among the motives figured in Aeschylus's *Prometheus Bound.*

In any case, invention makes for differentiation of social classes, and out of such differentiation arise social tensions which are expressed semi-narratively, semi-morally, in terms of "original sin" (that is, guilt intrinsic to interference with the universalizing of "justice," for justice is frustrated insofar as it cannot be made universal, and social inequality necessarily prevents it from being universal). So, whether you start with fire (equals invention) or with order (equals social inequality arising from the property structure that goes with the development of invention) you get such susceptibilities of conscience as equal "guilt" (hence call for purification, for which purgatorial fire is a symbolic specific). Or we could state our case thus: Even if you begin with the fire that went into mechanical inventions, somewhere along the line you must introduce fire as a ritual cleanser; and it is this *ritual* fire that we have to do with, when considering the poetic symbolizing of man's relation to authority (with the "guilt" implicit in social degree, or discrimination). Or, to try once more: The lime-kiln itself had to do with fire in the purely mechanical sense, but we are concerned with fire, not as the *conceptual* term for a purely natural process, but as an *idea,* a poetic symbol, a "spiritual" entity which the "natural" fire "stands for."

All told, then, concerning return-to-fire as a statement of essence in narrative terms, we have noted three orders of guilt: Connotations of pudenda (body-imagery); incest-awe (familial motives); embarrassments of social degree (the socio-anagogic motive). The examination brings us to a "jumping-off place," since it is a study of linguistic forms leading to the edge of the "metalogical" (the realm not beneath language but beyond language). It is "transcendental," in the Kantian sense, because it is concerned with the *ultimate* forms of an empirical element. Or, otherwise put: The *specifically* human situation being in the realm of symbol-using, it would require us to look for ways of peering into the reality-beyond-symbols by treating language *purely* as symbols.

Here is the paradox: We begin by the crudest of principles, *Words are mere words.* Nothing could be farther from "food," for instance, than a mere word for it. Nothing could be farther from "the ultimate ground of all possibility" than the mere word for that. Hence, above all, we would study the lore of sheer word-slinging (the essentially cynical fact that when one is not sorry, but says "I'm sorry," he may get credit even with himself for feeling sorry).

But to study the *internal relations* among such "slung words" (in their nature as "utterance" and "ejaculation") is to come upon a kind of *reality.* Thus, the word for "God" is but sheer *flatus vocis,* a worse than nothing, the symbol as an idealistic fog arising between symbolizer and symbolized; yet the *exact place* that that word has in a given verbal context *really is just what it is.* The other words that serve as modifiers for this one word (and they include words not just for ideas and images, but also for facts, attitudes, persons and personal relations) appear in exactly their given actual order.

For instance, when Hawthorne writes of "the private entrance to the infernal regions," then, after appropriate further "linguistic processing," speaks of a "gold radiance of the upper atmosphere" that "seemed almost as if a mortal man might thus ascend into the heavenly regions," the last thing that would occur to us would be to take "infernal regions" and "heavenly regions" as names for "real" places. As so considered, these terms are essentially one with the "mists" that are needed to qualify theological myths of Creation in terms of an initial verbal fiat. *But the steps from the writer's talk of the infernal to talk of the heavenly are real.* They are available to empirical study: Yet the *forms* (or rather, transformations through stages) disclosed by such study *are not themselves words used sheerly as correspondences* (as with the relation between, say, a table and the word for table.)

Thus, if one inspects the essence or form of the verbal journey, noting the internal relations among the parts and the nature (naturalness) of their sequence, one might come upon the "mystic initiation" *in* form and *through* form. Otherwise, one interprets linguistic reference too literally ever to see beyond its limitations as a *medium* (a means of mediation interposing itself as a "mist"). If one does not take this roundabout route, attempting rather, as with the unintended caricature of behaviorist psychologists, to disclose the more-than-linguistic by experiments the very form of which can disclose only the less-than-linguistic, one will never truly glimpse the extent to which less-than-linguistic natural objects possess, for man (the symbol-using species), hidden linguistic dimensions. The last way on earth to transcend the deceptions of *words* is by a mere "tough-minded" beginning with "things." For in such a scheme, the so-called "things" are allowed to smuggle in an undeclared verbal or symbolic content. In their capacity as symbol-using animals, men must approach "nature" by going "beyond the mist" (beyond the *double*-mist) of the verbal and the pre-verbal. (The verbal here is the realm that conceals symbols within its words for *things.* And the pre-verbal is the realm of infancy where verbal clarifications are gradually emerging through an intellectual fog, itself moralistically qualified by the "duties" of bodily hygiene and the "triumphs" of bodily "self-expression." [4])

Borrowing designs from the Kantian vocabulary, we could say that the words for things (and for operations in the realm of sheer place and motion) are *concepts;* but when such words are used in poetry, they are ideas (endowed with a purely linguistic, or dialectical aura that is absent from things in the strictly material sense). However, insofar as our lives are "crude first drafts of poems," there is always an ideal content lurking in the conceptual (or, we could say, there are ideal connotations implicit in the conceptual denotation).

Forms are a *journey.* Such a journey will not only involve a succession of stages. Also, there will be static relations among the parts (though one *may come upon* them by various routes that make them, too, seem like a development).

---

[4] We are *not* saying that adult motives are derived sheerly from conditions of the nursery. We *are* saying that the total expression of adult motives will necessarily include terms derived from conditions of the nursery. Indeed, often the poet may translate *civic* relations into terms that on their face contain few such motives, featuring merely the bodily and the personal. In these instances, the civic motives must be disclosed by such roundabout methods as we are here considering.

When we can offer various alternative routes for getting from one such internal relation to another, the probability is that we have not found the wholly adequate description.

Bodily (sensory); familial (personal); political, social, civic (hierarchal, making "socio-anagogically" for an "enigmatic" element in the "objects of everyday experience," endowing the presumably non-linguistic or extra-linguistic with a hidden linguistic dimension): these are the three orders of motives; but the journeys through this tangle, in the search for an essence beyond it, are not analyzable merely as, say, a set of steps from one to another, in whatever order one might choose. Rather, once a complex linguistic structure has arisen, there is also a state of simultaneous mutuality among the terms. For instance, fire as related to order, justice, authority (fire purgative to the hierarchal guilt) could link with the parental not merely by reason of the incest-awe (involving body-imagery of the sexual burning); also there would be the fact that parental terms themselves may personalize the principle of authority. Indeed, the possibilities are even subtler here: Given the normal resources of dialectic manipulation, norms of justice derived from the personal-familial can become antagonistic to "stately" justice (and can thus even be the matrix for a "higher" justice, as with the sister's pious refusal to obey the commands of the temporal ruler in Sophocles' *Antigone)*. Such considerations as this are involved in what we call the "static" relations.

But let us go back to inquire into the stages of the Hawthorne story (beginning purely with considerations of surface):

We would love to reduce it to five parts, with the peripety (point of farthest internality?) in part III. (Incidentally, in our analysis of the Keats Ode, in the *Grammar,* we assigned the peripety to stanza III, but stanza IV was in a sense an intensifying of the internal, as here the transcendent scene for the new act was dwelt upon.) In the case of "Ethan Brand," tentatively at least, the form (development, journey) seems best analyzable in six parts, with the last as a kind of epilogue.

I. Introduction. Lime-burner and his son. Scene: lime-kiln at night. Ethan Brand's laugh (the outward sign of his motivation). Description of the furnace (its intestine connotations, developed from talk of "the IDEA," the search for the Unpardonable Sin). Ethan is still in the offing, announced Siegfried-like, by his leit-motif (the laugh). The reader is not yet wholly certain whom the laugh announces, though he strongly infers. And we are explicitly told that this was the very kiln Ethan had formerly tended.

II. Enter Ethan Brand. His "illumination" (Satanic?). He places finger on his heart, as place of the Sin (Dimsdale had done likewise). Again the laugh (author expatiates on its fiendishness). For the in-our-next: Son is sent to summon Ethan's old cronies from tavern.

III. A kind of interlude? A marking-time, between the Son's departure and his return with Ethan's old acquaintances. Yet this pause, or arrest, is by no means "inefficient," a mere "filler." It is as profound as a (contextually defined) silence. Bartram and Ethan alone. Of a sudden, Bartram gets a fleeting sense of kinship with temptations. Possibly homosexual suggestions here, in the offing? (If only in the sense that Ethan is back; and Bartram, tending his own furnace, must represent a crude "masculine" aspect of himself. That is, there is such "homosexuality" as arises out of "narcissism," when Ethan communes with an alienated aspect of himself.) Along with the tentatives of the attitudinizing, there is the purely *doctrinal* formula. The problematical motive is defined as: "The Sin of an intellect that triumphed over the sense of brotherhood with man and reverence for God."

IV. The episode of the "old acquaintances"—This leads into the "performance" or "exhibition" theme. (Via the man whose daughter became a "circus-performer.") She is called "the Esther of our tale, the very girl whom, with such cold and remorseless purpose, Ethan Brand had made the subject of a psychological experiment, and wasted, absorbed, and perhaps annihilated her soul, in the process." Why Esther? We see no striking analogy to the Biblical Esther, who must be meant here. Is this "the *Hester* of our tale"? (Incidentally, lurking, prying, and noting his word "pry," which in its way is as essentially his as is the word "singular," we have often wondered whether "pry" could be the obverse of "Prynne," for all the shortening of the vowel.) Note also the analogies to the morbid, and fatal, experiments to which the husband subjected his wife in "The Birthmark." (Recall the importance of the "furnace" in the laboratory there.) Anyhow, the topic of this Esther-Hester-performer leads to the topic of the diorama (with the obscene protruding of the "gigantic, brown, hairy hand")—and this in turn leads to the incident of the "self-pursuing cur," after which the "worthies" leave.

V. The "worthies" are gone, dismissed by Ethan, who has also sent little Joe and Bartram to bed. He is now back to his beginnings, alone with fire (whatever that may stand for, as poetic idea, for it isn't just a scientific concept). Author now develops the purely *doctrinal* aspects of Ethan's guilt. (A good spot diplomatically, since the in-our-next quality is by now so well established, that the doctrinal will be tolerated. Indeed, the uncertainties dangling before the reader will make him even welcome it, as he might in a detective story welcome the discovery of the criminal; nay more, in his eagerness for doctrine, for the specifying of the offence, he might even be too willing, hence might be deceived into accepting the mere doctrine as an adequate statement of the case whereas, if it were enough, the rest would be but a burden.) [. . .] Finally, the "prophetic" (vatic) laugh comes into its own.

VI. Epilogue. The "separating out." Divided into:

(1) the "ascent" (the heavenly morning, purely in terms of *natural* imagery—i.e., the *depersonalized*, except insofar as natural images can be "mythic" transmogrifications of personal and social-political motives).

(2) the vestiges, "relics" (refuse, but purified), the "perfect, snow-white lime" and the "marble" heart (terms well worth remembering when you study snow and marble elsewhere in Hawthorne).

(3) the pragmatic cynicism (treated almost as glancingly as the hierarchal motive was, when on the doctrinal statement of the Sin, in Part V); Bartram on the *utility* of the rendered body, as sheer *lime.*

6

The Orestes Trilogy[1]

IN THE INTRODUCTORY PLAY, THE *AGAMEMNON*, Clytemnæstra, plotting with her paramour, kills her husband Agamemnon and Cassandra, the prophetess whom he had brought home as booty from the sack of Troy. Clytemnæstra justifies the murder on the grounds that, to obtain the victory for his armies, Agamemnon had slain their daughter, Iphigenia, on the sacrificial altar. The play ends with the Chorus praying for the son, Orestes, to appear and avenge his father's murder.

The second play, the *Libation-Bearers (Choëphoroe)*, begins with Orestes' arrival. He kills both the paramour (Aegisthus) and the mother. But though he has murdered his mother in righteous retaliation, as the play ends he is beginning to be tortured by remorse. (Dramatically, this torture was objectified by his seeing of the Furies, ancient goddesses that punish blood-guilt.) And he is told that, to be cured, he must journey to the oracle at Delphi, called the "navel" of the world.

The third play, the *Eumenides,* deals with Orestes' final absolution. The action begins at Delphi, where the Furies are still pursuing him, but have fallen asleep. It ends at Athens, where Orestes is finally absolved. And in the course of this absolution, the Furies themselves change their nature, as they shift their emphasis from the punishing of evil to the reward of good. Athena says that we are here witnessing the "first" trial for murder (a legal trial, in contrast with the earlier, feudal practice whereby a victim was avenged by kinsmen). And the development also allusively solemnizes a treaty of alliance recently

---

[1] From the manuscript *Poetics, Dramatistically Considered.* © The Kenneth Burke Literary Trust. Used by permission.

made between Athens and Argos. (Orestes came from Argos, but he is acquitted by an Athenian court.)

So much for the outline of the only surviving Greek trilogy. It offers special opportunities because Aristotle does not treat of the trilogy as a form, hence does not consider a "dialectical" progression whereby each play grows out of the preceding, or into the one that follows.

The equivalent of "original sin" in the *Oresteia* is the crime of Atreus, who slew the children of his brother, Thyestes, and served them to their father at a banquet which was supposedly held to celebrate the brothers' reconciliation. (There had been a prior offense, since Thyestes had seduced the wife of Atreus; but though this theft served as motive for Atreus's act of vengeance, his mode of retaliation was the first act that involved blood-guilt; hence the curse upon the House of Atreus derived from it rather than from the prior offense of Thyestes.)

What "logic of imagery" follows from this particular choice to symbolize the "original sin" that will serve as generating principle for the trilogy's form and style? Note, first, that it has to do with a matter of *eating.* The father is a kind of ogre-in-spite-of-himself: for as the result of his brother's treachery, he eats his children. We are told that when he discovers what he has done, he vomits in horror.

Psychoanalysis might suggest that the myth is a variant of the fantasy underlying the tale of Jack the Giant-Killer. But here the father-principle would be split in two, into "brothers," whereat the "good father" could still retain the function of the child-devouring Giant, but under forgivable conditions, since he had been tricked into his role by his other, the "bad uncle."

Also, since the whole work heads in the worship of the Olympian Zeus, it is fitting to remember, as we are reminded in the play, that Zeus also had been swallowed by his father, Saturn, but Saturn later disgorged his son as the result of an emetic deceptively administered by the mother, whereupon Zeus revolted, and set up a new era. And the same ambiguity is present here, since the "reign of Saturn" was also, by another tradition, identified with the golden age, which was celebrated during the annual rites of the Saturnalia, when master and servant changed places for the duration of the holiday. The double role of childhood, as happily protected and irritatingly confined, would seem symbolized here, along with dreams of a different social order.

In any case, whatever the original motives behind the myth of Thyestes, *on its face* it involves an imagery of biting, and throughout the work there are variants on this theme, in references to devouring, blood-sucking, disgorging, and the like. The Furies, that come to the fore near the end of the second play, and form the Chorus in the third, themselves represent the image in its extreme. For their basic role (they call themselves "Curses") is to objectify the vicious bite of conscience (cf. "remorse"); and to this end, fittingly, they are repeatedly referred to as "dogs." Similarly, in Clytemnæstra's dream, enigmatically fore-telling that her son is to kill her, she is nursing a serpent which sucks blood along with the maternal milk. The Furies, similarly, concentrate their nature in their "venom."

The dog image has a wider range, however. Besides the dogs that "hound" the guilty, there are the simply treacherous dogs, the loyal dogs, the subservient dogs, the alert dogs. At the opening of the first play, the Watchman speaks of himself as expectant, "like a dog."

The selection of eating or biting as the symbol for the underlying dynastic curse fits well with the dog image, as an "Aesopian" way of summing up characteristic human relationships. And above all, note how beautifully this image serves to represent a basic ambiguity of so-cial relations: the wavering line between loyalty and subservience (an essential concern, if drama is to be *civically* motivated).

Considering the dog image thus, we sense a flurry of motives when Clytemnæstra likens herself to a dog watching over the house. She is a woman, she is to kill, she is to be killed, and women (the blood-thirsty Furies) are to preside over her avenging (as indeed finally a woman, Athena, presides over the deal whereby the matricide is pardoned and the Furies accept a new abode, underground).

Here is a tangle, yet we can discern its strands. For, whatever the ultimate guilt may be, as regards the Olympian culture celebrated in the civic tragedies (ultimately pointing to *Zeus agoraios,* the parliamen-tary Zeus, as this trilogy explicitly does), there must also be the guilt towards *woman* as a class. In this trilogy, the transformations with re-gard to that problem are astounding, most notably in the dramatized legalism of the third play, with the hagglings whereby it is avowed that men are not really descended from women. The woman is but a nurse for the foetus. Accordingly, by this doctrine, strictly speaking, Orestes was not a matricide, for he had no mother; he had a father, and his mother was but a nurse who, we might say, served as mere incubator for the father's sperm. Similarly, Athena presides over the trial that frees Orestes; and she points out that she had no mother, since she was born from the head of Zeus. The "Justice" of the parliamentary Zeus is thus (not by interpretation, but explicitly in the text) essentially discriminatory, with regard to women, quite as was the culture itself, with its romantic love best expressed homosexually, as in the *Phaedrus* and in the poetry of Lesbian Sappho.

Let us first consider some psychoanalytic possibilities, not because we intend to use them, but because we want to get them out of the way. Various complications suggest themselves, as regards the ambiguous relation between parents and offspring that marks both the underlying dynastic curse and the murders enacted in the plays themselves. To begin with, we might interpret the original myth as a simple fantasy involving a primal fear of the father, a fear that is ironically confirmed by a moralistic device for exonerating the father. Here would be a remote analogue of the filial abnegation symbolized in Matthew Arnold's *Sohrab and Rustum*. Or we could imagine a kink hereby the fantasy arose as moralistic reversal of the motive symbolized in Jack the Giant-Killer. That is: An original impulse to assert one's will against the father would be translated into a fantasy of killing or eating him—and this in turn could be moralized by transformation into a retaliatory fantasy whereby the child rather than the parents was the victim. (It's always reasonable to look for a principle of retaliation in such plots, since so many lines in Aeschylus are variations on the theme of the *lex talionis*).

When the father is killed in the first play, clearly the son is not the direct agent of his death, since the killing is done by the mother, and the son does not enter the action until the second play. But one might conceivably still treat this as essentially a son's patricidal fantasy, moralized by deflection (that is, by imagining the offense as done by someone else, whom the son could then attack in righteous retaliation, without having to face the possibility that the mother was fulfilling a filial wish). In this connection it is worth noting that Orestes himself calls his mother a patricide, though she has killed her husband, not her father; and if she were acting as a surrogate for the son, this epithet would be astoundingly correct. But the authenticity of this passage has been questioned.

In any case, after Orestes has appeared on the scene, he expresses the wish that Agamemnon had been killed in battle at Troy, thus being spared the ignominious murder—whereat his sister Electra promptly says she wishes he had not been killed at all. We should note a further possible psychological subterfuge: Insofar as physical violence can stand for sexual violence, Orestes's slaying of Clytemnæstra could even represent a sexual attack in moralized disguise.

We do not intend to build on any of these possibilities. As regards justice, form, expectancy, we find in the logic of blood-guilt the conditions that prepare the audience for Orestes' killing of his mother. Here will be our stress. And this killing will in turn stir up personal problems of a sort that, in a work of such thoroughness (such "persecutional" thoroughness) will require a further set of manipulations, in a third play, to cure a sick conscience by changing the very nature of conscience itself. We want to watch how one particular tragic form unfolds.

There is a vexing shiftiness at the roots of the trilogy. The dramatist is looking back at feudal justice from the standpoint of civic justice. The myths he draws on could not have quite the same meaning in a civic setting as they had in the situations under which they arose. The tribal kind of family out of which the myths arose had already been greatly transformed. And such "archaizing" brings up motivational, puzzles that we could not hope to solve. For instance, cannibalistic imagery in a cannibalistic society should indicate motives much different from those of such imagery in a non-cannibalistic society. And if a story of "conscientious" killing emerges from a society where the blood-feud was the normal means of administering "justice," it could involve much different motives when read by people to whom forensic justice was the norm; for instance, it might take on many purely sexual connotations not present in the original situation. The same images, in the two situations, might evoke essentially different attitudes. So we shall try searching for motives more clearly "civic."

Thus, since the trilogy leads up to and away from the matricide, we should above all try to note what themes gravitate about this act. For instance, we focus upon that word "amphisbaena," uttered by Cassandra (who, as prophetess, is sure to state the essence) when she is trying to decide what the murderous Clytemnæstra should be called. For if Orestes is to slay an "amphisbaena" (naturally, for the best of reasons), we must certainly meditate upon that term, since by the rules of the myth Cassandra *cannot* be wrong.

Amphisbaens: from *amphis*, both ways; and *bainein*, to go. It is a serpent, in ancient mythology, beginning or ending at both head and tail alike. Meditating upon it, we may relevantly recall that in the play Clytemnæstra is called a serpent, as is Orestes (in her dream). On the side, we might recall the old formula: unless a serpent eats a serpent it will not become a dragon (*serpens nisi serpentem comederit, non fit draco*), though we'll not insist upon that one, since it is at best about the edges of the text. Nor will we insist upon the fact that such a design lends itself readily to the anal-oral ambiguities we considered before the "divide." However, we will most intensely insist upon the following:

When in the second play we hear the cry of Aegisthus, slain by Orestes off stage, and when Clytemnæstra has rushed in, asking what happened, the traditional messenger (here a servant) answers enigmatically: "The dead are killing the living, I say." But Clytemnæstra immediately calls the remark a riddle. For the expression so utilizes the resources of Greek grammar that it can also be interpreted in reverse: "The living is killing the dead." And it is deliberately designed to have this "amphisbaenal" nature.

She immediately interprets it in terms of the *lex talionis:* "We are to be killed by treachery, even as we killed." And she calls for an axe, to decide whether she is "victor or victim."

What are we to do with this moment? Each of the dramas has its turning point. But here is the point on which the whole trilogy turns. It is enigmatic, it is in its grammar an "amphisbaena"; and as a generating principle it is the very stock-in-trade of the tragic dramatist. Even in the seven extant plays, we could probably trace, literally, hundreds of variations on the formula. But the most concentrated spot we know of is in lines 308–314 of *The Libation-Bearers,* where the Chorus, referring to the Fates (Moirai), Zeus, fulfilment, and justice, give these three variants of the pattern: "Meet hate with hate [. . .] repay murder with murder [. . .] as he does, be it done unto him."

True, there will be manipulations. In the first play, a dismal genealogy will be announced whereby good times give rise to bad, and bad times perpetuate themselves. But we should not interpret this formula too absolutely. Rather, we should note how it provides, in the first play, a kind of statement that can be significantly revised in the third, where another kind of reversal is possible, and out of evil (as suffering) may emerge good (as release, purification, the exultant exalting of local justice and inter-civic pacts). And we should not overlook the ironically admonitory moment when the reformed Furies express the hope that the city will avoid *faction* (as indeed the tragic purge is helping it to do, at least for the duration of the play, and as long as the curative spell can hang on afterwards.) The statement (in *Eumenides*, 976–988) is tangled, perhaps "oracularly." But it ends on the hope that the citizens may unite in hating the enemy, whereat we can revert to a speech by Athena, on the same subject line 864: "May their wars be with foes abroad."

A notable "Delphic" or "oracular" expression occurs where Clytemnæstra is foretelling the victimization of Agamemnon. She has persuaded him, against his own wishes, to accept the ceremonious welcome, which he had said was more fitting for a god than for a man. But she would make him a god in the sense that she is to sacrifice him. And as he enters the palace, unknowingly going to his death, she utters her final prophetic formula (Ag. 973–4): "Zeus, Zeus, that fulfillest, fulfil these my prayers. To thee be the care of what thou wouldst fulfil." Of this word, "fulfil," more anon. For the moment note simply that its presence here in three forms (vocative case of adjective, present indicative, and infinitive: *teleie, telei, telein*) gives these two "final" lines a decidedly jingle-like quality. Indeed, since rhyme is not used in this poetry, we have almost the effect of a rhyming couplet when used in blank verse to mark a significant ending, for the two lines end on *telei* and *telein* respectively. There is the repetition of "Zeus." The words for "these my prayers" are quite repetitive in sound (*tas emas euxas,* a repetitive quality intensified by the fact that both by accent and by quantity, the emphasis is upon the syllable *as*). The expression here translated as "be the care" is a verb, *meloi.* The expression translated "wouldst" is a verb *melles.* The word for "to thee" is *soi,* which takes up the second vowel-sound of *meloi.* And this *oi* quality is intensified by addition of an almost meaningless enclitic *toi,* having the force of "in sooth," "verily." The *el* of *meloi* is in *teleleie, telei, melles,* and *tellein.*

> Zeû, Zeû, télele, tàs emàs euxàs télei,
> méloi dé toi soì tonper àn méllès teleîn.

Surely, it takes no knowledge of Greek forms to glimpse the tonal vibrancy of that couplet, or to appreciate its "Delphic" quality, in thus stating so vaguely a prophecy that the expectancies of the plot have already made drastically clear. And as to that word "fulfil": recall its presence in the New Testament (in the form, *tetéletai*), for Christ's last word: "It is finished." We shall later review in some detail the many ways in which this word recurs. For the tragedy out of which Aristotle developed his entelechial analysis is in its own way essentially entelechial. Indeed, we might consider Aristotle's notion of the entelechy as the exact philosophic equivalent of the tragic dramatist's concern with the many variants that *telos* comes upon, in the course of a complete tragic unfolding, as distributed among the various functions of the dramatis personae in their competitive cooperation towards a single end.

Likewise we can glimpse something beyond mere sententiousness in the many gnomic lines, as with formulas reduced to the ultimate like *pathei mathos* (knowledge through suffering). Summaries of motivation are similarly caught, as when Orestes, to say that Clytemnæstra, having killed her husband, was by the same token the slayer of his father, says almost telegraphically: "Husband-slayer slew my father" (though Greek grammar allows the sentence to be richer in tense here, and thus richer in relationships: the word for "husband-slayer," means, rather "one-having-slain-husband").

In stressing the "oracular" quality of Aeschylus's method, we have a further purpose in mind. We believe that it enables us to offer a *formal* means of linking Greek tragedy with the religious rites out of which it arose. And we would proceed thus:

Previously we spoke of "allusion" in tragedy (as with the implied allusion in Euripides' *Trojan Women,* and in the *Eumenides* the explicit allusion to Athenian justice and the pact with Argos). But there is another kind of allusion, explicitly informing the *style* of Greek tragedy: The constant allusion to the analogies between tragedy and religious rites of purification. Get our point here. We are *not* here discussing tragedy "genetically," in terms of its "origins." We are saying that the tragedy, *in its completion as a secular form,* is forever looking for ways to suggest underlying Bacchic modes of purification whereby even a murder done in hatred is shown to have the lineaments of a religious sacrifice, like a pious offering at the altar of some god.

In Chapter XVII of the *Poetics,* when discussing his remark that episodes must be "appropriate," Aristotle cites as an example (Euripides' *Iphigeneia in Tauris*) Orestes' "escape by means of the purification" (the only other place in the text, as we have previously noted, where there is mention of "catharsis"). However, he does not explain why this incident is so appropriate.

He did not explain because, to a Greek of that time, the example was self-evident. And it was self-evident, we submit, because it had an "appropriateness" of this sort: It shifted between secular and religious modes in ways whereby, though secular in motivation, it proceeded by the sophistication of religious modes. Iphigeneia, now a priestess of Artemis, had learned that the supposed stranger was her brother. But it has been decided that he is to be sacrificed. On the plea of cleansing him ritually in the sea as preparation for the sacrifice, she sets up a situation whereby they both can escape. The word for "escape" in the Aristotle passage is *soteria,* which in religious usage (as later in the New Testament) meant "salvation." Hence, the "appropriateness" of the episode is in its quality as a double *entendre.* It is not merely *derived* from the rites (in a sense whereby reference to the rites would be artistically irrelevant); it deliberately *alludes* to such matters, and gets some of its effect by secular analogies that are like ingenious variations on a theme (variations which, though developed far beyond the theme they are varying, yet contrive to keep the initial motive apparent).

Seen thus, the relation between this civic art-form and the Bacchic rites "out of which it arose" would not be simply a concern of anthropologists, historians, and the like, scientists who deal rather with the "background" of the tragedies than with the works "in and for themselves." Allusion, in the sense of formal analogy between religious rite and secular art, would be deliberately sought. Thus when Aeschylus, again and again, introduces metaphors of grapes, and other images or "prophetic" incidents of like temper, at moments where sacrifice is to be indicated, we are not merely "anthropologizing" if we note how the playwright points up the analogies between the secular killings and the religious mysteries. We are dealing with the very essence of the playwright's style, and with his means for attaining "propriety" in the development of his plot (hence means for fitting the plot to the logic of the audience's expectations).

We could cite minor allusions of this sort throughout. But just as, in Wagner's *Nibelungen* Cycle, one often finds the most revealing spots motivationally where the playwright in one play is giving the gist of another, so the passage that best illustrates our point is in the *Eumenides* (lines 459–463), where Orestes is summing up the *Agamemnon:* He says that Agamemnon did not perish honorably but was slain by his "black-hearted" mother, who "enfolded" him in a "crafty net" or snare, that still bears witness to his murder in the bath. And he admits he slew the woman who bore him (a three-word formula). The word for "crafty" here originally means spotted, mottled, dappled. And it is *also applied* to the "intricate" or "riddling" speech of oracles. The word translated as "enfolded" is none other than that most oracular of all, with such basic meanings as hide, conceal, cloak, keep secret, darken, make obscure (it is, in brief, the word from which we get "cryptic"). The word for witnessing is the one from which we get "martyr." And the cathartic implications are obvious, in the reference to Agamemnon's being slain in his bath.

Even the epithet "black-hearted," which at first glance seems so unambiguous, discloses interesting possibilities when you take a second look. For "black" is the epithet of the Earth-Mother, who will later be proclaimed the very source of the prophetic motive. It is the epithet of Night, celebrated in the text as a goddess. Indeed Clytemnæstra's first words (and in this art, first words are always pointed) refer to Mother Night. She uses for "Night" a traditional euphemism that means kindly or favorably disposed; she comes at dawn to announce the "glad" news that marks the beginning of the tragedy and that is explicitly described as having sped through the night. (That is, this news was hatching in the night as the proverb she cites refers to Dawn born of Night.) And we circle back to the details of the murder in another way, when we recall a notable observation about Demeter, the Earth-Mother, in the *Encyclopaedia Britannica* (Eleventh Edition): One of her epithets was "angry" (*erinys,* the very word that became personified in the name for the Furies); and there were rites celebrating her change from the "angry" to the "bather" (*lousia,* notable in that the word for "baths" in the present citation is *loutra*). We may thus even glimpse an analogy between the myth of her change from "angry" to "bather" and the change of the Furies from Erinyes to Eumenides. And Clytemnæstra's dreaded will-power may thus be seen to suggest "chthonian" sources (as the Earth-Mother was a chthonian deity, and the theme will be explicitly introduced in the second play, with reference to "chthonian Hermes," the principle of communication between the living and the nether-world). Nearly every important word of Orestes' summary is thus seen to suggest some fragment of the religious mysteries.

Further, just as the tragic character Pentheus gets his name from a function, *pentheo,* to mourn (as Euripides points out in his *Bacchae*), we might even catch the glimpse of a tragic function in the name "Agamemnon" (Steadfast). For the first half of his name is a word we have already discussed (meaning a *much* that can be *too much,* and so bring on envious disaster)—whereat we can glimpse allusion to Clytemnæstra's device for setting him up as a tragic victim by her overly honorific welcome, in providing for him a triumphal carpet that implied the same fate as did the net that would eventually ensnare him.[2]

If we thus look upon the tragedies as organized about a *methodic* use of allusions to religious rites, we get the point of the fairly well attested story that, despite Aeschylus's high repute in his adopted city (he was born at Eleusis, where the mysteries of the Earth-Mother were celebrated), at one time the Athenian populace became enraged with him for revealing inviolable secrets of Demeter-worship. (He is said to have been acting in one of his own plays, and was saved by fleeing to the altar of Dionysus in the orchestra, since his pious pursuers respected the rights of sanctuary.) Later he was acquitted, on the plea that he didn't know the things he had been saying were secrets. Such an art of allusion would obviously have both its advantages and its risks. But in any case, it draws upon religious allusions even when detailing what is, on its face, the most forbiddingly secular of crimes—and the discussion of such a poetic device would not involve solely a matter of "origins," and "derivations from extra-artistic sources," but would concern the *nature of the work as it is,* and the *logic of its style and form.*

Poetically, the stress upon the "oracular" (or "öneiromantic") has great stylistic advantage. Just as, in a joke, the last line is explosively significant, so in an "oracular" poetry there is always the goad to "packed" lines, lines that are "wiser than they know," in the elements they connote, or the destiny they foretell, or in proclaiming themselves as steps in the plot. By this last remark, we refer to the ways in which Aeschylus himself seeks to name in terms of plot the developments which a critic would name in terms of form. That is, the dramatist writing in such a tradition will find ways of saying, in effect: "This is an introduction," "This is a foreshadowing," "This is a summarization," "This is a peripety," "This is a discovery," and the like. And he will do so, not simply to point up the plot, but through a feeling that the progress through this series of steps in this order is itself the "essence" of the experience: the essence being not in this or that plot,

---

[2] It would be perfect for our purposes if the word for the net used in the slaying of Agamemnon in his bath could be shown to be also the name of a device used in the ritual sacrificing of animals on the altar.

but in the underlying process of initiation or cleansing common to all such plots.

Are we being too "Platonic" here? In any case, it is just as true that the story must be almost obsessively *this* story and none other. For only by being exclusively *this* story can it constantly mull over the details, until each is so saturated with the spirit of the others that the whole has unity. Yet, once such thoroughness is achieved, out of it, *beyond* it, there arises the "oracular" stress upon form as such, the profound persecutional necessity whereby, man being the symbol-using animal, the motives of his life disclose their obedience to the forms that go with symbol-using, that are "natural" to it; whereat, in following them, one is simultaneously free and compelled (quite as Clytemnæstra and Orestes act through deliberate choice, yet explicitly recognize that their notions of vindication would not allow them to act otherwise).

Form as form can readily degenerate into the weakest of art, sheer decorations; but when the "oracular" kind of attentiveness is keenest, it makes for a constant succession of pointed events (the discrete steps that sharpen one's awareness of the continuity). The movements of the Chorus doubtless contributed to such awareness: for as they turn from one direction to another, the poet almost spontaneously seeks for a corresponding turn in his idea—and to think of an art-form thus is to get a plot that moves like the ticking of a clock through time: each speech, or each stanza of a song, ticks the action one step forward; and such discreteness within the continuity makes for the kind of stylistic vigil that we have summed up as the "oracular" (at once soaked in detail and transcending detail).

Accordingly, one can make discoveries by asking "why" at every point. Why, for instance, does the first play have a Chorus of Elders, the second a Chorus of Captive Women, the third a Chorus of Furies? What formal "secret" underlies precisely that progression? Why does the first play open with a Watchman, the second with Orestes praying, the third with a Prophetess, whose devotions are interrupted by the discovery of the sleeping Furies? Why does the first play end on the dog image, here dyslogistically used; the second questioningly, on a count of three, with the ambiguities of salvation and doom; the third on the cry of exultation (immediately preceded, for a doubtless tremendously effective dramatic contrast, by the call for an awed silence)?

Even when our answers are not satisfactory, since not "complete," they do at the very least let us in flashes see down long corridors (and piously, since fearsomely—and fearsomely, since such a logic of symbol-using becomes a logic of persecution, with entanglement in the labyrinthine nets until or unless there is emergence into the stage of Peace, exulting in the public celebration of the great Pact). Here Form, Persecution, and Vindication tend to telescope into a single entity.

As regards the oracular pointedness we have in mind, see on what gong-like notes the three plays open. The first: "Gods." The second: "Hermes." (A passage preserved by the accident of its being quoted in a play of Aristophanes.) The third: "First." (That is, after the discipline of the *two preparatory plays*, in the *third* we are ready to begin at the beginning.)

But the opening words have more to commend then, even theatrically, as regards expectations. "Gods" (*Theous*) is in the accusative case; hence, as much as grammar could be, it is an incompletion. Add the verb, and you get: "Gods I beseech" (*aito*).

The second play begins with an invocation: "*Herme chthonie.*" Hermes of the nether-world. Here is the transitional play, fittingly introduced by Orestes' arrival on the scene. (At the end of the first play, the Chorus had devoutly expressed the hope that he would come to avenge his father's murder.) And the prayer to Hermes is most apt, since he is both the tutelary deity of those on journeys (as Orestes so compulsively was) and the power that communicates between the living and the dead. (In view of the parliamentary enlightenment which the third play is eventually to celebrate, we should also note that Hermes was the patron of the Athenian businessmen, and later, during factional disputes, a gang of hoodlums in sympathy with the old aristocracy were, one conspiratorial night, to symbolize their political sympathies by mutilating all the statues of Hermes. But Aeschylus was writing at an earlier date.)

As for the final oracular beginning, "First" (*Proton*): surely, coming where it does, it is the best of all. At the end of the second play, Orestes is told that he must travel to the temple of Apollo at Delphi. In accordance with ancient Greek tradition and the best modern psychiatry, the text refers to the centre-stone of this temple as the "navel" (*omphalos*) of the world. So, after the murder of his mother, to be cured Orestes must be thorough. He must go back to beginnings. (The word *proton* had also appeared in the very last speech of the previous play, where it referred to the fraternal crime which had brought the curse on the House of Atreus.)

As regards expectations, the word "First" naturally throws us forward, suggesting a second and a third, etc. But note the remarkable steps here, while recalling that Orestes committed his act under the tutelage of Apollo. First, says the Prophetess at Apollo's shrine, she honors the first-prophetess, Earth (Gaia, the Earth-Mother). Next after her, Themis, "for she received the gift of prophecy from her mother." Next, to the third in succession, with Themis's consent, Phoebe. And only then, after those three goddesses, the priestess of Apollo honors Apollo ("Phoebus, who has his name from Phoebe").

This prophetic killing of a woman (who somehow equals amphisbaena) thus takes us back to woman-woman-woman, beyond the male source of prophecy that had decreed the killing. In this poetry, concerned with the cathartic shedding of blood, such are the steps thus oracularly introduced. And at the very least, hearing them, we glimpse a formal attentiveness that leads to three beginnings as solemn as the first future-laden notes of a great symphony.

What of the endings? The propriety of the final exultation, as sharpened by the prior contrasting silence, is obvious. Apparently Aeschylus so contrived things that, towards the end of the play, the action spilled over into the audience, and engaged their participation as civic fellow-actors, so that the shouts in which the play came to its culmination could serve as incentive for the audience to join in.

As for the ending of the second play, what could be more appropriate? The last word is *ates* (that is: of folly, of blindness, of delusion, such delusion as is sent by the gods). Adding the noun to which it belongs, the expression is: "the fury of folly." And it appears in a question: When will this fury cease? More subtly still, when will it cease through being *lulled to rest?*

This, of a conscientious mother-killer!

As regards the ending of the first play. Apparently the text is corrupt, so that a couple of words are missing. It is tempting to think that the omissions were intentional. Clytemnæstra is making a final prophecy to the effect that she and her paramour will take over and set things in order. Accordingly one can imagine how the prophecy might have been deliberately obscured by an upsurge of the music. Such incompleteness of utterance, in an art that so greatly stressed completion, would stylistically, "oracularly," foretell the future of her prophecy. But it is probably the kind of effect least likely to be sought in Aeschylean drama, though Wagnerian music-drama tinkers with it constantly.

So much by way of general preparation. Let us now consider significant details of the plot while paying particular attention to the order in which they appear. (Let us "tick off" the more important of the discrete points that mark the work's continuity.) The social tensions which a cathartic drama thus exploits and releases are not ultimately resolved by such purely symbolic means. Insofar as the civic "pollution" which they are designed to ritually cleanse is intrinsic to the nature of the state, the semi-annual purges in the theatre could not bring permanent relief. For the situation outside the universe of the art-form still retained its characteristic goads and conflicts.

But though such tensions were like a hopelessly tangled ball of string that continued to be hopelessly tangled (a labyrinthine clutter of motives implying one another and forever circulating back upon themselves), the narrative sequence of an individual drama could separate these factors out, for the duration of the fiction and within the arbitrary conditions established by this one particular order of development. Things that go every which way could be made to go one way. Conditions that in life have no isolable parts, could be analyzed, or "broken down," into terms of one particular set of dramatis personae having interrelationships of one particular sort that unfold in one particular order. Elsewhere, most notably in our essay on "The First Three Chapters of Genesis," we consider how the principle of "cyclicality" incessantly prevails with regard to the inexpungeable and inexpugnable "guilt" of empire. But our task at this point is to watch exactly how such a condition, though static and ineradicable to human societies in the large, can in effect be "processed," and thus can seem to "get somewhere" (to go *from* there, *through* here, *to* that place yonder), once social entanglement that is without direction is translated into terms of the single, rectilinear sequence of one particular narrative or temporal artistic progression.[3]

The *Agamemnon* opens with the Watchman's speech, solemnly establishing the theme of Vigil, and introducing the formula for Clytemnæstra (who is feminine in heart, but masculine in counsel). After twenty-one lines, the speech suddenly breaks into the annunciation,

---

[3] Incidentally, our use of the word "static" to describe the "guilt" intrinsic to socio-political order reminds us of that astounding etymological irony whereby in ancient Greece the word *stasis* came to mean "revolution."

as the signal-fires are seen, proclaiming that Troy has fallen. May Agamemnon return soon. (But, psst! there are untoward things going on in this house. To those in the know, the Watchman will willingly speak; to the others, he has lost his memory.)

The situation thus being set, the Chorus of Elders introduces itself, and tragically meditates. Underlying their role, there is a notable dialectic whereby, in comparison with the hero, who is a vigorous warrior, the Elders are to be classed with children. That is, from one point of view, there is the progression from childhood, to manhood, to old age. But from another point of view, childhood and age are alike, since each in its way lacks the strength of manhood. For the most important tribal test is in the ability to bear arms, and children are not yet able while the elderly are no longer able.

We are not straining here. The Elders explicitly liken themselves to children in this respect, with the "oracular" addition that age is like a dream dreamed by day. (Aeschylus himself was a very old man when he wrote the *Oresteia*.) However, while the Chorus can thus serve a "regressive" purpose, partaking naturally of motives that shade off into infancy, within this similarity there is a very important difference. Age is more just than youth (an explicit Aeschylean principle)—and so, a Chorus of Elders will have exactly the attributes needed to set the mode of thought in a work that will come to a head in an almost legalistic concern with Justice, while forever digging back into the most infantile of fantasies to figure the ultimate essence of human threat and human vindication.

These Elders have the strength of Persuasion, they have the strength of Song, both divinely inspired—and they have the strength to proclaim the triumph of perfect heroes. (The adjective is a variant of our word *telos*.)

Here enters the first statement of the ultimate motivational problem: Agamemnon and Menelaus, in their sacking of Troy, are figured in an ominous vision of two eagles, one black, one white, devouring a pregnant hare. Thus, within the equations here set up, the first image of a destructive eating concerns not Thyestes' hideous destiny, but a warlike act of violence that is likened to the rapacity of predatory males attacking a pregnant female. And one of the males thus ominously introduced is returning home, to be slain by a woman. Admittedly, we don't wholly know what to make of this beyond its general tenor. But anyhow, there it is, and in the course of the trilogy, many details will be seen to bear upon it.

This motherly Troy, we may recall, was sacked for having taken the side of Helen in the great mythic dispute. So we may even catch a glimpse here, of the ambiguity that confuses the maternal woman and the erotic woman (mother and sweetheart), a confusion here expressed as a need to "slay" the mother in behalf of the son's possession of the sweetheart. (Dialectically, as we have observed in our *Rhetoric,* such imagery of violence can often be but a dramatized way of symbolizing transformation in general. That is: dialectically, the "slaying" of the maternal principle could here involve the attempt to dissociate the two kinds of woman. Tragedy naturally favors the imagery of the kill as a terminology in which to enact the idea of transformation, or "rebirth.") In any case, we are told that Artemis, the protectress of wild animals and their nurslings, *hates* this eagles' feast. (The verb for "hate" here has the root from which is derived the noun for the hellish "Styx.") And the Chorus is afraid lest she demand still further sacrifices.

Noting that Athena is here at odds with Zeus (who had favored the sacking of Troy), and that in her role as protectress of nurslings she may demand a further sacrifice, the Chorus beseeches Pan to deter her. The sacrifice about which they are apprehensive is in vaguely prophetic outline the disaster that is to follow. It will cause family strife, it will dissolve a wife's reverence for her husband; for there is a dreadful Wrath in the home, eager to avenge the death of a child (that is, Clytemnæstra will vindicate the murder by proclaiming it an act of retaliation for Agamemnon's sacrifice of her daughter, Iphigeneia).

This section is developed against a typical tragic formula, "Proclaim the dirge of mourning, but may the good prevail." It also includes the usual solemn sententiousness about "knowledge through suffering," which is here attributed to an ordinance of Zeus.[4] There is the usual scattering of the Great Persecutional Words (Right, Justice, Necessity, etc.) And as dramatic preparation for the next step in the play (Clytemnæstra's entrance), the Choric lamentation builds up most effectively the pitiableness of Iphigeneia's sacrifice, like a young goat on the altar. (The most telling detail perhaps is a reference to the

---

[4] The thought that one learns unforgettable lessons in the "school of hard knocks" provides a kind of technical ground for a belief in the tragic principle. But tragedy must go on digging into problems of motivation because suffering can also be "traumatic" enough to keep us *from* learning.

obstruction held across her mouth to stifle any cry that might have been a curse against Agamemnon's house, whereat she could strike back only by the look in her eyes, mutely begging for pity.)

We have already noted how her first speech, referring to the news of Troy's fall, is in the name of Mother Night. Then follows the first *formal* disclosure: the quick exchange of one-line questions-and-answers between the Chorus and Clytemnæstra (technically, a "stichomythia") as to the validity of the message indicated by the signal-fires. Anthropologists have pointed out that this form is a survival of the catechizing that figured at appropriate places in the religious mysteries. But reversing the emphasis, we would say that such stichomythia is deliberately "allusive," using for stylistic purposes a form that had definite connotations for the audiences of the time. The device, as thus adapted secularly, or Poetically, could point up a step in the plot by imparting a kind of *doctrinal* sharpness even to a narrative step.

Clytemnæstra's speech terminates in a sustained piece of epic-like narrative that forms a sturdy contrast with the jagged interchange just ended. She tells how the news of Troy's fall had advanced through the night, from one signal-fire to another. And there seems to be the first hint of an "amphisbaena" here; for the news spread by the signal fires is apparently racing against the fire of oncoming daylight. The news started after dark, but arrived before dawn. Hence, the victory is with "the one running first and last" (*protos* for "first"; and for "last," an adjective form of *telos*). Anyhow, in Clytemnæstra's next speech, there is a design that is half merger, half separating-out, as she imagines the last fighting at Troy, with the cries of victors and vanquished intermingled, yet distinguished by the difference in import (a design that is perfect example of what Coleridge meant by "imagination").

Clytemnæstra having expressed the hope that the conquerors did not commit acts of irreverence likely to enrage the local gods, the Chorus praises her manly prudence. (Dramatically, this masculine trait serves to make her later violent conduct seem more plausible to an audience that, unless otherwise prodded, spontaneously spoke of women in the same breath with slaves. But psychologically, the trait might be said to offer a bridging device whereby Clytemnæstra, in slaying Agamemnon, is acting as surrogate for a man, that is, for Orestes—hence, the deeper propriety of the "loose" usage whereby she is called a "patricide").

The Chorus next hails "Zeus the King, and Kindly Night," meditates on pious fears, and on Persuasion in the bad sense of the word;
and through an almost untranslatable tangle, likens war to a gold-mer-
chant (the upshot of the passage being the notion that war is a mode of
purification, as with the refining of gold). Though Aeschylus is said to
have asked only that he be remembered as a soldier, the Chorus here by
no means utters a simple glorification of war, but speaks sympathetically of those who secretly murmur against the Trojan carnage done
"for the wife of another."

However, where the diplomacy of catharsis is concerned, one must
always keep in mind the possibility that a dramatist is voicing a social
protest, not with the simple intention of getting it said, but rather as a
way of winning over members of the audience who are likely to resist
the work unless they are thus mollified. In his *Aeschylus and Athens,*
for instance, George Thomson offers quite convincing reasons for be-
lieving that the bold libertarian sentiments which edified Shelley in
Aeschylus's *Prometheus Bound* were but the preparation for later developments (in lost parts of a Promethean trilogy) which considerably
revised the attitudes stated so uncompromisingly in the one play still
extant. Thus, the sentiments as stated in the first play should be taken
not at face value, but as a function of their relationship to the entire cathartic process, culminating in ways whereby these originally excessive
(or "overflowing") attitudes were matured, or "purged." Of the three
great Athenian tragic playwrights, Euripides presumably went farthest
in the direction of a presentation that would offer such statements at
face value, rather than as diplomatic preparation for their subsequent
diplomatic purging.

The chorus here meditates much on the risk of pride that provokes
the wrath of the gods, observes that the Black Furies may pursue those
given to killing, opts for kinds of wellbeing humble enough not to
arouse envy; it hopes to be neither a despoiler, nor among those despoiled. In this speech, too, there have been good lines for the populace (Aeschylus being a kind of "Rooseveltian" who, though of patri-
cian descent, would, like Pericles, work with the machinery of democracy).

Next a Herald enters, and after long-winded honorings to the gods
(the playwright here coquetting with his audience, perhaps even semi-
comically, to delay the message) the Herald confirms Agamemnon's
victory and announces his arrival nearby. In accordance with the

ironic conventions of tragedy, he foreshadows bad times, by calling Agamemnon "happy." (The word is *eudaimon,* whereat we might recall Aristotle's subsequent strongly "eudaemonist" emphasis).

Next comes another disclosure-like stichomythia, this time an interchange between the Herald and the Chorus. It amounts to the proposition: Out of the Herald's joy, there arise in the Chorus misgivings.

When pressed, they answer with a formula: "Silence, to protect from harm." Or, more accurately: silence, medicine for harm. Let us even pause and copy out the syllables, today so obviously fatal: *to sigan pharmakon blabes.*

When Clytemnæstra enters (the next step in this formal predestination), she tellingly overdoes her expression of delight at Agamemnon's return. She advertises her fidelity, and sums up by calling herself a watch-dog of the house. (In this art, so essentially based on admonitions against excess, inclined even to think of mere success as excess, her overdoing is clear indication of a trend. And when the Herald, who is a crude fellow, praises her speech, he thus roundabout italicizes its bad auspices by deciding that, in a high-born wife, such *kompos* is not unfitting. (The word means noise, din, clash, hence derivatively, boastful speech.)

In the next minor developments, there are relevant references to the Furies and to Savior Fortune; with prophetic puns on Helen's name that make it equal to grasp, conquer, kill, seize, capture, hence leading to "bloody strife"; and with a variant of *telos,* most remarkably applied. (For this last detail, see lines 699–702, where it is said that Wrath, *menis,* in the fulfilling of its purpose, brought to Troy a *kedos*—whereat the text meditates upon the fact that this word, in Greek, fatally means both "marriage" and "sorrow.")

In a Choric song here, the sack of Troy is restated in another intensely relevant figure. The strophe speaks of a man who reared in his house a lion's whelp, "robbed of its mother's milk, yet still desiring the breast." Even so, it got much, being held in the arms like a nursing child.

In the antistrophe, it comes to maturity—whereat it spreads slaughter among the flocks, so that the house is defiled with blood. In this role, it is called a priest (*hiereus*) of ruin, that is, of *Ate,* one of our Persecutional Words, meaning distraction, bewilderment, folly, blindness, delusion; ruin, bane, pest. (Liddell and Scott says that it is less voluntary than *hubris*. But points out that Ate, as personified, was the daughter of Jupiter, goddess of mischief, author of all blind, rash actions and of their results, and having power even over her father.)

Similarly, *Ara*, feminine, is prayer, more usually a curse, rarely a blessing; hence, it also means the effect of a curse; thus also, mischief, ruin, and in Aeschylus is personified as goddess of Destruction or Vengeance (like Latin *Dira*), having the same office as the Erinyes. We thus now see the whole series: the great words for law and order; their other side, the words for retaliation, vengeance, vindication, ruin, and the bridging terms, like those for pollution (*miasma*), pride, folly, venom, piety (*sebas*), with their correctives in rites of purification (rites that, since they involve blood-sacrifices, are forever circling back into the feudal genealogy whereby conflict begets conflict)—and underlying it all, as a kind of unacknowledged word for Fate, stands the pattern of Consummation, repeatedly indicated in the many variants of *telos*.[5] Such, we submit, is the tragic translation of the term "Form," with its network of "proprieties" and "expectancies."

In antistrophe gamma of the Choric song we are now considering, *telos* appears with reference to prosperity that, having attained its end (*telesthenta*), gives birth to misery. In strophe delta, the pattern is developed in terms of *Hubris,* as Old Arrogance gives birth to Young Arrogance, which is to its parent like Black Curses.

In strophe gamma, the early gentleness of the lion whelp had been given a somewhat economic parallel, being likened to an early happy stage of wealth that later became ruinous. And after moralizings in accord with a favorite concern of Aeschylus (the relation between old power and raw new power), the theme next (antistrophe delta) takes on a somewhat demagogic guise, an appeal to the audience at large. Righteousness is said to gleam in humble smoky dwellings, not gilded mansions. The Chorus closes on the thought that Righteousness guides all things to their proper end (though the word here is not *telos* but *terma*).

The plot now takes a momentous leap forward. Agamemnon, predestined victim, enters with his prize, Cassandra. The Chorus is cautious in its greetings, saying that it would welcome him neither too

---

[5] A quick check discloses that variants of the word *telos* appear in the following lines of the first play: 65, 68, 105, 226, 314, 467, 532, 635, 700, 720, 745, 751, 807, 908, 972, 973 (twice), 974, 996, 1000, 1107, 1109, 1432, 1487, 1504.

much nor too little, but just enough (a scrupulosity that will later help underline the inauspicious nature of Clytemnæstra's overdone welcome). There is also the hint of an allusion to the Bacchic rites, perhaps too flitting to be noticed even by many of the audience: the Chorus, in a reference to "watered down affection," here borrows a figure from the diluting of wine.

Agamemnon, after similar concern about the proprieties of greetings (his first word is *proton*), refers to the blood-letting at Troy in a figure to do with the casting of ballots. It is the same word, *psephos,* about which the "primal" balloting of the third play will hinge. In the next stanza, noting that few can enjoy their friends' good fortune, he refers to the "venom of malice" (the word for venom here, *ios,* the word that throughout the play materializes the office of the Furies).

He also uses a formula ("as regards the City and the public gods," *pros polin te kai theous koinous*) which we consider basically relevant to our concerns with the stateliness of tragedy. Here we see the design in its perfection: How "the gods" can be a duplicate vocabulary for "the State," whereby political concerns can, as it were, be transcended by translation into mythic and mystical equivalents. In this same speech, Agamemnon spontaneously identifies his personal office with these two orders—then, speaking of a remedy (*pharmakon*) for political ills, he fleetingly suggests his end by a reference to the cure of ills by cautery or the knife. After further worry about the proprieties of worship (first of all, *prota,* being his greetings to the gods), he ends on a necessarily ill-omened expression of hope that victory will still stay with him.

The plot immediately takes another momentous step forward, as Clytemnæstra enters, overdoes her greetings, avows that she has wept so much she can weep no more, explains that she has sent Orestes away through fear of popular revolt if things went wrong; and then, after praying that envy (*phthonos*) be far removed, she ends by instructing her attendants to strew tapestries for Agamemnon to walk on. (Hint of the grape here: his path must be strewn with "purple"; also we note that, in the Iliad, both blood and death are called "purple.")

The motives could be ambiguous, since purple was royal. But Agamemnon does not relish this "barbarian" welcome. He is willing that she should revere him; "not as a god," however, "but as a man." Next, just as the relations between Chorus and Clytemnæstra, and between Chorus and Herald, had received "doctrinal" pointing in the quick one-line give-and-take of stichomythia, there is now a fatal dialogue of this sort between Clytemnæstra and Agamemnon, as she would persuade him to accept the over-ceremonious homage, and he demurs, fearing the disapproval of the people. The sympathies here are effectively turned in his direction, as he speaks of the people with respect while she is disdainful of them. Yet the altercation ends by her prevailing, as he yields reluctantly and with misgivings.

Previously, she had called herself a watchdog of Agamemnon's house; later she had called Agamemnon a watchdog of the fold; now she mixes talk of vestments dyed purple and talk of the dog-star (in the bad connotations of dog days). The passage seems peppered with allusion: there is mention of oracles, of reward for the saving of the soul, of leafage that will survive the scorching heat of the dog-star, of the bath at home-coming, and finally, explicitly, she speaks of Zeus making wine from grapes bitter at the time of ripening in the heat. As Agamemnon enters the palace, the passage ends on the ominous oracle-like formula we have previously cited, with its three forms: "fulfiller" [. . .] "fulfil thou" [. . .] and "to fulfil," and its obsessive repetitiousness of sound. Then she, too, leaves the stage.

The Elders now muse in great agitation. Against their will, they begin to sing prophetically. They are terrified by an uninterpretable dream. "Self-taught," they chant a "threnody of vengeance." They meditate on the thin line dividing health (*hygieia*) and disease (*nosos*). Twice there are variants of *telos* (996, and 1000) as the citizens hope against hope in hoping against fulfilment. And they observe that, once man's blood is spilled upon the earth, no spell can call it back. (In the third play, Apollo will develop this thought by pointing out that, whereas Zeus makes decisions that can be revoked, there is no revocation from the death which the Furies would visit upon their victims.)

Then Clytemnæstra, re-entering, addresses Cassandra, the captive princess, telling her to enter the palace. Clytemnæstra's speech is unfriendly, but she makes one characteristically Aeschylean remark: Cassandra, she says, was at least fortunate in that she had persons of long-standing wealth for masters, whereas the newly rich are crude and cruel in their treatment of slaves. Cassandra is silent. And after again pressing her to enter, since the victims are already waiting by the hearth for the sacrifice, Clytemnæstra herself impatiently leaves.

Having dwelt successively on the relations between Chorus and Clytemnæstra, Chorus and Herald, Clytemnæstra and Agamemnon, the play now concentrates on the relations between Chorus and Cassandra, an action that comes to a focus in the usual discovery-like stichomythia. Cassandra does not speak until the Chorus has proclaimed its pity for her, and appealingly likened her timidity to that of an animal just caught. (Incidentally, the "necessity" to which they say she should submit in slavery is *ananke,* the word that is elsewhere so resonantly *cosmologized* in the tragedies).

First inarticulate, then uttering enigmatic exclamations, next punning on Apollo's name, (she calls him her "Destroyer") she begins to speak fragments of prophecy, and gradually moves into a sustained narrative. In her gift of prophecy, she is said to be as keen-scented as a dog. She is said to retain the gift of prophecy, even in a soul enslaved. She puns on Clytemnæstra's name, deriving it from a verb that means "to intend" in the sense of scheming. She says that Clytemnæstra plans evil to her "kinsmen" *philoi,* a word that ranges in meaning from friends or loved ones to relatives by blood or marriage, and that Aristotle uses in his recipe for the kind of personal conflict best suited to the tragic plot). Twice, in her prophetic vision of Clytemnæstra's intention, she expresses it in terms of *telos* (1107, 1109). She helps keep the audience reminded that the scene is in the bath (a variant of the purification theme) And an excellent "amphisbaenal" touch is got, as she sees, like a prophecy, Atreus's original butchery of Thyestes' children, and Thyestes' eating of their flesh (an associational device that proclaims the imminent murder to be essentially the same in motivation).

So far, however, her vision of the murder is general. Later, her vatic clairvoyance will be used with maximum effectiveness. For whereas in most plays a "messenger" appears on the stage, to announce and describe the tragic horror after it had taken place, in the *Agamemnon* Aeschylus can make the recital doubly powerful because the incidents are being "prophesied" even while (as we know) the ambiguous preparation for "bath" and "sacrifice" are under way off stage. The connotations of her words for thus in general describing the imminent murder are remarkable in the complexity of motives they suggest so simply.

Let the woman be stoned, she cries, calling for an insatiable band or pack to shout exultantly over the victim. The word for band or pack here is *stasis.* The verb for exultant shouting was traditionally applied in the case of women crying to the gods in a loud voice, usually as a sign of joy. Quite obviously, it was "allusive," in applying to the women's shout of rebirth in the Bacchic revels. But still more remarkable is the fact that a form of this same verb will appear in the very last line of the entire trilogy (the change from Erinyes to Eumenides presumably having made it possible that the blood-thirsty glee of a conspiratorial band pursuing a sacrificial murderer with righteous indignation, could not feel free of the motivational ambiguities which still beset us at the time when Cassandra, who is herself soon to be murdered, is prophetically interpreting a murder in terms connoting ritual sacrifice).

Clearly, the poet seeks to add another connotation when, in lines 1125–1129, Cassandra sees a bull, gored by the black horn of his mate, who catches him in a robe, whereat he falls in a vessel of water, murdered by treachery in his bath. Here, clearly, Aeschylus would introduce suggestions of the sacrificial bull, merged with specific references to Clytemnæstra killing Agamemnon at his bath. The situation readily reveals the kind of motivational tangle that goes with the secularizing of the Bacchic rites. Though the bath is allusively a moment of ritual purification, it is first of all a bath in the secular sense of the term. Thus, an action that, from the purely secular point of view, involves a *murder,* contains an allusive dimension that equates it secondarily with a *religious sacrifice.* As regards this allusive dimension, Clytemnæstra is like a priestess scrupulously carrying out her appointed role, in honoring the gods by sacrificing a victim on the altar; yet as regards the new "enlightened" dimension of civic tragedy, she is merely acting like a criminal.

Au fond, this transformation of *sacrifice* (with its appropriate rationale) into crime (with a different rationale) would be somewhat like secularizing the Christian Mass in such a way that the priest who officiated was conceived of as trying to "wreak vengeance" on the sacrificial victim in whose honor the rite is being performed. It ambiguously converted a religious *sacrifice* into a secular *kill.* We say "ambiguously" because the transformation was not completed (as it usually is, say, in modern murder stories). Both orders of motives were still operating, an ambiguity all the more likely to prevail because, as with Agamemnon's formula regarding "the city and the public gods," the Athenians' civic motives were themselves strongly tinged with connotations of religious piety. Greek tragedy, we should remember, was played at a time when human sacrifices were still offered for cleansing the city of "pollution." And we should recall that catharsis by the ritual slaying of such *katharmata* was itself partially transformed into the more "enlightened" practice of reserving criminals for this role (in contrast with, say, the ritual sacrificing of virgins, the theme that figured in Agamemnon's sacrifice of Iphigeneia for the success of the war against Troy). The idea of a virgin as being "fit" for sacrifice because of her blamelessness would be totally different from the idea of a *katharma* who was fit for sacrifice because he had been condemned to death as a criminal.[6]

Since a dying is, roundabout, a birth (the end of one thing being by the same token the beginning of another); and since a mourning is also a marriage (in accordance with the two meanings of *kedos*, already explicitly noted by the dramatist); there are also references here to the new-born (1163) and to prophecies peering from behind a veil like a newly wedded bride (1178–1179). And that word for veil (*kalymma*) is certainly worth pondering, so far as "allusions" are concerned. For it is of the same root as *kalypto*, which appears in the clearly mystery-laden word, Apocalypse. The word *kalymma* also designates a round fishing net, hence may bring us back to the detail of the net that ensnared Agamemnon.

In this same passage, Cassandra's word for "prophecy" is *chresmos*. It is quite relevant to our purposes, in that Aristotle applies the etymologically related adjective, *chrestos,* to what he gives as the first requirement of a tragic character, usually translated "good." In line 940 of The Libation-Bearers, Orestes is called *pythochrestos* because of his relation to the Pythian, Apollo. Among other things, clearly the "good" character in tragedy must be of a sort that is "good" for the

---

[6] As regards this distinction between the choice of a victim because the victim is most blameless (the Christ-principle of victimage) and the choice of a victim because the victim is most blamable (the villainy-principle of victimage): Note that the tragic flaw (*hamartia*) serves as a neat midway stage between them. By this device (which was probably a significant variant of the principle of Achilles' heel), the victim could be a "good" man (*chrestos*) while at the same time being rationally sacrificeable as punishment for a fault. (His sacrifice became pitiful because he was felt to suffer greater misfortune than his mistake merited.) In Shakespeare's *Othello,* each of the three main characters exemplifies one of these principles. Desdemona is the perfectly blameless victim; Othello is the noble victim of a tragic flaw, an error in judgment; and Iago is the villainous victim who, we are assured, will be subjected to pitiless "torments" and "torture." Often in a tragedy there is also an *incidental* principle of victimage, for instance, in *Coriolanus* the supernumerary soldiers who get killed in the course of the hero's exploits and tergiversations.

tonalities of the oracular, with its relation to the genius of the Great Persecutional Words.

The use of the prophetess Cassandra to build up the audience's foreboding of the imminent murder is about as powerful a theatrical device as could be conceived. For besides the effectiveness in prophesying a calamity so near to fulfilment, there is the way in which Aeschylus uses Cassandra as a way of giving it added *dimensions* or *resonance.* For she can range through the whole history of the curse on the House of Atreus, endowing all developments, both past and yet to come, with the same dynastic "primal sin" (*protarchon aten*); and she can describe the murder in figurative language that fuses it with both ritual and criminal elements. Thus, in varied alternation between stichomythia and sustained speeches, Cassandra now brings all the motivational threads together: as in a dream, the murdered children, holding up the vitals of which their father had eaten; for this, vengeance was plotted by a cowardly lion (presumably Aegisthus, who was also a son of Thyestes); vengeful Clytemnæstra is referred to obliquely as a treacherous dog, licking the hand of the returning leader; it is here that she is called amphisbaena; or she is a two-footed lioness, bedding with a wolf in the absence of the noble male lion, and she will slay Cassandra too; her ways are like the preparing of a drug (that ambiguous word, *pharmakon,* connoting also the cures of magic); but another, a matricide, will come, as avenger, and here the idea of *telos* is figured in the image of a coping stone, or the final row of stones atop a wall. After the mention of her as an amphisbaena, which is perilous like a Scylla to mariners, or like a bitch of hell breathing war against her kinsmen, the word for the ritual shout of triumph appeared (line 1236); it was in connection with an image of the turn, the notion of peripety here being stated dramatically by a metaphor to do with the shout that arises with a changing tide of battle, here merged with the idea of Clytemnæstra's feigned joy at Agamemnon's homecoming, which in turn is merged with a term for safety, *soteria,* having hieratic connotations of "salvation." And having also prophesied her own death, Cassandra *exits.*

The Chorus too spoke of Agamemnon as returning home and, divinely honored, dying for the dead, though under conditions that will lead to further deaths. Then Agamemnon's first cry within is heard. And after the second cry, letting us know that he has been dispatched, you might think that the Chorus in their next deliberations, had read the prose of the assassins in *Murder in the Cathedral*. For twelve members, in succession, speak in the style of conferences on ways and means, proposing various contradictory policies that suggest a grim parody of parliamentary unction, vacillation, and delay (including the delay that takes the form of complaining at delay). Several speakers express fear that the violence may result in tyranny.[7] Following this passage, the bodies of Agamemnon and Cassandra are disclosed, with Clytemnæstra standing above her victims.

Many contemporary critics who put major stress upon the part played by prehistoric myth in the development of modern civilization usually get the order of things reversed here. They begin with theories about primitive *sparagmos*, and then treat typical modern analytic language as a "derivation" from such savage rites of "rending and tearing." But a dialectical approach, beginning the other way around, would first note that analysis is a resource natural to language; next would be a concern with such rites as *sparagmos*, that exemplify the analytic principle in one particular mode of action, with its corresponding rationale (in this case, presumably the notion that all participants could become consubstantial by devouring fragments of the same ritually prepared substance).

In the name of the feudal formula, "hate for hate," she vauntingly describes the killing of the man caught in the "evil wealth" of his garment like fish in a net. (Could this be a satanic variant of the formula, "not a fisher of fish, but a fisher of men"?) She likens his blood in the earth to spring rain on sown fields (thus clearly suggesting that some elements in the murder are analogous to a fertility rite); and in a personal parallel, the slain male's blood upon her is said to be like

---

[7] As for this development whereby the Elders fall into divided counsel on hearing Agamemnon's death cries: Presumably this is a sophisticated, secular analogue of the *sparagmos*, the moment of "rending and tearing" that is said to have taken place in the original Bacchic ceremony, when the victim that represented the god was picked into bits and devoured by the faithful. Though Poetics need not concern itself with such a genetic relationship between tragedy and its incunabula, one should isolate for comment the moment of *distraction as such*. Proper to the process of *transformation* there is a moment of disintegration; and when such *disintegration* is presented in terms proper to tragedy, it can well manifest itself as some form of *distraction*. (Primary example in English tragedy: the Porter scene following the murder in *Macbeth*.)

a spattering of dew. Later, when the Chorus has rebuked her for thus inviting the rage of the people, she asserts that Agamemnon's sacrifice of their daughter had itself been a pollution.

From now on, the playwright's concern is not so much with finishing off this play as with preparing for the immediate sequel. The Chorus gives its variant of the feudal pattern ("blow for blow"); Clytemnæstra is a "fiend" (*daimon*), there is a sense, she maintains, in which Agamemnon but seemed to have been killed by his wife, the real source of motivation being the primal curse on the House of Atreus. (The word here is *alastor,* which has, as its range of meanings: in general, avenger, persecutor, tormentor; hence, he who suffers from such vengeance; hence, the sinner, evil-doer, accursed and polluted man. The scope here in itself sums up the ambiguities of tragic sacrifice whereby, in the secularizing of the religious rites, murder can take on hieratic connotations even though the priestly, or *chrestos* role, as so defined, arouses moral indignation in the very ones for whom, as regards the catharsis of the blood-offering, the murder is enacted.)

The play ends soon after the appearance of the paramour, Aegisthus, who can feudal justify his part in the crime on the grounds that he is the third child of Thyestes. But the audience's sympathies are turned against him by his disdainful and defiant attitude toward the people. The bad relationship between Chorus and Aegisthus culminates in a snappy stichomythia, in which the Chorus likens his bragging beside Clytemnæstra to the boldness of a cock beside his hen. And after this "Aesopian" reduction, the play is abruptly ended by Clytemnæstra's reference to the Chorus's complaints as mere canine yapping. We have already discussed our risky hunch as to the possibility that the incompleteness of her final statement is due not to an imperfection in the codex but to a deliberate "unfinishedness," in accordance with the "prophetic" nature of the "oracular" style.

Perhaps the discussion of the first play in some detail will make it possible to treat of the other two summarily, despite their equal importance.

Why the Chorus of Slave Women, for figuring the motives of the second play? First, they suit well the themes of sufferance, lamentation, supplication, that go with any Aeschylean tragedy. Again, see the *Supplicants* for the several lines wherein the mimetics of beseechment are explicitly discussed, as a mode of appeal, a kind of pious diplomacy when dealing with Powers of any sort. And the very essence of

the motivation in this second, transitional play is a kind of Babylo-
nian captivity, a waiting for the moment of liberation, to be obtained
through the ambiguous sacrifice involving brother, sister, mother, and
the mother's paramour. (The sacrifice, we would say, is in the total
act—and it is made possible by being broken into these four major
roles, whereby a *state* can be transformed into a *process,* as the *parts*
into which it has been dramatically divided can be shown to act upon
one another. Hence, whatever the motionless "guilt" or "original sin"
may be, as thus broken into dramatic components it allows for a succession of *stages* that, in leaving things behind, can be experienced as
a purification.)

The Chorus's first speech also reaffirms our notion, stated previously, about the equating of women with what would now be called
the "unconscious." In their horrified reference to Clytemnæstra's prophetic dream, they use (in line 35) *muchothen,* (in line 38) *theothen.*
That is, to those two words for the inmost chamber for god, they add
the suffix–*then,* which means: coming from, or derived from. So here
is a good motivational cluster: woman, captivity, sufferance, lamentation, secrecy, dream, god-inspired, and fearsomely apprehensive. Add
the further appropriateness, that they can cry to the Earth Mother
(who is later to be named "first").

We shall pass up the many variants of the "tooth for a tooth, eye for
an eye" formula. But we should perhaps note that, in the first "doctrinal" interchange (*stichomythia*) between Electra and the Chorus, Electra refers to the coming avenger as either "juror" (*dicast*) or "justice-
bringer" (line 120). The terms point in quality towards the third play.
Like Orestes in his opening speech, she too prays to Hermes of the
nether-world (the principle of transition, or communication between
realms). And (for the psychoanalyst) after the second stichomythia,
discussing her discovery of the lock of Orestes' hair, she weeps copiously, saying that she feels as though pierced by a sword. Orestes vows
to the spirit of Agamemnon, "It shall be done" (our "telic" word, here
teleitai). The Chorus (387) hopes it will be able to shout over the slaying of Aegisthus and Clytemnæstra (again, a form of the word for the
ritual cry of rejoicing). At one point, contemplating the possible horrors, the Chorus exclaims that its insides are darkened at the words
it hears. The corresponding verb for these parts means: to eat the in-
wards of a victim after the sacrifice.

Electra tells Orestes that she was kept in her apartment (*muchos*) as a vicious dog in a kennel. The feudal pattern (461) gets half a turn for the better when Orestes says: "War shall match War, Right (*Dika*) shall match Right." The Chorus (471–474) meditates significantly that the curse on the House of Atreus must be cured not from without (*ektothen*) but of itself (though, as we have said , the division of the unitary guilt into distinct roles allows here for the many devices of the "scapegoat mechanism"). Orestes, praying in indignation to his dead father, begs to become ruler of his halls (478). Electra, when invoking her murdered father's aid, uses an interesting formula, as she calls children "voices of salvation [. . .] even for the dead." Clytemnæstra's dream (of giving birth to a serpent that drew in blood with its milk as she nursed it) is fittingly interpreted by Orestes in a stichomythia between him and the Chorus. Orestes (541) prays that this dream be fulfilled (*telesphoron*) in him. And the Chorus (551) having accepted his interpretation of the prodigy (*teraskopon*), the plot turns to the pragmatics of the case: The slayers are to be caught in the same snare. There is the hint of a prayer to Apollo here—enough, not too much, for though the god will later assume responsibility for Orestes' act, at this moment the act must be, above all else, a deliberate choice on Orestes' part. This Chorus of female slaves, meditating on horrors in general, decides that the worst transgression of all was committed by the women of Lemnos who, jealous of Thracian slaves, slew their husbands. Given the nature of Greek society, this moralizing seems a shrewd bit of public policy.

When we recall again the Porter scene in *Macbeth,* we realize that it is a notable reversal of the order in the *Choëphoroe.* For here, as Orestes pounds loudly at the door, calling to be admitted, the "knock of conscience" thus precedes the murder whereas in *Macbeth* it had followed. (However, in this play the knock is interpretable as a kind of "amphisbaena," too. For it can be taken either as an anticipation of the new horror, or as recollection of the previous one. Such doubleness of direction would go particularly well with this middle play, which contains the formula whereby either the dead can be said to kill the living, or the living the dead.) Clytemnæstra soon appears to welcome the supposed strangers—and a telling detail is inserted when, in her role as hostess, she promises them "warm baths." A little can count for much, at such moments.

She also speaks ambiguously about "revelry" in the house (698). But the word is allusive, for it is literally "bacchusing" (*bakcheia*), and she accompanies it, fittingly, with a reference to "iatric" hope. She avows that she is broken-hearted by the news of Orestes' death (which Orestes in disguise announces to her); yet she is a model of forgiveness, in assuring the supposed stranger that she will not hold the bad news against him.

The Chorus having prayed for a guileful form of Persuasion to take over, there enters (pathetically):

Orestes' old Nurse. She is a good-hearted soul, who talks too much; and, if you will believe us, she also rambles on about catharsis, which she conceives of , shall we say, in terms that have to do with the thinking of the body, specifically an infant's body. She even uses priestly terms here. For when noting how the infant, though sans speech, is moved by hunger, thirst, or the desire to wet (*lipsouria*), she says that she would be a prophetess (*promantis*) of its inclinations. But the bowels of the young child obey no one (they are *autarkes,* the word having connotations of absolute self-sufficiency or sovereignty). Hence she must sometimes combine the offices (*telos*) of nurse and laundress. This humorous passage (a succinct burlesque of Aeschylean motives) is serviceable relief for the solemnities of tragic sacrifice.

Perhaps the playwright added another trick here. For if the stichomythia, in its stylistic analogy with the doctrinal, assumes the accents of disclosure, then what would be the expectations, if the play at this point broke into such a style? We should think that, with stichomythia at this point, and the tradition of the Nurse dating back to Homer, the audience would expect her to recognize Orestes. And it would be high-class trifling when, instead, she hurries on her way, as thoroughly duped as Clytemnæstra. The result would be the usual dramatic advantage of such interludes: The play could now start towards the calamity afresh.

As soon as the Nurse leaves, the ominous note is resumed, in a long choral passage meditating solemnly on the entire sacrificial process, its innerness (here is *muchos* again), its final glad release. (At the end of the song, Aegisthus appears, talks vauntingly, and exits.)

Whatever may be the ultimate family patterns to which social motives might be reduced, in a work concerned with Justice in the grand style the social motives as such must figure prominently. Hence, the Chorus is busy identifying Orestes with the cause of freedom, and praying that he may soon possess his father's wealth, when Aegisthus's cry is heard. The murder is announced to Clytemnæstra in the amphisbaena-riddle we have already discussed—and soon after, Orestes, speaking of Aegisthus in comparison with his father, says that she shall lie with her paramour in death (the father-principle thus being as clearly disassociated into good and bad parts as it is in *Hamlet*).

Before he kills her, the usual motivational tangle is mentioned: (923) in a stichomythia, Orestes tells her that he is not killing her, she is killing herself. And she warns him about the "hounds of the mother" (the Furies), the "doctrinal" interchange ending on two "oracular" lines that foretell her fate obliquely.

During the silent violence off stage, the Chorus (941) calls for the ritual shout of triumph, also in a refrain Biblically exulting that the "light" has come and they are made "free." (At the end of this speech, Orestes will be disclosed standing above the two slain victims.) His speech justifying his act in avenging his father finally becomes transformed into a universalizing of his guilt: "I grieve for all things done and suffered, and for the entire race"; his "victory" has become "pollution" (*miasmata,* 1016–1017). A few lines further (1028) he will refer to his mother as a "patricidal pollution" (*patroktonon miasma*).

The motives pointing to the final play are now vigorously assembled: the rapid progress of remorse is materialized in Orestes' horror at the sight of "the mother's wrathful hounds"; they are loathsome, like Gorgons, and dripping with blood, to be saved, he must journey to the temple of Apollo (the "navel"); there is a need of further cleansing; a tempest has run its course (*etelesthe,* 1067); was Orestes a deliverance or a doom? When will the fury of disaster be lulled to sleep? So the play ends on a question.

The propriety of the Furies as the Chorus for the third play is obvious. First, in this pack of females that hounds its victims, the dog image comes to fruition. And if there is still a problem of conscience to be settled, then what better way to settle it than by putting the principle of conscience itself, as traditionally symbolized by the Furies, into a position whereby its own transformation could be dramatized? Whereas, in lesser dramatists, the lyric function threatens the dramatic function, Aeschylus here finds a way of making it as dramatic as possible, since the Furies change their nature—and the great civic accomplishment in this enterprise comes from the skill by which the transformation of conscience is interwoven with political motives. As a result the duplication of the State in the gods is dramatically presented as a derivation of the State from the gods. And with astounding ac-

curacy, the transformations of conscience are related to emergent political institutions. Poets or critics who have translated all their sociopolitical sympathies into aesthetic equivalents, and who are thus able
to smuggle in their politics under the slogan of "no politics," will find
little cause to think well of this third play.

We admit that, on another score, we found ourselves rebelling. The
third play seems so obsessed with gore, that in despair we began to
wonder whether ritual purification by "bloodless sacrifice" is humanly
possible. The thought made our earlier concern with "body-thinking"
look ludicrously domestic. However, things lightened somewhat when
we realized that, since there is no great *act* of violence in the play
(indeed since we have passed beyond such a stage in this trilogical
discipline), purely theatrical necessities required the poet to be even
more zestful than before in bloody *imagery*. And the Erinyes had to be
hellishly blood-thirsty, if only that, after *their* purgation, their transformation into Eumenides be felt by the audience as a sufficient step
forward. For even after their conversation, they are a gloom-loving lot,
in contrast with the Olympians, the "newer" gods.

Looking again at the *Choëphoroe* (1021–1023) we note how, puz-
zled as to how it all would end (*telei*) Orestes had likened himself to a
charioteer driving far outside his course. This figure refers ostensibly
to Orestes' rapidly mounting sense of guilt. He is distracted. But it
can also be interpreted as introducing a divisive design, a principle of
separation or splitting apart, that will distinctly characterize the third
play. For the turn from the first two plays to the third will involve a
notable change in the psychic accountancy by which the bookkeeping of the conscience will be regulated. And this will show in the very
form of the work. First, there must be the formal conditions for the
transformation whereby the Erinyes become Eumenides. Analogous
with this will be the division of the action into two scenes: Delphi (the
"navel," Pythonically concerned with the "interpretation of dreams"),
and Athens (involving forensic readjustments ultimately under the
sign of Zeus Agoraios, the principle of the parliament, and of distribu-
tive justice in contrast with the feudal mode of vengeance embodied
in the *Agamemnon* and *Choëphoroe*). This division will also be treated
in terms of a distinction between the "old gods" and the "new." And
as we have seen the primal curse previously translated into terms of
personal relationships (specifically, relations between parents and offspring), it is now to be treated explicitly in terms of civic relationships

(the dramatic situation here being such that, having passed beyond the stage of violence, the plot can treat of civic discord in a mixture of legalism and mythology that, by its conciliatory temper, gives us the reassuring sense of civic faction being transcended by civic unity).

We have already discussed the opening of the play, that begins with the three goddesses, next gets to Apollo, and weaves its way finally to Zeus the Fulfiller (289 *teleion*). The action proper begins with reference to the Furies asleep at the shrine (here appear both *muchos* and *omphalos*, inner sanctum and navel).[8]

The situation is reviewed for the audience, as the ghost of Clytemnæstra appears (she calls herself a dream), to chide the Furies for their drowsiness. They are finally goaded into zeal again, and will attest the vicious circle of their ways by uttering the hope that an avenger will come to punish Orestes. Their word for avenger here is *miastor*, that is polluter (177). Always, in this reckoning, vindication (as seen from one point of view) is pollution (as seen from another).

Apollo and the Furies haggle as to whether a wife's murder of her husband is worse than the murder of a blood-relative. And Apollo's speech (213–224) is revealing, in that it shows us how the stress upon "fulfilment" takes on *contractual* connotations. For though marriage is given connotations of fate (in being called *morsimos*, foredoomed), it is a contract, presided over by Zeus and Hera, the "Fulfillers," under the guardianship of Justice (*dike*). The speech ends on the statement that Athena will review Orestes' case (*dika*)—and soon thereafter the scene shifts to the temple of Athena, at Athens.

The general alignment here, pitting the "old" gods against the "new," seems reducible legalistically to the distinction between an absolute and a relative view of transgression. The Furies would punish forever; Orestes, backed first by Apollo and later by Athena, would contend that he has suffered enough. At the beginning of one speech (starting with line 276), he states the case in a seven word formula: "I,

---

[8] And we would pause on the word *teraskopos*, or interpreter of portents. Though it is here (62) applied to Apollo, we propose that this resonant word for *Traumdeuter* be taken into English. *Skopos*, watchman, observer; *teras*, miracle, sign, wonder, marvel, prodigy, potent, omen, and so finally monster. Our motto, when reading such oneiromantic literature, should be: Get thee a terascope; and be watchful of hermetics, to grow strong in hermeneutics. Aeschylus *compels* "terascopic" criticism. (We note there is already an obsolete word, teratic, meaning wonderful, ominous, prodigious. The terascopic would seek out all the stylistic ramifications of the teratlc.)

schooled in evils, learned many purgings." The Furies retort that they are just and upright, and will pursue him to the end (*teleos,* 320). Then follows a long Choral passage (321–396), beginning with an invocation to Mother Night, and twice referring to their kind of thoroughness (*teleioi,* 382; *teleon,* 393). Here they restate their role of bloody vengeance, in a vigorous summarizing passage that gets them sharply established, as preparation for the entrance of Athena (with her wholly different frame of justice) immediately thereafter.

Athena serves quite a diplomatic function here: For though the legalistic trial (in the name of Justice, *Dike*) will be held under her auspices, the final word of her first speech begins on "from afar" and ends on "themis," (a kind of Right which, according to Liddell and Scott, is related to legal Justice as Latin *jus* or *fas* are related to *lex*). Rational justice tends towards the pragmatic, and can end in the wholly non-magical kind of legislation we find in traffic regulations. At the other extreme are the magical "curses" of the Furies. But there are also the proprieties of custom, piously exacting their way, established by usage rather than by magistrates or legislatures—and they are summed up as Themis (the daughter and goddess who, at the opening of the play, was invoked by Apollo's priestess, next after the Earth-Mother). So Athena is evidently to help us keep rational law infused with the magic of custom, while yet avoiding the too-somber magic of the bloody Avengers.

Around this point, as regards "steps" in the development, we should note this neat progression: (1) The Chorus's statement of their role, in introducing themselves to Athena; (2) the stichomythia, involving Chorus and Athena, and ending on the Chorus's agreeing to a legal trial; (3) Athena's asking Orestes to speak for himself, on the grounds that the Furies have already stated their case; (4) Orestes' summary of the past, a kind of *logos* that (as we have previously indicated) vibrates with mystic double *entendres,* surrounding the murder with connotations of a ritual sacrifice; (5) and finally, Athena's speech (470–489), which begins with talk of *themis,* next discusses the role (*moira*) of the Furies, and ends on a series of technical terms to do with trial by jury. The procedure thus in sum interweaves primal guilt, propriety, and the machinery of rational law (even rationalistic law). In line 468, Orestes had stated his appeal to Athena in typical formularistic style: "You judge if just or unjust." "Judge" here was a verb form of the word

Krisis, as Athena uses another (487) when she talks of selecting her jurymen.

The Chorus of Furies, musing uneasily on the trial (490–565), helps remind us that we are witnessing a transition, or peripety. For in its opening line it speaks of turns now threatened. This entire song is remarkable in its ways of keeping sophisticated law infused with the magic of the primal. It points to the danger that Justice will be slighted, when individuals and the State are not trained to fear. In good Aeschylean tragic philosophy, (or Aristotelian philosophy, for that matter) it distrusts both anarchy and tyranny, advising in everything the middle way. It derives pride (*hybris*) from impiety (*dyssebia*), and situates true wealth in mental health. It sums up "entelechially": *kurion menei telos,* which seems to mean: "The end remains supreme," or perhaps "ripeness is all"?

After this, comes the pageantry of preparations for the trial. The stress throughout, as has been noted, is on the tragedy of spectacle, here perhaps not even tragedy at all, if we consider this play in isolation. Indeed, in its nature as reconciliation, as peace following hellish deeds and their purifying, it could even be comedy, in Dante's use of the term. And the "cathartic" vision of all classes united in a common procession is motivationally analogous to the Divine Pageant that Dante witnesses at the end of his climb through purgatory. Also, this "first" trial is by the same token a "Last Judgment." It is first and last in one, since it stands for the *essence* of trial, as defined by the norms of civic enlightenment.

Stichomythia comes into its own, in the interchange during which the Chorus questions Orestes like a trial lawyer questioning a witness. Here it's almost like the catechizing in which it presumably began. The most momentous line is probably Orestes' brief formula for Clytemnæstra as twice polluted, since her slaying of her husband was by the same token her slaying of his father. Orestes finally asks Apollo to decide (*krinon,* again our verb for "crisis") whether he had acted justly.

At one point in the trial, ritual motives underlying the murder of Agamemnon are so transformed as to be almost completely transcended. Apollo (625–639) makes this important distinction: In this woman's murder of a high-born man divinely empowered, the killing was not done gallantly, as when the Amazons slew, but occurred when the victim was in his bath, and when he was caught in a cunningly wrought robe. Here, at first sight, the hieratic connotations seem to have been swamped beneath stress upon the meanness of the deed. Yet, look again, and you see one most ingenious allusion; for the adjective that names the cunning of the robe is *daidalos*—whereupon we see relations between the net and mysterious Daedalian maze of the Minotaur.

To appreciate the skill of the poetic tactics here, we must, combine the following elements:

(1) The secular poem gets poetic effects by allusion to religious rites;

(2) Specifically, it transforms "sacrifice" into terms of "murder";

(3) Conversely, when treating of murder, it keeps vibrant the connotations of sacrifice;

(4) But legal rhetoric never seeks to present a case impartially; rather, the orator presents it in terms most favorable to his side;

(5) In the present poetic imitation of a trial, Apollo is depicted as acting like a trial lawyer, who would have the jury view the deed in the light most favorable to his client;

(6) Accordingly, he presents it in terms that picture it as a mean act;

(7) At this point, the secularization of the hieratic thus seems almost complete, since meanness is about as far as one can get from the solemnity of the priestly;

(8) The appeal as poetry thus resides in the poetic imitation of a rhetorical device (the orator's way of prejudicing a case);

(9) And to keep us reminded that it *is* such, the reference to the *Daedalian* is inserted, since this reference, likening the net to the maze, specifically brings us again into the connotations of mystery and ritual sacrifice surrounding the labyrinth of King Minos, and the Joycean artificer who wrought for him.

The Chorus makes a telling point (640–643) when observing that, whereas Zeus is supposedly so concerned about a father's death, he himself had cast his aged father Cronus into bonds. Whereupon Apollo, growing rhetorically indignant, draws the important distinction between the irrevocable (as with a slaying) and the decision that can be revoked (as with Zeus's confining of his father).

Soon after this (673–675) comes the most astounding manifestation of the tragic thoroughness. For if this culture is to be *essentially* patrilinear, the corresponding reformation of conscience must find the personal terms that will most accurately symbolize the political order. Examination of conscience for civic ends can go no further. Hence, in speaking for Orestes, Apollo questions whether matricide is even possible! The mother, he says, is but the nurse of the offspring. And he cites the fact that Athena, who presides over this trial, was born from the head of Zeus. "Justice" is thus said to be in essence patriarchal. The *biological* function of motherhood is thus "appropriately" interpreted in terms of legal reason (the Jovian intellect).

And when Athena tells the Athenians they are judging ("crisis-ing") the first trial for murder, "first" here is the narrative way of saying that this is an imitation of the formal principles underlying all such trials, the extension of which into corresponding personal terms implies a "conscientiously" legal revision of men's attitudes toward biological motherhood. Also this legal essence is materialized; for the Hill of Ares (that will in time bequeath us Milton's word "Aeropagetica") is the quasi-historic spot at which the trial is represented as being held.

Men will be deterred from wrong-doing, Athena says, by two motives: Reverence (*sebas*) and Fear (*phobos*). (She might as well have said: In this new order, the motives of tragedy will be left intact.) But one must revere neither anarchy nor tyranny. And one must cultivate fear, since there is no righteousness without it. And, given solemn respect for good government, the city and country will enjoy salvation. Ethically, the entelechial principle is here complete; in effect, taking greed for granted, the playwright through Athena asks: Just what blend of fear and reverence brings us to our best as citizens and human beings? In this spirit, Athena calls upon each man to take up his ballot.

While the balloting is in progress, dramatic action is maintained by squabbling between Apollo and the Chorus. An important polytheistic motive is solved in the direction of monotheism, as Apollo says that this oracles derive not only from him, but from Zeus. (The earlier derivation, from Gaia, Themis, and Phoebe, had ambiguously contained this conclusion, as the priestess, though detailing three goddesses as "first," had not concluded her prayer until she had wound from such beginnings to Zeus as the culmination. Might the change be in form the opposite to the amphisbaena? Might it be the transcendence that, forever being found, is also forever being lost, and then forever being glimpsed again, as men in thoroughness meditate to the point where they come upon the dreaming motives of the primal worm, the brainless digestive tract in which symbolic thought is still but a labyrinthine confusion, manifoldly possible, but by no single detail actualized?)

The theme of the Furies' purging is stated bodily in lines 729–730, another "telic" passage, in which Apollo prophesies that they will vomit their venom.

Athena announces that if the votes are tied (if the "crisis" is even), she will cast her ballot for acquittal (saying that she sides with the father on the grounds that she had no mother). And those judges to whom this *telos* is assigned are called upon to pour the ballots from the urn. In a three-line formula, Orestes wonders fearfully what the verdict will be. ("How trial crisised?"). Chorus invokes Night, the Dark Mother.

When the ballots are found even, and Athena has voted for acquittal, the final steps involve the appeasing of the Furies. Since they are older gods, and Athena is among the younger, points of propriety must be considered. But matters of etiquette are tactfully observed, and in ways that allow for spectacle. The possibility of dissension within the city is ritually exorcised. Many other good wishes for the citizenry are scattered about, from a bulging cornucopia of benevolence. (Zeus and Moira are working together, in the disposition of motives.) The final procession escorts the reformed Avengers to their new home underground in Athens (in the "subconscious" of the State?). And we end on the theatrical contrast, already noted, as the awed silence is followed by the final shout of exultation, proclaiming a civic sentiment in which the entire citizenry can be united. *Ololuxate!* Let the glad shout go up! The modern idealistic equivalent is probably the exultant cry, "*Seid umschlungen, Millionen,*" in Schiller's *Ode to Joy,* as used in the choral movement of Beethoven's Ninth Symphony, though we should recall that the Greek word was for a shout celebrating a rebirth due to a death.

Sociologically, one's first tendency would be to view the trilogy along these lines: There were ethical canons that went with tribal blood-guilt, and with the feudal ways of administering justice under such a code. But civic institutions had developed to the point where still further transformations were necessary. And in the *Oresteia*, Aeschylus works out a drama to this end.

But there is also a slightly different possibility. According to this view, the old tribal system had already been considerably obscured by the civic modes of justice. But these civic modes in turn had begun to show great weaknesses, marked by the emergence of sociopolitical conflicts (conflicts which, in the terminology of tragedy, were called *miasmata,* "pollutions").

Thus, Aeschylus's trilogy would be a diplomatic way of saying, in effect: "Fellow-citizens, you think conditions are bad now. But you don't know how well off you are. Just remember how harshly justice was administered in the old days. Then you'll realize the advantages of our civic enlightenment." Thus, on the principle of *reculer pour mieux sauter,* the dramatist contrived to consider uneasy *conditions now* in terms of drastic *conditions then.*

We have said that a social tension intrinsic to a given sociopolitical order is in itself a static condition, a formless mood or state, that merely lingers on, in aimless Daedalian complexity. It prevails until or unless the society so alters its way of living that the old tensions are replaced by new tensions intrinsic to the new situation. And these in turn will be like stagnant miasmatic swamps, trackless, aimless, and offering no firm foothold. A state of social tension just *is;* it has no natural divisibility into parts.

But once it has been translated by a poet or a philosopher into a set of differentiating terms variously interrelated, this stagnant *state* can be experienced rather as a *process.* And within the conditions of the terminology, such transforming of a state into a process can be in effect a *cleansing.* Things can be so separated out, that a part of the tangle can be left behind (at least within the conditions of the terminology).

For the Athenians, the Orestes trilogy must have been cathartic in that way. It analyzed their *contemporary* condition in terms of a comparison with an ominously idealized *past* condition. This design in itself endowed the *state* of "pollution" with a *direction,* which was in turn analyzed in terms of the characters who were variously related to the two feudal stories of guilt, sacrifice, and vindication. Thus, though in Aeschylus's day civic conflicts had already become sufficiently intense to seem miasmatically swampy, as conceived in terms of a contrast with feudal justice this very *problem* took on the quality rather of a *solution.* The contemporary modes of justice were thus seen as having *gone beyond,* or *transcended,* the earlier drastic ways.

The persuasiveness of this view was greatly heightened by the way in which an account of dynastic feuding was merged with vestiges of religious ritual so that an original rite of sacrifice took on connotations of sheer murder, as viewed from the standpoint of civic "enlightenment." And a concern with the tangle of motives involved in that transformation could replace a concern with the immediate tangle of motives besetting the contemporary city. We have tried at various points to indicate how in our opinion this confusion must have operated to endow the plays with an almost unspeakably complex motivational scope. But the best one can hope for is to catch a glimpse of that *status evanescentiae.* However, it is not hard to imagine with what eagerness the audience must have seized on Aeschylus's pageant-like solution, with all exultantly marching together *towards* a condition somehow felt to be a hopeful Next Phase, though actually the pageant had but pictured the essence of civic practices already prevailing. However, by this view of them in their essentiality, their "firstness," they were "cleansed," and the audience was cleansed by contagion.

There is one notable formal consideration we don't quite know what to do with, but surely it is significant. What shall we make of the fact that Orestes does not appear at all in the first play, though he is mentioned? True, the *Agamemnon* is so constructed that his presence is not needed, and thus would be an impediment. But there seems something remarkable in the fact that the play was so constructed.

The only observation we have thought of which does have some bearing on the design concerns the fact that in one notable respect Orestes' absence from the first play helps knit the three plays together. From the standpoint of the relation between feudal justice and civic justice, note that the first two plays are set off against the third. For only the first two have slayings, and the third is concerned with problems of private conscience and civic consciousness that are resolved *after* the slayings. On the other hand, the second and third plays are set off against the first, from the standpoint of the fact that the son, Orestes, is the major character of these two, but does not appear at all in the play that enacts the slaying of his father by his "patricidal" mother.

From the psychoanalytic point of view, perhaps the son's absence from the first play might be taken as remote evidence that the "manly"

Clytemnæstra is *au fond* his surrogate, thereby further motivating his "noble indignation" when he avenges as though from without an act that could also be secretly intrinsic to his own motives. This possibility would be further increased by his assertion that *he* was not slaying Clytemnæstra, she was *slaying herself.* The most obvious explanation for this remark, of course, is the notion that by her guilt she had brought punishment upon herself. But the remark could be interpreted more roundabout in accordance with the notion that, if Clytemnæstra had been a surrogate for a "patricidal" son in the first play, the son's secret identification with her crime would in effect make her action his. Thus in the second play, when punishing her, he would in effect be punishing himself by proxy. And it would then be appropriate, in this roundabout sense, for him to say that she was punishing herself. It would be a circuitous way of saying that he was punishing himself.

Fundamentally, however, we are not here concerned with a "psychoanalytic" matter so much as a lexical, or "logological" one. Our reasoning is along these lines: The feudal principle of retaliation forever circles back upon itself (each "pollution" being corrected by an act that, is in turn a "pollution"). If you telescope this process, you get the amphisbaena-like reversibility that has the design of the reflexive, an act doubling back upon itself, a "process" that "gets nowhere," cleansing guilt in ways that cause more guilt.

The trilogy seemed to offer an escape from this vindicatory treadmill, by transforming the nature of conscience (a change symbolized in the transformation of the Furies, to match the instituting of the "first" trial). But if we view the entire trilogy as *one continuous process,* itself capable of being telescoped into a single character, or identity, then a quite different possibility emerges.

In this sense, quite as the original tension or "pollution" is essentially formless, so the entire complexity of the trilogy is reducible to a unitary essence in which all aspects of the work imply one another, since they all participate in the same universe of discourse, and are all saturated with its unifying principle.

In this sense, the entire tangle of interwoven motives forever turns upon itself, so that father Agamemnon, mother Clytemnæstra, paramour Aegisthus, sister Electra, and ego Orestes would all be but fleeting aspects of the same over-all Daedalian motive. And such telescoping should be expected to reveal itself at strategic moments, such as the time when Orestes tells Clytemnæstra that the son's murder of the mother is in reality her act of suicide, quite as the mother's murder of her husband had been called an act of patricide.

All told, from the logological point of view, everything probably boils down to this paradox: In one sense, language is a collective medium, which the individual acquires from his group, and which in its collective nature ties the individual forever to collectivist thinking, the conceiving of human "rationality" in terms of the sociopolitical ingredients embedded in the nature of the symbols he learns from his group. In another sense, language is solipsistic, a separate dictionary of mutually interrelated terms taking form in each man's mind, living while he lives and dying when he dies. To match the solipsistic nature of such interwoven symbolism "macrocosmically," there are the "microcosmic" solipsistic counterparts one finds in particular symbol-systems, such individual universes of discourse as we glimpse when we consider the Aeschylean trilogy as a whole, and think of its basic unity as in effect as a *telescoping* of its dramatic differentiations, their merging into a single principle (itself inexpressible, but felt by us to the extent that we feel the work to be self-consistent).

To round things out, one further consideration is in order. Recall that it was traditional for the tragic trilogy to be in turn followed by a satyr-play. Thus, this astoundingly thorough search for completion was in turn felt to require a completion.

The satyr-play that completed this particular trilogy has been lost. From the standpoint of those who would systematically lurk, and would piously spy upon great texts, this is perhaps the greatest loss in all history. For though we do know that the satyr-plays were of precisely such characters as were treated solemnly in the tragedies, the most symmetrical possibility of all would be the discovery of a satyr-play that burlesqued the *very same* characters which had been treated heroically in the tragic trilogy preceding it. Such an arrangement would be most civilized; it would complete the completing perfectly.

In any case , the use of a satyr-play to end on, reminds us that tragic solemnity itself, as a literary species, needs a solution beyond itself. Though the trilogy seeks heroic ways of adapting grand gestures to civic conditions, there is also a sense in which heroic gesturing as such is intolerable. If tragedy (with its peculiar modes of dignification) makes for catharsis, there is also a sense in which it leaves us in still further need of catharsis. And the satyr-play, which completed the cycle, would seem to have performed this function.

We might say that it produced a kind of catharsis by totally changing the rules. Instead of trying to resolve all the problems that arise from the particulars of a given tragic dignification, the dramatist in his satyr-play throws out tragic dignification per se. He thus gets freedom by a flat refusal to accept any of the norms that had caused the embarrassment.

However, such a radical solution requires that the chase begin all over again. For the group needs its solemnities, quite as it needs its hilarities. So, six months later: three more trilogies, in turn "corrected" by three more satyr-plays.

7

Othello: An Essay to Illustrate a Method[1]

OTHELLO	Will you, I pray, demand that demi-devil
	Why he hath thus ensnared my soul and body?
IAGO	Demand me nothing. What you know, you know.
	From this time forth I never will speak word.
LODOVICO	What, not to pray?
GRATIANO	Torments will ope your lips. (5.2.307–12)

I

IAGO AS KATHARMA

OTHELLO: ACT 5, SCENE 2. DESDEMONA, FATED CREATURE, marked for a tragic end by her very name (Desdemona: "moan-death") lies smothered. Othello, just after the words cited as our motto, has stabbed himself and fallen across her body. (Pattern of Othello's farewell speech: How he spoke of a "base Indian" [356],[1] and we knew by that allusion he meant Othello. When it was told that he "threw

---

[1] Reprinted by permission of *The Hudson Review* 4.2 (Summer 1951), 165–203. © 1951 by Kenneth Burke. We are grateful to Scott L. Newstok, editor of *Kenneth Burke on Shakespeare* (West Lafayette, IN: Parlor Press, 2006) for allowing us to use the bracketed line numbers and make other editorial corrections based on his meticulous work on *"Othello*: An Essay to Illustrate a Method."

148

a pearl away" [356], for "threw away" we substituted "strangled," and for the pearl, "Desdemona." Hearing one way, we interpreted another. While he was ostensibly telling of a new thing, thus roundabout he induced us to sum up the entire meaning of the story. Who then was the "turbaned Turk" [362] that Othello seized by the throat and smote? By God, it was himself—our retrospective translation thus suddenly blazing into a new present identity, a new act here and now, right before our eyes, as he stabs himself.) Iago, "Spartan dog, / More fell than anguish, hunger, or the sea" (371–72), is invited by Lodovico to "Look on the tragic loading of this bed" (373). *Exeunt omnes* with Iago as prisoner, we being assured that they will see to "the censure of this hellish villain. / The time, the place, the torture" (378–79). Thus like the tragic bed, himself bending beneath a load, he is universally hated for his ministrations. And in all fairness, as *advocatus diaboli,* we would speak for him, in considering the cathartic nature of his role.

Reviewing, first, the definition of some Greek words central to the ritual of cure:

Katharma: that which is thrown away in cleansing; the offscourings, refuse, of a sacrifice; hence, worthless fellow. "It was the custom at Athens," lexicographers inform us, "to reserve certain worthless persons, whom in case of plague, famine, or other visitations from heaven, they used to throw into the sea," with an appropriate formula, "in the belief that they would cleanse away or wipe off the guilt of the nation." And these were *katharmata*. Of the same root, of course, are our words *cathartic* and *catharsis*, terms originally related to both physical and ritual purgation.

A synonym for *katharma* was *pharmakos*: poisoner, sorcerer, magician; one who is sacrificed or executed as an atonement or purification for others; a scapegoat. It is related to *pharmakon*: drug, remedy, medicine, enchanted potion, philtre, charm, spell, incantation, enchantment, poison.

Hence, with these terms in mind, we note that Iago has done this play some service. Othello's suspicions, we shall aim to show, arise from within, in the sense that they are integral to the motive he stands for; but the playwright cuts through that tangle at one stroke, by making Iago a voice at Othello's ear.

What arises within, if it wells up strongly and presses for long, will seem imposed from without. One into whose mind melodies spontaneously pop, must eventually "hear voices." "Makers" become but "instruments," their acts a sufferance. Hence, "inspiration," "afflatus," "angels," and "the devil." Thus, the very extremity of inwardness in the motives of Iago can make it seem an outwardness. Hence we are readily disposed to accept the dramatist's dissociation. Yet villain and hero here are but essentially inseparable parts of the one fascination.

Add Desdemona to the inseparable integer. That is: add the privacy of Desdemona's treasure, as vicariously owned by Othello in manly miserliness (Iago represents the threat implicit in such cherishing), and you have a tragic trinity of ownership in the profoundest sense of ownership, the property in human affections, as fetishistically localized in the object of possession, while the possessor is himself possessed by his very engrossment (Iago being the result, the apprehension that attains its dramatic culmination in the thought of an agent acting to provoke the apprehension). The single "mine-own-ness" is thus dramatically split into the three principles of possession, possessor, and estrangement (threat of loss). Hence, trust and distrust, though *living in* each other, can be shown *wrestling with* each other. *La propriété, c'est le vol.* Property fears theft because it is theft.

Sweet thievery, but thievery nonetheless. Appropriately, the first outcry in this play was of "thieves, thieves, thieves!" (1.1.79) when Iago stirred up Desdemona's father by shouting: "Look to your house, your daughter, and your bags. / Thieves, thieves!" (80–81)—first things in a play being as telltale as last things. Next the robbery was spiritualized: "you have lost half your soul" (87). And finally it was reduced to imagery both lewd and invidious: "an old black ram / Is tupping your white ewe" (88–89), invidious because of the social discrimination involved in the Moor's blackness. So we have the necessary ingredients, beginning from what Desdemona's father, Brabanzio, called "the property of youth and maidhood" (173). (Nor are the connotations of *pharmakon*, as evil-working drug, absent from the total recipe, since Brabanzio keeps circling about this theme, to explain how the lover robbed the father of his property in the daughter. So it is there, in the offing, as imagery, even though rationalistically disclaimed; and at one point, Othello does think of poisoning Desdemona [4.2.194].)

Desdemona's role, as one of the persons in this triune tension (or "psychosis"), might also be illuminated by antithesis. In the article on the Fine Arts (in the eleventh edition of the *Encyclopaedia Britannica*) the elements of pleasure "which are not disinterested" are said to be:

> the elements of personal exultation and self-congratu-
> lation, the pride of exclusive possession or acceptance,
> all these emotions, in short, which are summed up in
> the lover's triumphant monosyllable, "Mine." (Colvin
> 357)

Hence it follows that, for Othello, the beautiful Desdemona was not an aesthetic object. The thought gives us a radical glimpse into the complexity of her relation to the audience (her nature as a rhetorical "topic"). First, we note how, with the increased cultural and economic importance of private property, an aesthetic might arise antithetically to such norms, exemplifying them in reverse, by an idea of artistic enjoyment that would wholly transcend "mine-own-ness." The sharper the stress upon the *meum* in the practical realm, the greater the invitation to its denial in an aesthetic *nostrum*.

We are considering the primary paradox of dialectic, stated as a maxim in the formula beloved by dialectician Coleridge: "Extremes meet." Note how, in this instance, such meeting of the extremes adds to our engrossment in the drama. For us, Desdemona *is* an aesthetic object: We never forget that we have no legal rights in her, and we never forget that she is but an "imitation." But *what* is she imitating? She is "imitating" her third of the total tension (the disequilibrium of monogamistic love, considered as a topic). She is imitating a major perturbation of property, as so conceived. In this sense, however aloof from her the audience may be in discounting her nature as a mere playwright's invention, her role can have a full effect upon them only insofar as it draws upon firm beliefs and dark apprehensions that not only move the audience *within* the conditions of the play, but prevail as an unstable and disturbing cluster of motives *outside* the play, or "prior to" it. Here the "aesthetic," even in negating or transcending "mine-own-ness," would draw upon it for purposes of poetic persuasion. We have such appeal in mind when speaking of the "topical" element. You can get the point by asking yourself: "So far as catharsis and wonder are concerned, what is gained by the fact that the play imitates *this particular tension* rather than some other?"[2]

---

[2] It will become clear, as we proceed, that we by no means confine our analysis of appeal to such "topical" consideration. But "topics," as discussed in Aristotle's *Rhetoric,* mark one of the points where the work, over and above the appeal of its internal relations, appeals by reference to "non-aesthetic" factors. The "allusive" nature of the work need have no literal bearing at all.

In sum, Desdemona, Othello, and Iago are all partners of a single conspiracy. There were the Enclosure Acts, whereby the common lands were made private; here is the analogue, in the realm of human affinity, an act of spiritual enclosure. And might the final choking be also the ritually displaced effort to close a thoroughfare, as our hero fears lest this virgin soil that he had opened up become a settlement? Love, universal love, having been made private, must henceforth be shared vicariously, as all weep for Othello's loss, which is, roundabout, their own. And Iago is a function of the following embarrassment: Once such privacy has been made the norm, its denial can be but promiscuity. Hence his ruttish imagery, in which he signalizes one aspect of a total fascination.

So there is a whispering. There is something vaguely feared and hated. In itself it is hard to locate, being woven into the very nature of "consciousness"; but by the artifice of Iago it is made local. The tinge of malice vaguely diffused through the texture of events and relation-

---

That is, it would be "allusive," and correctly allusive, in the sense we have in mind, even though you could prove that in all the history of Western culture no single "Blackamoor" ever arose to such office as Othello's, married a white woman, and as the result of jealous misunderstandings, strangled her.

Longinus's *On the Sublime* offers us the bridge we want, for getting from the recognized use of topics in Rhetoric to their possible unrecognized presence in Poetry. For on many occasions he cites instances of oratory, but treats them as instances of poetry.

Critics systematically recognized that orators employed "topics" to "move" audiences in the practical meaning of the word "move" (inducing them to make practical decisions, etc.). But when they came to the analysis of poetry (with its purely aesthetic way of being "moving"), instead of reference to "topics" they shifted the stress to "imagery." (Longinus, himself is a good instance of this change, as his treatise, in contrast with the low rating placed on imagination in classical works generally, assigns to images and imagination the high place they attain in nineteenth-century idealism and romanticism.)

"Images," however, are but one aspect of 'topics'.' And the shift of terms conceals a continuity of function. Or, otherwise put: if the topic is said to figure in the appeal when a given line of oratory is being analyzed, what happens to such appeal when this same line is appreciated purely as poetry? Does the topical appeal drop out of the case entirely? Or are such considerations retained, but in disguise, as critics focus the attention upon "imagery," with its varying capacity for inducing moods or forming attitudes?

ships can here be condensed into a single principle, a devil, giving
the audience as it were flesh to sink their claw-thoughts in. Where
there is a gloom hanging over, a destiny, each man would conceive of
the obstacle in terms of the instruments he already has for removing
obstacles, so that a soldier would shoot the danger, a butcher thinks
it could be chopped, and a merchant hopes to get rid of it by trading.
But in Iago the menace is generalized. (As were you to see man-made
law as destiny, and see destiny as a hag, cackling over a brew, causing
you by a spell to wither.)

In sum, we have noted two major cathartic functions in Iago: (1)
as regards the tension centering particularly in sexual love as property
and ennoblement (monogamistic love), since in reviling Iago the audience can forget that his transgressions are theirs; (2) as regards the
need of finding a viable localization for uneasiness (*Angst*) in general,
whether shaped by superhuman forces or by human forces interpreted
as superhuman (the scapegoat here being but a highly generalized form
of the overinvestment that men may make in specialization). Ideally, in
childhood, hating and tearing-at are one; in a directness and simplicity
of hatred there may be a ritual cure for the bewilderments of complexity; and Iago may thus serve to give a feeling of integrity.

These functions merge into another, purely technical. For had Iago
been one bit less rotten and unsleeping in his proddings, how could
this play have been kept going, and at such a pitch? Until very near
the end, when things can seem to move "of themselves" as the author
need but actualize the potentialities already massed, Iago has goaded
(tortured) the plot forward step by step, for the audience's villainous
entertainment and filthy purgation. But his function as impresario
takes us into matters that must be considered rather in terms of internal development.

II

IDEAL PARADIGM

As regards internal relations, let us propose the following ideal paradigm for a Shakespearean tragedy:

ACT I: Setting the situation, pointing the arrows, with first un-
mistakable guidance of the audience's attitude towards the *dramatis
personae*, and with similar setting of expectations as regards plot. Thus
we learn of Cassio's preferment over Iago, of Iago's vengeful plan to

trick Othello ("I follow him to serve my turn upon him. . . . But I will wear my heart upon my sleeve / For daws to peck at. I am not what I am" [1.1.42, 64–65]). Also we learn of Desdemona as the likely instrument or object of the deception. Usually, in this act, various strands that are later to be interwoven are introduced in succession, with minimum relation to one another, though an essential connection is felt: for instance, the incidents in the Council Chamber of scene 3 will set up, in Othello's departure for battle, such conditions as, the audience already realizes, are suited to Iago's purposes (the situation thus implicitly containing his act).

Act 2: Perhaps the most nearly "novelistic" act of a Shakespearean play? While events are developing towards the peripety, the audience is also allowed to become better acquainted with a secondary character much needed for the action. "Humanization," even possibly character-drawing for its own sake, as the second act of *Hamlet* might be entitled "Polonius" (the five being: "The Ghost," "Polonius," "The Play-within-a-Play," "Ophelia Pitiful," and "The Duel"). If act 1 of *Othello* could be called "Iago Plans Vengeance," act 2 would be "Cassio," or better, "Cassio Drunk," since his use in sharpening our understanding of all the relationships must also be eventful in itself, as well as performing some function that will serve as a potential, leading into the third act.

Or might the best way to approach the second act be to treat it as analogous to the introduction of the second theme in the classical sonata-form? Perhaps the most revealing example of the second act, thus considered, is in Corneille's *Cinna* (c. 1639). In the first act we have seen Cinna plotting against the life of the Emperor (Auguste). The woman whom he loves has demanded that he lead this conspiracy. The Emperor had mistreated her father, and she would have vengeance, though the Emperor has sought to make amends by being kind and generous to her personally. Hence, her lover, to prove himself "worthy" of her (what could a Cornelian tragedy do without that word, *digne!*) must conspire against the Emperor, with whom he stands in good favor. He plans the assassination for love. When officiating at a public sacrifice, he will make the Emperor the victim instead. Just before the first act ends, one of the conspirators enters with the news that Cinna and the other main conspirator, Maxime, have been summoned by the Emperor. The act ends on general consternation among the conspirators. They fear that their plot has been discovered.

In act 2, however, the plot is moved forward by a startling development. Auguste, who has not appeared in the first act at all, now
confides to Cinna and Maxime that he is weary of rule. He would
lay down his office, turning it over to Cinna and Maxime. (And to
complete the irony of the situation, he also talks of plans for having
Cinna marry Emilie, the very woman for whose love Cinna has vowed
to slay him.) He "aspires to descend" (*aspire à descendre*), a good variant of the "mounting" theme which we always watch incidentally in
our search for motives. Thus, one editor quotes Louis Racine, in his
Mémoires: "'Note well that expression,' my father said with enthusiasm
to my brother. 'One says *aspire to rise (aspirer à monter)*; but you must
know the human heart as well as Corneille did, to be able to say of an
ambitious man that he aspires to descend.'"

The Emperor's unexpected decision, in all simplicity and affection,
to make the conspirators rulers in his stead, is a *second theme* of the
most startling sort. As contrasted with the expectations established at
the end of act 1 (the conspirators' fears that their conspiracy had been
discovered), this development is so abrupt as almost to be a peripety.
And the situation is so set up that whereas Cinna and Maxime had,
heretofore, been united despite a divergency of motives, they are now
put at odds. Maxime would now abandon the conspiracy; but Cinna
would carry it through regardless, since it is the price of his marriage
to vengeance-minded Emilie. In this kind of drama, almost each scene
discloses something that jerks the characters into a new relationship
(somewhat as, with the slow turning of a kaleidoscope, there is a succession of abrupt changes, each time the particles fall suddenly into a
new design). But the change from the conspiracy theme of the first act
to the abdication theme of the second is so exceptionally marked that
it illustrates our point about the second theme even to excess.

Incidentally, as regards Shakespearean forms generally, we suppose
that the relation between "second theme" and "double plot" should
best be studied along the lines of Mr. Francis Fergusson's speculations
about "analogy" in drama, in his recently published *Idea of a Theater*
(1949).

ACT 3: The Peripety. In act 2, after Cassio had been established unmistakably as chivalrous in the extreme towards Desdemona, Iago had
promised us in an aside: "He takes her by the palm. Ay, well said—
whisper. With as little a web as this I will ensnare as great a fly as Cassio. Ay, smile upon her, do. I will gyve thee in thine own courtship"

(2.1.168–71). Accordingly, we might call act 3 "The Trap Is Laid." Or perhaps, "The Mock Disclosure," since here Iago causes Othello to see with his own eyes things that are not—and with this diabolic epiphany the play rises to a new level of engrossment.

Iago's manipulations of Othello's mind are like the catechizing of him in a black mass, as the pace of the play increases through their raging stichomythia; and in the handkerchief the solemn enunciation of the false doctrine has its corresponding revelation of the "sacred object."

Note, incidentally, how cautiously the dramatist has released the incidents of his story. Before Iago works on Othello as regards Desdemona, we have seen him duping Cassio, then Montano, and even to some extent his confederate Roderigo; also we have seen him molding Othello's misjudgment of Cassio; and only then do the direct attacks upon Othello's confidence in Desdemona begin. Thus, through seeing Iago at work, the audience has been led carefully, step by step, to believe in the extent of his sinister resources, before the fullest dramaturgic risks (with correspondingly rich rewards) are undertaken. Only now, presumably, the dramatist feels that he has prepared the audience to accept the possibility of Othello's ensnarement.

References to the Cornelian structure might also assist us here. One Corneille editor who sums up the structure of the five acts could be translated freely thus:

> The first act makes clear the location of the action, the relations among the heroic figures (their situation), their interests, their characteristic ways, their intentions.
>
> The second gets the plot under way (*commence l'intrigue*).
>
> In the third, it reaches its full complication (literally, "it ties itself").
>
> The fourth prepares the untying (*dénouement*).
>
> And in the fifth act this resolution is completed.

The formula does not quite fit the particulars of *Cinna*. We do not know of Auguste's intentions until the second act; and we do not know until the third that Maxime is secretly in love with Emilie. So some of the development is got by *gradual revelation* of the character's designs.

However, the paradigm can help us glimpse a difference, in the third act, between a Cornelian "tying" and a Shakespearean "peripety." After all the workings at cross-purposes, the discovery that Maxime is in love with Emilie does serve to add the final complication. But this is hardly a reversal, such as we underwent at the beginning of act 2. Rather it is more like putting on "the last straw," by taking the final step in the directions already indicated. In contrast, recall the great peripety scene in *Julius Caesar,* Antony's speech to the mob (3.2). Here no such timely releasing of information is involved: as against the Cornelian transformation-by-information, we watch the transformations taking place before our eyes while we follow the effects of Antony's ingenious oratory. Similarly in *Othello,* the great scene in the third act where Iago finally springs the trap, involves no new disclosures, so far as the audience is concerned. We simply witness (with a pleasurable mixture of fear and admiration) a mounting series of upheavals, as Iago works his magic on the Moor.

ACT 4: "The Pity of It." Indeed, might we not, even as a rule, call this station of a Shakespearean tragedy the "pity" act? There can be flashes of pity wherever opportunity offers, but might the fourth act be the one that seeks to say pity-pity-pity repeatedly? Thus, after the terror of Gloucester's eyes being torn out in act 3 of *King Lear,* there is the pity of his blindness in act 4, while the audience is likewise softened by the sweet tearfulness of Lear's reunion with Cordelia (father and daughter meeting like child and mother). In the same act of *Measure for Measure,* Mariana is pensively silent while the boy sings "Take, O take those lips away" (4.1.1). In *Hamlet,* the corresponding stage is Ophelia's fatal bewilderment. In *Macbeth,* it is the killing of Macduff's son. And so on. Here, when Desdemona says to Othello, who has just struck her, "I have not deserved this" (4.1.236), she almost literally repeats the Aristotelian formula for pity (that we pity those who suffer unjustly). And, after the slight flurry of hope when Othello, talking with Emilia, gets a report of Desdemona not at all like the one Iago had led him to expect, Desdemona's "willow" song (4.3.38–54) is particularly sad because, in her preparations for Othello's return ("He says he will return incontinent" [4.3.11]), there are strong forebodings (making her rather like a victim going willingly towards sacrifice). She seems doubly frail, in both her body and her perfect forgiveness—an impression that the audience will retain to the end, so that the drama attains maximum poignancy when Othello, hugely, throttles her.

In *Cinna*, it is in the fourth act that Auguste learns of the treachery. Pity here takes the modified form of manly grief, as he in a great soliloquy first accuses himself, then gradually moves towards a monarchic resolution (*"O Romains! ô vengeance! ô pouvoir absolu! . . ."*). Then it undergoes another modification, as the Empress begs Auguste to treat the conspirators with mercy. And in this tragedy, too, I believe, we might select the fourth as the "pity act."

The reference to modifications in *Cinna* also reminds us that sometimes the pity can be used purely as a device to "soften up" the audience. The pity we feel for Desdemona singing the willow song is of this sort. At other times it can be used to motivate some act of vengeance on the part of some character in the play, as with Macduff on hearing of his son's death.

Act 5 is, of course, the bringing of all surviving characters to a final relationship, the resolution, in accordance with the original pointing of the arrows, arrows pointed both rationalistically, by intrigue, and through a succession of ideas and images (topics) that direct the play into one channel of associations rather than another, thereby "setting the tone," and getting new implications from the sum of the many passing explicit references. When Othello says, "Put out the light, and then put out the light" (5.2.7), is he but making the scene for the act, hence finding a device for killing her three times (for even without this, she dies twice, as were the second time a weak nervous twitch following a previous strong expulsion)? Or is this, ritually, a double darkness, imaginally saying that his enclosed mind is now engrossed with still narrower enclosure?

This analysis of the form does not cover all the important fields of investigation, even as regards the succession of acts (or succession of stages, insofar as the present explicit division into five acts may have been the work of editors, rather than of the playwright). There is a kind of ritualistic form lurking behind a drama, perhaps not wholly analyzable in terms of the intrigue. That is, the drama (like such a Platonic dialogue as the *Phaedrus*) may be treated formally as a kind of "initiation into a mystery"—and when approached exclusively in such terms, the analysis of the intrigue alone is not adequate. The mythic or ritual pattern (with the work as a *viaticum* for guiding us through a dark and dangerous passage) lurks behind the "rational" intrigue; and to some degree it requires a different kind of analysis, though ideally the course of the rational intrigue coincides with the course of the work, considered as *viaticum*.

Viewed in these terms, the first act would be "the way in." It states the primary conditions in terms of which the journey is to be localized or specified this time. The same essential journey could be taken in other terms; hence, there must be a point at which we glimpse the essence of the mystery as it lies beyond all terms; but this point can be reached only by going thoroughly into some one structure of terms. For though the ritual must always follow the same general succession of stages regardless of the intrigue, this course is repeated each time in the details proper to a particular intrigue. There is perhaps nothing essentially "irrational" about the stages of initiation; however, they may seem so, as contrasted with the rationality of the intrigue (with its need to present the natural development in terms of probability and necessity).

The second act (the introduction of the "second theme") would seem analogous to the definite pushing-off from shore. Of course, the very opening of the play was, in one sense, a pushing-off from shore, the abandoning of one realm for another. But once this decision has been taken, within its own internality there is another kind of departure when the second theme has entered, and we now do indeed feel ourselves under way (as though the bark had suddenly increased its speed, or suggested a further certainty in its movements).

In the peripety of the third act, the principle of internality confronts its very essence. Here is the withinness-of-withinness. It corresponds to the moment in the *Phaedrus* where Socrates has talked ecstatically of the soul as self-moving, as the "fountain and beginning of motion" (451), and of a wing (a most unwinglike wing, by the way, with capacities that would also lend themselves well to psychoanalytic interpretation) (452–53); and precisely following these topics, he arrives at "the heaven which is above the heavens" (453) (the *hyperouranion*, which, by our notion, would figure the withinness-of-withinness); and he now comes forward with the enunciation of the principle that has been secretly directing our voyage: "There abides the very being with which true knowledge is concerned; the colorless, formless, intangible essence, visible only to mind, the pilot of the soul" (453). (Before moving on from his principle of oneness to his doctrine of the hierarchic order which he would deduce from this principle, he further drives it home imaginally by talk of an ultimate feasting "in the

interior of the heavens" [454]. He has thus brought together, and fused
with his rational principle of oneness: flight in the sense of betterment;
flight in the sense of sexual exaltation; and the notions of substantial
contact that draw upon suggestions of feasting for many reasons both
normal and perverse, the basic normal reason doubtless being the la-
tent memory of the infant's sense of wholly joyous contact while feed-
ing at the breast.)

Reverting now to the drama: In the third act, containing the peripety in a five-part form, we should arrive at some similar principle of
internality. The principle is revealed at its best, perhaps, in *Hamlet*,
since the play-within-a-play of the third act so clearly figures the withinness-of-withinness that we have in mind. The design is almost as
clearly revealed in *Julius Caesar*, for Antony's speech before the Roman
populace is similarly a kind of play-within-a-play. And to say as much
is to see how the same principle informs the third act of *Othello*, with
Iago here taking the role of Antony and Othello the role of the mob
moved by his eloquence. However, as contrasted with the ecstatic moment of internality in the *Phaedrus*, here we confront a monstrous
mock-revelation, in accordance with Iago's promise, at the end of act 1:
"Hell and night / Must bring this monstrous birth to the world's light"
(1.3.385–86). ("O, it is monstrous, monstrous!" [3.3.95] exclaims
Alonso a few lines before the end of the third act in *The Tempest*, a
play so greatly unlike *Othello* in attitude, since the destinies there are
all in the direction of easement, but so greatly like it in one notable
dramaturgic respect, since Prospero is even more influential than Iago
in overseeing the development of the plot.)

What of the rite from here out? I take it that, from this point on, we
are returning. We shall get back to the starting point, though with a
difference, somewhat as with a child who, having gone the magic circle
in the Old Mill at the amusement park, steps from the boat, walks
past the same ticket booth that he had passed before entering: everything is literally the same as it was before, yet somehow everything is,
in essence, altered.

There is presumably to be some kind of splitting, a "separating
out." Something is to be dropped away, something retained, the whole
history thereby becoming a purification of a sort. Seen from this point
of view, the "pity act" reveals further possibilities. From the standpoint
of intrigue, we noted how it might serve to motivate vengeance in one
of the *dramatis personae*, or how it might serve to "soften up" the audi-

ence so that they would be more thoroughly affected by the butchery still to come. But from the standpoint of the "initiation," the pity may be viewed as one aspect of the "separating out," preparing us, in one way or another, to relinquish those figures who are to die for our edification.

The last act would complete this process. And it would "release" us in the sense that it would transform the passion into an assertion. For in a tragedy of sacrifice, the assertion need not be got through the *rescuing* of a character; more often it comes through the playwright's felicity in making sure that the character "dies well" (within the conditions of the fiction)—or, as regards the "separating out," the character whom we would disclaim must in some ultimate sense be destroyed, threatened, or branded. But, all told, the rite is complete when one has become willing to abandon the figures who vicariously represent his own tension. The work thus parallels what we have elsewhere cited a sociologist as terming a "ritual of riddance." It is a requiem in which we participate at the ceremonious death of a portion of ourselves. And whatever discomforts we may have experienced under the sway of this tension in life itself, as thus "imitated" in art it permits us the great privilege of being present at our own funeral. For though we be lowly and humiliated, we can tell ourselves at least that, as a corpse, if the usual rituals are abided by, we are assured of an ultimate dignity, that all men must pay us tribute insofar as they act properly, and that a sermon doing the best possible by us is in order.

III

DRAMATIS PERSONAE

First, as regards the rationality of the intrigue, the *dramatis personae* should be analyzed with reference to what we have elsewhere called the agent-act ratio. That is, the over-all action requires contributions by the characters whose various individual acts (and their corresponding passions) must suit their particular natures. And these acts must mesh with one another, in a dialectic of cooperative competition. So, in filling out the analysis of the *dramatis personae*, we should look for the acts, attitudes, ideas, and images that typify each of the characters (citing from the text, and discounting with regard to the role of the person that makes the statement). By the principle of the agent-act ratio, the dramatist prepares for an agent's act by building up the corresponding properties in that agent, properties that fit him for the act. Often, Shakespeare's great economy in attributing to a character only the traits needed for his action has led to misunderstanding about his methods: he is praised as though he aimed at "character-drawing" in the more novelistic sense. His characters' "life-like" quality, the illusion of their being fully rounded out as people, really derives from his dramaturgic skill in finding traits that act well, and in giving his characters only traits that suit them for the action needed of them. Often, purely situational aids are exploited here. Thus, much of Lucio's saliency in *Measure for Measure* derives from his ironic situation in forever slandering the Duke, or telling the Duke lies about his relations to the Duke, not knowing (as the audience does know) that he is talking to the Duke (3.1.335–415; 4.3.140–65).

If the drama is imitating some tension that has its counterpart in conditions outside the drama, we must inquire into the dramatic analysis of this tension, asking ourselves what it might be, and how the dramatist proceeds to break down the psychosis into a usable spectrum of differentiated roles. That is, we must ask how many voices are needed to provide a sufficient range of "analogies" (with the over-all tension being variously represented in each of them). Though Iago-Othello-Desdemona are obviously the major trio here, a complete analysis would require us also to ask how each of the minor characters reflects some fragment of the tension (while serving, from the standpoint of the intrigue, to help the three major persons dramatically communicate with one another).

Thus, briefly, Brabanzio is handy in relating the tension to an earlier stage, when Desdemona was her father's property. We follow a change from father-daughter to husband-wife—and this history also supplies a kind of tragic flaw for Desdemona, a magic mark against her, and one that Iago will use likewise, to further the intrigue. For the first suspicion of Desdemona had been uttered by none other than her own father:

> Look to her, Moor, if thou hast eyes to see.
> She has deceived her father, and may thee. (1.3.291–92)

Dramaturgically speaking, there had been this one false note, as regards Desdemona. Even if it had escaped the notice of the audience, the dramatist reconstructs it when Iago says to Othello: "She did deceive her Father, marrying you . . ." (3.3.210), etc.

The Duke, besides his convenience for details of the plot, provides ways for better identifying the psychosis, or tension, with matters of State (a dignification that, as we shall show later, is particularly important in this play).

Roderigo (marked by Iago's line, "Put money in thy purse" [1.3.333]), helps build up by contrast Desdemona's *spirituality* of property. (Emilia's coarseness similarly contributes, as does Bianca's disreputableness.) Roderigo is also handy in providing Iago with a confidant (and thereby allowing for a further mark against Iago, who is seen to be deceiving even him).

Cassio's role as "second theme" is obvious. We should also note how he bridges the high motives and the low, as his reverence for Desdemona is matched by his cynical attitude towards Bianca. Though we shall not here study the relations and functions of the minor characters in detail, perhaps we could most quickly indicate what we are here aiming at, if we noted two possible directly contrasting ways of dealing with Cassio.

In accordance with what we might call the "novelistic" approach to the *dramatis personae* (as a set of character-portraits), one might remark that, although Cassio was in many ways an admirable man, unfortunately he could not hold his liquor. Then one might remark that Iago, who happened to be a scheming wretch, took advantage of Cassio's weakness, to set him at odds with Othello.

But for our purposes the observations should be reversed thus: If Iago is to set Cassio at odds with Othello, the playwright must provide for Iago some plausible way of getting a hold on Cassio. And he can provide such a hold by endowing Cassio with this weakness (whereby Cassio's necessary befuddlement will be "characteristic" of him, while the playwright can further motivate the development situationally by staging the scene at a time of general revelry, when Cassio might be most likely, in the audience's opinion, to take a drink against his better judgment, at Iago's prodding).

It has been suggested that Othello's motives might have been explained on the basis of his status as a parvenu. By antithesis, this notion serves excellently to indicate the sort of approach we think should be employed in this section of the *dramatis personae*. The notion gains further credence from the fact that Iago himself discusses such a condition with relation to his disgruntlement with Cassio: "Preferment goes by letter and affection, / And not by old gradation, where each second / Stood heir to th' first" (1.1.35–37). And though such unsettlement is certainly to be considered always, as a possible motive complicating the magic of class relationships in Elizabethan times, for our purposes we should turn the matter around, putting it thus:

One notable aspect of the tension Shakespeare is exploiting is the lover's sense of himself as a parvenu. For ennoblement through love is a new richness (a notable improving of one's status, a destiny that made love a good symbol for secretly containing the political aspirations of the bourgeois as *novus homo*). Hence, in breaking the proprieties of love into their components, in dramatically carving this idea at the joints, we should encounter also in Othello as lover the theme of the newly rich, the marriage above one's station. And misgivings (which could be dramatized as murderous suspicions) would be proper to this state, insofar as the treasured object stands for many things that no human being could literally be. So, in contrast with the notion of the play as the story of a black (low-born) man cohabiting with (identified with) the high-born (white) Desdemona, we should say rather that the role of Othello as "Moor" draws for its effects upon the sense of the "black man" in every lover. There is a converse ennoblement from Desdemona's point of view, in that Othello is her unquestioned "lord." And could we not further say that such categorical attributing of reverence to the male (in a social context of double sexual standards) necessarily implies again some suspicions of inadequacy. The very sovereignty that the male absolutely arrogates to himself, as an essential aspect of private property in human affection, introduces a secret principle of self-doubt—which would be properly "imitated" in the ascribing of "inferior" origins to Othello, even in the midst of his nobility. And though the reader might not agree with this explanation in detail, it can serve in principle to indicate the *kind* of observation we think the analysis of the *dramatis personae* requires. For, in contrast with the novelistic "portrait gallery" approach to Shakespeare's characters, so prevalent in the nineteenth century, one should here proceed not from character-analysis to the view of the character in action, but from the logic of the *action as a whole*, to the analysis of the character as a recipe fitting him for his proper place in the action (as regards both the details of the intrigue and the imitating of the tension by dramatic dissociation into interrelated roles).

Since A. C. Bradley was one of the best critics who tended to approach Shakespeare "novelistically," we might develop our position best by commenting on some of his comments. Thus, when Bradley writes "Desdemona's sweetness and forgiveness are not based on religion" (V.147fn1), I can think of no remark better fitted to deflect attention from the sort of approach I have in mind. To arouse our pity here, Shakespeare places Desdemona in a sacrificial situation wherein she gives herself up as a gentle victim, with malice towards none. We have mentioned Aristotle's formula, that men pity those who suffer unjustly (*Poetics* 1453a5–6). But Shakespeare's usage involves a further motive. For pity is extracted most effectively from the spectacle of suffering if the tormented, at the very height of the torment, forgives the tormentor. The scene in which she sings the willow song (4.3.38–54) casts her perfectly in the role of one preparing meekly for sacrifice. And her sorrow is in the same mode when, having been fatally attacked by her husband, she speaks as her parting words: "Commend me to my kind lord. O, farewell!" (5.2.133). Here Shakespeare goes as far as he can towards making her conduct Christlike. And this *exploiting* of a religious pattern as a part of the playwright's design upon the audience's sympathies is a much more important detail about Desdemona as a character-recipe than the fact that, literally, she is not strong on theological references.

On the other hand, the playwright is always careful to see that, however austere the perfectly piteous offering may be, the audience is not confined to such exacting responses. There are others in the play who will help the audience to have its vengeance straight. The "hellish villain" (5.2.378) is excoriated before their very eyes by his own wife. And he is to be tortured: it is a promise. Similarly, in *King Lear*, even as the pitiful burdens of the old man's helplessness begin to mount upon us, the audience is audibly gratified, murmuring contentedly, when Kent lets loose his manly invective against Oswald.

But Bradley does make a remark usable for our purposes when he says of Emilia:

> From the moment of her appearance after the murder to the moment of her death she is transfigured; and yet she remains perfectly true to herself, and we would not have her one atom less herself. She is the only person who utters for us the violent emotions

> which we feel, together with those more tragic emo-
> tions which she does not comprehend. (VI.197)

To be sure, Bradley is here still talking as though there had been some
surprising change in her *character*, whereas we would have him approach such matters more directly, in terms of a transfiguration in
her *role*. Because of her relation to Iago within the conditions of the
play, because of the things she alone knows, she is in the best position
to take over the vindictive role we eagerly require of *someone* at this
point. Or, you could state it thus: Some disclosures are due, she is in
a position to make them, and if she makes them venomously, she will
do best by our pent-up fury, a fury still further heightened by the fact
that Desdemona died Christlike.

But when Bradley writes of Emilia, "what could better illustrate
those defects of hers which make one wince, than her repeating again
and again in Desdemona's presence the word Desdemona could not
repeat . . ." (VI.197), here is sheer portraiture, and done in a way that
conceals the functioning of the play. The dramatist must continually
keep vibrant with the audience, as an essential element in the psychosis, the animal words for sexuality. Iago, of course, carries the main
burden of this task. But when he is not about, others must do it for
him. It is important that the audience simultaneously associate Desdemona with such motives, and dissociate her from them. Here is the
very centre of the tension. Iago does not often speak to Desdemona;
and even when he does, within the conditions of the play he could not
plausibly speak to her thus, without lowering her in our esteem. But
Emilia is perfectly suited to maintain this general tenor of the imagery,
so necessary for retaining the exact mixture of pudency and prurience
needed for exploiting the tension. And besides thus keeping the motive vigorous, Emilia's use of such terms gives Desdemona's avoidance
of them a *positive* or *active* character—and activation, actualization, is
sought for always.

At first glance, one might expect us to welcome Thomas Rymer's
notion that Emilia's remarks, after the willow scene, are designed
merely as relief ("that we may not be kept too long in the dumps,
nor the melancholy Scenes lye too heavy, undigested on our Stomach"
[158]). But the theory of "comic relief" has been repeated too often to
be trustworthy. And at the very least, we might look at it more closely.
In one sense a tragic playwright should have no interest in giving his
audience "comic relief." At least, we'd expect him to be as overwhelm-

ingly and protractedly tragic as he could, without risk that the audience might rebel.

In forms such as Cornelian tragedy, "comic relief" was ruled out by the conditions of the game. The conventions required that the ceremonious gesture be sustained throughout. So-called "comic relief," on the other hand, allows for a shift in tonality that permits the dramatist to relax the tension without risking the loss of the audience's interest. He can turn suddenly to a different mode, which allows him later to start building anew from a lower intensity. In this respect, the device at least gives relief to the *dramatist*. But we would suggest this possibility: Rather than treating such a device merely as "comic relief," might one discern in it a subtler diplomacy? When the audience is carried beyond a certain intensity, it threatens to rebel, for its own comfort. But the playwright might engage it even here too, by shifting just before the audience is ready to rebel. However, he will shift in ways that subtly rebuke the audience for its resistance, and make it willing afterwards to be brought back into line. For in the "comic relief," he makes sure that the rebellion is voiced by "inferior" characters, as when Emilia, very nearly at the end of the fourth act, throws doubt on the entire system of "values" motivating Othello, Desdemona, and Iago, all three.

Desdemona has said, "Wouldst thou do such a deed for all the world?" (4.3.66)—and Emilia answers, "The world's a huge thing. It is a great price for a small / vice" (67–68). She continues in this vein, and as the act ends, this motive is strong with us. Yet she here utters the basic heresy against the assumptions on which this play is built. What of that? We would explain the tactics thus:

A tragic plot deals with an *excessive* engrossment. Hence, many average members of the audience might be secretly inclined to resist it when it becomes too overwrought. Accordingly, one might think it unwise of the dramatist to let their resistance be expressed on the stage.

However, Emilia is present among the big three as an average mortal among the gods. Thus, though in her role she represents a motivation strong with the audience, she is "low," while tragedy is "high." Hence in effect she is suggesting that any resistance to the assumptions of the tragedy are "low," and that "noble" people will choose the difficult way of Desdemona. And since, by the rules of the game, we are there for elevation, *her* voicing of our resistance protects, rather than endangers, the tragic engrossment. For the members of the audience, coming here to be ennobled, would bear witness to their high spiritual state by fearing the right things, as Aristotle in the *Nichomachean Ethics* (c. 350 BCE) reminds us that there is a nobility in fear when we fear properly (1115a12–13).

But let us return to Bradley. When discussing the contrast between Iago's "true self and the self he presented to the world in general," Bradley writes: "It is to be observed . . . that Iago was able to find a certain relief from the discomfort of hypocrisy in those caustic or cynical speeches which, being misinterpreted, only heightened confidence in his honesty. They acted as a safety-valve, very much as Hamlet's pretended insanity did" (VI.177).

Just as I was trying to make clear why I think these remarks malapropos, Bradley helped me by bringing in this reference to Hamlet's "pretended insanity." Passing over the fact that Hamlet's use of insanity as a ruse, while playing for time to avenge the murder, was part of the traditional story from which Shakespeare presumably adapted his own play, we would note other kinds of tactical considerations here.

Thus, when analyzing the plays of Shaw, we have noticed that, by introducing the use of a cantankerous character among the *dramatis personae*, Shaw could always guarantee himself a certain minimum of flurry on the stage. If nothing else was going on, he could let this character exercise for a while, in spirited Shavian fashion, until the plot was ready to resume. In *The Cocktail Party* (1950), Eliot gets a similar effect by a situational device. It is doubtful whether his personal temperament includes the kind of spirited character that came easy with Shaw. But within his means, he could get an equivalent effect situationally, by vexations, as characters enter at the wrong moment, return suddenly when they are supposed to have left for good, phone or call from the other room inopportunely, the whole adding up to a series of interruptions that is a secular equivalent of mortification, and contrives at the very least to keep things amusingly stirred up. Now, why could we not similarly note that Hamlet's malingering is an excellent device for maintaining a certain minimum of dramatic tension? And the device could serve further to give his utterances an oracular tone. For oracles traditionally speak thus ambiguously; hence the tomfoolery, combined with Hamlet's already established solemnity, could well help place his remarks under the sign of a fate-laden brooding.

The device also aided well in covering up one great embarrassment of the work. For the job of delaying Hamlet's vengeance until the fifth act, whereas he was so clearly in a physical position to kill the king in the first, and had unmistakably established the king's guilt in the third, threatened to arouse the audience's resentment. But the problematical aspect of Hamlet (made picturesque and convincing by the gestures of madness) could be of great assistance to the playwright. And only insofar as the tactics of delay were acceptable would the continuation of the play be possible. On the other hand, if it was necessary to explain Hamlet's pretended insanity as a "safety-valve," why did not so articulate a playwright as Shakespeare stress the point?

Bradley says of Iago: "Next, I would infer from the entire success of his hypocrisy—what may also be inferred on other grounds, and is of great importance—that he was by no means a man of strong feelings and passions, like Richard, but decidedly cold by temperament. Even so, his self-control was wonderful, but there never was in him any violent storm to be controlled" (VI.177).

Here again, looking at the matter from the standpoint of the principle we would advocate, we note rather that Shakespeare has no need for a turbulent figure like Othello here. Iago is properly the principle of steely suspicion that works upon the passions. And if he already has a complete function to perform in accordance with such a character, why should Shakespeare shower irrelevant traits upon him?

Shakespeare is making a play, not people. And as a dramatist he must know that the illusion of a well-rounded character is produced, not by piling on traits of character until all the scruples of an academic scholar are taken care of, but by *so building a character-recipe in accord with the demands of the action that every trait the character does have is saliently expressed in action or through action.* Here is the way to get "actualization." And such dramatic perfection of expression, whereby the salient traits are expressed in action, may then induce us to fill in (by inference) whatever further traits we may consider necessary for rounding out the character. The stress upon character as an intrinsic property, rather than as an illusion arising functionally from the context, leads towards a nondramatic explanation. And one can end by attributing to a character certain traits, or trends of thought, for which no line of text can be directly adduced as evidence.

I do not object categorically to such impressions. I would merely suggest that the line of inquiry with relation to them should be altered. *They are the preparatory material for critical analysis, not the conclusions.* If the critic feels that the spectacle of the character in action leads him

spontaneously to round out the character, in his own mind, by inferences that Shakespeare has not explicitly sought to establish as motives
in the play, then his job should be not just to show that he makes such
inferences, nor just to record his exaltation in the contemplation of
them; but rather he should aim to explain how, by the few traits which
are used for the actualizing of a role, the playwright can produce the
illusion of a rounded character.

Whereas it has become customary to speak of Shakespeare's figures
as of living people, the stupidest and crudest person who ever lived is
richer in motivation than all of Shakespeare's characters put together—and it would be either a stupidity or a sacrilege to say otherwise. It
is as an artist, not as God, that he invents "characters." And to see him
fully as an artist, we must not too fully adopt the Coleridgean view of
art as the "dim analogue of creation."

The risk in "portraiture" of the Bradleyan sort (and Samuel John-
son has done it admirably too, also with reference to *Othello*) is that
the critic *ends* where he should *begin*. As Jimmy Durante has so relevantly said, "Everybody wants to get into the act." In this sense, impressionistic criticism would write the work over again. Let the critic
be as impressionistic as he wants, if he but realize that his impressions
are the *beginning* of his task as a critic, not the *end* of it. Indeed, the
richer his impressions the better, if he goes on to show how the author
produced them. But the great risk in "conclusive" statements about a
work is that they give us the feeling of *conclusions* when the real work
of analysis still lies before us.

Bradley even asks us to "look more closely into Iago's inner man"
(VI.178). The expression almost suggests that Iago is so real, one might
profitably hire a psychoanalyst to get at the roots of him. And in the
same spirit, after noting that "Shakespeare put a good deal of himself
into Iago" (VI.189), Bradley continues: "But the tragedian of real life
[*sic!*] was not the equal of the tragic poet. His psychology, as we shall
see, was at fault at a critical point, as Shakespeare's never was. And so
his catastrophe came out wrong, and his piece was ruined" (VI.189).

When Bradley says of Iago, "He was unreasonably jealous; for his
own statement that he was jealous of Othello (1.3.369–70) is confirmed by Emilia herself (4.1.152), and must therefore be believed"
(VI.176), here we would offer another kind of purely poetic consideration, in contrast with Bradley's novelistic portraiture. In line with
Francis Fergusson's discussion of "analogy" in his analysis of *Hamlet*

(*Idea of a Theater* 94–142), we would note that Iago is here placed in a position analogous to that which is finally forced upon Othello. Such analogy at the very least gives greater consistency to a work, carrying out the principle of repetitive form, by varying a theme. But it does more. For the area of similarity between Iago and Othello here serves also to point up the great difference between them. (Coleridge reminds us dialectically that *rivales* are opposite banks of the same stream.) Hence, Iago's *ignoble* suspicions by contrast make Othello's suspicions seem *more noble*, thereby helping induce us to believe that he killed Desdemona not just in jealousy, but for the sake of "honor." Or, otherwise put: here is the principle of the "reflector," discussed in one of Henry James' prefaces. If you have several characters all looking at the *same* object, you can thereby point up the differences in their perceiving of it. And in attributing to Iago a suspicion analogous to the one he would arouse in Othello, the poet thus is in his way using the "reflector" principle. Also, at the very least, Iago's suspicion helps motivate his vindictiveness, and "rationally." For in situations where "honor" is taken as a primary motive, it usually follows that *vengeance* can serve as "rational" motivation of an act (a point to be remembered always, when considering motivations purely on the level of the intrigue).

But let us, in concluding this section, make sure that we do not take on more burdens than we must. To read Stanislavsky's notes on the staging of *Othello* (1948) is to realize that, in our novel-minded age at least, the actor is helped in building up his role by such portraiture as Bradley aims at. We will hypothetically grant that the novelistic method may be best for aiding the actor to sink himself in his role. Give him a "physical task," such as Stanislavsky looks for, to make sure that in each scene he can operate on something more substantial and reliable than his mood and temperament. Then, once you have made sure of this operational base, allow for as much novelistic improvising as can give the actor a sense of fullness in his role. Maybe so. But we would still contend that, *so far as the analysis of the playwright's invention is concerned*, our proposed way of seeing the agent in terms of the over-all action would be required by a dramaturgic analysis of the characters.

IV

Peripety

This section, to be complete, should trace the development of the plot,
stressing particularly the ways in which the playwright builds up "potentials" (that is, gives the audience a more or less vague or explicit "in
our next" feeling at the end of each scene, and subsequently transforms
such promises into fulfillments). The potentialities of one scene would
thus become the actualizations of the next, while these in turn would
be potentials, from the standpoint of unfoldings still to come.

Bradley's remark, "Iago's plot is Iago's character in action" (VI.190)
is excellent, unless it tempts us, as it did him, to reverse the order of
our inquiry, looking at Iago's conduct as though it were the outgrowth
of his character, rather than looking at his character as having been so
formed by the playwright that it would be a perfect fit for the kind of
conduct the play required of him. But in any case, since Iago's schem-
ings are to be appreciated as such, and since they form the plot itself,
the audience is somewhat invited to watch the plot as plot.

However, we shall here confine ourselves mainly to the peripety,
act 3, scene 3.

Iago has promised so to manipulate the meaning of events that
Othello will be led to misinterpret what goes on before his very eyes
(and the eyes of the audience, who know exactly the nature of his errors). Iago now faithfully fulfills his promise; and after proper preparation of the audience under the guise of preparing Othello, he finally
becomes like a fiend goading an elephant, making the ungainly beast
rear on its hind legs, thrash in bewilderment, and trumpet in anguish.
As the scene begins, no suspicion of Desdemona has crossed Othello's
mind (unless you except the warning of Brabanzio's which at least had
brought up the topic, as ambiguous foreshadowing, in Othello's presence).

In the first scene of the third act, after mild horseplay with clown
and musicians, a strong potential was established: Iago got his wife to
arrange for Cassio's meeting with Desdemona. Never missing an opportunity to keep the innuendoes vibrant, the playwright has Emilia
tell Cassio of Othello's desire "To take the saf'st occasion by the front"
(47) for reinstating Cassio. Thus with the assurance that Cassio will
be where we need him, there follows a brief scene of seven lines, wherein the playwright helps Iago help the playwright get Othello prop-

erly placed. Then, along with the usual references to Iago as "honest" (3.3.5) (which, since they call for an easy kind of translating, thereby also help induce the audience to collaborate in the making of the play) we hear Desdemona assuring Cassio that she will importune Othello in his behalf. (For potential, as regards "Cassio's suit" [26], she states her intentions fatally: "thy solicitor shall rather die / Than give thy cause away" [27–28].) We are now ready for the grand interweavings, as Othello and Iago enter at a distance, Cassio leaves, and Iago mutters, "Ha! I like not that" (33).

OTHELLO	What dost thou say?
IAGO	Nothing, my lord. Or if, I know not what.
OTHELLO	Was not that Cassio parted from my wife?
IAGO	Cassio, my lord? No, sure, I cannot think it,
	That he would steal away so guilty-like
	Seeing your coming.
OTHELLO	I do believe 'twas he.
DESDEMONA	How now, my lord?
	I have been talking with a suitor here,

["suitor"—ill-starred word!]

	A man that languishes in your displeasure.
OTHELLO	Who is't you mean?
DESDEMONA	Why, your lieutenant, Cassio (34–45)

[who, we vibrantly learn, "hath left part of his grief" (54) with her.]

Thus, by his stutterings, Iago has taken an incident actually neutral, and made it grim for Othello. The audience now has a pattern for creating vigorously: *translating* (the inducement to an audience's self-persuasion that resides in the use of dramatic irony). Desdemona continues to importune (and the playwright helps her help Iago by having her, in the course of remarks, say to Othello: "What, Michael Cassio, / That came a-wooing with you, and so many a time / When I have spoke of you dispraisingly / Hath ta'en your part" [71–74]). After Desdemona has left, Othello sums up the motivations perfectly: "Excellent wretch! Perdition catch my soul / But I do love thee, and when I love thee not, / Chaos is come again" (91–93). Whereupon, Iago resumes his pattern, making noncommittal remarks that invite Othello to do the committing for himself:

IAGO   My noble lord.

OTHELLO   What dost thou say, Iago?

IAGO   Did Michael Cassio, when you wooed my lady,
                Know of your love?

[We now see the full dramatic utility of Desdemona's reference to Cassio "a-wooing."]

OTHELLO   He did, from first to last. Why dost thou ask?

IAGO   But for a satisfaction of my thought,
                No further harm.

OTHELLO   Why of thy thought, Iago?

IAGO   I did not think he had been acquainted with her.

OTHELLO   O yes, and went between us very oft.

IAGO   Indeed?

OTHELLO   Indeed? Ay, indeed. Discern'st thou aught in that?
                Is he not honest?

[Fatal word. If the devil Iago is honest, then Cassio and Desdemona, being honest, will be devils.]

IAGO   Honest, my lord?

OTHELLO   Honest? Ay, honest.

IAGO   My lord, for aught I know.

OTHELLO   What dost thou think?

IAGO   Think, my lord?

OTHELLO   'Think, my lord?' By heaven, thou echo'st me
                As if there were some monster in thy thought
                Too hideous to be shown! Thou dost mean something.
                I heard thee say even now thou liked'st not that,
                When Cassio left my wife. What didst not like?
                And when I told thee he was of my counsel
                In my whole course of wooing, thou cried'st
                        'Indeed?'
                And didst contract and purse thy brow together
                As if thou then hadst shut up in thy brain
                Some horrible conceit. If thou dost love me,
                Show me thy thought. (94–120)

Here the Moor's magnificent upsurge is built around his own description of Iago's tactics. Thus not only is the device used, but in a dramatized way the audience is informed that it is being used, and what its nature is.

Thence to a new device: Iago, to bring up the theme of jealousy, doubts himself, blames himself, begs Othello to make due allowances: "As I confess it is my nature's plague / To spy into abuses, and oft my jealousy / Shapes faults that are not" (151–53). The topic is thus introduced, under the guise of asking that it be avoided. A drastic variant of the *praeteritio* and one that will soon be developed further, as Iago proves himself a master of the "Say the Word" device, whereby the important thing is to see that the summarizing word, the drastically relevant motivating title is spoken. For in its nature as imagery, inviting one to make oneself over in its image, no "no" can cancel it; it could only be abolished by another image—not by a negative, but by a still stronger positive, and the only stronger one, as we shall see later, will not overwhelm it, but will serve as the ultimate reinforcement of it.

Meanwhile, after some near-puns on treasure ("Who steals my purse steals trash" [162], etc. . . . "But he that filches from me my good name" [164], etc.), near-puns, since they half suggest other kinds of repository, likewise to be conceived in association with one's good name—next Iago can exploit directly the topic that he had introduced roundabout: "O, beware, my lord, of jealousy. / It is the green-eyed monster which doth mock / The meat it feeds on" (169–71). But now he is gathering momentum, and he rounds out his statement by adding another term, "cuckold" (171), just as a topic, not yet explicitly pointed. And he contrives to "Say the Word" by another route: "Good God the souls of all my tribe defend / From jealousy!" (179–80).

Then, as regards the audience, Othello makes the next important contribution: "Think'st thou I'd make a life of jealousy, / To follow still the changes of the moon / With fresh suspicions?" (181–83). The involvements of property here take a momentous step forward. By the catamenial theme, time and the very motions of the heavens begin to interweave themselves with Othello's endangered treasure; or, otherwise put, the personal and social nature of such property now begins to move towards ultimate transmogrification, made part of nature, and cosmologized.

But now a new tack is needed. Othello must show strong resistance, too. Otherwise, this bullfight will not be spectacle enough. So after himself introducing the topic of "goat" (184), which Iago will exploit later, he swings into revolt against these ingeniously inculcated obsessions, ending on a demand for proof.

During the discussion of proof, Iago adopts the role of one who is himself looking for proof. Iago is not arguing with Othello ever (quite as a good dramatist would never think of arguing with his audience). Rather, he takes the role of one who is joining with Othello to get the matter clear, and would himself rejoice if his suspicions were proved wrong. But, as if half grudgingly (after having talked of feminine deception generally), he does recall how Desdemona had once deceived her father. He glancingly suggests that Othello is not "Of her own clime, complexion, and degree" (235). He contrives to keep the theme going by a hint of a pun his author was much given to, as he speaks of "her country forms" (242). Then he leaves the stage (whereat Othello can sum up by musing, "This honest creature doubtless / Sees and knows more, much more, than he unfolds" [247–48]); then returns to make a special point of the plot potential, in asking that Othello leave Desdemona free to meet with Cassio.

Left alone this time, Othello muses on the problems of his sweet property:

> O curse of marriage,
> That we can call these delicate creatures ours
> And not their appetites! I had rather be a toad
> And live upon the vapour of a dungeon
> Than keep a corner in the thing I love
> For others' uses. (272–77)

And as Iago had previously told Roderigo that "they say base men being in love have then a nobility in their natures more than is native to them" (2.1.212–13), so Othello here likewise considers love in hierarchic terms: "Yet 'tis the plague of great ones; / Prerogatived are they less than the base" (3.3.277–78).

Then, after Desdemona has made her invaluable contribution to the plot by losing her handkerchief, ("Your napkin is too little" [291], Othello had said), and Iago has come into possession of it (informing the audience that he will "in Cassio's lodging lose this napkin, / And let him find it" [325–26]), Othello sums up the major cluster of his motives, yielding now frankly to his suspicions:

> O, now, for ever
> Farewell the tranquil mind, farewell content,
> Farewell the plumèd troops and the big wars
> That makes ambition virtue! O, farewell,
> Farewell the neighing steed and the shrill trump,
> The spirit-stirring drum, th'ear-piercing fife,
> The royal banner, and all quality,
> Pride, pomp, and circumstance of glorious war!
> And O, you mortal engines whose rude throats
> Th'immortal Jove's dread clamours counterfeit,
> Farewell! Othello's occupation's gone. (352–62)

In accordance with our method, we cannot lay too much stress upon this speech. For the audience is here told explicitly what the exclusive possession of Desdemona equals for Othello, with what "values" other than herself she is identified. Here they are listed: Ambition, virtue, quality, pride, pomp, circumstance, glory, and zest in his dangerous occupation. Within the magnificently emotional utterance, there is thus an almost essay-like summary. Over and above what she *is*, Othello tells us in effect, here are the things she *stands for*. All these nonsexual elements are implicit in her sex, which is enigmatically, magically, by the roundabout route of courtly mystery, the emblem of them. For such reasons as this, he could later call himself "An honourable murderer" (5.2.300), saying that he did "all in honour" (301) in slaying the charismatic figure who once had announced her intention "to preserve this vessel for my lord" (4.2.86). (In the fourth act, a similar identification will be mentioned briefly: "O, the world hath not a sweeter creature! / She might lie by an emperor's side, and command him tasks" [4.1.176–77].)

When he threatens to turn his fury against Iago, as he spasmodically doubts his own torrents of doubt, Iago now lets loose upon the audience Shakespeare's best rhetoric of *enargia*, in bringing the particulars of infidelity before Othello's, and thus the audience's, very eyes, first obliquely, then finally by his lie that implicates Desdemona in the lascivious movements and treacherous mutterings attributed to Cassio in his sleep.

Now is the time for the *materializing* of these fatal errors, concentrated in the handkerchief as their spirit made manifest. Iago: "but such a handkerchief— / I am sure it was your wife's—did I today / See Cassio wipe his beard with" (3.3.442–44). Within the explicit conditions of the plot, it has been charged with fatal implications—whereat the scene, like the raging Pontic (456) which Othello likens to himself (no ebb tide, all flood), now takes its "compulsive course" (457), with "violent pace" (460), while amidst shouts of "black vengeance" (451), "hollow hell" (451), "aspics' tongues" (454) and "bloody thoughts" (460), Iago and Othello come to kneel together, swearing vengeance and loyalty in vengeance—and then, finally, once more, a variant of the "Say the Word" device, introducing the theme while ostensibly speaking against it:

IAGO   My friend is dead.
              'Tis done at your request; but let her live.
OTHELLO   Damn her, lewd minx! O, damn her, damn her!
              Come, go with me apart. I will withdraw
              To furnish me with some swift means of death
              For the fair devil. (476–81)

Kneeling together, and well they should, for they are but two parts of a single motive—related not as the halves of a sphere, but each implicit in the other.[3]

V

"THE WONDER"

So much ado, so much stress, so much passion and repetition about an Handkerchief! Why was not this call'd the *Tragedy of the Handkerchief?* . . . We have heard of *Fortunatus his Purse,* and of the *Invis-*

---

[3] Note that, as the scene progresses, Iago's part in the development gradually diminishes. And his contribution is in inverse ratio to Othello's increasing engagement. At first he must act vigorously, to set Othello into motion. But once Othello has been fully aroused, and is swinging violently, Iago's role is reduced to a series of slight additional pushes, each just enough to maintain the sweeping rhythm of Othello's passion.

ible Cloak, long ago worn thread bare, and stow'd up
in the Wardrobe of obsolete Romances: one might
think, that there were a fitter place for this Handkerchief, than that it, at this time of day, be worn on
the Stage, to raise every where all this clutter and turmoil. Had it been *Desdemona*'s Garter, the Sagacious
Moor might have smelt a Rat: but the Handkerchief
is so remote a trifle, no Booby, on this side *Maurita-
nia*, cou'd make any consequence from it.

Desdemona dropt her Handkerchief; therefore
she must be stifl'd.

Here we see the meanest woman in the Play takes
this *Handkerchief* for a *trifle* below her Husband to
trouble his head about it. Yet we find, it entered into
our Poets head, to make a Tragedy of this *Trifle*.

—*Thomas Rymer [160, 163]*

"Sure there's some wonder in this handkerchief," Desdemona had con-
fided to Emilia; "I am most unhappy in the loss of it" (3.4.98–99).
And well she might be. For the handkerchief will sum up the entire
complexity of motives. It will be public evidence of the conspiracy
which Othello now wholly believes to exist (and which, according to
our notions on the ironies of property, *does* exist). And by the same
token, it will be the privacy of Desdemona made public. If she is enigmatic, emblematic, the gracious fetish not only of Othello, but of all
who abide by these principles of spiritual ownership, then her capital
as a woman is similarly representative, the emblem of her as emblem.
Hence, this handkerchief that bridges realms, being the public surrogate of secrecy, it is an emblem's emblem—and in his belief that
she had made a free gift of it to another, Othello feels a torrential
sense of universal loss. Since it stands for Desdemona's privacy, and
since this privacy in turn had stood magically for his entire sense of
worldly and cosmological order, we can readily see why, for Othello,
its loss becomes the ultimate obscenity. But there is a further point to
be considered, thus:

Aristotle has said that accidents are best accepted in a tragedy when
they are placed before the play's beginning, unless they can be made
to seem fate-guided (*Poetics* 1454b4–8). Explicitly, there is no attempt
here to show that the handkerchief is lost and found by supernatural

guidance. The bluntness of the convenience is tempered by two devices of the plot: (1) Othello, by talking about it, calls the audience's clear
attention to it when it falls; (2) since Emilia finds it and gives it to Iago,
rather than Iago's finding it himself after having talked of wanting it,
the addition of this intermediate step provides a certain tactful modulation between Desdemona's losing it and Iago's getting it. (Also, incidentally, this roundabout approach supplies complications that will
later enable the plot to operate somewhat "of itself," when things must
turn against the great impresario, Iago, Emilia having been given the
information that leads to the exposing of him.)

But our main point is this: There is a kind of magic in the handkerchief, for the audience as well as for Othello—and this property serves
as the *equivalent* of a fate-guided accident (the miraculous). It is this
miraculous ingredient in the handkerchief that makes the audience
willing to accept, so late in the play, the accident whereby Iago came
into possession of it after giving notice that he wanted it. Or we'll state
our position in modified form: Insofar as the accident is resented, the
audience has not felt the equivalent for the fate-guided that we have
in mind.

As we began with the subject of pollution (the subject of catharsis),
so here, when on the subject of wonder (the other great lure of tragedy),
we must return to it. Some psychoanalytic theorists have written of
instances where, in dreams, the various secretions of the human body
may become interchangeable. "The gist of the matter," Freud says, "is
the replacement of an important secretion . . . by an indifferent one."
And in accordance with this principle, we believe that some of the
"wonder" in this object derives from such ambiguities, which Othello
had been made to suggest remotely when he said to Desdemona, "I
have a salt and sorry rheum offends me. / Lend me thy handkerchief"
(3.4.49–50). Perhaps we are looking too closely; but the adjective "salt"
previously appeared in Iago's expression, "As salt as wolves in pride"
(3.3.409), used when first stirring Othello to jealousy. (*Oxford English Dictionary*—Pride: mettle or spirit in a horse, 1592; sexual desire,
"heat," esp. in female animals, 1604.) A related usage appears in act 2,
scene 1, where Iago, lying to Roderigo about Cassio, speaks of "his salt
and most hidden loose affection" (233–34).

In any case, we can see for a certainty how Shakespeare proceeds
to identify the handkerchief at the beginning of the fourth act, where
Iago shifts from talk of one "naked with her friend in bed" (4.1.3) to

talk of a hypothetical handkerchief. And the playwright bluntly rein-
forces the identification by having Othello fall "into an epilepsy" (47)
precisely from the strain of repeating, in great frenzy, this same drastic
association of ideas which Iago had imposed upon him. As with the
speech that ended, "Othello's occupation's gone," a simple "essayistic"
listing of associated topics underlies the expression here too. Indeed,
since the intensity of Othello's agitation calls properly for a disregard
of syntax, the speech at the beginning and the end does merely state
the topics to be associated in our minds:

> Lie with her? Lie on her? We say 'lie on her' when
> they belie her. Lie with her? 'Swounds, that's ful-
> some!   Handkerchief—confessions—handkerchief.
> . . . Pish! Noses, ears, and lips! Is't possible? Confess?
> Handkerchief? O devil! [*He falls down in a trance.*]
> (34–36, 40–41)

Shakespeare thus does all he can to make sure that this object be
the perfect materialization of the tension which the play is to exploit,
or "imitate." Again, note that it has both intimate and public aspects,
being sometimes tucked away, sometimes held in full view. It thus has
likewise the pontificating attributes best suited to such an object, and
to the kind of mock-revelation it is to supply.

Othello mostly carries on the work of endowing it, for the audience, with a full range of magic properties. Thus, while speaking of it
to Desdemona, in warning her belatedly against its loss, he uses such
resonant expressions as these, all turned in the direction of the magical: "Egyptian" . . . "to my mother" . . . "charmer" . . . "subdue my
father" . . . "but if she lost it" . . . "She, dying, gave it me" . . . "To lose't
or give't away were such perdition / As nothing else could match" . .
. "magic" . . . "A sibyl that had numbered in the world / The sun to
course two hundred compasses" (one should also contrive to implicate
the story meteorologically) . . . "prophetic fury" . . . "dyed in mummy"
. . . "conserved of maidens' hearts" (3.4.54–72). (And, he could add,
what all these ingredients are but deflections of: Vessel now standing for a hierarchic nest of roles; the public emblem of Desdemona's
privacy, which principle in turn is but the concentrate of Desdemona,
herself charismatically infused, visibly, tangibly, embodying the tensions, or mysteries of property, as thus personalized with a grace in

Desdemona that sets off, and is complemented by, the Othello-Iago grandeur).[4]

Truth, too, is implicated here, terrifyingly. In ownership as thus conceived, our play is saying in effect, there is also forever lurking the sinister invitation to an ultimate lie, an illusion carried to the edge of metaphysical madness, as private ownership, thus projected into realms for which there are no unquestionably attested securities, is seen to imply also, profoundly, ultimately, estrangement; hence, we may in glimpses peer over the abyss into the regions of pure abstract loneliness. All this condition follows from the fact that, if Cassio had wiped his beard with the handkerchief, as Iago lyingly said he had, then by the logic of the emotions, by the mad-magical-metaphysical principle of *falsus in uno, falsus in omnibus* (particularly when the supposed falsity involved a one that itself stood for an *all*), then this beard had by the same token obscenely scratched against Desdemona's cheek or pillow.

And, as projected absolutely, all culminated in a last despairing act of total loneliness. Hence, Othello's suicide said, in the narrative terms for the defining of essence, that investment as so conceived is essentially reflexive; for this great male lover, surprisingly, goaded by a man, ends on an imagery of self-abuse, doing himself violence as, having seized "by th' throat" a "circumcisèd dog," he "smote him thus" and thereby "threw a pearl away" that possessed a richness other than the tribal (5.2.364–65, 356). So Othello is "beside himself," as he must be, for one portion of himself to slay the other, and as he was "in principle," when Iago had kneeled with him in joint vows of vengeance, a posture that was a lie, when considered rationalistically in terms of the

---

[4] As for Rhymer's assertion that the handkerchief is trivial: Shakespeare answered it in advance when Desdemona, talking to Cassio about Othello's agitation, says that some such concern a, matters of state must have "puddled his clear spirit." (III, iv, 140.) For in such cases (we would call them hierarchically motivated) "Men's natures wrangle with inferior things,/Though great ones are their objects." In thus pleading for the emblematic, she puts heroically what Rhymer puts meanly. In effect, she says to the audience: "You, who have come here for tragic ennoblement, remember that Othello's tragic excess is noble." (Incidentally, our term "excess" here is used advisedly. The Greek word hubris, often used to designate the hero's "tragic flaw," is in many contexts translated "excess." Indeed, a river on the rampage is said to "hubrize," whereat we might relevantly recall Othello likening his mood to the violence of the "Pontick sea.")

intrigue only, but was profoundest truth, as regards its purely ritual design.

Thereafter, the play must be brought to a close swiftly. In a summarizing couplet Othello will say, as regards the underlying design of the major theme: "the kiss, the kill; the kill, the kiss." Cassio, the second theme, will reaffirm the hierarchic motive in its purity: "For he was great of heart" (371). And to Lodovico is entrusted the job of recapitulating the connotations generally: "O bloody period!" (366) . . . "the tragic loading of this bed" (372) . . . "O Spartan dog" (371) (for Iago is called a dog only a few lines after Othello's ingenious reference to another figure, a "circumcisèd dog," which the audience interpreted as an allusion to himself, had terminated startlingly in a twist of sense whereby the *allusion* could merge into an *act* here and now; and since he called this hypothetical figure a Turk [362], we might properly recall that Iago earlier, in banter with Desdemona, had referred to himself as a Turk [2.1.117]) . . . "the fortunes of the Moor . . . succeed on you" . . . "the censure of this hellish villain" . . . "The time, the place, the torture" (5.2.376–79) . . .

> Myself will straight aboard, and to the state
> This heavy act with heavy heart relate. (380–81)

VI

RELATED PLAYS BY SHAKESPEARE

This essay is not complete. For present purposes, it need not be, since to some extent one can also illustrate a procedure by noting what is still needed. In the *Dramatis Personae* section (III), bulky as it became, we didn't abide by our requirements, in getting the full recipe for the characters and noting how they mesh. And the relation between potentials and actualizations of plot could have been considered throughout the play.

The first and fifth sections deal with topical matters that point beyond the work. The second seeks to meet the tests of discussion in terms *of kind*. The third and fourth stress internal analysis of particulars.

We try to treat of diction indirectly, when considering an author's general diplomacy of presentation. But insofar as even a thorough job of this sort would leave some important stylistic matters still untreated, perhaps a special section (as in Aristotle's *Poetics*) would be required. For instance, we found no place in this scheme to discuss that passage where Iago, interpreting to Roderigo Cassio's reverential conversation with Desdemona, remarks: "Didst thou not see her paddle with the palm / of his hand? Didst not mark that?" (2.1.245–46). Why "paddle" is so good there, I can't figure out; but it is certainly genius in its devil-Iago felicity. On the other hand, we could probably have included under a full treatment of potentials the place where, after Othello has kissed Desdemona, Iago confides in an aside to the audience: "O, you are well tuned now, / But I'll set down the pegs that make this music, / As honest as I am" (2.1.196–98). Elsewhere Iago always builds up the potentials by stating explicitly what he intends to do. But at this point, using *imagery* rather than an *explicit statement* about his designs, he merely establishes the potential "in principle." He keeps things positively turned in the desired direction. But the dramatist would proceed too bluntly, without sufficient modulations into an act, if Iago here had stated exactly what he intended to do. This is a good illustration of a case where vague imagery is superior to clear ideas, in pointing the arrows. (Often novelists begin thus, when adumbrating a destiny. In the novel form, because of the slow developments possible to it, a much higher percentage of such potentials is admissible. But usually the Shakespearean kind of drama must point more "efficiently." And I believe this is the only case in the play where Iago states his designs in such purely "attitudinal" fashion.)

However, much of the stylistic element still not treated would fit well in a sixth section we would include, concerned with the respects in which the expressions of this play overlap upon the expressions in other plays by the same author.

For instance, do not our remarks on the ultimate interchangeability of Othello and Iago gain further support from the fact that, in *Titus Andronicus*, the figure of Aaron merges important aspects of the two? (Or, more accurately stated, the aspects have not yet been dissociated.) For there the black man is the villain: "this barbarous Moor, / This ravenous tiger, this accursèd devil" (5.3.4–5). He calls his own child "thick-lipped slave" (4.2.174), as Roderigo called Othello "thick-lips" (1.1.66). He calls himself a "black dog" (5.1.122), and at one place is referred to ironically as "pearl" (5.1.42), in a speech that next animadverts to the "base fruit of his burning lust" (5.1.43). We are told that

"Aaron will have his soul black like his face" (3.1.204). And the theme of the *handkerchief* seems here adumbrated gruesomely, in all that has to do with the lopping-off of *hands* (whereat, incidentally, we are reminded that, when we were first expecting Othello to ask Desdemona about the handkerchief, in a delay by a kind of semi-surprise, he says instead, "Give me your hand" [3.4.34]). And when Marcus wipes the tongueless Lavinia's tears with a handkerchief, Titus refers to it as a "napkin" (3.1.140). Such a cluster of details would require us eventually to look for a wider theory of terminology that included this work as well.

In the case of *Titus Andronicus*, the issue is complicated by scholars' doubts as to what portions of the work should be attributed to Shakespeare. But in considering the whole problem of hierarchy, as it came to a head in the speech on Othello's threatened loss of "occupation" if he lost Desdemona, we should examine, in *Troilus and Cressida,* Ulysses' speech on "the specialty of rule" (1.3.77). Here, after having proceeded in the usual fashion, implicating "The heavens themselves, the planets, and this centre" (85), in the human order, he concludes: "Take but degree away" (109) and "This chaos, when degree is suffocate, / Follows the choking" (125–26) (surely no accidental recurrence of such topics as are central to *Othello*). Again, Ulysses speaks of "appetite" as a "universal wolf" that "Must make perforce an universal prey, / And last eat up himself" (121, 123–24). Should we not here remember Iago's reference to "wolves in pride" (3.3.409), or Emilia: "They are all but stomachs, and we all but food. / They eat us hungrily, and when they are full, / They belch us" (102–3)—while she refers to jealousy as "a monster / Begot upon itself, born on itself" (156–57), thus in another way bringing us back to the theme of the reflexive. (Indeed, in the last analysis, what are we to make of the fact that the most perfect dramatic form *is* reflexive in nature, as things seem rounded out perfectly in ironic histories whereby the "engineer" is "Hoised with his own petard"?)

But references to hierarchy, in such terms as we have been considering, remind us also of Menenius Agrippa's allegory at the beginning of *Coriolanus*: "There was a time when all the body's members, / Rebelled against the belly" (1.1.85–86) . . . —whereat we are tossed back to *Titus Andronicus* again, in the reference to "Lucius, son to old Andronicus, / Who threats in course of this revenge to do / As much as ever Coriolanus did" (4.4.65–67).

Or, we find cause to bring in *Measure for Measure*, which seems surprisingly much like *Othello*, in the kind of tension it exploits (the use of a sexually "virtuous" character to suggest prurient thoughts), Angelo in that case taking upon himself the burden of the audience's illicit suggestibility, and the Duke having somewhat the role of impresario which Iago had carried in the apportionment of the tasks in his play. Or, further, the ambiguities of the black man, as implicated in Iago, point back likewise to the Sonnets, where "black beauty" (127.3) in a woman is celebrated with such agitation, in contrast with the poet's gallant delight in the love of a "fair" man.

Here is the area of speculation where "all the returns are not yet in." The purpose would be to go beyond the terminological integration of a single play, in search of an over-all motivational scheme that might account for the shifts from one work to another. I admit that here all tends to grow nebulous. I use the word deliberately, thinking of great gaseous masses out of which solid bodies presumably emerge. But we should keep peering into these depths too, the farthest reaches of our subject. For here must lie the ultimate secrets of man, as the symbol-using animal.

8

The Vegetal Radicalism of Theodore Roethke[1]

PERHAPS THE BEST WAY-IN IS THROUGH the thirteen flower poems that comprise the first section of *The Lost Son*. The two opening lyrics, "Cuttings" and "Cuttings (Later)," present the vital strivings of coronated stem, severed from parental stock. Clearly the imagistic figuring of a human situation, they view minutely the action of vegetal "sticks-in-a-drowse" as

> One nub of growth
> Nudges a sand-crumb loose,
> Pokes through a musty sheath
> Its pale tendrilous horn.

The second of the two (that sum up the design of this particular poetic vocation) should be cited entire, for its nature as epitome:

> This urge, wrestle, resurrection of dry sticks,
> Cut stems struggling to put down feet,
> What saint strained so much,
> Rose on such lopped limbs to a new life?
> I can hear, underground, that sucking and sobbing,
> In my veins, in my bones I feel it,—
> The small waters seeping upward,

---

[1] "The Vegetal Radicalism of Theodore Roethke" was first published in the *Sewanee Review*, vol. 58, no. 1 (Winter 1950): 68–108. © 1950, 1978 by the University of the South. Reprinted with permission of the editor.

> The tight grains parting at last.
> What sprouts break out,
> Slippery as fish,
> I quail, lean to beginnings, sheath-wet.

Severedness, dying that is at the same time a fanatic tenacity; submergence (fish, and the sheer mindless nerves of sensitive plants); envagination as a homecoming.

To characterize the others briefly: "Root Cellar" (of bulbs that "broke out of boxes hunting for chinks in the dark," of shoots "lolling obscenely," of roots "ripe as old bait"—a "congress of stinks"); "Forcing House" (a frantic urgency of growth, "shooting up lime and dung and ground bones" [. . .] "as the live heat billows from pipes and pots"); "Weed Puller" (the poet" "Under the concrete benches, / Hacking at black hairy roots,—/ Those lewd monkey-tails hanging from drainholes"); "Orchids" ("adder-mouthed" in the day, at night "Loose ghostly mouths/ Breathing"; "Moss-Gathering" (the guilt of moss-gathering); "Old Florist" (genre portrait, lines in praise of a man vowed to the ethics of this vegetal radicalism); "Transplanting" (a companion piece to the previous poem, detailing *operations* in ways that appeal to our *sensations*); "Child on Top of a Greenhouse" (the great stir below, while the young hero climbs, smashing through glass, the wind billowing out the seat of his britches); "Flower-Dump" (the picturesqueness greatly increased by a strong contrast, as the catalogue of the heap and clutter ends on a vision of "one tulip on top / One swaggering head / Over the dying, the newly dead"); "Carnations" (where the theme shifts to talk of "a crisp hyacinthine coolness, / Like that clear autumnal weather of eternity,"—a kind of expression as we shall later try to indicate, not wholly characteristic of this poet).

From this group we omitted one item, "Big Wind," because we want to consider it at greater length. It reveals most clearly how Roethke can endow his brief lyrics with intensity of action. Nor is the effect got, as so often in short forms, merely by a new spurt in the last line. No matter how brief the poems are, they progress from stage to stage. Reading them, you have strongly the sense of entering at one place, winding through a series of internal developments, and coming out somewhere else. Thus "Big Wind" first defines the situation (water shortage in greenhouse during storm) with a five-line rhetorical question. Next come fifteen lines describing the action appropriate to the scene, the strained efforts of those who contrive to keep the pipes supplied with hot steam. Then the substance of this account is restated in a figure that likens the hothouse to a ship riding a gale. And after eleven lines amplifying the one turbulent metaphor, there are two final lines wherein the agitation subsides into calm, with a splendid gesture of assertion. We cite the summarizing image, and its closing couplet:

> But she rode it out
> That old rose-house,
> She hove into the teeth of it,
> The core and pith of that ugly storm,
> Ploughing with her stiff prow,
> Bucking into the wind-waves
> That broke over the whole of her,
> Flailing her sides with spray,
> Flinging long strings of wet across the roof-top,
> Finally veering, wearing themselves out, merely
> Whistling thinly under the wind-vents;
> She sailed into the calm morning,
> Carrying her full cargo of roses.

The unwinding of the trope is particularly fortunate in suggesting transcendence because the reference to the "full cargo of roses," even as we are thinking of a ship, suddenly brings before us a vision of the greenhouse solidly grounded on terra firma; and this shift apparently helps to give the close its great finality. Thus, though you'd never look to Roethke for the rationalistic, the expository steps are here ticked off as strictly as in the successive steps of a well-formed argument. And thanks to the developmental structure of such poems, one never thinks of them sheerly as descriptive: they have the vigor, and the poetic morality, of action, of form unfolding.

To round out this general sampling, we might consider a poem written since the publication of *The Lost Son*. It is "The Visitant," and in contrast with "The Big Wind," which is robust, it possesses an undulance, a hushedness, a contemplative, or even devotional attitude, that makes of love an almost mystic presence. Roethke here begins with such a natural scene as would require a local deity, a genius loci, to make it complete. Hence, as the poem opens, the place described is infused with a numen or pneuma, a concentration of spirit just on the verge of apparition.

The work is divided into three movements: the first anticipatory, the third reminiscent, the second leading through a partly secular, yet gently pious, theophany. The mood is beautifully sustained.

The introductory stanza evokes a secretive spot by a stream, at a time of vigil ("I waited, alert as a dog") while, with a shift in the slight wind (figuring also a breath of passion?), "a tree swayed over water." Nine lines establishing expectancy, a state of suspension as though holding one's breath. ("The leech clinging to a stone waited.")

The second stanza is of the "coming." We quote it entire:

> Slow, slow as a fish she came,
> Slow as a fish coming forward,
> Swaying in a long wave;
> Her skirts not touching a leaf,
> Her white arms reaching toward me.
> She came without sound,
> Without brushing the wet stones,
> In the soft dark of early evening,
> She came,
> The wind in her hair,
>   The moon beginning.

The wind is thus there too, so the ambiguities of the advent may now presumably stand also for erotic movements sometimes celebrated by poets as a "dying." The swaying tree of the first stanza has its counterpart in the swaying "fish" of the second.

The third stanza is of the same scene, now retrospectively: The spirit is there still, but only through having been there, as in the first stanza it was there prophetically. Thus, at the end:

> A wind stirred in a web of appleworms;
> The tree, the close willow, swayed.

The peculiar mixture of tension and calm in this poem is of great felicity. The talk of "swaying," the key word repeated in each stanza, has its replica in the cradle-like rhythm. And the whole effect is gratifyingly idyllic, even worshipful.

As a comment on method, we might contrast "The Visitant" with another poem where Roethke was apparently attempting, in a somewhat "essayistic" manner, to trace the birth of Psyche. It begins

> The soul stirs in its damp folds,
> Stirs as a blossom stirs,
> Still wet from its bud-sheath,
> Slowly unfolding.

Cyclamen, turtle, minnow, child, seed, snail—each in turn is exploited to define how the spirit moves, "still and inward." The lines are the poet's *De Anima:* and the emergent soul is seen ultimately in terms of an inner Snail-Phallus. As there is a mind's eye, a spirit breath, an inner ear, so he would seem to conceive a kind of transcendent sex-within-sex, the essence of pure snailhood ("outward and inward" [. . .] "hugging a rock, stone and horn" [. . .] "taking and embracing its surroundings"). But though the poem is almost a review of Roethke's favorite images, it is far less successful in combining Psyche and Eros than "The Visitant." For it is weaker in action, development, being rather a series of repetitive attempts to arrive at the same end from different images as starting point. Roethke could have got to this poem by translating the theories of mystical theology directly into his own impressionistic equivalent. In "The Visitant" he has moved beyond such mere correspondences by introducing a dramatic situation and building around it. A comparison of the two poems shows how the essayistic (that moves toward excellence in Pope) could be but an obstruction to Roethke.[2]

We have said that the mention of "coolness" and "eternity" was not characteristic of Roethke's language. We meant this statement in the strictest sense. We meant that you will rarely find in his verse a noun ending in "-ness" or "-ity." He goes as far as is humanly possible in quest of a speech wholly devoid of abstractions.

To make our point by antithesis: glancing through Eliot's "Burnt Norton," we find these words:

> abstraction, possibility, speculation, purpose, deception, circulation, arrest, movement, fixity, freedom,

---

[2] Since this comment was written, the poem has been greatly revised, mainly by omission of about half its original contents. In its final form, there is a progression of but three images (blossom, minnow, snail) culminating in a catachresis ("music in a hood"). One epithet ("a light breather") is lifted from the body of the poem to be used as title. And the last six lines diminish gradually from ten syllables to two. The poem has thus finally been assimilated, has been made developmental.

compulsion, *Erhebung* without motion, concentration without elimination, completion, ecstasy, resolution, enchantment, weakness, mankind, damnation,
consciousness, disaffection, stillness, beauty, rotation,
permanence, deprivation, affection, plentitude, va-
cancy, distraction, apathy, concentration, eructation,
solitude, darkness, deprivation, destitution, property,
dessication, evacuation, inoperancy, abstention, ap-
petency, silence, stillness, co-existence, tension, im-
precision, temptation, limitation.

If Roethke adheres to his present aesthetic, there are more of such
expressions in this one Quartet of Eliot's than Roethke's Vegetal Radicalism would require for a whole lifetime of poetizing.

In one poem, to be sure, they do cluster. In "Dolor," lines detailing
the "tedium" of "institutions" (notably the schoolroom), we find, besides these two words: sadness, misery, desolation, reception, pathos,
ritual, duplication. But their relative profusion here explains their absence elsewhere, in verse written under an aesthetic diametrically opposed to such motives. (In one place he uses "sweetness" as a term of
endearment, yet the effect is more like an epithet than like an abstract
noun.)

Accordingly, in the attempt to characterize Roethke's verse, you
could profitably start from considerations of vocabulary. The motive
that we have in mind is by no means peculiar to this one poet. It runs
through modern art generally. And though few of the artists working
in this mode are interested in formal philosophy, the ultimate statement of the problem would take us back to some basic distinctions in
Immanuel Kant's *Critique of Pure Reason:* notably his way of aligning
"intuitions," "concepts," and "ideas."

If you perceive various sensations (of color, texture, size, shape,
etc.), you are experiencing what Kant would call "intuitions of sensibility." If you can next "unify" this "manifold" (as were you to decide
that the entire lot should be called a "tree"), in this word or name
you have employed a "concept of the understanding." "Intuitions" and
"concepts," taken together, would thus sum up the world of visible,
tangible, audible things, the objects and operations of our sensory experience. And because of their positive, empirical nature, they would
also present the sensible material that forms the basis of a poetic image

(however "spiritual" may be the implications of the poet's language in its outer reaches).

"Intuitions" and "concepts" belong to Kant's "Aesthetic" and "Analytic" respectively. But there is also a purely "Dialectical" realm, comprising "ideas of reason." This is the world of such invisible, intangible, inaudible things as "principles." The various "isms" would be classed as "ideas of reason." In carrying out an idea, men will at every turn deal with the concrete objects that are represented in terms of "intuitions" and "concepts"; yet the idea itself is not thus "empirical," but purely "dialectical," not available to our senses alone, or to measurement by scientific instruments.

Do not these distinctions of Kant's indicate the direction which poetry might take, in looking for a notable purification of language? If one could avoid the terms for "ideas," and could use "concepts" only insofar as they are needed to unify the manifold of "intuitions," the resultant vocabulary would move toward childlike simplicity. And it would be cleansed of such unwieldy expressions (now wielded by politicos and journalists) as: capitalism, fascism, socialism, communism, democracy (words unthinkable in Roethke's verse, which features rather: cry, moon, stones, drip, toad, bones, snail, fish, flower, house, water, spider, pit, dance, kiss, bud, sheath, budsheath, ooze, slip-ooze, behind which last term, despite ourselves, we irresponsibly keep hearing a child's pronunciation of "slippers").

Kant's alignment was designed primarily to meet the positivistic requirements of modern technological science. And since he himself, in the *Critique of Judgment,* talked of "aesthetic ideas," the issue is not drawn by him with finality. The modern lyric poet of imagistic cast might even with some justice think of himself as paralleling the scientific ideal, when he stresses the vocabulary of concrete things and sensible operations; yet the typical scientist language, with its artificially constructed Greek-Roman compounds, seems usable only in a few sophisticated gestures (as with the ironic nostalgia of a Laforgue). This much is certain, however: Whatever the complications, we can use the Kantian distinctions to specify a possible criterion for a purified poetic idiom. The ideal formula might be stated thus: *A minimum of "ideas," a maximum of "intuitions."* In this form, it can sum up the Roethkean aesthetic. (The concept would be admitted as a kind of regrettable necessity.)

For further placements (as regards the problems of linguistic purity set by urbanization), we might think of Dante's *De Vulgari Eloquentia*, Wordsworth's Preface to the Lyrical Ballads, and D. H. Lawrence's cult of the "physical" as contrasted with the "abstract."

Dante introduced the criterion of the infantile in the search for a purified poetic idiom. Choosing between learned Latin and the vernacular, he noted that the "vulgar locution" which infants imitate from their nurses is "natural" and "more noble," hence the most fit for poetry. But though he set up the infantile as a criterion for preferring Italian to a learned and "artificial" language, his criteria for the selection of a poetic vocabulary within Italian itself encompassed a quite mature medium. Thus, the ideal speech should be "illustrious, cardinal, courtly, and curial"; and in such a language, one would necessarily introduce, without irony or sullenness, many "ideas of reason." Indeed, what we have called the "infantile" criterion of selection we might rather call a search for the ideal mother tongue (had it not been for the Fall, Dante reminds us, all men would still speak Hebrew, the language of the Garden of Eden). That is, we could stress its *perfection*, its maturity and scope (its "mother wit"), rather than its *intellectual limitations* (though in the first great division of labor, separating those who specialize in being males and those who specialize in being females, the class of womanhood would seem to be the "more noble," so far as concerned its associations with the *medium* of poetry). The ideal language, we might say, was under the sign not of the child but of the Virgin Mother; though even, had the infant Jesus been the ultimate term for the motivation here, his essential kingliness would have been enough to derive the illustrious, cardinal, courtly, and curial from the infantile alone, as so modified.

In any case, as early as Dante's time, though prior to the upsurge of the industrial revolution, the division of labor was sufficiently advanced for him to assert that each kind of craftsman had come to speak a different language in the confusion of tongues caused during work on the Tower. The diversity of languages was thus derived from specialization, quite as with particular technical idioms today—and the higher the specialized activity, Dante says, the more "barbarous" its speech. His principle of selection could thus acquire a new poignancy later, when the learned language he had rejected had become an essential part of the vernacular itself, and when the relation between mother and child is not formally summed up in the infancy of a universal ruler (though, roundabout, in furtive ways, there are the modern mothers who are by implication ennobled, in giving birth to offspring they encourage to be child-tyrants).

By the time of Wordsworth's preface, after several centuries of progressively accelerated industrialization, the search for a principle of selection, for a "purified" speech, involves another kind of regression, a romantic reversion, not just to childhood simplicity, but also to "low and rustic life." For in this condition, "the essential passions of the heart [. . .] can attain their maturity, are less under restraint, and speak a plainer and more emphatic language." Though Wordsworth is talking of the rustic life itself, approaching the problem in terms of language (as Wordsworth's own explicit concern with selection entitles us to do), we should stress rather the imagery drawn from "the necessary character of rural occupations." Such imagery, he says, would be "more easily comprehended" and "more durable"; and by it "our elementary feelings" would be "more forcibly communicated," since "the passions of men are incorporated with the beautiful and permanent forms of nature."

Wordsworth is also explicitly considering another threat to poetry, the journalistic idiom which by now has almost become the norm with us, so that poets are repeatedly rebuked for not writing in a style designed to be used once and thrown away. Thus, on the subject of the causes that now act "with a combined force to blunt the discriminating powers of the mind," bringing about "a state of almost savage stupor," Wordsworth writes:

> The most effective of these causes are the great national events which are daily taking place, and the increasing accumulation of men in cities, where the uniformity of their occupations produces a craving for extraordinary incident, which the rapid communication of intelligence hourly gratifies.

"The rapid communication of intelligence hourly"; this is Wordsworth's resonant equivalent for "journalism." In such an expression he does well by it, even while recognizing its threat to poetic purity as he conceives of such purity.

He goes on to state his belief that, despite his preference for the ways of pretechnological nature as the basis for a poet's imagery, "If the time should ever come when what is now called Science [. . .]

shall be ready to put on [. . .] a form of flesh and blood, the Poet will lend his divine spirit to aid the transfiguration." Maybe yes, maybe no. Though concerned with the purification of vocabulary for poetic purposes, Wordsworth does not show (or even ask) how the technological idioms themselves can be likened to the language learned at the breast.

We should note, however, one major respect in which the terms of the new technology are in spirit a language close to childhood. For they have the quality of death rays and rocket ships, and other magical powers the thought of which can make the child wonder and in his imagination feel mighty. Indeed, the pageantry of the technological (the new lore of the giant-killers) can appeal to the infantile, long before there is any concern with such romances of love as, variously, concern Dante, Wordsworth, and Roethke, all three. What you put around a Christmas tree reflects no longer the mystery of the Birth, but the wonders of modern technological production. So, surprisingly, we glimpse how a poet's nursery language may be more mature than at first it may seem. It may be no younger than the adolescent in spirit, though this adolescence is on the side that leans toward the universal sensibility of childhood (and of the maternal) rather than toward the forensic, abstract, and journalistically "global."

A bridge-builder, no matter how special his language, has successfully "communicated" with his fellows when he has built them a good bridge. In this respect, the languages of the technological specialties confront a different communicative problem than marks the language of the specialist in verse. And even if, with Wordsworth, you believed in the ability of poetry to poetize any conditions that modern technology might bring into being, you could question whether this result could be got through the Wordsworth aesthetic. Hence, a century later, D. H. Lawrence, whose flower poems could have been models for Roethke, warns against a kind of abstraction from the physical that accompanies the progress of scientific materialism.

The doctrine infuses all of Lawrence's writings. But one can find it especially announced in his essay, "Men Must Work and Women as Well," reprinted in the Viking Portable. We think of statements like these: "Mr. Ford, being in his own way a genius, has realized that what the modern workman wants, just like the modern gentleman, is abstraction. The modern workman doesn't want to be interested in his job. He wants to be as little interested, as nearly perfectly mechanical, as possible." [. . .] The trend of our civilization is "towards a greater and greater abstraction from the physical, towards a further and further physical separateness between men and women, and between individual and individual." [. . .] Such displays even as "sitting in bathing suits all day on a beach" are "peculiarly non-physical, a flaunting of the body in its non-physical, merely optical aspect." [. . .] "He only sees his meal, he never *really* eats it. He drinks his beer by idea, he no longer tastes it." [. . .] "Under it all, as ever, as everywhere, vibrates the one great impulse of our civilization, physical recoil from every other being and from every form of physical existence." [. . .] "We can look on Soviet Russia as nothing but a logical state of society established in anti-physical insanity.—Physical and material are, of course, not the same; in fact, they are subtly opposite. The machine is absolutely material, and absolutely anti-physical—as even our fingers know. And the Soviet is established on the image of the machine, 'pure' materialism. The Soviet hates the real physical body far more deeply than it hates Capital." [. . .] "The only thing to do is to get your bodies back, men and women. A great part of society is irreparably lost: abstracted into non-physical, mechanical entities."

One may object to the particulars here; the *tendency* Lawrence discusses is clear enough. And though machinery (as viewed in psychoanalytic terms) may stand for the pudenda, and though the abstractions of technology and finance may even make for a compensatory overemphasizing of the sexual (Love Among the Machines), Lawrence was noting how the proliferation of mechanical means makes for a relative withdrawal, for a turn from intuitive immediacy to pragmatist meditation; hence his crusade against the intellect (and its "ideas").

As a novelist, Lawrence confronted this problem in all its contradictoriness. His crusade against the intellect was itself intellectual, even intellectualistic. Along with his cult of simplicity (which, going beyond Dante's infantile-maternal criterion and Wordsworth's rustic one, became a super-Rousseauistic vision of ideal savagery) there was his endless discussion of the issue. But though few modern novels contain a higher percentage of talk that might fall roughly under the heading of "ideas," (talk under the slogan, Down With Talk), in his verse he sought for images that *exemplified* the state of intuitive immediacy rather than expatiating on the problem of its loss. For whereas the novels dealt with people, the verse could treat of animals and inanimate beings that imagistically figured some generalized or idealized human motive (as with the heroic copulation of whales and elephants, or the social implications in the motions of a snapdragon). All told, he loquaciously celebrated the wisdom of silent things—for the yearning to see beyond the intellect terminates mystically in the yearning to regain a true state of "infancy," such immediacy of communication as would be possible only if man had never spoken at all (an aim often sought in sexual union, though both sexual barriers and the breaking of those barriers are preponderantly conditioned by the many "ideas of reason" that are the necessary result of language and of the social order made possible by language).

All told, then, we can see in Roethke's cult of "intuitive" language: a more strictly "infantile" variant of the Dantesque search for a "noble" vernacular; a somewhat suburban, horticulturist variant of Wordsworth's stress upon the universal nature of rusticity; and a close replica of Lawrence's distinction between the physical" and the "abstract."

With "prowess in arms" (*Virtus*) he is not concerned. The long poems, still to be considered, are engrossed with problems of welfare (Salus), though of a kind attainable rather by persistent dreamlike yielding than by moralistic "guidance of the will." *As for Venus,* in Roethke's verse it would seem addressed most directly to a phase of adolescence. The infantile motif serves here, perhaps, like the persuasive gestures of sorrow or helplessness, as appeal to childless girls vaguely disposed toward nursing. The lost son's bid for a return to the womb may thus become transformed into a doting on the erotic imagery of the "sheath-wet" and its "slip-ooze." And in keeping, there is the vocabulary of flowers and fishes (used with connotations of love), and of primeval slime.

We have considered representative instances of Roethke's poetic manner. We have viewed his choice of terms from the standpoint of three motivational orders as described by Kant. And we noted three strategic moments in the theory of poetic selectivity (Dante on the infantile, Wordsworth on the rustic, Lawrence on the physical) . Now let us ask what kind of selectivity is implicit in Roethke's flower images (with their variants of the infantile, rustic, and physical).

In particular, what is a greenhouse? What might we expect it to stand for? It is not sheer nature, like a jungle; nor even regulated nature, like a formal garden. It is not the starkly unnatural, like a factory. Nor is it in those intermediate realms of institutional lore, systematic thanatopses, or convenient views of death, we find among the relics of a natural history museum. Nor would it be like a metropolitan art gallery. It is like all these only in the sense that it is a museum experience, and so an aspect of our late civilization. But there is a peculiar balance of the natural and the artificial in a greenhouse. All about one, the lovely, straining beings, visibly drawing sustenance from ultimate, invisible powers—in a silent blare of vitality—yet as morbid as the caged animals of a zoo.

Even so, with Roethke the experience is not like going from exhibit to exhibit among botanic oddities and rarities. It is like merging there into the life-laden but sickly soil.

To get the quality of Roethke's affections, we should try thinking of "lubricity" as a "good" word, connoting the curative element in the primeval slime. Thus, with him, the image of the mire is usually felicitous, associated with protection and welcome, as in warm sheathlike forms. Only in moments of extremity does he swing to the opposite order of meanings, and think rather of the mire that can hold one a prisoner, sucking toward stagnation and death. Then, for a period of wretchedness, the poet is surprised into finding in this otherwise Edenic image, his own equivalent for Bunyan's slough of despond.

Flowers suggest analogous human motives quite as the figures of animals do in Aesop's fables (except that here they stand for relationships rather than for typical characters). The poet need but be as accurate as he can, in describing the flowers objectively; and while aiming at this, he comes upon corresponding human situations, as it were by redundancy. Here was a good vein of imagery to exploit, even as a conceit: that is, any poet shrewdly choosing a theme might hit upon hothouse imagery as generating principle for a group of poems. Yet in this poet's case there was a further incentive. His father had actually been a florist, in charge of a greenhouse. Hence, when utilizing the resources of this key image for new developments, Roethke could at the same time be drawing upon the most occult of early experiences. Deviously, elusively, under such conditions the amplifying of the theme could also be "regressive," and in-turning.

The duality, in the apparent simplicity, of his method probably leads back, as with the somewhat mystic *ars poetica* of so many contemporary poets, to the kind of order statuesquely expressed in Baudelaire's sonnet, *"Correspondances,"* on mankind's passage through nature as through "forests of symbols," while scents, sounds, and colors "make mutual rejoinder" like distant echoes that fuse "in deep and dusky unity."

In "Night Crow," Roethke states his equivalent of the pattern thus:

> When I saw that clumsy crow
> Flap from a wasted tree, A shape in the mind rose up:
> Over the gulfs of dream
> Flew a tremendous bird
> Further and further away
> Into a moonless black,
> Deep in the brain, far back.

One could take it as a particularized embodiment of a general principle, an anecdote of *one* image standing for the way of all such images, which are somehow felt twice, once positivistically, and once symbolically.

In this connection, even one misprint becomes meaningful. In "Weed Puller," he writes of flowers "tugging all day at perverse life." At least, that is the wording presumably intended. The line actually reads: "tugging at pre-verse life." In Roethke's case, this was indeed a "pre-verse" way of life. In the flowers, their hazards and quixotisms, he was trained to a symbolic vocabulary of subtle human relations and odd strivings, before he could have encountered the equivalent patterns of experience in exclusively human terms. As with those systems of pure mathematics which mathematicians sometimes develop without concern for utility, long before men in the practical realm begin asking themselves the kind of questions for which the inventor of the pure forms has already offered the answers; so, in the flower stories, the poet would be reverting to a time when he had noted these forms before he felt the need for them, except vaguely and "vatically."

The opposite way is depicted in a drawing (we falsely remembered it as a caricature) printed in *L'Illustration* and reproduced in Matthew Josephson's book on Emile Zola. It is entitled "Zola Studying Railroad Life on a Locomotive; Drawing Made on the Scene, During a Voyage Between Paris and Le Havre, When He Was Seeking the Living Documents for his Novel, *La Bête Humaine*." Zola, standing, stiffly erect, between the cabin and the coal car, dressed in a semiformal attire that would suit a doctor or a lawyer of that time, is all set to make the trip that would supply him with certain required documentary observations for a "scientific" novel.

What, roughly, then, is the range of meaning in Roethke's flowers? In part, they are a kind of psychology, an emphatic vocabulary for expressing rudimentary motives felt, rightly or wrongly, to transcend particular periods of time. Often, in their characters as "the lovely diminutives," they are children in general, or girls specifically. When we are told in "The Waking" that "flowers jumped / Like small goats," there is a gracing of the bestial motive referred to as "the goat's mouth" in the "dance" of "The Long Alley," section three. The preconscious, the infantile, the regressive, the sexual—but is there not in them a further mystery, do they not also appeal as a pageantry, as "positions of pantomime," their natural beauty deriving added secular "sanctification" from the principle of hierarchy? For the thought of flowers, in their various conditions, with their many ways of root, sprout, and blossom, is like the contemplation of nobles, churchmen, commoners, peasants (a world of masks). In hothouse flowers, you confront, enigmatically, the representation of status. By their nature flowers contribute grace to social magic—hence, they are insignia, infused with a spirit of social ordination. In this respect they could be like Aesop's animals, though only incipiently so. For if their relation to the social mysteries were schematically recognized, we should emerge from the realm of intuitions (with their appropriate "aesthetic ideas") into such "ideas of reason" as a Pope might cultivate ("whatever is, is right" [. . .] "self-love, to urge, and reason, to restrain" [. . .] "force first made conquest, and that conquest, law" [. . .] "order is heaven's first law" [. . .] "that true self-love and social are the same"). A Roethke might well subscribe to some such doctrine, notably Pope's tribute's to "honest Instinct"—but in terms whereby the assumptions would, within these rules of utterance, be themselves unutterable.

Other of the shorter poems should be mentioned, such as "My Papa's Waltz," which is dashing, in its account of a boy whirled in a dance with his tipsy father; "Judge Not," a more formalistic statement than is characteristic. Some of the short pieces come close to standard magazine verse. "The Waking" risks a simple post-Wordsworthian account of pure joy. And "Pickle Belt," recounting "the itches / Of sixteen-year-old lust," while not of moment in itself, in its puns could be listed with the crow poem, if one were attempting to specify systematically just how many kinds of correspondence Roethke's images draw upon. But mostly, here, we want to consider the four longer pieces: "The Lost Son," "The Long Alley," "A Field of Light," and "The Shape of the Fire."

Roethke himself has described them as "four experiences, each in a sense stages in a kind of struggle out of the slime; part of a slow spiritual progress, if you will; part of an effort to be born." At the risk of brashness, we would want to modify this description somewhat. The transformations seem like a struggle less to be born than to avoid being undone. Or put it thus: The dangers inherent in the regressive imagery seem to have received an impetus from without, that drove the poet still more forcefully in the same direction, dipping him in the river who loved water. His own lore thus threatened to turn against him. The enduring of such discomforts is a "birth" in the sense that, if the poet survives the ordeal, he is essentially stronger, and has to this extent *forged himself* an identity.

The four poems are, in general, an alternating of two motives: regression, and a nearly lost, but never quite relinquished, expectancy that leads to varying degrees of fulfillment. In "Flight," the first section of "The Lost Son," the problem is stated impressionistically, beginning with the mention of death ("concretized," of course, not in the name of "death," which would be at the farthest an abstraction, at the nearest an abstraction personified, but circumstantially: "At Wood-lawn I heard the dead cry"). When considering the possible thesaurus of flowers, we were struck by the fact that, in the greenhouse poems, there was no overt reference to the use of flowers for the sickroom and as funeral wreaths. Deathy connotations are implicitly there, at the very start, in the account of the Cuttings, which are dying even as they strain heroically to live. And there is the refuse of "Flower Dump." But of flowers as standing for the final term of human life, we recall no mention. Roethke has said that he conceives of the greenhouse as symbol for "a womb, a heaven-on-earth." And the thought of its vital internality, in this sense, seems to have obliterated any conscious concern with the uses to which the products of the florist's trade are put. In any case his present poem, dealing with a lyric "I" in serious danger, fittingly begins in the sign of death.

The opening stanza, however, contains not merely the theme of deathlike stagnation. There is also, vaguely, talk of moving on:

> Snail, snail, glister me forward,
> Bird, soft-sigh me home.

In the society of *this* poet's lowly organisms, there is a curative element, incipiently. And throughout the opening section, with its images of rot and stoppage, there is likewise a watching and waiting. Even a rhetorical *question* is, after all, subtly, in form a *quest*. Hence the call for a sign ("Out of what door do I go, / Where and to whom?"), though it leads but to veiled oracular answers ("Dark hollows said, lee to the wind, / The moon said, back of an eel," etc.), transforms this opening section ("The Flight") into a hunt, however perplexed. Thus the stanza that begins "Running lightly over spongy ground," is followed by one that begins, "Hunting along the river." The section ends on a riddle, in terms contradictory and symbolic, as befits such utterance. The connotations are Sphinx-like, oracular; the descriptions seem to touch upon an ultimate wordless secret. What is the answer? Put all the disjunct details together, and; for our purposes, we need but note that the object of the quest is lubricitous (in the mode of furtive felicity). End of Section One.

Section Two: The Pit—nine lines, in very subdued tonality, about roots—in general an amplification of the statement that the poet's search is radical. We cite the passage entire, since it is a splendid text for revealing the ingenuity of Roethke as Rhetorician:

> Where do the roots go?
> Look down under the leaves.
> Who put the moss there?
> These stones have been here too long.
> Who stunned the dirt into noise?
> Ask the mole, he knows.
> I feel the slime of a wet nest.
> Beware Mother Mildew.
> Nibble again, fish nerves.

Considered as topics ("places" in the traditional rhetorical sense), the stanza could be reduced to a set of images that variously repeat the idea of the deep-down, the submerged, the underground. Roots [. . .] "under the leaves" [. . .] stones long buried beneath moss [. . .] the sound of moles burrowing [. . .] these are details that variously repeat the same theme in the first six lines. The last three, while similar in quality (the dank, hidden, submerged, within), add a further development: the hint of incipience, ambiguously present in lines seven and eight ("I feel" and "Beware"), comes clear in line nine: "Nibble again, fish nerves."

For the moment confining ourselves to the first six: note how this series of lyric images is dramatized. Surprisingly, much is done by a purely Grammatical resource. Thus, the underlying assertion of the first couplet (this mood is like roots, like under-the-leaves) is transformed into a kind of "cosmic" dialogue, split into an interchange between two voices. The next restatement (it is like moss-covered stones) is broken into the same Q-A pattern, but this time the answer is slightly evasive, though still in the indicative ("These stones have been here too long," a "vatic" way of suggesting that the mood is like stones sunken, and covered heavily). The third couplet (it is like the sound of moles burrowing) is introduced by a slightly longer and more complex form of question. (The first was where-roots-go, the second who-put-moss-there, and the third is who-stunned-dirt-into-noise, a subtly growing series). Also the answer is varied by a shift into the imperative ("ask the mole").

All this questioning and answering has been as if from voices in the air, or in the nature of things. But the turn in the last three lines is announced by a shift to the lyric "I" as subject. The image of mildew is made not only personal, but "essential," by being named as "Mother Mildew." The indicative in line seven ("I feel") shifts to imperatives in lines eight and nine ("Beware" and "Nibble"); but whereas in the first of these imperatives the topic (mildew) appears as object of the command, in the second the topic ("fish nerves") is given as subject.

Thus, though the stanza is but a series of restatements, it has considerable variety despite the brevity of the lines and despite the fact that each sentence ends exactly at the end of a line. And the Grammatical shifts, by dramatizing the sequence of topics, keep one from noting that the stanza is in essence but a series of similarly disposed images (symbolizing what Roethke, in a critical reference, has called "obsessions").

As for the closing line, the more one knows of the fish image in Roethke's verse, the more clearly one will feel the quality of incipience in the nibbling of "fish nerves."

The third section, "The Gibber," might (within the conditions of a lyric) be said to culminate in the *act* that corresponds to the attitude implicit in the opening scene. It is sexual, but reflexively so: the poet is disastrously alone. Listening, "by the cave's door," the poet hears an old call ("Dogs of the groin / Barked and howled," and sinister things, in the mood of a Walpurgisnacht, call for his yielding in a kind of death). Against a freezing fear, there is a desperate cry for infantile warmth. "I'm cold. I'm cold all over. Rub me in father and mother." The reflexive motif is most direct, perhaps, in the lines: "As my own tongue kissed / My lips awake." The next lines (Roethke has called them a kind of Elizabethan "rant") culminate in shrilly plaintive inventory of the hero's plight:

> All the windows are burning! What's left of my life?
> I want the old rage, the lash of primordial milk!
> Goodbye, goodbye, old stones, the time-order is going,
> I have married my hands to perpetual agitation,
> I run, I run to the whistle of money,
>> the lamentation being summed up, by a break in a different rhythm:
> Money money money
> Water water water

Roethke's Vegetal Radicalism is not the place one would ordinarily look for comments on the economic motive. Yet you can take it as a law that, in our culture, at a moment of extreme mental anguish, if the sufferer is accurate there will be an accounting of money, too. It will be at least implicit, in the offing—hence with professional utterers it should be explicit. So, the agitation comes to a head in the juxtaposing of two liquidities, two potencies, one out of society, the other universal, out of nature. (And in the typical dichotomy of aestheticism, where the aesthetic and the practical are treated as in diametrical opposition to each other, does not this alignment encourage us to treat art and the rational as antitheses? For if money is equated with the practical and the rational, then by the dialectics of the case art is on the side of an "irrational," nonmonetary Nature.)

After a brief rush of scenic details (cool grass, a bird that may have gone away, a swaying stalk, the shadow of a worm, undirected clouds— all developed by the Grammatico-Rhetorical method we noted in "The Pit") the section ends on a world of white flashes, which the poet finally characterizes as of the essence of cinder "falling through a dark swirl." Into the funnel: down the drain. The dream-death. Though the second section was entitled "The Pit," here actually is the poem's abysmal moment, after which there must be a turning.

Hence, Section Four, "The Return." Recovery in terms of the "father principle." Memory of a greenhouse experience: out of night, the coming of dawn, and the father. After the description of the dark, with the roses likened to bloody clinkers in a furnace (an excellently right transition from the ashes theme at the close of the previous section to the topic of steam knocking in the steam pipes as a heralding of the advent), the movement proceeds thus (note that the theme of white is also kept and appropriately transformed):

> Once I stayed all night.
> The light in the morning came up slowly over the white
> Snow.
> There were many kinds of cool
> Air.
> Then came steam.
> Pipe-knock.
> Scurry of warm over small plants.
> Ordoung! ordnung!
> Papa is coming!

We happen to have seen a comment which Roethke wrote on this passage, and we cite it for its great use in revealing his methods:

> Buried in the text are many little ambiguities that are not always absolutely necessary to know. For instance, the "pipe-knock." With the coming of steam, the pipes begin knocking violently, in a greenhouse. But "Papa," or the florist, often would knock his own pipe (a pipe for smoking) on the sides of the benches, or the pipes[. . .] . Then, with the coming of steam (and "papa"—the papa on earth and heaven being blended, of course) there is the sense of motion in the greenhouse—my symbol for the whole of life, a womb, a heaven on-earth.

Recalling De Quincey's comments on the knocking at the gate after the murder scene in Macbeth, and recalling that we have just been through a "suicide" scene, might we not also include, among the connotations of this sound, the knock of conscience? Particularly in that the return to the paternally (or "superegoistically") rational is announced in terms of an admonition (*Ordnung! ordnung!*)—and we should note, on the side, as a possible motivating factor in Roethke's avoidance of ideational abstraction, that this German word for order is one of his few such expressions, though here it has practically the force of an imperative verb, as "sweetness," in another context, was not in function an abstract noun but rather a name, an epithet of personal endearment. (Roethke has said that he had in mind the father's Prussian love of discipline, as sublimated into the care of flowers; and he wanted to suggest that the child, as a kind of sleepy sentry, "jumped to attention at the approach.")

The final section (sans title) amplifies the subject of illumination (that we have followed from darkness, through "white flashes," to dawn). But its opening suggests its unfinishedness (as with a corresponding midstage in Eliot's *Four Quartets*):

> It was beginning winter,
> An in-between time [. . .]

And after talk of light (and reflexively, "light within light") the poem ends on his variant of religious patience and vigil, as applied to the problem of superegoistic rationality:

> A lively understandable spirit
> Once entertained you.
> It will come again.
> Be still.
> Wait.

Again the funnel, in the narrowing-down of the lines. But not, this time, the funnel of darkness that had marked the end of Section Three. There has been a coming of light after darkness, a coming of warmth after cold, a coming of steam after powerlessness, a coming of the father and of his superegoistic knock—and now at the last a fuller coming is promised. And within the rules of this idiom, "understandable" is a perfect discovery. It is perhaps the only "intellectualistic" word (the only word for "rational") that would not have jarred in this context.

All four of the long poems follow this same general pattern. Thus, "The Long Alley" begins with a sluggish near-stagnant current (from sources outside the poem we have learned that this brooding, regressive stream is "by the edge of the city"). Direction is slight but it is there:

A river glides out of the grass. A river or serpent.
A fish floats belly upward,
Sliding through the white current,
Slowing turning,
Slowly.

But the way out is roundabout, a way in. Next there are apostrophes to an absent "kitten-limp sister," a "milk-nose," a "sweetness I cannot touch," as our hero complains that he needs "a loan of the quick." And the stanza ends narcissistically. In the third section, after a plea again reflexively addressed ("Have mercy, gristle") there is an agitated "dance," a simulated *argutatio lecti* (Catullus 6, 11) conveyed somewhat impressionistically, symbolically, enigmatically. After this "close knock," again struggling toward warmth ("Sweet Jesus, make me sweat," a musically felicitous cry, in that the last word is an umlaut modification of the first: sw——t sw——t), there is a somewhat idealistic vision, a gentle name-calling, in which girls ("tenderest") are "littlest flowers" with "fish-ways," while the talk of light ("drowsing in soft light" [. . .] "Light airs! A piece of angels!") prepares for the closing stanza with its talk of warmth. The progress of the sections might be indicated by these summarizing lines: (1) "My gates are all caves"; (2) "Return the gaze of a pond" (an ingenious inversion of the Narcissus image); (3) "I'm happy with my paws"; (4) "The tendrils have me"; (5) "I'll take the fire."

The shortest of the four long poems, "A Field of Light," begins similarly with "dead water" and evolves into a celebrating of "the lovely diminutives," while the poet walked "through the light air" and "moved with the morning." The mood is most succinctly conveyed, perhaps, in the line: "Some morning thing came, beating its wings." The poem is in three stages: (1) The "dead water," but almost pleasantly, a "watery drowse"; (2) the question-like and questionable act ("Alone, I kissed the skin of a stone; marrow-soft, danced in the sand"); (3) Exhilarated sense of promise.

However, despite the alleviation here, in the final poem, "The Shape of the Fire," the entire course is traveled again. Indeed, if we can accept the ingenious suggestion of one commentator (Mr. Bill Brown, a student in a poetry class of Roethke's), the line "An old scow bumps over black rocks" is about as regressive as human memory could be. It suggests to him "the heart-beat of the mother," as the fetus might hear it dully while asleep in the amniotic fluid, the ultimately regressive baptismal water. (Such reminiscence from prenatal experience would be a purely naturalistic equivalent for the "clouds of glory" that Wordsworth Platonically saw the infant memory "trailing" from its "immortal" past.) In any case, at the very least, the line suggests the state of near-stagnation, a stream so low that a boat of even the shallowest draught scrapes bottom. And after a reflexive section ("My meat eats me," while before this there was but half a being, "only one shoe" and "a two-legged dog"), and a section on vigil ("The wasp waits"), and one to announce awakening promise ("Love, love sang toward," a pleasantly impressionistic idyll of early happiness at the age when childhood was merging into puberty), now the boat can again figure, but transfigured, to assert direction:

> To stare into the after-light, the glitter left on the lake's surface,
> When the sun has fallen behind a wooded island;
> To follow the drops sliding from a lifted oar,
> Held up, while the rower breathes, and the small boat drifts quietly shoreward;
> To know that light falls and fills, often without our knowing,
> As an opaque vase fills to the brim from a quick pouring,
> Fills and trembles at the edge yet does not flow over,
> Still holding and feeding the stem of the contained flower.

Thus, at the end, the cut flower with which the book began. And though the image of the gliding boat (as contrasted with the bottom-scraping one) has moved us from stagnation to felicity (here is a resting on one's oars, whereas Shelley's enrapt boats proceed even without a rower), note that the position of the poet in the advancing craft is backward-looking. Still, there is testimony to a delight in seeing, in contrast with Baudelaire's poem on Don Juan crossing the Styx, similarly looking back: Charon steered the craft among the shades in torment,

> *Mais le calme héros, courbé sur sa rapière,*
> *Regardait le sillage et ne daignait rien voir.*

As for all the possible connotations in light, as used in the final illumination of the Roethke poem, spying, we may recall that the last line of the second section was: "Renew the light, lewd whisper."

All told, to analyze the longer poems[3] one should get the general "idea" (or better, mood or *attitude*) of each stanza, then note the succession of images that actualize and amplify it. Insofar as these images are of visible, tangible things, each will be given its verb, so that it have sufficient incidental vividness. But though, in a general way, these verbs will be, either directly or remotely, of the sort that usually goes with the thing (as were dogs to bark, or pigs to grunt), often there may be no verb that, within the conditions of the poem, the noun objectively requires.

For instance, at the beginning of "The Shape of the Fire," there is a line "A cracked pod calls." As an image, the cracked pod belongs here. It is dead, yet there is possibility of a new life in it. Hence, topically, the line might have read simply "A cracked pod." Similarly, there is the line, "Water recedes to the crying of spiders." If spiders stand in general for the loathsome, the line might be translated formalistically: "The principle of fertility is overcome by the principle of fear." However, though pods may rattle, and spiders may weave or bite or trap flies, pods don't call and spiders don't cry.[4]

In considering this problem most pedestrianly, we believe we discovered another Rhetorical device which Roethke has used quite effectively. That is, whenever there is no specific verb required, Roethke resorts to some word in the general category of *communication*. Thus, though "shale loosens" and "a low mouth laps water," a cracked pod

---

[3] Incidentally, there are records of "The Long Alley," and "The Shape of the Fire," as read by the author (Poetry Room, Harvard College Library: The *Harvard Vocarium Records*). Some of the tonalities are strikingly like those in the record of Joyce's readings from *Anna Livia Plurabelle*.

[4] Though our "formalistic" version here would be acceptable as a "first rough approximate of the meaning, there are further possibilities in the offing. Psychoanalytically, insects are said to figure often in dreams as surrogates for children. And in an earlier version of the lyric, "Judge Not,," a reference to "the unborn, starving in wombs, curling" had used the same image: the fetuses were described as curling "like dried spiders." The line, "Water recedes to the crying of spiders" might thus, if trailed far enough, bring us into the region of the birth trauma, as figuring an infant cry at separation from the placental bath. And since the line is immediately followed by "An old scow bumps over black rocks," the child as crying spider could fit well with the already cited interpretation of this second line. (The matter of the order would not be all-important. In the elliptical style, the stages of a development may readily become reordered.)

calls, spiders and snakes cry, weeds whine, dark hollows, the moon and salt say, inanimate things answer and question and listen or are listened to. To suggest that one thing is of the same essence as another, the poet can speak of their kissing, that is, being in intimate communion (a device that has unintended lewd overtones at one point where the poet, to suggest that he is of the essence of refuse, says, "Kiss me, ashes," a hard line to read aloud without disaster, unless one pauses long on the comma). The topic is clouds? Not clouds that billow or blow, but that would just *be?* The line becomes: "What do the clouds *say?*"

There are possible objections to be raised against this sort of standard poetic personifying, which amounts to putting a communicative verb where the copula is normally required, or perhaps one could have no verb at all. But it does help to suggest a world of natural objects in vigorous communication with one another. The very least these poetic entities do is resort to "mystic participation." The poet's scene constitutes a society of animals and things. To walk through his idealized Nature is to be surrounded by figures variously greeting, beckoning, calling, answering one another, or with little groups here and there in confidential huddles, or strangers by the wayside waiting to pose Sphinx-like questions or to propound obscure but truth-laden riddles. One thus lives as though ever on the edge of an Ultimate Revelation. And as a clear instance of the method as a device for dramatization, consider a passage in "The Lost Son," which, topically considered, amounts to saying, "This is like dying in a weedy meadow, among snakes, cows, and briars," but is transformed by communicative verbs thus:

> The weeds whined,
> The snakes cried,
> The cows and briars
> Said to me: Die.

Somewhat incongruously, we have expressed the underlying statement in terms of simile. Yet similes are very rare in Roethke. The word "like" appears, unless we counted wrong, but three times in the four long poems; "as," used as a synonym for "like," occurs not much oftener. Indeed, one way to glimpse the basic method used here is to think, first, of simile, next of metaphor, and then (extrapolating) imagine advancing to a further step. Thus, one might say, in simile, "The toothache is like a raging storm," or metaphorically, "The rag-

ing tooth." Or "beyond" that, one might go elliptically, without logical connectives, from talk of toothache to talk of ships storm-tossed
at sea. And there one would confront the kind of *ars poetica* in which
Roethke is working.

The method may be further extended by the use of a word in accordance with pure pun-logic. Thus, if in "reach" you hear "rich," you
may say either "reach me" or "rich me" for the reach that enriches.
("Rich me cherries a fondling's kiss.")

Much of this verse is highly auditory, leaving implicit the kind of
tonal transformations that Hopkins makes explicit. And often the el-
lipses, by weakening strictly logical attention, induce the hearer to
flutter on the edge of associations not surely present, but evanescently
there, and acutely evocative (to those who receive poetry through ear
rather than eye).

Surely in a poem still to be considered, "God, give me an ear" is a
barely audible extending of the sense in "God, give me an ear" (here
the tonal effect is surest if approached through visual reading); and
in the same poem, "tree" and "time" have been "irresponsibly" transposed, with suggestive effects, thus: "Once upon a tree / I came across
a time." "The ear's not here / Beneath the hair" (in the opening stanza
of Section Two, "The Shape of the Fire") is tonal improvising, which
leads one vaguely to think of the ear as surrogate for a different order
of receptacle. And in the lines immediately following ("When I took
off my clothes / To find a nose, / There was only one / For the waltz
of To, / The pinch of Where"), besides "to" in the sense of "toward,"
there are suggestions of "two" (here present in its denial, but the meaning most prominent to an auditor who does not have the page before
him), while there are also connotations of "toe" as in toe dance (which
in turn stirs up a belfry of bat-thoughts when we consider the narcis-
sistic nature of this particular "toe dance," recall similarly the "last
waltz with an old itch" in "The Long Alley," and then flutter vaguely
in the direction of the infantile "polymorphous perverse" as we think
of the briskly and brilliantly conveyed corybantics in the brief lyric,
"My Papa's Waltz," the account of a child snatched up and whirled ri-
otously in a dance by his tipsy father). And since "t" is but an unvoiced
"d," we believe that, on the purely tonal level, "God" may be heard
in "gate." In any case, in "The Long Alley" there are but three lines
elliptically separating "this smoke's from the glory of God" and "My
gates are all caves."

Though Roethke's lines often suggest spontaneous simplicity, and though the author has doubtless so cultivated this effect that many lines do originally present themselves in such a form, on occasion the simplicity may be got only after considerable revision. Thus, in an early version of "The Shape of the Fire," there had been a passage:

> The wind sharpened itself on a rock. It began raining.
> Finally, having exhausted the possibilities of common sense,
> I composed the following: [. . .]

"It began raining" was later changed to "Rain began falling." An earlier version had been, It rains offal, but this, though more accurate, had to be abandoned presumably because of its closeness to "It rains awful." Eventually the reference to rain was dropped completely—for if the essence perhaps better omitted. The second and third lines were changed to: "Finally, to interrupt that particular monotony, / I intoned the following." Both versions thus sounded self-conscious and formalistic, whereas the final version is naively vatic:

> The wind sharpened itself on a rock;
> A voice sang: [. . .]

The "I" of the versifier at work has been replaced by a cosmically communicating "voice."

Stanley Kunitz, reviewing *The Lost Son and Other Poems* in *Poetry*, justly observes:

> The sub-human is given tongue; and what the tongue
> proclaims is the agony of coming alive, the painful
> miracle of growth. Here is a poetry immersed in the
> destructive element. It would seem that Roethke has
> reached the limits of exploration in this direction,
> that the next step beyond must be either silence or
> gibberish. Yet the daemon is with him, and there is
> no telling what surprises await us.

Reverting, in this connection, to our talk of intuitions, concepts, and ideas, and recalling the contrast between the vocabulary of these poems and that of Eliot's *Quartets*, we might put the matter thus, in seeking to characterize Roethke's "way":

There is a realm of motives local to the body, and there is a possible ultimate realm, of motives derived from the Ground of All Existence, whatever that may be. In between, there are the motives of man-made institutions, motives located generally in the terminologies of technology, business, politics, social institutions, and the like. Here are many titular words, abstractions, "ideas of reason," to name the realm midway between the pains, pleasures, appetites of the individual body and the Universal Ground.

Since the body emerges out of nature, its language seems closer to the ultimate realm of motives than do the abstractions of politics. However, the pleasures, pains, fears, and appetites of the body are all, in subtle ways, molded by the forms of the political realm; hence what we take as "nature" is largely a social pageant in disguise. But the vocabulary of traffic regulation is alien to the "noble" speech of childhood emerging from infancy. (Parker Tyler, so often excellent in his insights, convincingly points to the "aristocratic" element in Charlie Chaplin's child motif. And Nietzsche, in his *Genealogy of Morals,* might better be talking of a child when he cites, as his example of the aristocrat, the person whose resentment "fulfils and exhausts itself in an immediate reaction, and consequently instills no *venom*," while this resentment "never manifests itself at all in countless instances," since "strong natures" cannot "take seriously for any length of time their enemies, their disasters, their misdeeds," and forgive insult simply because they forget it.)

In any case, as tested by the simplicity of the "natural" vocabulary, the forensic sub-Ciceronian speech is "barbaric." And though we may, by roundabout devices, disclose how politics, through the medium of family relations, affects the child's experiences at the very start of life, the ideas are certainly not there—hence the "purest" vocabulary is that of the emotionally tinged perceptions (the "intuitions of sensibility").

But how much of human motivation is the poet to encompass in his work? Or, next, how much is he to encompass directly, explicitly, and how much by implication, by resonances derived from sympathetic vibrations in the offing? There comes a time, in life itself, when one flatly confronts the realm of social hierarchy (in the scramble to get or to retain or to rewardingly use money, position, prestige). Will one, then, if a poet, seek to discuss these motives just as flatly in his poetic medium? Or will he conceive of poetry by antithesis (as so many of our poets, now teaching poetry, place it in direct antithesis to their means of livelihood, hence contending that the "aesthetic" is precisely what the "didactic" is not)?

It is not for critics, in their task of characterization, to legislate for the poet here. It is enough to note that there are several methods of confronting the problem, and that Roethke's work has thoroughly and imaginatively exemplified one of them. He meets, in his way, the problem which Eliot met in another by expanding his poetry to encompass theological doctrine, and thereby including a terminology which, within the Roethke rules, would be ungainly (unless used ironically—and children don't take to irony). Eliot added winds of doctrine. Roethke "regressed" as thoroughly as he could, even at considerable risk, toward a language of sheer "intuition."

However, our use of the Kantian pattern will deceive us, if we conclude that such intuitions really do remain on the level of "sensation." For not only do they require the "concept" (as a name that clamps intellectual unity upon a given manifold of sensations); they also involve motives beyond both sense and understanding: we go from intuitions of a sensory sort to intuitions of a *symbolic* sort (as with the motives of the "unconscious" which make variously for fusion, confusion, diffusion). In scholastic usage, by "intuition" was meant the recognition that something is as it is. The term was not restricted merely to sense perception. Not only would color, sound, or odor be an intuition; but there would be intuition in the recognition that two and two make four, or that a complex problem is solvable in a certain way, or that a science rests on such and such principles. Applied to modern poetizing, the word might also be used to name a situation when the poet chooses an expression because it feels right, though he might not be able to account for the choice rationalistically. The judgment would rely on such motives as are, under favorable circumstances, disclosable psychoanalytically, or may be idealistic counterparts of hierarchic motives (a "beauty" involving *social* distinction between the noble and the vulgar, mastery and enslavement, loveliness and crassness); and there may also be included here responses to the incentives of pun-logic.

Thus, if in one context the image of a flower can stand for girlhood in general, and if in other contexts a fish can have similar connotations, in still other contexts flower and fish can be elliptically merged (for reasons beyond the fact that the one can be plucked and the other caught), producing what we might call a "symbolic intuition" atop the purely sensory kind. Or we might consider such idealistic mergers a symbolist variant of the "aesthetic idea" (as distinguished from "ideas of reason" in the more strictly rationalist sense). They are "fusions" if you like them, "confusions" if you don't, and "diffusions" when their disjunction outweighs their conjunction. And they are a resource of all our "objectivist" poets who use "positive" terms to elicit effects beyond the positive. Particularly we are in a purely idealistic (rather than positivistic) order of intuitions when we extend the motifs, going from fish to water and from flower to warmth or light, and hence from water to motions that are like pouring, or from flowers to motions that are like swaying (so that a sudden influx of birds might be a symbol descending through the fish-water-girl line, or a swaying tree might descend through the flower-warmth-girl side of the family, the two branches being reunited if the tree is swaying over water, after talk of a swaying fish).

This is the liquescent realm in which Roethke operates. But by eschewing the "rationality" of doctrine (a "parental principle" which one may situate in identification with father governments or mother churches, or with lesser brotherhoods themselves authoritatively endowed), the poet is forced into a "regressive" search for the "superego," as with talk of being "rubbed" [. . .] "in father and mother." Eliot could thus "rub" himself in dogma, borrowed from the intellectual matrix of the church. But Roethke, while avidly in search of an essential parenthood, would glumly reject incorporation in any cause or movement or institution as the new parent (at least so far as his poetic idiom is concerned). Hence his search for essential motives has driven him back into the quandaries of adolescence, childhood, even infancy. Also, as we have noted elsewhere, the search for essence being a search for "first principles," there is a purely technical inducement to look for definition in terms of one's absolute past; for a *narrative* vocabulary, such as is natural to poetry, invites one to state essence (priority) in *temporal* terms, as with Platonist "reminiscence"—an enterprise that leads readily to "mystic" intuitions of womb heaven and primeval slime

The battle is a fundamental one. Hence the poems give the feeling of being "eschatological," concerned with first and last things. Where their positivism dissolves into mysticism, they suggest a kind of phallic pantheism. And the constant reverberations about the edges of the images give the excitement of being on the edge of Revelation (or suggest a state of vigil, the hope of getting the girl, of getting a medal, of seeing God). There is the pious awaiting of the good message—and there is response to "the spoor that spurs."

Later poems repeat the regressive imagery without the abysmal anguish. Thus, in "Praise to the End!" our hero, expanding in a mood of self-play ("What a bone-ache I have" [. . .] "Prickle-me" [. . .] "I'm a duke of eels" [. . .] "I'll feed the ghost alone. / Father, forgive my hands" [. . .] "The river's alone with its water. / All risings / Fall") follows with snatches of wonder-struck childhood reminiscence mixed with amative promise:

> Mips and ma the mooly moo,
> The like of him is biting who,
> A cow's a care and who's a coo?—
> What footie does is final.

He ends by asking to be laved in "ultimate waters," surrounded by "birds and small fish." And a line in the opening ("stagnation") section of "The Long Alley" ("My gates are all caves") is now echoed in an altered form happy enough to serve in the upsurge of the final stanza: "My ghosts are all gay." Along with the nursery jingles, some lines are allowed to remain wholly "unsimplified":

> It's necessary, among the flies and bananas, to keep a
> constant vigil, For the attacks of false humility take
> sudden turns for the worse.

"Where Knock Is Open Wide" is a placid depiction of childhood sensibility and reverie, in a post-Blake, post-Crazy Jane medium close to the quality of Mother Goose, with many "oracular" lines, in Sibylline ways near to the sound of nonsense. The poem progresses thus: thoughts about a kitten (it can "bite with its feet"); lullaby ("sing me a sleep-song, please"); dreams; the parents; an uncle that died ("he's gone for always" [. . .] "they'll jump on his belly"); singing in infancy; an owl in the distance; "happy hands"; a walk by the river; a fish dying in the bottom of a boat ("he's trying to talk"); the watering of roses ("the stems said, Thank you"). But "That was before. I fell! I fell!" Thereafter, talk of "nowhere," "cold," and "wind," the death of birds, followed by a paradigm of courtship: "I'll be a bite. You be a wink. / Sing the snake to sleep." And finally: "God's somewhere else. / [. . .] Maybe God has a house. / But not here."

The title, though borrowed, is extremely apt in suggesting the kind of motivation which Roethke would reconstruct for us. Recall, for instance, Coleridge's distinction between "motive" and "impulse" (a distinction later revised somewhat in his theological writings, but clearly maintained while his reasoning was in accordance with the aesthetic of "The Eolian Harp"). By "motives" Coleridge meant such springs of action as derive from "interests." Bentham's utilitarian grounds of conduct, for instance, would be "motives." But "impulse" is spontaneous, a response free of all *arrière-pensée,* all ulterior purpose. Here, the answer would be as prompt as the call, would be one with the call. In the world of the adult Scramble, such a state of affairs would indeed be a happy hunting ground for hunters—and whoever is in fear of loss must, at the startling knock on the door, hasten to hide the treasure before opening. However, in the theme of childhood reverie, as ideally reconstructed, the poet can contemplate an Edenic realm of pure impulsiveness.

Yet perhaps it is not wholly without *arrière-pensée.* For is the motivation here as sheerly "regressive" as it may at first seem? Is not this recondite "baby-talk" also, considered as rhetoric, one mode of lover-appeal? And considering mention of the wink and the bite in connection with talk of the fall, might we not also discern an outcropping of double meanings, whether intended or not, in reference to a "mooly man" who "had a rubber hat" and "kept it in a can"? The cloaking of the utterance in such apparent simplicity may not prevent conception of an adult sort here, particularly as the lines are followed immediately by talk of "papa-seed."

What next? The placid evocation of childhood might well be carried further (the period of anguished evocations has presumably been safely weathered). Further readings in mystic literature could lead to more developments in the materializing of "spirit" (as in "The Visitant"). But a turn toward the doctrinaire and didactic (the socially "global" as against the sensitively "ultimate") would seem possible only if all this poet's past methods and skills were abandoned.

There is another already indicated possibility, however, which we might define by making a distinction between "personification" and "personalization." And we might get at the matter thus:

Though Roethke has dealt always with very concrete things, there is a sense in which these very concretions are abstractions. Notably, the theme of sex in his poems has been highly generalized, however intensely felt. His outcries concern erotic and autoerotic motives generically, the Feminine as attribute of a class. Or, though he may have had an individual in mind at the moment, there is no personal particularization in his epithets, so far as the reader is concerned. He courts

Woman, as a Commoner might court The Nobility (though of course he has his own "pastoral" variants of the courtly, or coy, relation).

But because his imagism merges into symbolism, his flowers and fishes become Woman in the Absolute. That is what we would mean by "personification."

By "personalization," on the other hand, we would mean the greater *individualizing* of human relations. (Not total individualizing, however, for Aristotle reminds us that poetry is closer than history to philosophy, and philosophy seeks high generalization, whereas historical eras, in their exact combination of events, are unique.) In any case, we have seen one recent poem in which Roethke has attempted "personalization" as we have here defined it: "Elegy for Jane (My student, thrown by a horse)." Though not so finished a poem as "The Visitant," it conveys a tribute of heartfelt poignancy, in a pious gallantry of the quick confronting the dead, and ending:

> If only I could nudge you from this sleep,
> My maimed darling, my skittery pigeon.
> Over this damp grave I speak the words of my love:
> I, with no rights in this matter,
> Neither father nor lover.

Perhaps more such portraits, on less solemn occasions, will be the Next Phase? Meanwhile, our salute to the very relevant work that Roethke has already accomplished, both for what it is in itself, and for its typicality, its interest as representative of one poetic way which many others are also taking, with varying thoroughness.[5]

---

[5] I had long planned to revise this article (which was published sixteen years ago). I had hoped to bring it up to date by discussing Theodore Roethke's later work, and to make some of my original observations more precise. But I have finally decided to leave the piece just as it was, along with its several fumblings. For I cannot better contrive to suggest the rare, enticing danger of Roethke's verse, as I felt it then, and still do. Looking back now, in the light of his body's sudden yielding into death, can we not see the end vatically foretold when the connotations of vibrancy in his image of the fish become transformed into connotations of putrescence? And, if the heart stops at a moment of total mystic drought, do we not find that moment ambiguously and even jauntily introduced, through the delightful lines on 'The Sloth"? With both this essay and the one following, my memory of voice and manner is imperious in ways that I have not at all been able to indicate.

9

Policy Made Personal: Whitman's Verse and Prose-Salient Traits[1]

THE PLAN HERE IS TO CONSIDER FIRST Whitman's statement of policy in *Democratic Vistas*. Even there his views of history, society, and nature are personalized somewhat. But the full job of personalization is done in his *Leaves of Grass*, which is to be considered in a second section. And finally, since both of these sections are general in their approach, a third section will put the main stress upon one poem, "When Lilacs Last in the Dooryard Bloom'd." Throughout, however, we shall proceed as much as practicable by the inspection and comparison of contexts. Unless otherwise specified, all words or expressions in quotation marks are Whitman's. (Perhaps a better subtitle would be: On Interrelations Among Key Terms in Whitman's Language.)

I. VISTAS

The design of Whitman's essentially idealistic thought is neatly indicated in the three stages of historical unfolding he assigns to "America, type of progress." This alignment seems a handy place to spin from.

The first stage was embodied in the Declaration of Independence, the Constitution, and its Amendments. It "was the planning and putting on record the political foundation rights of immense masses of people [. . .] not for classes, but for universal man."

[1] Reprinted with permission from *Leaves of Grass, One Hundred Years After*. 1955. Ed. Milton Hindus. Stanford, CA: Stanford University Press, 1966. 74–108. © 1983 by Milton Hindus.

220

The second stage is in the "material prosperity" that resulted after the democratic foundations had been laid: "wealth, labor-saving machines [. . .] a currency," etc.

A third stage, still to come but "arising out of the previous ones," would bring about the corresponding "spiritualization" of the nation's sheerly material development.

The first and third stages are in the realm of idea, or spirit. The second stage is in the realm of matter. Writing his essay a few years after the close of the Civil War, he placed himself and his times in stage two, a time marked by "hollowness at heart," lack of honest belief in "the underlying principles of the States," "depravity of the business classes," while all politics were "saturated in corruption" except the judiciary ("and the judiciary is tainted"). "A mob of fashionably dressed speculators and vulgarians [. . .] crude defective streaks in all the strata of the common people [. . .] the alarming spectacle of parties usurping the government [. . .] these savage, wolfish parties[2] [. . .] delicatesse [. . .] polite conformity [. . .] exterior appearance and show, mental and other, built entirely on the idea of caste" [. . .] in sum: "Pride, competition, segregation, vicious wilfulness, and license beyond example, brood already upon us."

One could cite many other statements of like attitude. But the idealistic design of his thinking permitted him without discouragement to take full note of such contemporary ills, and perhaps even to intensify them as one step in his essay. For against the dissatisfactions of the present, he could set his "planned Idea," a promise for the future. Since "the fruition of democracy, on aught like a grand scale; resides altogether in the future," he would "presume to write, as it were, upon things that exist not, and travel by maps yet unmade, and a blank." Thus, the technically negative nature of the "fervid and tremendous Idea" is made in effect positive, so far as *personal* considerations go. By seeing contemporary conditions in terms of future possibilities, in "vistas" that stressed "results to come," he could treat "America and democracy as convertible terms," while having high hopes for both.

---

[2] Since political parties are themselves a point at which present organization and future promises meet, we might expect him to waver here, and he does. Thus: "I advise you to enter more strongly yet into politics"—but also "Disengage yourself from parties." The wavering even invades his syntax, when he says that he knows "nothing grander, better exercise, better digestion, more positive proof of the past, the triumphant result of faith in human kind, than a well-contested American national election."

He says, "It is useless to deny" that "Democracy grows rankly up the thickest, noxious, deadliest plants and fruits of all—brings worse and worse invaders—needs newer, larger, stronger, keener compensations and compellers"; but, in line with post-Hegelian promises, he saw in any greater challenge the possibility of a correspondingly greater response.

In sum, then, as regards the basic design of his thinking, the Vistas found elation in a project for the "spiritualization of our nation's wealth." (He likes words like "richness" and "luxuriance," words that readily suggest both material and spiritual connotations, gaining resonance and persuasiveness from this ambiguity.) "The extreme business energy, and this almost maniacal appetite for wealth prevalent in the United States, are parts of amelioration and progress," he says (in terms that, of all things, suggest Marxist patterns of thought with regard to material development under capitalism); but a different order of motives is manifest in the statement (he would probably have said "promulgation") of his ideal: "offsetting the material civilization of our race [. . .] must be its moral civilization."

If, by very definition, one can view all materially acquisitive behavior in terms of ideal future fulfillment, it follows that the poet could contemplate with "joy" the industrious industrial conquest of the continent. Not until late in life (after his paralytic stroke) does this "ecstatic" champion of the "athletic" and "electric" body turn from identification with the feller of trees (as in *Song of the Broad-Axe*) to identification with the fallen tree itself (as in *Song of the Redwood-Tree*), though he always had fervid ways of being sympathetic to child, adult, and the elderly. Our point is simply that the zestfulness of the typical Whitman survey could follow logically from his promissory principle, his idealization of the present in terms of the future.

Halfway between the realm of materials amassed by his countrymen's "oceanic, variegated, intense, practical energy" and the realm of spirit, or idea, we might place his cult of the sturdy human body, its "spinal," "athletic," "magnetic" qualities and the "appetites" that make for "sensuous luxuriance." (As the recipe also called for a male type "somewhat flushed," we dare wonder ironically whether his notion of the perfect "manly" temperament also concealed a syndrome of symptoms, an idealistic recognition, without realistic diagnosis, of the hypertension that must have preceded his paralysis. Surely, prophesying after the event, we might propose that Whitman's headlong style should involve high blood pressure as its nosological counterpart.)

For an "over-arching" term here, Whitman could speak of "nature" in ways that, while clearly referring to the materialistic on one side, also have pontificating aspects leading into a Beyond, along Emersonian lines. (In fact, toward the close of the *Vistas,* one is often strongly reminded of Emerson's earlier and longer transcendentalist essay, *Nature,* first published in 1836.) Democracy was Nature's "younger brother," and Science was "twin, in its field, of Democracy in its." But such equations were idealistically weighted to one side: for while "Dominion strong is the body's; dominion stronger is the mind's."

Somewhere between the grounding of his position in time, and its grounding in eternity, there is its grounding in terms of personality (two of his special words to this end being "identity" and "nativity").

For grounding in time, one obvious resource is a contrast with some previous time (antithesis being one of the three major stylistic resources, as we are informed in Aristotle's *Rhetoric*). But though "democracy" is thus pitted against "feudalism," Whitman admonishes that "feudalism, caste, ecclesiastical traditions [. . .] still hold essentially, by their spirit, even in this country, entire possession of the more important fields." For "All smells of princes' favors." And "The United States are destined either to surmount the gorgeous history of feudalism, or else prove the most tremendous failure of time." Whereas now we tend to think of Shakespeare as poignantly at the crossing between the feudal and the modern, the antithetical genius of Whitman's scheme led him to say: "The great poems, Shakespeare included, are poisonous to the idea of the pride and dignity of the common people." For though Shakespeare was conceded to be "rich," and "luxuriant as the sun," he was the "artist and singer of feudalism in its sunset." In contrast, Whitman called: "Come forth, sweet democratic despots of the west." And being against "parlors, parasols, piano-songs," he matched his praise of the "divine average" by words against "the mean flat average." Declaring, "We stand, live, move, in the huge flow of our age's materialism," he quickly added, "in its spirituality." And "to offset chivalry," he would seek "a knightlier and more sacred cause today." In so far as the claims of traditional culture were effete and pretentious (and "for a single class alone"), he admonished against "Culture"—and later, apologists of Nazism could take over the tenor of his slogans by the simple device of but half-hearing him.

As for eternity: His attacks upon traditional ecclesiastical forms were stated in terms of an "all penetrating Religiousness" that vigorously proclaimed its scorn of "infidels." He always identified democracy with what he called "the religious element," however that might differ from the norms of conventional churchgoing (and it differed greatly, as regards its relation to his cult of the "body electric").

His notion of "succession" (a eulogistic word that sounds nearly like his very dyslogistic one, "secession") we have already touched upon. It is in line with the typical nineteenth-century doctrine of permanent evolution, into ever higher forms, a design that falls in the realm of time, so far as the manifestations of history are concerned, but that would be above time, in so far as its operation were constant. "The law over all, the law of laws, is the law of successions; that of the superior law, in time, gradually supplanting and overwhelming the inferior one." Fittingly, the essay reverts to this "law" in the paragraph-long closing sentence, where America, "illumined and illuming," is saluted in terms of the ideal future, when she will have "become a full-formed world, and divine Mother, not only of material but spiritual worlds, in ceaseless succession, through time—the main thing being the average, the bodily, the concrete, the democratic, the popular, on which all the superstructures of the future are to permanently rest."

The lines succinctly assemble the main components of his Ideal Matrix, or "divine Mother." (And what better words for an *ending* than "permanently rest"?) But the personalizing of this "Mother" (the democratic creed) will take on attributes not strictly germane to either the politics of democracy or the personality of motherhood.

The logic of his terminology centers in his emphasis upon the individual person ("rich, luxuriant, varied personalism"). In proclaiming that "the ripeness of religion" is to be sought in the "field of individuality," and is "a result that no organization or church can ever achieve," he automatically sets up the dialectical conditions for a principle of division matched by a principle of merger. While his brand of "personalism" will "promulge" the "precious idiocrasy and special nativity and intention that he is, the man's self," all such individual selves are to be joined in democratic union, or "cohesion"; and the result is "ensemble-Individuality," an "idiocrasy of universalism," since the "liberalist of today" seeks "not only to individualize, but to universalize." And while the aim is to formulate "one broad, primary, universal, common platform," he says, "even for the treatment of the universal" it is good "to reduce the whole matter to the consideration of a single self, a man, a woman, on permanent grounds."

In sum: There is "the All, and the idea of All, with the accompanying idea of eternity" (the poems will speak of "the all-mother," and the "Mother of All"). And in silence, in the "solitariness of individuality," one can "enter the pure ether of veneration," to "commune" with the "mysteries" and the "unutterable." Or (as regards the timely), "individuality" and its "unimpeded branchings" will "flourish best under imperial republican forms" (for the grandeur of spiritualized democratic "expansion" will make for an "empire of empires").[3]

So we have the "idea of perfect individualism," of "completeness in separation," with its dialectical counterpart: "the identity of the Union at all hazards." Not only must man become "a law, a series of laws, unto himself"; also "the great word Solidarity has arisen." The "individualism, which isolates" is but "half only," and has for its other half the "adhesiveness or love, that fuses." Thus, both of these trends (contradictory or complementary?) are "vitalized by religion," for you in your solitude can "merge yourself" in the "divine." (A sheerly politico-economic variant of this dialectic for fitting the one and the many together is in his statement: "The true gravitation-hold of liberalism in the United States will be a more universal ownership of property, general homesteads, general comfort-a vast, inter-twining reticulation of wealth.")

But if the three stages are handiest as a way into the underlying idealistic *design* of Whitman's thinking, perhaps the most succinct *doctrinal* passage is this:

"Long ere the second centennial arrives, there will be some forty to fifty States, among them Canada and Cuba. When the present century closes, our population will be sixty or seventy millions. The Pacific will be ours, and the Atlantic mainly ours. There will be daily electric communication with every part of the globe. What an age! What a land! Where, elsewhere, one so great? The individuality of one nation must then, as always, lead the world. Can there be any doubt who the

---

[3] "It seems as if the Almighty had spread before this nation charts of imperial destinies, dazzling as the sun yet with many a deep intestine difficulty, and human aggregate of cantankerous imperfection—saying, lo! the roads, the only plans of development, long and varied with all terrible balks and ebullitions." Might not these lines serve well as motto for his *Song of the Open Road,* and as indicating a notable ingredient in his cult of the roadway generally?

leader ought to be? Bear in mind, though, that nothing less than the mightiest original non-subordinated SOUL has ever really, gloriously led, or ever can lead."

Then comes the very important addition, in parentheses: "This SOUL-its other name, in these Vistas, is LITERATURE." Then follows typical talk of "ideals," and of a "richness" and "vigor" that will be in letters "luxuriantly."

The essay's opening reference to "lessons" attains its fulfillment in these views of Whitman on the didactic or moralizing element in his ideal literature, its social service in the training of personalities. By the "mind," which builds "haughtily," the national literature shall be endowed "with grand and archetypal models," as we confront the "momentous spaces" with a "new and greater personalism," aided by the "image-making faculty."

Here, then, is the grand mélange: "Arrived now, definitely, at an apex for these Vistas," Whitman sees in dream "a new and greater literatus order," its members "always one, compact in soul," though "separated [. . .] by different dates or States." This band would welcome materialistic trends both "for their oceanic practical grandeur" and "for purposes of spiritualization." And by "serving art in its highest," such a "band of brave and true" would also be "serving God, and serving humanity."

Such a literature would affirm the "fervid comradeship," "adhesive love," between man and man that Whitman so strongly associated with his evangel of democracy. And as for woman, the "prophetic literature of these States," inspired by "Idealism," will train toward "the active redemption of woman," and "a race of perfect Mothers."

He offers four portraits of ideal female types: a servant, a businesswoman, a housewife, and a fourth that we might call a grand old lady ("a resplendent person [. . .] known by the name of the Peacemaker"). It is particularly relevant to look more closely at this fourth figure.

Whitman has just been referring to "that indescribable perfume of genuine womanhood [. . .] which belongs of right to all the sex, and is, or ought to be, the invariable atmosphere and common aureola of old as well as young." The next paragraph begins: "My dear mother once described to me [. . .] ," etc. Eighty years old, this fourth type of personality that his mother is said to have described was a kind of grandmotherly Whitman. She had lived "down on Long Island." She was called the "Peacemaker" because of her role as "the reconciler in the

land." She was "of happy and sunny temperament," was "very neigh-
borly"; and she "possessed a native dignity." "She was a sight to look
upon, with her large figure, her profuse snow-white hair (uncoifed by
any head-dress or cap) [. . .] and peculiar personal magnetism"—and
when reading the word on which the recital of his four "portraits"
ends, might we not fittingly recall that Whitman's poems are dotted
with references to the "electric" and "magnetic" ?

We consider this all of a piece: the steps from "the indescribable
perfume of genuine womanhood," to "My dear mother, "to the grandmotherly figure in which this entire set of portraits culminates (and
thus toward which the series might be said to have tended from the
start). Frankly, we stress the point for use later, when we shall be considering the scent of lilacs, "the perfume strong I love," mentioned in
commemoration of the poet's great dead democratic hero. Meanwhile,
a few more considerations should be noted, before we turn from his
prose statement of policy to its personalizing in his verse.

We should recall his principle of cultural *ascesis* (the notion that
"political democracy" is "life's gymnasium [. . .] fit for freedom's ath-
letes," and that books are "in highest sense, an exercise, a gymnast's
struggle"). It is easy to see how thought thus of a *studious athleticism*
might, on the one hand, proclaim "health, pride, acuteness, noble aspirations" as the "motive-elements of the grandest style"; on the other
hand, given the "appetites" that go with such exercisings and exer-
tions, the poet might find no embarrassments in equating democracy
with the grandeur of ever expanding empire.

But there is one mild puzzler to be noted with regard to the
Whitman cult of democratic expansionism. When saying that the
"spine-character of the States will probably run along the Ohio, Mis-
souri and Mississippi rivers, and west and north of them, including
Canada," he describes the "giant growth" thus: "From the north, intellect, the sun of things, also the idea of unswayable justice, anchor
amid the last, the wildest tempests. From the south the living soul, the
animus of good and bad, haughtily admitting no demonstration but
its own. While from the west itself comes solid personality, with blood
and brawn, and the deep quality of all-accepting fusion."

One automatically waits for some mention of the east here-but there
is none. Interestingly enough, one of the poems ("To the Leaven'd Soil
They Trod") discusses "vistas" and *ends* on a similar design:

> The prairie draws me close, as the father to bosom broad
>   the son,
> The Northern ice and rain that began me nourish me to the
>   end,
> But the hot sun of the South is to fully ripen my songs.

Presumably, the poet mentions only three points of the compass, since he was born in the East, and was so *tendency-minded*. And perhaps, since the Vistas contain the equation, "the democratic, the west," the East is, by the dialectical or rhetorical pressures of antithesis, the vestigially and effetely "feudal," except in so far as it is inspirited by the other three sources of motivation. (South, by the way, is in Whitman's idiom the place from which "perfume" comes. As regards North, we must admit to not having fully done our lessons at this time.)

A few further points, before turning from the *Vistas to the Leaves:*

In connection with the notion of guidance through literature, Whitman writes: "A strong mastership of the general inferior self by the superior self, is to be aided, secured, indirectly, but surely, by the literatus." And we might remember this word "mastership," to puzzle over it, when in the poem of the "Lilacs" he says: "Yet the lilac with mastering odor holds me," even though we may not quite succeed in fitting the passages to each other.

And we should note Whitman's words in praise of a strong political digestion, since they bear so directly upon the relation between his design and his doctrine: "And as, by virtue of its cosmical, antiseptic power, Nature's stomach is fully strong enough not only to digest the morbific matter always presented [. . .] but even to change such contributions into nutriment for highest use and life—so American democracy's."

Such faith in the virtues of a healthy appetite is doubtless implied when, on the subject of political corruption, Whitman assures us that "the average man [. . .] remains immortal owner and boss, deriving good uses, somehow, out of any sort of servant in office." (Or, more generally, here is the encouragement of the sprout-out-of-rot principle.) At every step along the way, whatever tax is levied by their Lordships, Favoritism and Dishonesty, it remains a fact that Democracy does build its roads and schools and courthouses—and the catalogue of its accumulations, when listed under one national head, becomes truly "oceanic" and "over-arching." But at the mention of catalogues, we might well turn to a survey of the verse.

II. Leaves

No two opening lines of a poet's work ever indicated more clearly the sheer dialectics of a position than in the "Inscription" with which *Leaves of Grass* begins:

> One's-Self I sing, a simple separate person,
>   Yet utter the word Democratic, the word En-Masse.

For a poet generally so voluble, this entire poem of eight lines is astoundingly efficient. Note how the second stanza (proclaiming that "physiology" is equally important with "physiognomy" and "brain," and that he sings "The Female equally with the Male") ambiguously translates his code into its corresponding *sexual* terms. Then, in the third stanza, he merges life, work, God's laws, song, and his futuristic cult of the present, all under the sign of strong motives and hopeful attitudes:

> Of Life immense in passion, pulse, and power,
> Cheerful, for freest action form'd under the laws divine,
> The Modern Man I sing.

The main themes that are lacking are: (1) his merging of birth and death in the allness of the mother, and (2) his stress upon perpetual passage (what would Whitman do without the word "pass" or its components: "I come and I depart" ?). And, of course, the notable equating of democracy with the love of male for male is manifest here only if we read as a double *entendre* his words about Male and Female (though most likely they were not so intended).

In his "oceanic" accumulation of details, the catalogues that characterize most of his longer poems (such as *Salut au Monde!*), there is the "spiritualization" of matter. Here is his primary resource for those loosely yet thematically guided associations of ideas which enable him to "chant the chant of dilation or pride." Of such spiritual possessions, he has "stores and plenty to spare." Who was more qualified than Whitman to write a *Song of the Exposition* with its closing apostrophe to the "universal Muse" and maternal Union: "While we rehearse our measureless wealth, it is for thee, dear Mother"? In effect, the Whitman catalogue locates the rhetorical device of amplification in the very nature of things.

It is possible that, after long inspection, we might find some "over-arching" principle of development that "underlies" his typical lists. Al-ways, of course, they can be found to embody some principle of repeti-tive form, some principle of classification whereby the various items fall under the same head (as with the third stanza of the *Salut*, for instance, which races through a scattering of nationalities, with a scat-tering of details hastily allotted to each: the Australians "pursuing the wild horse," the Spanish semipleonastically dancing "with castanets in the chestnut shade," "echoes from the Thames," "fierce French liberty songs," and so on, ending with the Hindoo "teaching his favorite pupil the loves, wars, adages, transmitted safely from poets who wrote three thousand years ago"). Some critic might also discern a regular canon of *development* in such "turbulent" heapings. Meanwhile, in any case, there are the many variations by internal contrast (as with varying rhythm and length of line, or as the variations on "out of" the open-ing lines of "Out of the Cradle Endlessly Rocking": out of, over, down from, up from, out from, from the, from your, from under, from those, from such, borne hither). And even where *epanaphora* is extreme, there are large tidal changes from stanza to stanza, or rhetorical forms that suggest the shifting of troops in military maneuvers.

> Melange mine own [. . .] Omnes! Omnes! [. . .] the
> word En-Masse[. . .] the One formed out of all [.
> . .] toward all [. . .] made ONE IDENTITY [. . .]
> they shall flow and unite [. . .] merge and unite[. . .]
> to merge all in the travel they tend to [. . .] All, all,
> toward the mystic ocean tending [. . .] Song of the
> Universal [. . .] O public road[. . .] to know the uni-
> verse itself as a road [. . .] along the grand roads of the
> universe [. . .] All, all, for immortality [. . .] it makes
> the whole coincide [. . .] I become part of that, what-
> ever it is [. . .].

—such lines state the "omnific" principle behind the aggregates of the catalogues.

To such a cult of the "divine average," good will and good cheer sometimes come easy:

> "I love him, though I do not know him . .. . I know
> not where they go; / But I know they go toward the
> best [. . .] surely the drift of them is something grand

> [. . .] illustrious every one [. . .] Great is Wealth—
> great is Poverty [. . .] Flaunt away, flags of all nations!
> [. . .] I believe materialism is true, and spiritualism is
> true—I reject no part [. . .] I do not see one imperfec-
> tion in the universe [. . .] the venerealee is invited."[4]

He thinks happily of "easily written, loose-fingered chords," and "the loose drift of character, the inkling through random types." He assures us, in hale and hearty camaraderie: "I turn the bridegroom out of bed, and stay with the bride myself"—nay more: "My voice is the wife's voice." His gusto suggests something like a cheerleader's at a chess tournament when he proclaims: "Hurrah for positive science! Long live exact demonstration!" But the tactics are much subtler when, addressing a locomotive, he says: "Law of thyself complete, thine own track firmly holding."

In a poet capable of maintaining "this is Ocean's poem," a poet "aware of the mighty Niagara," the principle of joyously infused oneness can be centered in various terms of high generalization:

> "the greatness of Religion [. . .] the real and perma-
> nent grandeur of These States [. . .] efflux of the Soul
> [. . .] great City [. . .] transcendental Union [. . .]
> teeming Nation of nations [. . .] the immortal Idea [.
> . .] Sex" (which "contains all" [. . .] "every hour the
> semen of centuries").

—all such subjects serve as variants on his theme of unified diversity. "Underneath all, Nativity" ("I swear I am charmed with nothing except nativity, / Men, women, cities, nations, are only beautiful from nativity"), by which he meant the individual being's uniqueness of identity ("singleness and normal simplicity and separation"). When he thinks of "Death, merged in the thought of materials," he swears "there is nothing but immortality!" When he "wander'd, searching among burial places," he "found that every place was a burial place." All "to the Ideal tendest"; "Only the good is universal"; "All swings around us. / I have the idea of all, and am all and believe in all"; "He resolves all tongues into his own."

---

[4] But not always. In *Song of the Open Road* we are told: "No diseas'd person, no rum drinker or venereal taint is permitted here."

In his prophetic role as "Chanter of Personality," he can use the Idea of Allness as justification for his claim to act as the spokesman for all: "I act as the tongue of you; / Tied in your mouth, in mine it begins to be loosened." Corresponding to "the great Idea, the idea of perfect and free individuals," an idea for which "the bard walks in advance," there are the many forms of idealized "appetite." These range from thoughts of a gallant and adventurous launching of "all men and women forward with me into the Unknown," to the notion of normal physical sensations programmatically made excessive, an abnormality of super-health:

> "Urge, and urge, and urge [. . .] complete abandon-
> ment [. . .] scattering it freely [. . .] athletic Democracy
> [. . .] ecstatic songs [. . .] the smoke of my own breath
> [. . .] the boundless impatience of restraint [. . .] un-
> mitigated adoration [. . .] I inhale great draughts of
> space [. . .] tumbling on steadily, nothing dreading
> [. . .] give me the coarse and rank [. . .] fond of his
> sweetheart, relishing well his steak [. . .] aplomb in
> the midst of irrational things [. . .] turbulent, fleshy,
> sensual, eating, drinking, and breeding."

In earlier versions of this last set honorifically describing himself, "turbulent" had been "disorderly." And we glimpse something of his rhetorical tactics when we recall that "I am he who goes through the streets" later became "I am he who walks the States." He gains concreteness in such inventions as "love-juice," "limitless limpid jets of love," and "life-lumps." Or analogies between the physical body and what J. C. Ransom has called the world's body are exploited in such statements as "Through you I drain the pent-up rivers of myself" (elsewhere he similarly speaks of "pent-up, aching rivers").

When we turn from the physical body and the world's body to the body politic, we note how such concretizing of the "democratic" code almost automatically vows the poet to imagery of a homosexual cast. For if Democracy is to be equated with "the manly love of comrades," and if such love is to be conceived *concretely,* in terms of bodily intimacy, such social "adhesiveness" ("the great rondure, the cohesion of all") that he advocates is almost necessarily matched by many expressions of "robust love" that would be alien to the typical heterosexual poet, as conditioned by our mores. And though the sex of his lover is not specified in the startling section 5 of *Song of Myself,* the many similarly motivated poems in *Calamus* give reason enough to assume that he is here writing of a male attachment, as with the "hugging and loving bed-fellow" of section 3 (though this passage may also be complicated by infantile memories of the mother). In any case, we should note, for what little it may be worth, that in *The Sleepers* Whitman associates the "onanist" with the color "gray," the same color with which he associates himself ("gray eyes" and "gray-necked"), while the "hermit thrush" singing in the "swamps" of the "Lilacs" poem is "gray-brown" (though "smoke" and "debris" here are also gray; and there are other grays that are still further afield). The directest association of himself with an onanistic motive is in the last two lines of "Spontaneous Me." Also, he uses a spiritual analogue (frequently encountered in devotional verse) when, concerning his literary motive, he apostrophizes his tongue: "Still uttering—still ejaculating—canst never cease this babble ?"

As regards the poetic I, who would "promote brave soldiers," has "voyagers' thoughts," would "strike up for a New World," is "he that aches with amorous love," would "dilate you with tremendous breath," or "buoy you up": here his motives and motifs get their summarization in his title of titles, *Leaves of Grass.* Accordingly, one direct way into his verse is to ask what associations clearly cluster about these two nouns, "leaves" and "grass" (which are related to each other as individuals are to the group, thus being in design like his term in the *Vistas,* "ensemble-Individuality," though in that formula the order is reversed). Here we are at the core of his personalizing tactics. And, typically, it is in his *Song of Myself* that he specifically offers answers to the question, "What is the grass?" (As indication that he would here be the Answerer to a fundamental question, he tells us that it has been asked by a child.) In section 6 of this poem, he offers several definitions:

First, he says of grass: "I guess it must be the flag of my disposition, out of hopeful green stuff woven." Other references to "stuff" in this poem are:

> voices [. . .] of wombs and of the father-stuff
> This day I am jetting the stuff of far more arrogant republics
> I am [. . .]
> Maternal as well as paternal, a child as well as a man,

Stuff'd with the stuff that is coarse and stuff'd with the
stuff that is fine."

Elsewhere we have noted "I pour the stuff to start sons and daughters
fit for these States," and "these States with veins full of poetical stuff."
Interestingly enough, all other three references to "flag" in this poem
are in contrast with "hopeful green." There are "flag-tops [. . .] draped
with black muslin" to "guard some corpse"—and twice the word is
used as a verb, in the sense of "droop": "Did you fear some scrofula
out of the unflagging pregnancy?" and "The hounded slave that flags
in the race." (Note that "draped" is an ablaut form of "drooped" and
"dropt.")

Second: "Or I guess it is the handkerchief of the Lord, / A scented
gift and remembrancer designedly dropt, / Bearing the owner's name [.
. .] " We have noted no other references to handkerchiefs in Whitman,
though there is always *Othello* in the offfing! But the verb "dropt"
recalls the "drooped" and "dropt" of the "Lilacs" poem (which also
refers to "inlooped flags with the cities draped in black") and since the
matter of *scent* also links these two contexts, we shall wait for further
leads here when we specifically deal with this theme. So far as the internal organization is concerned, by the way, we might note that the
reference to the "owner's name" attains an enigmatic fulfillment near
the end of the poem, when the poet decides that his motive "without
name [. . .] a word unsaid," though "To it the creation is the friend
whose embracing awakes me."

Other meanings he offers are: "I guess the grass is itself a child"; [. .
.] "or I guess it is a uniform hieroglyphic, / [. . .] Growing among black
folks as among white." Again, it seems like "the beautiful uncut hair
of graves"—and as Whitman frequently shuttles back and forth along
the channel of affinity that links love and death or womb and tomb,
his next stanza, beginning "Tenderly will I use you curling grass," contrives by quick transitions to go from "the breasts of young men" to
"mothers' laps." In the following stanza, grass is related to both "the
white heads of old mothers," and "the colorless beards of old men,"
while a reference to "the faint red roofs of mouths" leads to the specifically poetic motive, in the mention of "uttering tongues."

Near the close of the poem (section 49) the theme of grass as the
"hair of graves" is developed further ("O grass of graves"), while the
connotations are generally of a maternal, or even obstetrical sort, in
the references to the "bitter hug of mortality," the "elder-hand press-

ing," and the "accoucheur" who helps bring about "the relief and escape" through Death.

The scent theme figures here likewise, thanks to a bit of rhetorical alchemy. For after apostrophizing the "Corpse" as "good manure," the poet assures us: "but that does not offend me, / I smell the white roses sweet-scented and growing," whereat the associations, taking their lead from the vital connotations of the participle "growing," shift into quite a different order: "I reach to the leafy lips, I reach to the polish'd breasts of melons." And do we not find tonal vestiges of "leafy" in the two similar-sounding words of the next line: "And as to you Life I reckon you are the leavings of many deaths"?

To trail down the various uses of the verb "leave," in the light of the possibility that it may secondarily involve motives intrinsic to the noun "leaves," would take us on a longer journey than we could manage now. But let us look at a few. Consider, for instance, in *Song of Myself,* section 3: "As the hugging and loving bed-fellow sleeps at my side through the night [. . .] / Leaving me baskets cover'd with white towels swelling the house with their plenty." In this context for "leaving," the hug is not overtly maternal, though the food connotations suggest that it may be secondarily so, quite as the "baskets" in this passage might correspond food-wise to the "polish'd breasts of melons" in the other. And similarly, in *Song of Myself,* section 6, an implicit food motive seems to guide the steps from "curling grass" to "the breasts of young men," and thence finally via "mothers" to "mouths," with a final turn from the nutriently oral to the poetically eloquent, in "uttering tongues." Yet, as regards "swelling the house with their plenty": we might recall that in "I Sing the Body Electric" we find the step from "love-flesh swelling and deliciously aching" to "jets of love hot and enormous," and two pages later: "There swells and jets a heart" (after talk of "blood" that might well bear study in connection with the talk of blood in the poem beginning "Trickle drops! my blue veins leaving! / O drops of me! trickle, slow drops, / Candid from me falling, drip, bleeding drops"). So the "hug" of Death or bed-fellows seems sometimes maternal, sometimes "democratic," or indeterminately something of both.

But our main intention at this point was to consider some more obvious cases where we might seem justified in adding the verb forms to our inquiry into the various major meanings of "leaves." Perhaps the perfect *pontificating* case is in *Starting from Paumanok,* where the line,

"*Take my leaves America*" suggests something midway between "receive my offerings" and "put up with my constant departures." Or in so far as Whitman sometimes uses "blade" as a synonym for "leaf," there is another kind of bridge between noun and verb when, in "Scented Herbage of My Breast," in connection with male love, he says: "Emblematic and capricious blades I leave you." And before moving on, we'd like to consider one more context where the verb form seems quite relevant to our concerns. We have in mind the passage on Death, the "hug of mortality," the "sweet-scented," and Life as "the leavings of many deaths," a development that is immediately preceded by the lines (except for fifteen words):

> I find letters from God dropt in the street, and every one is
>   sign'd by God's name,
> And I leave them where they are [. . .]

This is in section 48 of *Song of Myself.* Though this longest poem is sometimes entitled "Walt Whitman," we have said that there is in it a *problem of name* (that is, a problem of *essence,* of *fundamental motivation;* and we would base our position, naturally, upon the fact that, as the poet nears his windup, he centers upon the problem of locating a substance "without name"). But, relevantly reverting to the context where the word "name" first appears, we find it precisely in that passage (of section 6) where he speaks of the Lord's "scented" handkerchief, "bearing the owner's name," and "designedly dropt."

There are the many obvious places where the leaves are the leaves of books (a usage that fits well with a pun on utterance, in the notion of a tree's "uttering" leaves). A three-line poem in *Calamus* embodies this usage incidentally, in the course of a somewhat secretive confession:

> Here the frailest leaves of me and yet my strongest last-
>   ing,
> Here I shade and hide my thoughts, I myself do not ex-
>   pose them,
> And yet they expose me more than all my other poems.

The word "calamus" itself is apparently within the same orbit, and even allows us to watch "flag" for signs of similar meaning, since calamus is "sweet flag," of which our dictionary says: "The root has a pungent, aromatic taste, and is used in medicine as a stomachic; the leaves have an aromatic odor, and were formerly used instead of rushes to strew on floors." Thus, we might assume that "calamus" is one of his "scent" words, though our incomplete reading has not as yet given us a clear title to this assumption. However, we can cite a one-page poem ("These I Singing in Spring") in which the mention of "calamus-root" accompanies such clearly scent-conscious references as "smelling the earthy smell," "lilac, with a branch of pine," and "aromatic cedar" (calamus-root here being specified as "the token of comrades"). Since "calamus" is the Latin word for "reed," we also dare note inklings of grassiness in the "reedy voice" of the hermit thrush that warbles through the "Lilacs" poem.

"Herbage" clearly belongs here—as in "Scented Herbage of My Breast" (though the subsequent references to "tomb-leaves," "body leaves," "tall leaves," and "slender leaves [. . .] blossoms of my blood," while they are clear as radiations from the leaf motif, are somewhat vague in themselves). Herbage for grass is matched by feuillage for leaves; and as judged by the assemblage of details in *Our Old Feuillage,* leaves can be any item that he includes in his surveys and poetic catalogues, here called "bouquets" ("Always [. . .] All sights [. . .] All characters [. . .] "; "Always the free range and diversity—always the continent of Democracy"; and "Encircling all, vast-darting up and wide, the American Soul, with equal hemispheres, one Love, one Dilation or Pride").

Leaves are sometimes called "blades"; and the blade of the broadaxe is called a "gray-blue leaf" (thereby adding the *gray* strand—and since the axe was "to be leaned and to lean on," we recall: "I lean and loafe at my ease observing a spear of summer grass"). Besides adding "spear" to our radiations, we note that "lean and loafe" are here attitudinally identical. But further, lo ! not only is "loafe" tonally an ablaut form of "leaf"—change the unvoiced "f" to its voiced cognate, "v," and you have the close tonal proximity between "loafe" and "love."

"Leaves" and "grass" cross over into the scent category, in the reference to roots and leaves as "perfume," or in lines such as "The prairie-grass dividing, its special odor breathing," and "The sniff of green leaves and dry leaves [. . .] and of hay in the barn"—or the reference to "words simple as grass" that are "wafted with the odor of his body or breath."

Nowhere do we recall encountering such connotations as in the 129th Psalm, "Let them be as the grass upon the housetops, which withereth afore it groweth up"; or in Isaiah 40: "The grass withereth,

the flower fadeth: because the spirit of the Lord bloweth upon it: surely the people is grass."

We should note two other major principles of unity:

First, there are the references to the "first," a common poetic and
narrative device for the *defining of essence*. Perhaps the central example
is his line: "I speak the password primeval, I give the sign of democracy." The more familiar we become with Whitman's vocabulary, the
more condensed this line is felt to be. Identity is proclaimed quasi-
temporally, in the word "primeval." Such firstness is further established in terms of the poetic I as spokesman for a public cause. But
the more closely one examines the word "sign" in Whitman, the more
one comes to realize that it has a special significance for him ranging
from signs of God ("and every one is sign'd by God's name, / And I
leave them where they are") to such signs as figure in a flirtation. (In
"Among the Multitude," for instance: "I perceive one picking me out
by secret and divine signs / [. . .] that one knows me. / Ah lover and
perfect equal," as per the ambiguously "democratic" kind of equality
especially celebrated in the *Calamus* poems.) "Password" is notable for
merging one of his major verbs with the term that sums up his own
specialty (elsewhere he has "passkey").

When proclaiming "a world primal again," he characteristically
identifies it with the "new," the "expanding and swift," and the "turbulent." Another variant of such quasi-temporal firstness is in his term
"nativity," as with "Underneath all, Nativity." And often references to
the "child" serve the same reductive function (as with "Years looking
backward resuming in answer to children").

Lines such as "Unfolded out of the folds of the woman, man comes
unfolded," and "Out of the cradle endlessly rocking" reveal how readily such essentializing in terms of the "primal" can lead into the realm
of the maternal (which may range from the sheer abstract principle of
Union to the personally "electric," "magnetic," or "athletic"). And we
might discern a "democratic" variant of the attitude implicit in the
German epithet *wohlgeboren,* when he temporally defines his personal
essence thus: "Starting from fish-shape Paumanok where I was born, /
Well-begotten, and rais'd by a perfect mother."

There is a notable variant of the temporal idiom in "Crossing
Brooklyn Ferry." For as the literal crossing of the river becomes symbolically a vision of crossing into the future, so the poet becomes a
kind of essentializing past, defining the nature of his future readers.

In "With Antecedents," we see how this temporal or narrative mode of defining essence can fit into the dialectics of *logical* priority (priority in the sense that the first premise of a syllogism can be considered prior to the second premise). For while, as his very title indicates, he is concerned with the temporally prior, he reduces his temporal sequence in turn to terms of "all" when he says: "We stand amid time beginningless and endless, we stand amid evil and good, / All swings around us."

In his *Song of the Open Road,* which calls upon us continually to "reach" and "pass," and "to merge all in the travel they tend to," he uses a reverse kind of temporal priority; namely, seniority: "old age, calm, expanded, broad with the haughty breadth of the universe, / old age, flowing free with the delicious near-by freedom of death." (The broad-breadth pair here could lead us into his notable breast-breath set.) But with the subject of Death, we come upon another kind of summing up, since it names the direction in which the "ever-tending" is headed. ("Tend" is as typical a Whitman word as "pass," though it occurs much less frequently.) So, let us consider Whitman's poetizing of Death. But since Death is the Great Positive-Seeming Negative, perhaps we might best consider it with relation to the poet's use of the negative in general.

The incidence of negatives is probably highest in the poems of the *Calamus* period; at least, in many places here they come thick and fast. There is almost an orgy of not's and nor's in "Not Heaving from My Ribb'd Breast only," as sixteen of the poem's seventeen lines so begin, while one line contains a second. Since the poem is composed of a single periodic sentence about "adhesiveness" (the "pulse of my life"), we should certainly be justified in asking whether there may be a substantive relation in these poems between the negative and the resolve to celebrate democracy with songs of "manly attachment." (See also particularly in this same series: "Not Heat Flames Up and Consumes"; "City of orgies"; "No Labor-Saving Machine"; or the way in which a flat "no" serves as fulcrum in "What Think You I Take My Pen in Hand ?")

It might also be worth noting that the *Calamus* theme of the "subtle electric fire that for your sake is playing within me" produces two significant and quite appealing instances of anacoluthon: "City whom that I have lived and sung in your midst will one day make you illustrious," and "Oh you whom I often and silently come where you are that I may be with you." (We mention anacoluthon here because, tentatively, though not for certain, we incline to believe that the figure indicates a certain deviousness in thinking, hence may remotely indicate a "problematical" motive.)

A more orthodox strategy of deflection (almost a *diplomacy*) is to be seen in another poem of the *Calamus* series, "Earth, My Likeness." Beginning on the theme of the analogy between the poet's body and the earth as a body, the poet then avows a questionable motive in himself, after figuratively attributing a like motive to the earth:

> I now suspect there is something fierce in you eligible to
>   burst forth,
> For an athlete is enamour'd of me, and I of him,
> But toward him there is something fierce and terrible in me
>   eligible to burst forth,
> I dare not tell it in words, not even in these songs.[5]

In *Song of Myself* (section 44) there is an absolute negative, identified with a "first":

> Afar down I see the huge first Nothing, I know I was even
>   there,
> I waited unseen and always, and slept through the lethargic
>   mist,
> And took my time, and took no hurt from the fetid carbon.
> Long I was hugg'd close—long and long.

---

[5] The lines contain many notable terms. First, since they twice say "eligible," we might remember the connotations here when we come upon the word elsewhere. Thus, when winding up *Our Old Feuillage,* Whitman writes: "Whoever you are ! how can I but offer you divine leaves, that you also be eligible as I am ?" or in *By Blue Ontario's Shore,* see "All is eligible to all." And recalling the "lessons" on which *Democratic Vistas* began, note in *Starting from Paumanok:* "I sat studying at the feet of the great masters, / Now if eligible O that the great masters might return and study me." The repetition of "fierce" might recall the "fierce old mother" and "savage old mother" of "Out of the Cradle Endlessly Rocking." Also "liberty songs" were fierce. The poem gives us some specific meanings for "athlete," to be remembered even though the word can be extended to an "athletic matron." And the movement ends in the negative, with relation to his own verse.

Immediately after, the thought is developed in terms of the maternal. For instance: "Cycles ferried my cradle," and "Before I was born out of my mother generations guided me," lines that overlap upon even the sheer titles of *Crossing Brooklyn Ferry* and "out of the Cradle Endlessly Rocking." The word "hugg'd" might remind us of the previously quoted reference to "the hugging and loving bed-fellow [. . .] / Leaving me baskets," etc. (section 3). Or there was the "hug of mortality" in section 49, and the death-smell that "does not offend me" and was quickly replaced by talk of the "sweet-scented."

Section 12 in *Starting from Paumanok* has some interesting involvements with the negative. First the poet addresses his femme, Democracy. In her name he will make both the "songs of passion" and the "true poem of riches." He will "effuse egotism," and will show that male and female are equal.

We might note that such equality of sex could mean one thing as applied to the body politic, but something quite different if applied to the individual personality. For within the individual personality, an "equality" of "male" and "female" motives could add up to an ambivalence of the *androgynous* sort, as it would not, strictly in the realm of politics. Yet we must also bear in mind the fact that, however close language may be to the persuasions and poetics of sexual courtship, language as such is nonsexual; and in so far as motivational perturbations arising from purely linguistic sources become personalized in terms of any real or imagined distinctions between "male" and "female," such sexual-seeming differentiations should be inadequate to the case; hence, any purely *linguistic* situations that happened to be stated in sexual terms (involving either sexual differentiations or sexual mergers) should have elements that could be but *prophetically glimpsed* beyond a terminology formed by sexual analogies.

For instance, though language necessarily has a realm of dialectical resources wholly extrinsic to sexuality, there is the ironic linguistic fact that concrete bisexual imagery may be inevitable, if a poet, let us say, would give us not at one time the image of *mother* and at another the image of *father,* but would rather seek to localize in concrete imagery the idea of *parent.* At the very least, thinking of such a linguistic embarrassment along psychoanalytic lines, we might expect some kind of merger or amalgam like that in Whitman's exclamation: "Mother! with subtle sense severe, with the naked sword in your hand." (And after the analogy of "spears" of grass, we might well have swords of grass, too, not forgetting the naked broad-axe. Further, a poet given to homosexual imagery might well, when writing of his verbal art, glimpse the wholly nonsexual quandaries that lie in the bed of language, far beyond any and all sociopolitical relations.) [6]

But we were on the subject of the negatives in section 12 of *Starting from Paumanok*. Immediately after the poet has proclaimed the equality of male and female, and has vowed that he will prove "sexual organs and acts" to be "illustrious," the negatives come piling in. He will show that "there is no imperfection in the present, and can be none in the future," and that "nothing can happen more beautiful than death." The next stanza has a negative in four of its five verses, and the positive line is introduced by a disjunctive conjunction:

> I will not make poems with reference to parts,
> But I will make poems, songs, thoughts, with reference to
>   ensemble,
> And I will not sing with reference to a day, but with refer-
>   ence to all days,
> And I will not make a poem nor the least part of a poem
>   but has reference to the soul,
> Because having look'd at the objects of the universe, I find
>   there is no one nor any particle of one but has reference
>   to the soul.

Whereas the Whitman negative, at one extreme, seems to involve the notions of No-No that trouble the scruples of "manly love" (scru-

---

[6] See *Der Monat,* Juni 1954, Heft 69: *Die Alten Ägypter,* by J. A. Wilson, page 277: *Ein anderer, irdischerer Text macht aus der Erschaffung von Schu und Tefnut einen Akt der Selbstbefleckung Atums—ein deutlicher Versuch, mit dem Problem fertig zu werden, wie ein Gott allein, ohne dazugehörige Göttin, etwas zeugen soll.* And on page 280, returning to the theme of a creation *"aus einer Selbstbefleckung des Schöpfergottes,* a creation made *"aus seinem Samen und seinen Fingern,"* the author next says (and we consider this a thoroughly substantial association): *Wir sahen ja schon, wie das Aussprechen eines Namens an sich ein Schöpfungsakt ist.* We have many times been struck by the fact that the creative word could be called parthenogenesis or *Selbstbefleckung,* depending on whichever sexual analogies the analogizer preferred; but this is the first time we ever encountered so heroic a version of such thinking. And we are particularly struck by the writer's turn from the subject of this self-involved physical act on the part of a wholly independent god to the subject of creation by verbal fiat.

ples that somehow connect with thoughts of the maternal and, of course, with the problem of his identity, or "nativity," as a poet), in the above quotation we see how such matters fade into purely technical considerations. For if the *particulars* of life are positive, then the "ensemble" or "soul" would be correspondingly negative; or if you considered the "ensemble" positive, then the "parts" would be negative (as with Spinoza's principle: *omnis determinatio est negatio*). Or in a fluctuant medium such as Whitman's, where the issues need not be strictly drawn, the talk of parts and wholes may merely call forth a general aura of negativity. However, once we consider this problem from the standpoint of the distinction between positive and negative, we should note the dialectical resources whereby, above the catalogues of positive details that characteristically make up so many of his poems, there should hover some summarizing principle—and this principle would be "negative," at least in the sense that no single detail could be it, though each such positive detail might partitively stand for it, or be infused with its spirit. (The problem is analogous to that of negative theology.)

When the technical principles of positive and negative are projected into their moralistic counterparts (as good and evil), the poet can assert by the doubling of negatives, as in "I will show that there is no imperfection." And if you will agree that death is negative (in so far as it is the privation of life), then you will note double negativity lurking in the statements that "nothing can happen more beautiful than death," or "Copulation is no more rank to me than death is."

Sometimes the *principle* of negativity is present, but in a positive seeming statement that is really a denial of a social negative, as with "the bowels sweet and clean," Or "perfect and clean the genitals previously jetting." Or here is a line that runs heretically counter to vast sums expended in the advertising of deodorants for people who think that their vague sense of personal guilt is to be eliminated by purely material means: "the scent of these armpits aroma finer than prayer." In keeping with this pattern, he can also celebrate the "joy of death," likening it to the discharging of excrement ("My voided body nothing more to me, returning to the purifications"). Similarly, farther afield, as though boasting of virtues, he can tell of the vices that were "not wanting" in him ("the wolf, the snake, the hog," among others). For he "will make the poem of evil also," for "I am myself just as much evil as good, and my nation is"—whereat, expanding further, "and I say there is in fact no evil." Accordingly, "none can be interdicted, / None but are accepted."

At one point in *Song of the Open Road* he formulates the principle in general terms, in ways suggesting Hegel: "It is provided in the essence of things that from any fruition of success, no matter what, shall come forth something to make a greater struggle necessary," a principle that could provide good grounds for feeling downcast, if one were so inclined. Elsewhere, "after reading Hegel," he avows: "the vast all that is called Evil I saw hastening to merge itself and become lost and dead." And in keeping with the same design, he could praise the earth because "It grows such sweet things out of such corruptions."

In sum, Whitman would programmatically make all days into a kind of permanent Saturnalian revel, though celebrating not a golden age of the past, but rather the present in terms of an ideal future. And, in poetically personalizing his program, he "promulges" democracy in terms of a maternal allness or firstness and fraternal universality ambiguously intermingling in a death hug that presents many central problems for the patient pedestrian analyzer of The Good Gray Poet's terminology.

But when we remind ourselves that the Roman Saturnalia traditionally involved a ritualistic reversal of roles, with the slaves and servants playing as masters for a day while the masters playfully took orders, we wonder whether the ironic bitterness of Whitman's poem, "Respondez! Respondez!" (first published in 1856 as "Poem of the Proposition of Nakedness") might be studied as a kind of Saturnalia-in-reverse.

"Let the slaves be masters! let the masters become slaves!" he exhorts—but this call to the answerer is phrased rather in the accents of outrage. "Let the cow, the horse, the camel, the garden-bee—let the mudfish, the lobster, the mussel, eel, the sting-ray, and the grunting pig-fish—let these, and the like of these, be put on a perfect equality with man and woman!"

In this almost splutteringly ferocious poem, the nation is surveyed wholly without benefit of his normal "spiritualization":

> Stifled, O days, O lands ! in every public and private corruption!
> Smothered in thievery, impotence, shamelessness, mountain-high;

> Brazen effrontery, scheming, rolling like ocean's waves
>   around and upon you, O my days! my lands! [. . .]
> —Let the theory of America still be management, caste,
>   comparison! (Say! what other theory would you?)

And so on, and so on. "Let there be money, business, imports, exports, custom, authority, precedents, pallor, dyspepsia, smut, ignorance, unbelief!"

As for this sullen poem in which he stylistically turns his usual promulgations upside down, we perhaps have here the equivalent of such reversal as marks the mystic state of "accidie." In any case, of all his negatives, this poem would seem to have been one that carried him quite outside his characteristic literary role. It shows how very harsh things could seem to him, in those days, when for a moment he let himself look upon the conditions of his day without the good aid of his futuristic IDEA.

III. LILACS

Having considered Whitman's political philosophy in general, and the general way in which he personalized his outlook by translation into the rapt editorializing of his verse, we would here narrow our concerns to a close look at one poem, his very moving dirge, "When Lilacs Last in the Dooryard Bloom'd," perhaps the poem of his in which policies and personalizations came most nearly perfectly together.

The programmatic zestfulness that marks Whitman's verse as strongly as Emerson's essays encountered two challenges for which it had not been originally "promulged": the Civil War, and the valetudinarianism forced upon him by his partial paralytic stroke in 1873.

Before these developments, his stylistics of "spiritualization" had provided him with a categorical solution for the problem of evil as he saw it. Except for the outlaw moment of "Respondez! Respondez!" (or its much briefer form, "Reversals") his futuristic idealizing could readily transform all apprehensions into promises, and could discern a unitary democratic spirit behind any aggregate of natural or man-made places or things that added up to national power and prowess. This same principle was embodied in the random samplings that made up his poetic surveys and catalogues (which do impart a note of exhilaration to his text, even though one inclines to skim through them somewhat as when running the eye down the column of a telephone directory). And whatever guilt was left unresolved by his code could be canceled by the accents of perfervid evangelism (notably in his celebrating of "adhesiveness").

But since the entire scheme was based upon an ideal of all-pervasive and almost promiscuous Union, the motives of secession that culminated in the Civil War necessarily filled him with anguish. And even many of the inferior poems in *Drum-taps* become urgent and poignant, if read as the diary of a man whose views necessarily made him most sensitive to the dread of national dismemberment. Here, above all, was the development in history itself which ran harshly counter to the basic promises in which his poetry had invested. He reproaches not himself but "America": "Long, too long [. . .] / you learned from joys and prosperity only." And, in slightly wavering syntax, he says the need is henceforth "to learn from crises of anguish."

Yet in one notable respect, his doctrines had prepared him for this trial. In contrast with the crudity of mutual revilement and incrimination that marks so many contemporary battles between the advocates of Rightist and Leftist politics, Whitman retained some of the spontaneous gallantry toward the enemy that sometimes (as in Chevy Chase) gives the old English-Scottish border ballads their enlightening moral nobility. And whatever problematical ingredients there may have been in his code of love as celebrated in the *Calamus* poems, these motives were sacrificially transformed in his work and thoughts as wound-dresser ("I have nourished the wounded and soothed many a dying soldier" [. . .] "Upon this breast has many a dying soldier leaned to breathe his last" [. . .] "Many a soldier's loving arms about this neck have cross'd and rested, / Many a soldier's kiss dwells on these bearded lips").

Similarly, when ill health beset him, though it went badly with one who had made a particular point of celebrating the body at the height of its physical powers, here too he had a reserve to draw upon. For his cult of death as a kind of all-mother (like the sea) did allow him a place in his system for infirmities. Further, since death was that condition toward which all life *tends,* he could write of old age, "I see in you the estuary that enlarges and spreads itself grandly as it pours in the great sea"—and though this is nearly his briefest poem, it is surely as *expansionist* a view as he ever proclaimed in his times of broad-axe vigor. We have already mentioned his new-found sympathy with the fallen redwood tree. Other identifications of this sort are imagined in his lines about an ox tamer, and about a locomotive in winter (he now wrote "recitatives").

As for the lament on the death of Lincoln: here surely was a kind of Grand Resolution, done at the height of his powers. Embodied in it, there is a notable trinity of sensory images, since the three major interwoven symbolic elements—evening star, singing bird, and lilac— compose a threeness of sight, sound, and scent respectively. Also, perhaps they make a threeness of paternal, filial, and maternal respectively. Clearly, the star stands for the dead hero; and the "hermit" bird, "warbling a song," just as clearly stands for the author's poetizing self.

But whereas vicarious aspects of star and bird are thus defined within the poem itself, we believe that the role of the lilac is better understood if approached through an inquiry into the subject of scent in general, as it figures in Whitman's idiom.

In the section on *Vistas,* we put much store by the passage where, after referring to "that indescribable perfume of genuine womanhood," Whitman next speaks of his mother, then proceeds to describe an elderly lady, a "resplendent person, down on Long Island." We consider this set of steps strongly indicative, particularly in so far as many other passages can be assembled which point in the same direction. And though Whitman's associations with scent radiate beyond the orbit of the feminine, maternal, and grandmotherly, we believe that his terms for scent have their strongest motivational jurisdiction in this area, with the *Calamus* motive next.

In this Lincoln poem, the lilac is explicitly called "the perfume strong I love." The sprigs from the lilac bushes ("to perfume the grave of him I love") are not just for this one coffin, but for "coffins all." And the Death figured in such lilac-covered coffins is called a "Dark Mother." In "Out of the Cradle Endlessly Rocking," where there is the same identification of the maternal and the deathy, the development is built about the account of a solitary "he-bird [. . .] warbling" for his lost mate, quite as with the mournful warbling of the hermit thrush— and the incident is said to have taken place "When the lilac-scent was in the air and Fifth-month grass was growing."

The cedars and pines in the "recesses" of the swamp where the hermit thrush is singing are also explicitly included in the realm of scent, as evidenced by the lines: "From the fragrant cedars and the ghostly pines"; "Clear in the freshness moist and the swamp-perfume"; "There in the fragrant pines and the cedars dusk and dim." See also, in *Starting from Paumanok,* that poem of his origins and of his femme Democracy: having heard "the hermit thrush from the swamp-cedars, / Solitary, singing in the West, I strike up for a New World." But it is the lilac that holds the poet "with mastering odor," as he says in the Lincoln poem.

In another poem, *A Broadway Pageant* (and one should think also of broad-axe and broad breast), there is a passage that clearly brings out the identification between scent and the maternal, though in this case the usage is somewhat ambiguous in attitude, whereas by far the great majority of references to scent in Whitman are decidedly on the favorable side: "The Originatress comes, / The nest of languages, the bequeather of poems, the race of eld, / Florid with blood, pensive, rapt with musings, hot with passion, / Sultry with perfume." (His word "florid" here could be correlated with a reference to "Florida perfumes," in a poem on Columbia, "the Mother of All.") In this same poem, near the end, there is a passage about "the all-mother" and "the long-off mother" which develops from the line: "The box-lid is but perceptibly open'd, nevertheless the perfume pours copiously out of the whole box." Psychoanalytically, the point about identification here could be buttressed by the standard psychoanalytic interpretation of "box," and thus perhaps by extending the same idea to the coffin—but we would prefer to stress merely the sequence of steps in this passage itself, while noting that the terms for derivation ("out of") take us once again back to the "Cradle" poem.

Consider also this passage, near the windup of *Song of Myself:*

> The past and present wilt—I have fill'd them, emptied
>   them,
> And proceed to fill my next fold of the future.
> Listen up there ! what have you to confide to me ?
> Look in my face while I snuff the sidle of evening [. . .]

Does not "snuff the sidle" here suggest the picture of a youngster nosing against the side of the evening, as were the evening an adult, with a child pressing his face against its breast? In any case, "fold" is a notable word in Whitman, with its maternal connotations obvious in the line where the syllable is repeated almost like an *idée fixe:* "Unfolded out of the folds of the woman, man comes unfolded," an expression that also has the "out of" construction. Another reference, "Endless unfolding of words of ages," leads into talk of acceptance

("I accept Reality and dare not question it, / Materialism first and last imbuing")—and two lines later he speaks of "cedar and branches of lilac." Recall also the traditional association of the feminine with matter (as in Aristotle). In the "Lilacs" poem, immediately before the words "dark mother," death is called "cool-enfolding."

In one of the *Calamus* poems, a reference to "perfume" follows immediately after the line, "Buds to be unfolded on the old terms," and there are other lines that extend the area of the perfume beyond the feminine and maternal to the realm of manly adhesiveness, and to his poetic development in general, as in "In Cabin'd Ships at Sea": "Bear forth to them folded my love, (dear mariners, for you I fold it here in every leaf)."

There are many other references, direct and indirect, which we could offer to establish the maternal as a major element in the lilac; theme. But we believe that these should be enough to prove the point.

Imagine, then, a situation of this sort:

A poet has worked out a scheme for identifying his art with the ideal of a democratic "empire" that he thinks of as a matrix, an All-Mother, a principle of unity bestowing its sanctions upon a strong love of man for man, an "adhesiveness" generally "spiritual," but also made concrete in imagery of "athletic" physical attachment. Quite as God is conceived as both efficient cause and final cause, so this poet's unitary principle is identified with both a source from which he was "unfolded" (the maternal origins "out of" which his art derived) and an end toward which he "ever-tended" (death, that will receive him by "enfolding" him, thus completing the state of "manifold ensemble" through which he had continually "passed," by repeatedly "coming" and "departing"). A beloved democratic hero has died—and the lyric commemoration of this tragic death will be the occasion of the poem.

How then would he proceed, within the regular bounds of his methods and terminology, to endow this occasion with the personal and impersonal *dimensions* that give it scope and resonance ? (For a good poem will be not just one strand, but the interweaving of strands.)

Note, first, that the poem involves several situations. There is the commemorated situation, the death of the hero, as made specific in the journey of the coffin on its last journey. There is the immediate situation of the commemorating poet, among a set of sensory perceptions that he associates, for us, with the hero's death. There is the national scene that he can review, after the fashion of his catalogues, when charting the journey of the coffin (and when radiating into other details loosely connected with this). Near the end, a national scene that had *preceded* the hero's death will be recalled (the time of civil war, or intestine strife, that had accounted historically for the tragic sacrifice). And in the offing, "over-arching" all, there is the notion of an ultimate scene (life, death, eternity, and a possibility of interrelationships in terms of which immediate sensory images can seem to take on an element of the marvelous, or transcendent, through standing for correspondences beyond their nature as sheerly physical objects). The reader shifts back and forth spontaneously, almost unawares, among these different scenes, with their different orders of motivation, the interpenetration of which adds subtlety and variety to the poem's easy simplicity.

The three major *sensory* images are star, bird, and bush (each with its own special surroundings: the darkening Western sky for the "drooping" star, the "recesses" of the swamp for the "hermit" bird, the dooryard for the lilac, with its loved strong perfume—and for all three, the evening in "ever-returning spring"). As regards their correspondences with things beyond their nature as sheerly sensory images: the star stands for the dead loved hero (in a scheme that, as with so much of the Wagnerian nineteenth century, readily equates love and death). The bird crosses over, to a realm beyond its sheerly sensuous self, by standing for the poet who mourns, or celebrates, the dead hero (while also ambiguously mourning or celebrating himself).

And what of the third image, the scent of lilac? It fits the occasion in the obvious sense that it blooms in the springtime and is a proper offering for coffins. And though it is from a realm more material, more earthy, than sight or sound, it has a strong claim to "spirit" as well, since scent is *breathed*. (Passages elsewhere in Whitman, such as "sweet-breathed," "inhaling the ripe breath of autumn," and "the shelves are crowded with perfumes, / I breathe the fragrance," remind us that references to breathing can be secondarily in the scent orbit, and often are in Whitman's idiom.)

Though, in the lore of the Trinity, the Father is equated with power, the Son with wisdom, and the Holy Spirit with love, it is also said that these marks of the three persons overlap. And similarly, in this trinity (of star, bird, and bush) there are confusions atop the distinctions.

In so far as the bird stands for the poet whose art (according to the *Vistas*) was to teach us lessons, the bird would correspond to the son, and wisdom. The star, in standing for the dead Lincoln, would surely be an equivalent of the father, implying power in so far as Lincoln had been a national democratic leader. Yet the nearest explicit attribution of power, the adjective "strong," is applied only in connection with the *lilac,* which would be analogous to the third person of the trinity, the holy spirit (with the notable exception that we would treat it as *maternal* whereas the Sanctus Spiritus is, *grammatically* at least, imagined after the analogy of the masculine, though often surrounded by imagery that suggests maternal, quasi-Mariolatrous connotations) .

The relation of lilac to love is in the reference to "heart-shaped leaves." Since the evening star is unquestionably Venus, the love theme is implicitly figured, though ambiguously, in so far as Venus is feminine, but is here the sign of a dead *man*. As for the "solitary" thrush, who sings "death's outlet song of life," his "carol of death" is a love song at least secondarily, in so far as love and death are convertible terms. Also, in so far as the bird song is explicitly said to be a "tallying chant" that matches the poet's own "thought of him I love," the love motif is connected with it by this route.

But the words, "song of the bleeding throat," remind us of another motive here, more *autistic,* intrinsic to the self, as might be expected of a "hermit" singer. Implicit in the singing of the thrush, there is the theme most clearly expressed perhaps in these earlier lines, from *Calamus:*

> Trickle drops ! my blue veins leaving!
> O drops of me! trickle, slow drops,
> Candid from me falling, drip, bleeding drops,
> From wounds made to free you whence you were prison'd,
> From my face, from my forehead and lips,
> From my breast, from within where I was conceal'd, press
>   forth red drops, confession drops,
> Stain every page, stain every song I sing, every word I say,
>   bloody drops,
> Let them know your scarlet heat, let them glisten,
> Saturate them with yourself all ashamed and wet,
> Glow upon all I have written or shall write, bleeding drops,
> Let it all be seen in your light, blushing drops.

Do we not here find the theme of utterance proclaimed in and for itself, yet after the analogy of violence done upon the self?

Regrettably, we cannot pause to appreciate the "Lilacs" poem in detail. But a few terministic considerations might be mentioned. There is the interesting set of modulations, for instance, in the series: night, black murk, gray debris, dark-brown fields, great cloud darkening the land, draped in black, crepe-veiled, dim-lit, netherward black of the night, gray smoke, gray-brown bird out of the dusk, long black trail, swamp in the dimness, shadowy cedars, dark mother, dusk and dim— all in contrast with the "lustrous" star. (If you will turn to *Song of Myself,* section 6, you will find the "dark mother" theme interestingly foreshadowed in the "dark [. . .] darker [. . .] dark" stanza that serves as a transition from "mothers' laps" to "uttering tongues.") And noting the absence of Whitman's distance-blue, we find that he has moved into the more solemn area of lilac, purple, and violet. Note also the spring-sprig modulation.

There are many devices for merging the components. At times, for instance, the swampy "recesses" where the bird is singing are described in terms of scent. Or sight and scent are intermingled when "fragrant cedars" are matched with "ghostly pines" at one point, and "fragrant pines" are matched with "cedars dusk and dim" at another. And of course, there is the notable closing merger, "Lilac and star and bird twined with the chant of my soul," a revision of his "trinity" in the opening stanzas, where the bird does not figure at all, the third of the three being the poet's "thought of him I love."

Prophesying after the event, of course, we could say that the bird had figured *implicitly* from the very first, since the bird duplicates the poet, though this duplex element will not begin to emerge until section 4, where the bird is first mentioned. But once the bird has been introduced, much effectiveness derives from the poem's return, at intervals, to this theme, which is thus astutely released and developed. One gets the feel of an almost frenzied or orgiastic outpouring, that has never stopped for one moment, and somehow even now goes unendingly on.

One gets no such clear sense of progression in the poem as when, say, reading *Lycidas.* But if pressed, we could offer grounds for contending that section 13 (the mathematical center of the poem) is the point of maximum internality. For instance, whereas in sections 4 and 9, the thrush is "warbling" *in* the swamp, here the song is said to come *from* the swamps,: *from* the bushes, *out of* the dusk, *out of* the cedars and pines (a prepositional form which we, of course, associate with the maternal connotations it has in the opening stanzas of "out of the Cradle Endlessly Rocking"). Thus, one might argue that there is a crucial change of direction shaping up here. Also, whereas section 4 had featured the sound of the bird's song, and section 9 had added the star along with talk of the bird's song, in section 13 we have bird, star, and lilac, all three (plus a paradox which we may ascribe at least in part to the accidental limitations of English—for whereas we feel positive in associating lilac with the feminine or maternal, the poet writes of the "mastering" odor with which the lilac holds him).

We could say that the theme of the cradle song, or "Death Carol" (that follows, after a brief catalogue passage) had been implicitly introduced in the "from's" and "out of's" that characterize the first stanza of section 13. But in any case, a clear change of direction follows this movement, with its theme of death as "dark mother." And since we would make much of this point, let us pause to get the steps clear:

As regards the purely sensory imagination, the theme (of the "Death Carol" as cradle song) is developed in the spirit of such words as soothe, serenely, undulate, delicate, soft, floating, loved, laved. And whereas there is no sensory experience suggested in the words "praise! praise! praise!" surely they belong here wholly because of the poet's desire to use whatever associations suggest total relaxation, and because of the perfect freedom that goes with the act of genuine, unstinted praise, when given without ulterior purpose, from sheer spontaneous delight.

What next, then, after this moment of farthest yielding? Either the poem must end there (as it doesn't), or it must find some proper aftermath. The remaining stanzas, as we interpret them, have it in their favor that they offer a solution of this problem.

As we see it, a notable duality of adjustment takes place here (along lines somewhat analogous to the biologists' notion of the correspondence between ontogenetic and phylogenetic evolution, with regard to the stages that the individual foetus passes through, in the course of its development).

In brief, there are certain matters of recapitulation to be treated, purely within the conditions of the poem; but if these are to be wholly vital, there must be a kind of *new* act here, even thus late in the poem, so far as the momentum of the poet is concerned. And we believe that something of the following sort takes place:

In imagining death as maternal, the poet has imagined a state of ideal infantile or intra-uterine bliss. Hence, anything experienced after that stage will be like the emergence of the child from its state of Eden into the world of conflict. Accordingly, after the "Death Carol," the poet works up to a recital in terms of armies, battle flags, the "torn and bloody," "debris," etc. Strictly within the conditions of the poem, all these details figure as recollections of the Civil War, with its conditions of strife which accounted historically for the hero's death. But from the standpoint of this section's place *after* the imagining of infantile contentment, all such imagery of discord is, in effect, the recapitulation of a human being's emergence into the intestine turmoils of childhood and adolescence.

After this review of discord, there is a recapitulation designed to bring about the final mergings, fittingly introduced by the repetition of Whitman's password, "passing." There had been much merging already. Now, in the gathering of the clan, there is a final assertion of merger, made as strong and comprehensive as possible. The "hermit song" is explicitly related to the "tallying song" of the poet's "own soul." The "gray-brown bird" is subtly matched by the "silver face" of the star. Our previous notion about the possible pun in "leaves" (as noun and verb) comes as near to substantiation as could be, in the line: "Passing, I leave thee lilac with heart-shaped leaves." There is a comradely holding of hands.

So, with the thought of the hero's death, all is joined: "the holders holding my hand"; "lilac and star and bird twined with the chant of my soul"; "and this for his dear sake," a sacrifice that ends on the line, "The fragrant pines and cedars dusk and dim"—nor should we forget that the sounds issuing from there came from the "recesses" of the "swamp-perfume." [7]

---

[7] Five lines from the end, the expression "Comrades mine and I in the midst," restating in slight variation the words of section 14, "I in the middle with companions," might be used as an indication of the way in which the poet's terms radiate. In *Calamus* there is a poem that also has the expression, "I in the middle." One will also find there "lilac with a branch of pine," "aromatic cedar," the themes of singing and plucking (to match "A sprig with its flower I break"), and a reference to "the spirits of friends dead or alive." In *A Broadway Pageant,* there also appears the expression "in the middle." But just as the other usage had been a bridge into the theme of comradely

The first line of a Whitman poem is usually quite different rhythmically from the lines that follow. The first line generally has the formal rhythm of strict verse, while even as early as the second line he usually turns to his typical free-verse style. (*Song of the Broad-Axe* is an exception to the rule, as it opens with no less than six lines that do not depart far from the pattern: long-short/ long-short/ long-short/ long, as set by the verse: "Weapon, shapely, naked, wan.") We copied out a batch of first lines, just to see how they would look if assembled all in one place, without reference to the kind of line that characterizes most notably the poet's catalogues. When reading them over, we noted that they are so much of a piece, and gravitate so constantly about a few themes, one might make up a kind of Whitman Medley, composed of nothing but first lines, without a single alteration in their wording. Here is one version of such an arrangement. It is offered as a kind of critical satyr-play, to lighten things after the tragic burden of our long analysis:

> First O Songs for a Prelude
>
> Lo, the unbounded sea!
> Flood-tide below me! I see you face to face!
> In cabined ships at sea,
> Out of the cradle endlessly rocking,
> Over the Western sea hither from Niphon come
> As I ebb'd with the ocean of life,
> Facing west from California's shore,
> Give me the splendid silent sun with all his beams full-daz-
>   zling.
> O to make the most jubilant song !
> A song for occupations!

---

attachment, here the context is definitely in the maternal orbit. This same stanza contains the reference to the perfume that "pours copiously out of the whole box," and "venerable Asia, the all-mother." In the "Lilacs" poem, the theme of copious pouring is distributed differently. In section 13, the bird is told to "pour" its song. In section 7, the idea is transferred to the breaking of the lilac: "Copious I break, I break the sprigs from the bushes, / With loaded arms I come pouring for you"—whereat again we would recall that the first reference to the "shy and hidden bird," with its "song of the bleeding throat," followed the line, "A sprig with its flower I break."

A song of the rolling earth, and of words according,
I hear America singing, the varied carols I hear.
These I singing in spring collect for lovers,
Trickle drops ! my blue veins leaving!
America always ! Always our old feuillage!
Come, said the Muse,
Come my tan-faced children.
(Now list to my morning's romanza, I tell the signs of the
　　Answerer.
An old man bending I come upon new faces,
Spirit whose work is done—spirit of dreadful hours!
Rise, O days, from your fathomless deeps, till you loftier,
　　fiercer sweep.)
As I pondered in silence,
Starting from fish-shape Paumanok where I was born,
From pent-up aching rivers;
As I lay with my head in your lap camerado,
Thou who has slept all night upon the storm;
Vigil strange I kept on the field one night,
On the beach at night
By blue Ontario's shore.
I sing the body electric,
Weapon shapely, naked, wan,
Scented herbage of my breast,
Myself and mine gymnastic ever,
Full of life now, compact visible,
I celebrate myself and sing myself;
Me imperturbe, standing at ease in Nature.
On journeys through the States we start,
Among the men and women, the multitude,
In paths untrodden,
The prairie grass dividing, its special odor breathing—
Not heaving from my ribbed breast only,
Afoot and light-hearted I take to the open road.
You who celebrate bygones,
Are you the new person drawn toward me ?
Whoever you are, I fear you are walking the walks of
　　dreams.
Behold this swarthy face, these gray eyes;

Passing stranger! you do not know how longingly I look
    upon you.
Respondez! Respondez!
Here, take this gift—
Come, I will make the continent indissoluble.
O take my hand, Walt Whitman!
As Adam early in the morning
To the garden anew ascending.

Part 3

By and Through Language, Beyond Language

10

A Socioanagogic Approach to Literature: Selections from "Linguistic Approach to Problems of Education" [1]

BASIC ORIENTATION

BEGINNING ABSOLUTELY, WE MIGHT DEFINE MAN as the typically language-using, or symbol-using, animal. And on the basis of such a definition, we could argue for a "linguistic approach to the problems of education." Or we could settle for much less, merely pointing to the obviously great importance of the linguistic factor as regards both education in particular and human relations in general.

LANGUAGE IN EDUCATIONAL THEORY

For symmetry's sake, we would build upon the more thoroughgoing of these positions. Yet, for prudence' sake, we would remind the reader: Even if he will not go so far with us, there are still many points in favor of restoring (however differently) the great stress once placed

---

[1] "A Socioanagogic Approach to Literature: Selections from 'Linguistic Approach to Problems of Education.'" 1955. *Modern Philosophies and Education: Fifty-Fourth Year Book of the National Society for the Study of Education.* Ed. Nelson B. Henry, Chicago: Published by the Society and distributed by University of Chicago Press, 1955, 54, Pt. I, 259–303. Reprinted by permission of National Society for the Study of Education.

upon language in educational theory. (Recall that the medieval *trivi-um* comprised grammar, rhetoric, and logic or dialectic.)

In either case, whether the more thoroughgoing or the less thoroughgoing of these positions is adopted, we shall be considering our subject in terms of symbolic action. We shall look upon language-using as a mode of conduct and shall frame our terms accordingly. We could call this position "dramatistic" because it thus begins with a stress upon "action." And it might be contrasted with idealistic terminologies, that begin with considerations of perception, knowledge, learning. In contrast with such *epistemological* approaches, this approach would be *ontological,* centering upon the *substantiality* of the *act.* Also, a "dramatistic" approach, as so conceived, is *literal,* not *figurative.* Man literally is a symbol-using animal. He really does approach the world symbol-wise (and symbol-foolish).[2]

But a "dramatistic" approach, with its definition of man as the typically language-using or symbol-using animal, points two ways. First, the principles of symbol-using must be considered in their own right, as a separate "realm" or "dimension" (not reducible to "nature" in the nonverbal or extraverbal sense of the term). Second, the formula should warn us not to overlook the term "animal" in our definition. Man *as an animal* is subject to the realm of the extra-verbal, or nonsymbolic, a realm of material necessity that is best charted in terms of *motion.* That is, in his sheer animality, man is to be described in terms of *physical* or *physiological;* notion, as contrasted with the kind of terms we need for analyzing the realm of verbal action.

Professor Brubacher has touched upon an analogous problem, when referring to the classical definition of man as "rational animal." As regards those who "subscribed to a humanistic theory of education,"

---

[2] Our views represent a "semanticism" mainly in the sense that the emphasis is *linguistic.* But this essay does not propose to be a survey of the field. And, in one most notable respect, it runs directly counter to typical "semanticist" procedures. The late Korzybski's teachings, for instance, centered about an attack upon what he called "elementalism." Another word for it would be "substance-thinking." While sharing his distrust of such thinking (political "racist" theories are drastic enough grounds for such distrust), we take it that the principle of substance (and consubstantiality) cannot be eliminated from language accordingly, we would seek rather for terms designed to make its presence as obvious as possible. Kant treated "substance" as a universal form of the *mind;* correspondingly, we would at least treat "substance-thinking" as a universal motive of *language.*

he says: "They held with Aristotle that the distinctive nature of man which set him off from other animals was his rationality. The principal function of education, therefore, was to develop this rationality."

In general, this partial *non sequitur,* in leading some thinkers to overstress the differentia (man's "rationality"), led others to an antithetical overstress upon the genus (man's "animality"). And if we are to abide by our somewhat similar definition, we must watch lest, in our zeal to bring out the *formal* considerations of the differential (language-using, or symbol-using), we slight the *material* considerations of the genus (animal). Or, otherwise put: We must guard lest, in our zeal for a terminology of *action,* we overlook the areas properly chartable in terms of *motion.*

Accordingly, a "dramatistic" terminology built about this definition for man will not exalt terms for "action" to the exclusion of terms for "motion." If, by the physical realm, we mean the nonverbal ("subverbal" or "extraverbal") realm, then the *physical realm* is properly treated in terms of motion. And "action" (ethics, "personality," and the like) will be confined to the realm of symbol-using, with its appropriate principles. Thus, a "dramatistic" perspective, as so conceived, would *decidedly not* oblige us to treat of "things" in the terminology proper to "persons" or vice versa.

The problem is complicated by the fact that, while there can be motion without action (as with a falling material object, or the operations of some purely mechanical device), there can be no action without motion (as one cannot think or speak or carry out a decision without a corresponding set of sheerly neural and muscular goings-on). Thus, there is a sense in which every human act is merged with its sheerly physical or physiological ground. For instance, whereas the *actions* of a game are motivated by the logic of the rules, such acts also involve the sheer physical *motions* of the players and their instruments, in varying quantitative distribution about the field. (*Nulla actio sine motione.* A team can't win a game unless it knows how to "throw its weight around.")

Or consider cases where moral attitudes affect physiological functioning (as when emotional disturbances produce disorders of the bodily organs). Here the realm of action (and its "passions"!) is seen to infuse the realm of motion in ways grotesquely analogous to the powers of a "grace" that, according to the theologians, "perfects" nature.

Thus, though the realms of "action" and "motion" are *discontinuous* in so far as the "laws" of action are not in strict principle reducible to the "laws" of motion (quite as the rules of grammar could not properly be reduced to terms suitable for electronics), the two realms must be *interwoven* in so far as man's *generic animality* is experienced by him in terms of his specific "symbolicity."

Suppose, for instance, that we tried to conceive of "property" in as purely "physical" a sense as possible. We might note respects in which an organism "accumulates private property" by adapting to its particular needs certain portions of its environment. *Its* food, *its* air, *its* water, *its* sunlight, *its* space, *its* shelter, *its* mate—some or all of these things may be "appropriated," in accordance with the specific nature of the organism. In this sense, assimilation could be said to involve a purely *physiological* kind of "private property," however mutual may be the relationships prevailing among various organisms, or "substances," in their "ecological balance."

Here is the realm of "animality," of sheer physical "necessity." If the organism is denied the proper "motions" of assimilation or digestion needed for its survival, it dies. It *must* take into itself alien substances, in accordance with the nature of *its* substance. Some degree of such purely *material* appropriation, with the many material "motions" involved in these processes, is necessary to sheer animal survival. And man, as an animal, confronts the same necessities.

Think next of the many ways whereby such rudimentary needs are transcended, once we move into the realm of "symbolic action." Here we come upon the vast structure of "rights" and "obligations" that takes form when "property" is conceived *legalistically* (as with the "legal fictions" of a modern financial corporation, which the courts treat as a "person"). Surely no one would hold that the "needs" of such a "body" are reducible purely to terms of a few biological necessities. Ownership, as so conceived, involves a fantastically intricate network of purely *symbolic* operations, as evidenced by the army of *clerics* who in one way or another are occupied with promulgating, recording, interpreting, and enforcing the sheerly *man-made* laws of property.

To consider this realm intelligibly, we must discuss symbolic manipulations as such. For obviously, they have a "perfection" of their own, a formal resourcefulness that transcends the nonsymbolic or extrasymbolic realm of purely biological functioning. And such a realm of "personality" goes so far beyond the needs of sheer "animality," that whereas a physical organism can "biologically own" only so much as it can take into its body, or as it can by purely physical powers deny to another, a member of the symbol-using species may "symbolically own" resources that, in his capacity as sheer physical organism, he could not exhaust in a million lifetimes.

Indeed, once ownership becomes modified by the conditions of purely symbolic action, a realm of fantasy and paradox arises. Does a great leader, for instance, "own" his office as head of a state? Or is he not rather "owned" by his subjects who consider themselves "consubstantial" with him, so far as their sense of participation in a common cause is concerned? Whatever your answer to this quandary may be, you will grant that such thoughts confront us with a great *drama of human relations*. For quite as a state is held together physically by a network of purely *material* communicative resources (things that exist and operate in accordance with the laws of *motion*), so this network itself is guided in its construction and control by a network of purely *symbolic* acts and symbol-guided purposes, ranging from the lowly processes of bookkeeping and accountancy to the over-all terminology of "right," "justice," "beauty," "propriety," "truth," the "good life," etc., in which the logic of a given social order comes to an ideal, theoretic head.

Above sheer human animality, then (above man's genus as rooted in the laws of material motion), there has been erected a social complexity that could not have existed without the aid of man's differentia (his capacity for symbolic action). And in this sense, though we would warn against the temptation to forget the genus in our concern with the differentia, we would hold that the proper approach to the genus is *through* the study of symbolic action, as such action takes form in the drama of human relations. Otherwise, for reasons that we shall consider as we proceed, the failure to detect the full scope of the "linguistic dimension" in human affairs and human attitudes obscures our understanding of both the linguistic and the extralinguistic. According to the position here advocated, there is a "pageantry" in objects, a "socioanagogic" element imposed upon them, so far as man is concerned, because man necessarily approaches them in accordance with the genius of his nature as a symbol-human species. Since language is social in the political, administrative sense, the purely physical sociality of nonlinguistic things thus subtly partakes of this purely symbolic spirit, so far as human dealings with "nature" are concerned.

Here is the problem at the bottom of our search, as at the bottom of a well. Our motto might be: By and through language, beyond language. *Per lingcam, praeter linguam.*

The "dramatistic" is to be distinguished from the "dramatic," in that drama proper is the symbolizing or imitating of action, whereas the "dramatistic" is a critical or essayistic analysis of language and thence of human relations generally, by the use of terms derived from the contemplation of drama.

But the dramatistic can take great dramas as its point of departure. They provide the set forms in conformity with which we would construct our terminology. Since the real world of action is so confused and complicated as to seem almost formless, and too extended and unstable for orderly observation, we need a more limited material that might be representative of human ways while yet having fixity enough to allow for systematic examination.

In this respect, great dramas would be our equivalents of the laboratory experimenter's "test cases." But this kind of "controlled conditions" would differ from the arbitrary controls of a typical laboratory experiment. The losses are obvious, the gains less so, unless one stops to realize how hard it is to set up laboratory conditions for establishing instances of symbolic action that, while having a form sufficiently stable to be methodically observable, are also sufficiently complex and mature to be representative of human motives.[3]

But we may be on less cogent ground when laying primary emphasis upon the examining of written texts. Professor Benne[4] has tellingly raised this objection in correspondence, pointing to the many elements besides the literary text that figure in a dramatic performance, and suggesting that the present writer's occupational psychosis as a specialist in literature may be partly responsible for this textual emphasis. To be sure, though we can at least point to the example of Ar-

---

[3] From the "dramatistic" point of view, for instance, experiments with animals would be categorically suspect, since animals are not typically linguistic; and experiments with children would be categorically suspect, since children are not sufficiently mature. Such material might serve suggestively, but it could not possibly have all the "dimensions" needed for the analysis of any complete linguistic performance. And we work on the assumption that our test cases should intrinsically possess such a range.

[4] Educational Consultant: Professor Kenneth Benne, Boston University, Boston, Massachusetts.

istotle, who rated the text of a drama higher than its performance, we must never forget that many fresh exegetical insights come of witnessing actual performances (as when we compare different actors' readings of the same lines); and a sympathetic auditor may be mysteriously moved by a performance given in a language he doesn't even know). Yet, although histrionic and choreographic elements (tonal, plastic, and scenic) contribute critically to the enjoyment and understanding of drama, don't all such modes of expression regularly build their logic *about the interpretation of the text itself?*

Professor Benne has further objected that we tend to neglect the fertile field of drama-like situations in real life (situations that may arise spontaneously, or may be set up partly by the deliberate cunning of an impresario; as with some "candid" radio and television programs). This is a particularly important objection, since education is so largely in the realm of public relations generally. Our point here is simply that one should not *begin* a "dramatistic" analysis with such cases. But co-ordinates *developed from the analysis of formal drama* should certainly be applied to fluctuant material of this sort. Further, such applications, made by a different class of specialists, should reveal notable respects in which the drama-like situations of real life *differ* from drama proper (a difference probably centering in the fact that situations in real life lack *finality*, except in so far as life happens to "imitate art"). Professor Benne's desire to place more weight upon drama-like situations in life ("a playground fight, for example") led us to realize that, given the new recording devices for motion and sound, such new-style documents do resemble the text of a formal drama, in allowing for repeated analysis of a single unchanging development (an "action" that, in its totality, remains always the same). Here, in effect, the new means of recording, or "writing," have extended the realm of the "text" into areas that once lay beyond it. Such material comes close to the "textual" ideal we have in mind; since an observer can repeatedly observe the identical object, thus having the best opportunity to mature his observations.

Still (in an "occupationally psychotic" way) we feel that the written word comes nearest (so far as "records" go) to a merging of "linguistic anatomy" with "linguistic physiology." For single words (many of which are recurrent in the given text) are in their singularity quite "dead"; yet they are very much "alive," as regards their ways of taking part contextually with one another. And in the beginning of our culture was the assurance that in the beginning was the word.

On the other hand, we do not by any means equate "symbol-using" with "word-using." All the arts, such as music, painting, sculpture, the dance, even architecture, are in various ways and to varying degrees symbolic activities. Verbal symbol-using (like its variant, mathematics) enjoy a special place among the lot because the individual word has a kind of conceptual clarity not found in individual notes, colors, lines, motions, and the like (except in so far as these are in effect *words,* as with the conventionalized doctrinal representations in some traditional ritual dance).

In this connection, Professor Benne has suggested that the justification for featuring language among symbolic media may "lie in the fitness of word-symbols for the *criticism* and *analysis* of the others, including word-symbols themselves." This observation suggested to us another step in the same direction, thus: Inasmuch as education merges into the philosophy of education, we may note that verbal symbols are the best medium for "philosophizing" about anything. [259–266]

Language and Problems of Human Relations

[. . .] But for our over-all principles, we necessarily select terms so highly generalized that they apply to work greatly varying in quality (just as both an "excellent" play and a merely "representative" one might be said to have beginning, middle, and end, or to be written in blank verse, or to be a tragedy).

All told, the project approaches the problem of human relations through a study of language in its four major aspects: (a) the logical or indicative; (b) the rhetorical or persuasive; (c) the poetic; (d) the ethical or personal. But only some of the theories and rules of thumb on which this essay is based are directly relevant to the philosophy of education. And in trying to decide which parts of this material should be stressed here, we shall follow the very helpful lead of an article by Professor Benne, "Toward a Grammar of Educational Motives," published in the January, 1947, issue of *Educational Forum.* The article is built around a review of the present writer's book, *A Grammar of Motives,* which outlines the "dramatistic" view of language and of motivational problems generally. The article makes the following main points:

The *Grammar* "may be read as a reaction against 'scientistic' attempts to 'reduce' the explanation of human conduct to the influence of various conditions and causes—physical, chemical, biological or generally environmental." Burke "finds an irreducible minimum of terms necessary to the adequate discussion of human motivation," and he derives these "from his analysis of dramatic action." There are five such terms, which " 'point' in any human action to an actor, a scene, some agency (means), a purpose, as well as the over-all action in which the other terms are united."

Again, "Whatever the various motivations of the semanticists, one may see Burke as a semanticist, seeking to give an interpretation of meaning and its transformations in a 'dramatistic' as opposed to the 'scientistic' perspective which has prevailed in most semantic studies."

"Still another approach" might stress the fact that "in focusing on the language of *any* discussion of motives," the book "is a 'grammatical' approach to discourse about motives." Hence, "on this view, various philosophies become 'casuistries' seeking only to apply these grammatical principles in and to 'the case' of some actual and given cultural situation." Accordingly, Burke attempts a " 'casuistry' of his own, taking major philosophic systems as 'cases' and developing their distinctive characters in terms of their varying stress upon one or another of the terms of his pentad," as materialism features the "scenic" element in motivation, idealism stresses "agent," pragmatism "agency" (instrument), mysticism "purpose," and realism "act." (We might here add that the book also stresses the ways whereby the terms become functions of one another: Thus, by the "scene-act ratio" is meant a statement where the substance of an act is said to have been potentially or analogously present in the scene, and to be derived from the scene; similarly, an "agent-act" ratio derives the quality of the act from the corresponding nature of the agent; the "purpose-agency ratio" concerns the relation of consistency or consubstantiality between end and means; etc.)

The project as a whole (including portions still to be published) aims at an "extended comic treatment of human relations, of the 'foibles and antics of 'the Human Barnyard.' " Reaffirming "the parliamentary process," it is motivated by a "humanitarian concern to see how far conflict (war) may be translated practically into linguistic struggle and how such verbal struggle may be made to eventuate in a common enactment short of physical combat."

Other details noted: "encouraging tolerance by speculation"; a "Neo-Liberal Ideal" that proposes to accept with ironic indignation "the development of technology, a development that will require such a vast bureaucracy (in both political and commercial administration) as the world has never before encountered"; would "confront the global situation with an attitude neither local nor imperialistic"; and is designed to embody its attitude in a method of linguistic analysis.

In his "howevers" (and howevers are of the essence in this perspective) Professor Benne finds that Burke's book is not sufficiently "normative, preferential." But there is a partial however to this however: "Nevertheless, one can find implicit norms in his description of his method," as with Burke's stress upon the *dialectical,* which is equated with "dramatism" at one end and with "scientific method" at the other, and with an over-all complexity of view that is ironic. (For irony "arises when one tries, by the interaction of terms upon one another, to produce a development which uses all the terms," in the methodic search for "a 'perspective of perspectives' in which the values of each partial perspective are in some measure preserved.")

Calling the book "a methodology of practical judgment," Professor Benne next refers to another work, *The Discipline of Practical Judgment in a Democratic Society* (by Raup, Benne, Smith, and Axtelle), which "attempts to do justice to the meaning of Burke's pentad of dramatistic terms in the act of judgment, though without the employment of his terminology." These two books "seem fruitfully to supplement each other"; and they "make at least a beginning in this task of the interpretation of rationality and of contemporary symbolic adequacy." Or, in sum: " 'Symbolic adequacy' can only be developed," and "mastery of our linguistic resources (which are ultimately our rational resources) can be achieved if acquired in the dramatic perspective of the significant conflicts of our time."

Among other considerations stressed in this perspective, we might list briefly: Their systematic concern with the principle of "identification" that prevails, for instance, when ruler and subjects, however disparate their ways of living, feel themselves united in some common cause; the gleams of "mystery" and corresponding feelings of guilt that arise when beings of different status are in communication; the modes of *symbolic purification* ingrained in the nature of symbolic action, and culminating in acts of *victimage;* the principle of *completion* to which language vows us, as when we round out a judgment upon others until it returns upon the self (cf. the Kantian "categorical imperative"); the verbal resources of *transcendence,* implicit in the initial momentous fact that the word transcends the thing it names; and, above all, the workings of that marvel of marvels, not present in nature, and found only in the resources of symbolism, the *negative* (with its "completion" or "perfection" in the "thou shalt not").

The approach to human relations through the study of language in terms of drama makes such concerns primary and seeks to build a systematic terminology to treat of human quandaries in such a spirit. It contends that the basic motives of human effort are concealed behind the clutter of the machinery, both technological and administrative, which civilization has amassed in the attempts to live well. It contends that by a methodic study of symbolic action men have their best chance of seeing beyond this clutter, into the ironic nature of the human species. Yet it seeks to be as instrumentalist as the instrumentation it would distrust. But while it would completely grant that terminologies of motion are properly cultivated those fields of applied science dealing specifically with aspects of motion (as the physical sciences), it would categorically resist any quasi-positivistic tendencies to treat of the human realm in such terms.

We must here leave many relevant questions unanswered. But we might close this section by a reference to the kind of "short-cut" which we consider primary, where the analysis of particular linguistic structures is concerned:

We refer to the notion that the study of symbolic action in particular literary works should begin with the charting of "equations." That is: When you consult a text, from which you hope to derive insights as regards our human quandaries in general, you begin by asking yourself "what equals what in this text?" And then, next, "what follows what in this text?"

The study of such "equations" is a way of *yielding without demoralization*. One cannot know in advance what the "equations" are to be (what "hero" is to equal, what "villain" is to equal, what "wisdom" is to equal, etc.).[5] Yet in one's search for such "equations," which the author himself *spontaneously exemplified* rather than upheld as conscious doc-

---

[5] As for the importance of such an emphasis, consider the difference between the equation "reason equals respect for authority" and the equation "reason equals distrust of authority." Such equations are studied, first of all, in a non-normative, nonpreferential way, the assumption being that the best function of education is in giving us a free approach to such linkages, which otherwise tend to call forth automatic responses, making us in effect somnambulists.

trine, one is guided by method. Accordingly, such analysis is no mere surrender, though it does set up a preparatory stage in which one wholly "yields" to the text.

Having thus, without heckling, systematically let the text say its full say, even beyond what its author may have thought he was saying, we have the basic admonition as regards man, with relation to his specialty, "symbolic action." We see "exhortations" of terrifying importance being prepared for, even when a writer has no such intentions in mind. For, if certain elements equal "good" and certain elements equal "bad" (or, what is often more important, if certain elements equal "socially superior" and certain elements equal "socially inferior"), then in contemplating the "dynamics" of such "equations" (their implied hortatory value), do we not contemplate the very essence of human foibles?

And, at least within the ideality of our educational pursuits, are we not thereby admonished to watch and wait—and not just preceptorially, but technically?

"Dramatism," the approach to the human situation "linguistically," in terms of symbolic action, fulfils its purposes only in so far as it makes methodical the attitude of patience. The "dramatic" may thunder. It should. The "dramatistic," in a commingling of techniques and hypochondriasis, will "appreciate" man's ways of thundering.

Educational Aims and Values

Education, as so conceived, would be primarily admonitory. It would seek to become a sophisticated and methodized set of parables, or fables. Noting how man's distinctive trait, his way with symbols, is the source of both his typical accomplishments and his typical disabilities, education as so conceived would be first and foremost "of a divided mind," and would seek to make itself at home in such divisiveness.

Far too often, education is wholly under the sign of the promissory. The serious student enters school hoping to increase his powers, to equip himself in the competition for "success," to make the "contacts" that get him a better-paying job. Vocational courses almost inevitably confirm such an attitude, since their main purpose is to perfect technical ability, to teach special skills.

The "humanistic" aspect of the curriculum is usually approached in the same spirit, even by those who think of themselves as opponents of the vocational emphasis. The courses are expected in some way or other to help students "get ahead" as individuals. Humanistic education thus becomes the attempt to teach and to acquire the kind of "insignia" that are thought to be proof of cultural election.

This pragmatic emphasis may not always be individualistically motivated. With the project of *The Republic* for the training of the guardians, for instance, the emphasis was rather in the direction of Plato's yearning that education might serve for the triumph of all Greek states, united in a common cause against the "barbarians." And nationalistic emphases in general would belong here; for although there is conceivable an ideal world of nationalisms that would be related to one another as peacefully as the varied portraits in an art gallery, we need no very difficult fables to admonish us about the ever-ready dialectical resource whereby national "*differences*" may become national "conflicts."

Only a truly "universal" attitude toward educational purposes can modify this intrinsically *competitive* emphasis. Such an attitude would be grounded in the thought that all mankind has a major stake in the attempt to discipline any tendencies making for the kind of war now always threatening. In this spirit, we would aim at the discovery of methods that would be a *technical* equivalent of such uneasiness as, in religious terms, has been called the "fear of God." And we would seek for a *technical* equivalent of "mortification" thereby hoping to make active and mundane a kind of scruples now too often confined to the separate realm of the cloister.

But such "technicalizing" would produce notable changes of emphasis, since we are here discussing purely *secular* modes of education. In this realm, the pious "fear of God" would be replaced by a partially impious "fear of symbol-using" (that is, an ironic fear of the very resourcefulness that is man's greatest boast). And "mortification" in the religious sense would have, as its secular "dramatistic" analogue, a methodic distrust of competitive ambitions which goad us either as individuals or as groups. Or, more accurately: We would try, *at least within the limited orbit of theory, or contemplation,* to perfect techniques for doubting much that is now accepted as lying beyond the shadow of a doubt.

A mere inculcating of "tolerance," "good will," "respect for the rights of others," and such, cannot be enough. Such attitudes are all too airily "positive." And the educational training here advocated would be in its very essence *negative,* as negative as the Ten Commandments.

Yet its negativity would be of a paradoxical sort; we might label it "Faustological, since it would center in the study of ambition as a *disease*. At the same time it would concede that we had all better be very very ambitious and sufficiently exacting in our ambitiousness to cancel off the many prompter ambitions that, given the new weapons, threaten to destroy us.

The *pragmatic,* the *admonitory,* and the *appreciative* thus merge. For we would study the means by which men have been able to increase their assertiveness; thereby we should be "appreciating" human genius, yet doing so with fearsomeness (albeit a fearsomeness which our technical approach enables us to temper in the kindly spirit of comedy, while we tentatively seek to develop ways of looking upon us all as fools rather than as knaves). But in such tripleness of emphasis, the admonitory (the "negative") is to be treated as "foremost among the equals."

The aim, then, is to droop, at least *ad interim* (within the special conditions of the educational enterprise, considered as but one stage of a person's life)—but to droop so methodically, with such an emphasis upon method, that each day can bristle with assertions, as we attempt to perfect our lore of the human scramble (what Goethe calls the *Zeitenstrudel,* and Diderot the *grand branle*).

Education, as so conceived, would brood, as with the Flaubert who wrote *L'Education Sentimentale.* But in its attempts to perfect a technique of brooding, it would learn to cherish the documents as never before. No expunging of records here. All must be kept, and faithfully examined; and not just that it may be approved or disapproved, but also that it be considered as a challenge to our prowess in placing it within the unending human dialogue as a whole.

If we temporarily risk being *stopped* by such a discipline, let us realize that the discipline is ideally designed precisely to that end. Education must not be thought of merely as a means of preparing students for market, though that's what much of it now is. Education must be thought of as a *technique of preparatory withdrawal,* the institutionalizing of an attitude that one should be able *to recover at crucial moments,* all along the subsequent way.

Admittedly, this view of education as a kind of smiling hypochondriasis presents some difficulties. The promissory, by its very nature, likes to look forward. And there is apparently danger lest youth would either too greatly resist such doctrines as a mere "counsel of despair," or would accept them only too thoroughly, if a whole educational program were undertaken in such a spirit. Perhaps, the world being what it is, this enterprise could be but one course in a curriculum, rather than the guiding principle behind educational policy in general. But if so, at least it would be conceived of as a kind of "central" or "over-all' course, a "synoptic" project for "unifying the curriculum" by asking the students themselves to think of their various courses in terms of a single distinctive human trait (the linguistic) that imposes its genius upon all particular studies.

Also, there can be much very active enjoyment in approaching the precious documents from this point of view. When the mortifying "fear of man as symbol-user" has been "comically" *technicalized,* such an attitude does not by any means close our horizons but opens many new vistas, making all aspects of symbolic activity somehow "contemporary" with us.

"Drooping," as so qualified, can be quite muscular.

EDUCATIONAL PROCESS, METHODOLOGY

Primarily, we are ever to be on the lookout for grammatical and dialectical resources in general, while inspecting particular works for the discovery of special cases that forever keep threatening our frame of generalizations. In this respect, the procedure is not different from the traditional modes of inquiry and placement. But it has a somewhat "existentialist" aspect, in that we constantly re-begin from unique experiences (since each book that we take as our point of departure leads into our generalizations from one unique set of conditions, and accordingly compels us to see them in a perspective never quite duplicated, if we take any other book as our "informing experience"). Later, when discussing the negative, we shall consider another point at which this position closely parallels the existentialist one, if we have interpreted it correctly.

The study is thus built pedagogically about the "indexing" of some specific "symbolic structure," in the attempt to study the nature of a work's internal consistency and of its unfolding. But in contrast with courses in "literary appreciation," the generalizations at which we aim are not confined to a concern with the work's "beauty." Our quest concerns its linguistic nature in general; and then, beyond that, the insight it may afford into man's ways as symbol-user.

We proceed on the assumption that the "perfect case" for analytic purposes as a definitive literary text. This view, in turn, is doubtless but a variant of the traditional analogy whereby "nature" was likened to a "scripture" which would be legible if one but knew the language it was written in. In this case, the "signs" manifested by a human personality or by a social incident (or social order, or social movement, or cultural trend in general) would be treated as relatively obscure aspects of motivational structures that are least obscure in literary texts. There would thus be no difference *"principle"* between textual analysis and social analysis. But though textual analysis would be the "ideal norm" here, there is no reason why specialists in other sciences could not apply the same procedures, *mutatis mutandis,* to their subjects (as with Freud's systematic attention to the "free associations" of his patients, or the use of questionnaires in polls of public opinion). Our major difference (if there is any essential difference!) is in the over-all direction we would give to such procedures.

When the great executive has finished his murder thriller, and relaxed into a well-earned sleep after having gone, by a certain disciplinary route, from the killing of the victim to the killing of the mystery, our vigil has but begun. We must ask: "What does the victim equal? . . . What does the killer equal? . . . What does the virtuously or disingenuously instigatory heroine equal? . . . What are the stages of this journey?" etc.

And we do this, not just to learn something about the given work, but ultimately in the hope of learning something about the ways in which the "personality" of the work relates to the "personality" of a social order; and then, in accordance with our project for methodic drooping, we look for ways whereby the work embodies, however assertively, even militantly, the *malaise* of a given property structure (with the goads, and "mortifications," and demands upon our "patience," and invitations to victimage, that are intrinsic to any such order).

Tragedies are quite convenient for our purposes, since we accept Aristotle's statement that tragic poetry aims at a kind of "catharsis"— and the explicitly civic, stately, or courtly nature of the tragedies traditionally accepted as great, makes easier our search for routes that clearly link mere "personal equations" with the "great persecutional words," such as fate, law, right, justice, Themis, Moira, Nemesis, necessity. But other species of expression are also inspected for kinds of catharsis or transcendence proper to their nature.

There are principles and rules of thumb to guide the task of "indexing." And one has available a set of at least partially coordinated statements about the nature of symbolic action in general. With this to start from, teacher and class are on a voyage of discovery together. Ideally, we keep open the channels that take us back and forth between general principles and casuistry, and, whereas certain methods for tracking things down have already been developed, teacher and class are engaged in a joint enterprise for perfecting these. But, whereas the original reading might have sought to track down a "villain," we rather would seek to track down the nature of the author's idea of "villainousness" conceived not just historically, with regard to the "climate of opinion" that prevailed in a given social order but, universally or formally, with regard to the modes and motives of such symbolizing in general.

We proceed by systematically "suffering" a given text, in the hope of discovering more about the symbolic activity in its particular sufferance. "Formal discipline" is identical with the carrying out of such an investigation. "Truth" is absolute, in the sense that one can categorically make assertions about certain basic resources and embarrassments of symbols. It is nearly absolute, as regards certain "factual" statements that can be made about the terms of a given work. It is highly problematical, as regards the question that ultimately concerns us most: What is the nature of a symbol-using animal? Here, at least ideally, however emphatic we may become on the spur of the moment, we adopt as our primary slogan: "All the returns aren't in yet." And we would continue to keep alive this attitude (the "Deweyite" emphasis) by embodying it in methods that practically *compel* one to be tentative, at least during the preparatory stage when one is trying to locate all the significant correlations in a book, without deciding whether they are "good" or "bad," but trying rather simply to find out exactly what they *are*.

Since every course in the curriculum is a symbolically guided mode of action, a placement of all courses from the standpoint of symbolic action violates none of them, though with regard to many scientific disciplines the linguistic approach can be irksome to instructors who would persuade themselves and their classes that they are talking about "objective reality" even at those times when they happen to be but going through sheerly linguistic operations. Since every specialty has its terminology, it can be studied like any poem or philosophic treatise, for its "equations." And, indeed, if you inspect any given scientific writer's terminology closely enough, you can hope to find the bridges that join his purely technical nomenclature with the personal realm.

But though such statements are required for a full account of human action in the realm of physical motion, a "dramatistic" approach by no means requires that laws of motion as such be equated with action. Indeed, we have tried to show how the very self-consciousness of our stress upon action forces us to distinguish action from sheer motion (a distinction that is obscured, for instance, in Aristotle's term *kinesis,* though that very ambiguity is helpful in warning us how the two usages can cross, as when Aristotle himself "dramatistically" discusses the realm of physics in terms of "action" and "passion").

Though the student would not be abiding by the spirit of the enterprise if he merely set about such a fragmentary search as often characterizes doctoral theses, in all methods there is a large percentage of "neutrality," in the sense that a theory of ballistics could be called "neutral," since it could be employed by either side to slay the other. Accordingly, analysis can be carried into lines that take us far from our primary search (any method being ambiguous enough in its potentialities to become detached from the attitude for which it was designed).

Indeed, one can even imagine situations where, even if mankind did amass an authoritative lore on the odd kinds of "somnambulism" to which our nature as symbolists makes us susceptible, there might arise some calamitously endowed "throw-back" who used it all to make things worse rather than better, somewhat as when rules for the cure of souls are transformed into the techniques of "psychological warfare." For, since every point of view has its corresponding "pragmatics," this dilemma of the ambiguities in power or method is not confined to pragmatism. And, at least, the admonitory aspects of our position can prevent us from thinking of any human resource, such as "mind," "spirit," "eloquence," "imagination," "intellect," "understanding," "rationality," as intrinsically good, rather than as prone to the trickeries (and the grandeurs!) of the symbolic order upon which such resources so strongly rely.

The principle of "negativity" which is basic to the "dramatistic" approach, being essentially of a "repressive" nature (in contrast with liberal practices that often seemed to do all in their power to avoid the spirit of the thou-shalt-not), this approach must cope with the great threat to student interest that goes with such a concern. However, as contrasted with earlier modes of scholastic regimentation, it says no with a difference. It says no *by studying "no,"* by trying systematically to discover just how vast a domain the principle of negativity does actually govern, despite our assumptions to the contrary. Nor is such an investigation undertaken purely in the hope that, by such insight, one may be better qualified to emancipate one's self from the "reign of no." One must take it for granted that negativity of some sort is inevitable to social order, as conceived and constructed by an inveterately symbol-using species. And one must remember that the "negatives" of property and propriety are very "positive" in the sense that they affirm the given society's co-operative norms. Negatives shared in common can be like wealth shared in common.

It is not for us a question whether man is naturally good or naturally depraved; it is simply a question of realizing that, as animality in general comprises a set of positive needs, appetites, and gratifications (ultimately reducible to terms of material motion), so the distinctive trait of man, his way with symbols, or languages, centers in his ability to use the negative of "conscience," a symbolically guided ability that is also interwoven with the thou-shalt-not's, or no-trespassing, of property. [267–278]

[. . .] A linguistic approach to the study of human relations, on the other hand, would suggest rather the possibility that we are "poets all." Maybe, then, with a typically symbol-using creature, no solution of his difficulties but a *perfectly symbolic one* could content him, no matter how practical or normal he may think of himself as being.

The educational process as here conceived is guided by this ironic likelihood: That man can be content with nothing less than perfection, and that a typically symbol-using species will conceive of perfection in a way that is essentially symbolic, somewhat as "angels" are sheer "message." Our study of poetic ritual for instance, would be guided by this notion. And some of Santayana's ingenious conceits, concerning the aspirations of the spirit to so transcend material conditions that the mind dissolves into the realm of pure being, would be interpreted by us linguistically as the ultimate human hankering for a condition so thoroughly in keeping with man's differentia that his generic animality would be transformed into a perfect symbol-system. A visible burlesque of such transcendence is seen in the Cyberneticists' dream of reducing all mental operations to their counterparts in the order of *pure* motion. And we all know of journalistic critics who read books so fast and write on them so quickly, their minds are hardly more than a telephone exchange where messages automatically converge and are automatically rerouted. [281–282]

[. . .] We can never sufficiently emphasize, however, that we are thinking of education as a tentative, preparatory stage in life, not as a final one. It is final only in the sense that it possesses it own kind of completeness and thus, ideally, should be recoverable at all stages in one's life. For it develops to perfection one stage in the confronting of a problem, the stage where one steps aside as thoroughly as possible and attempts, in the spirit of absolute linguistic skepticism, to meditate upon the tangle of symbolism in which all men are by their very nature caught.

The corresponding methods of interpreting man's entanglement have been sloganized by us elsewhere as the "socioanagogic," since a primary aim here is to discover in what respects the objects of this world are enigmatic emblems of man's relation to the social order (that is, in what respects they may possess for man a "symbolic' character, over and above their nature as sheer *things*). Since language, however manipulated by the individual user, is essentially a collective or social product, the powers of the social order will inevitably be manifested in it, quite as these powers can only be developed by the use of linguistic resources. A social philosophy, as so conceived, would be built about four orders: the verbal or linguistic; the sociopolitical; the natural; the supernatural. And we shall end this section by briefly indicating the relation we think they bear to one another. [287–288]

[. . .] But there is a paradox upon which a dramatist philosophy of social motivations lays great emphasis: Whereas we are by the nature of the case compelled to see the part that the other three orders of terms play in the terminology of the supernatural order, and whereas we are familiar with the transcendentalist dialectic of a writer, say, like Emerson, who contrives to interpret the many agencies of the everyday world as all variously embodying a single supernatural purpose, it is much harder to detect the ways in which the linguistic, and social orders affect our ideas of the natural order. And this is the enigma, above all others, with which dramatism, as a social philosophy, is engrossed.

By the socioanagogic emphasis in linguistic criticism, we refer to a concern with the ways in which the structure of the social and linguistic orders affects the metaphors men use for the supernatural order and colors the "empirical reality" which men think they perceive in the natural order. We believe that the natural order is profoundly infused with symbolism, "mystery," and "divinity" of a purely secular and social sort, however transcendent its gleam may sometimes seem to be. Here, we believe, is a major source of man's exorbitant goads and false exaltations. We believe it to be a major source of the scramble so incessantly plaguing great nations that most persons seem to take it as "the norm," sometimes assuring us that man is "naturally predatory," and sometimes in unconscious sacrilege interpreting such worldly struggle as an evidence of man's "divine discontent." [289]

[. . .] There is no tangle so hopeless that it cannot, with the symbol-using species, become the basis for a new ingenious assertion that transcends it, by the very nature of linguistic assertion. No way of life can be so wretched, corrupt, or even boring that some expert symbol-user or other can't make it the subject matter of a good book. Wherever you might moralistically exclaim, "How awful!" there is the opportunity for the aesthetic to answer spiritedly, "But how *delightfully* awful!"

In sum, there is the transcendence in expression as such (the point emphasized in the Crocean aesthetic). Atop that, there is the transcendence implicit in the processes whereby the work "purifies itself" in the course of its unfolding. And beyond that, there is transcendence by the various ways whereby we feel ourselves similarly purified while undergoing the imaginary discipline of the story's action and passion (undergoing such either as spontaneous spectators or as students, or both). And so, each time we inspect a great work of human thought (that is, a great symbolic exercising), we can be delighted by the manifestations of its genius, a skill whereby even the accents of lamentation can be transformed into the pleasurable. [292]

[. . .] But, ideally at least, viewed in "the absolute," an educational program of this sort would come closer to such promises as were once called the *consolatio philosophiae*. Admonition would make of education a watching and waiting, appreciation would seek out the positive attitudes that corrected such negatives. Its great stress upon linguistic skepticism would imply that it is not designed to make up the student's mind for him. For it could not arrogate to itself the right (or assume that it had the ability) to anticipate the *particularity* that characterizes an individual's decisions. [294]

[. . .] Such, then, is what we take to be the nature of education as preparation for adult life." The obligations of order hang over us, even if we would revolt against order. Out of such predicaments, ingenious fellows rise up and sing; thus promptly have all our liabilities been by symbol-using converted into assets. Similarly aesthetic, from this point of view, is any way of analytically *enjoying* the ways of rising up and singing. These ways may be "diagnostic," as all education in one sense is. And so we are led back to the realm of the admonitory.

And finally, and above all, in keeping with our "socioanagogic" search for the ways in which the magic of the social order infuses men's judgments of the beautiful (quite as it infuses their ethics and their perception of even "natural" things) we watch everywhere for the manifestations of the "hierarchal" motive, what Ulysses, in *Troilus and Cressida,* calls "degree." It is only "by degree," he declaims, that communities, schools, brotherhoods, businesses, inheritance, the prerogatives of age and office, even the regularities of nature, "stand in authentic place." Accordingly, "Take but degree away, untune that string, / And, hark! what discord follows; each thing meets / In mere oppugnancy." And later, with a strange imagistic paralleling of *Othello,* he sums up: "Chaos, when degree is suffocate, / Follows the choking." We cite from this long passage, not exactly to reaffirm the Shakespearean answer, but to recall how vast, in the perspective of Shakespearean drama, was the scope of question. [295]

11

Goethe's *Faust,* Part I[1]

IN AN EARLIER SECTION OF THIS ESSAY, to be found in the *Chicago Review* for Fall, 1954, I proposed that four "offices" (derived in part from Cicero's "three offices of the orator) be considered as essential to the analysis of poetic symbolism. The first office is that of teaching or informing; the second, that of pleasing; the third, that of moving of the agent. It is with the fourth of these, and specifically with the work's "personality" as expressed symbolically and socially determined, that I am concerned here; and I am to show how the symbolizing of perfect victimage relates to the "entelechial" principle natural to the genius of language.

I. THE OUTLINE OF THE WORK, AS PAINTED FOR OUR PURPOSES

An elderly man, sick of sheer intellectual knowledge, regretful that worldly delights and honors have passed him by, makes a pact with the devil. The devil, restoring his youth, shall empower him to seduce a guileless girl. After agreeing to a pact, but before encountering the girl, with the aid of diabolic magic he takes part in a tipsy revel of adolescents and also visits a Witches' Kitchen. Then follows the carefully paced seduction, which results in the seducer's killing of the girl's

---

[1] This essay first appeared in *Chicago Review.* "Goethe's *Faust,* Part I." *Chicago Review* 9.1 (Spring 1955): 40–72. Used by permission. "Goethe's *Faust,* Part I" later appeared in *Language as Symbolic Action.* Berkeley, CA: University of California Press, 1966. 139–62.

brother and in her half-mad disgrace and death, after she has in madness drowned her illegitimate child. The mounting turmoil of the plot culminates in an episode of Pandemonium, a perverse "preternatural" orgy that stylistically completes the episodes of the tippling students, of Hell's Kitchen, and of the man's furious debate with himself in a forest cavern. Also, its riot impressionistically duplicates a quasi-revolutionary outbreak, here "channelized" in sexual terms. Of this sexual story we could say that it recounts how a wealthy man seduced a trusting girl of modest means by whom he was deemed "noble"; how his wealth had seemed to her capable of making her look like a "lady of nobility"; and how her guileless ways of failing to protect her sexual treasure had made her seem to him like an "angel."

II. Negatives (or, rather, a Few of the More Notable Ones)

In the "Prologue in Heaven," the Lord classes Mephistopheles among the spirits that deny (*verneinen*). And when Mephistopheles discloses himself to Faust for the first time, he calls himself the spirit that always denies (*Ich bin der Geist, der stets verneint*). In the riot of Walpurgis Night, Faust calls Mephistopheles the "spirit of contradiction" (*Geist des Widerspruchs*). And the nature of the motives in the Witches' Kitchen is epitomized in the crazy mathematical design of a computation that nonsensically adds up to nothing.

But we should also note that Gretchen's first words are negatively couched, as she somewhat curtly says to Faust that she is neither a lady nor beautiful and can go home unaccompanied: *Bin weder Fraulein weder schön / Kann ungeleitet nach Hause gehn*. But subsequently we hear her admitting to herself how much she has been impressed by the talk of the great man, who makes her feel ashamed by comparison, while all she can do is say yes to everything he tells her: *Beschämt nur steh' ich vor ihm da, / Und sag zu allen Sachen ja*. Unlike the devil, she could not steadily deny. We might also note that the devil, in perhaps the most patly character-drawing device of all drama, pays handsome tribute to her in an aside, pityingly apostrophizing her as "thou good and innocent child" (*du guts unschuldigs Kind*), his negative here being couched almost in the accents of a doting parent.

In the first stanza of his opening speech, Faust had lamented that we can know nothing (*dass wir nichts wissen können*). Later he contemplates suicide, as a possible dissolution into nothingness (*ins Nichts*). And in the garden with Gretchen, when discussing the advisability of total yielding (*sich hinzageben ganz*), he had avowed that the delight must be forever, since its end would be disaster: "No, no end! No end!" (*Nein, kein Ende! Kein Ende!*). Later, when reproaching himself for his impetuosity, he calls himself homeless and a monster (literally, "unhoused" and an "un-man": *der Unbehauste* [. . .] *der Unmensch*).

Gretchen's initial negative is understandable enough, as likewise the poetic justice of the disaster that went with her turn from nay to yea. Faust's negatives apparently involved philosophic speculations, plus his rhetorical adapting of these to the ends of certain worldly gains (here epitomized in the seducing of Gretchen). But the central consideration, for our purposes, is the negativity of Mephistopheles.

In the "Prologue in Heaven," the Lord explains why he does not hate the likes of Mephistopheles. Man inclines too easily toward sloth, he says (*Des Menschen Tätigkeit kann allzuleicht erschlaffen*); and the devil serves as a companion, to keep men prodded into action. Previously the Lord had given Mephistopheles permission to tempt Faust, since man can be expected to err as long as he keeps striving (*es irrt der Mensch solang' er strebt*).

III. Striving (*Streben*)

With this reference to striving we have not only a theme but more specifically a *term* that we can trace in zigzags throughout the entire work. We have explicit authority in the text for connecting it with both "the Lord" and the "spirit of negation, or contradiction." And, if only because the play is for the most part in rhymes, we find the word itself quickly becoming interwoven with two others that rhyme with it: "soaring" (*Schweben*) and "life" or "living" (*Leben*). "Weaving" (*Weben*) figures secondarily. So far as sheer letters go, this "fatal" word is but *Schweben* without the initial *sch*.

To dispose of the more general motivational problem before tying ourselves down to purely "concordantial" connections, we should note, first of all, that the "Prologue in Heaven" makes no pretences whatever to an esoteric religious vision. Goethe is portraying a "heavenly" court, to be sure; but in the spirit of a conceiver of a *fiction,* of a masque or conceit, not in that of a pious prophet who might say that he is reporting on an actual dialogue in Heaven. In particular, we would lay great store by Mephistopheles' soliloquy, on which the Prologue ends. He likes to see the Old Man (*den Alten*) now and then, he says, and is careful never to break with him. And "it's quite decent of so great a lord to be so human when talking with the devil" (*Es ist gar hubsch von einem grossen Herrn, So menschlich mit dem Teafel selbst zu sprechen*). Clearly, this is the way an underling talks of his superior, as when the clerk feels proud that the boss has acted toward him "like a good fellow."

The "heavenly prologue" is thus seen to be the mythically transmogrified replica of a quite worldly situation: The three angels ("messengers") praising the Lord are analogous to three loyal ambassadors in audience with the monarch. And Mephistopheles is the inevitable nay that matches the three devoted angels' unswerving yea. We thus begin with a dramatized paradigm of an administrative center, a masquelike depiction of its "essence": the authority, the loyal underlings, the resistant underling (with the authority recognizing that there is a sense in which the resistant underling plays a necessary role in the authoritative structure). We should add: To the purely internal ends of greater vividness, the "heavenly scene" is cosmologized by the three angels' references to the astronomical heavens, which are as splendid (literally, "lordly," *herrlich*) as on the first day of the Creation.

There is an alternative prologue, the "Prologue in the Theatre." There, the theatrical manager would correspond to the Lord, the dramatic poet would be analogous to the angels, and the jester, or *lustige Person*, would match Mephistopheles. But the change of persons here naturally leads also to a slight dislocation of the three functions, so that the correspondences between the two matrices are not exact.

As for the "*Streben*-nexus," (the "courtly" motive localized in a few key words), the most famous *strebt* passage appears early in the drama, when Faust is talking to his bluntly devoted disciple, Wagner. Faust tells him man is born with a desire that presses forward and up (*hinauf und vorwärts*). There follows a transitional reference to skylarks; then comes the noted set piece, of the spread eagle that soars (*schwebt*) and the crane that over waters homeward strives (*strebt*). Next comes Faust's avowal that two motives ("souls") dwell within his breast—and out of that speech in turn evolves the appearance of the poodle, the first manifestation of Mephistopheles. (Though Wagner sees it only as a dog, while Faust from the start senses in it something vaguely portentous, the two views agree to this extent: Wagner lays great emphasis upon the subservience of the animal; and immediately after the "fog" has been dispelled, Mephistopheles presents himself in the guise of a person eager to *serve* Faust as his *master: Was steht dem Herrn zu Diensten?*) Later, when sizing up Faust's susceptibilities, Mephistopheles muses, "Fate has given him a spirit that ever presses forward irrepressibly" (*ungebändigt*). There is talk of overhasty striving that overleaps man's earthly pleasures. And "soaring" follows, in connection with the idea of unappeasable appetite.

In the "Prologue in Heaven," *schwebt* had appeared in a notable connection. The Lord, when addressing the loyal angels, likened eternal living to the condition of becoming (*das Werdende*); and he told them they must strengthen with enduring thoughts whatever wavers (the word *schwebt* itself vacillates among such meanings as soar, hover, and waver). But the most important further reference occurs in the episode of Walpurgis Night. Here, the riotous ride is said to take place among a whirlpool of fantastically inhuman creatures, a swirl (*Strudel*) that strives upward (*strebt nach oben*). Everything is so topsy-turvy in this incident, you think you're pushing and you're being shoved (*Du glaubst zu schieben, und du wirst geschoben*). Whereat we are reminded that, in the "Prologue in the Theatre," the dramatic poet refers to a *Strudel* into which the surging multitude draws us against our wills. And in the Dream that forms an intermezzo to the Walpurgis Night section, there is a quatrain recited by the crane (recall him in the earlier "striving" passage): He says that, because he loves to fish in both clear and muddy waters, that's why you see this pious gentleman mixing with the devil (a variant of the "two souls" theme).

IV. In Sum, On the Play as "Characteristic"

The foregoing observations should serve at least to indicate the sort of symbolism that figures in the work as a "natural sign" of the author (the work as approached in terms of the "fourth office"). However, in studying it as the portrait of a personality we aim to begin with the broadest possible frame of reference. The fact that Goethe was a romantic poet who became a minister of state would be relevant, certainly. But even if we knew nothing about him as a private citizen we should still want to contend that the "Prologue in Heaven" is a dramatized paradigm of the "courtly situation," the administrative motive reduced to a "basic design." Intrinsic to this, we would say, are problems of negativity variously classifiable in purely critical terms and here figured in terms of dramatic imitations (characters variously acting).

Even if we did not know that Goethe had translated Diderot's *Neveu de Rameau* or did not know that, in his capacity as an elderly statesman, he greatly feared and condemned such disorders as came to a head in the French Revolution, we should look for evidences of the "hierarchal psychosis" (of the "social pyramid") which we believe figures essentially in every work. (Indeed, we choose a full-bodied work such as this because, in its great intellectual clarity, it can clearly reveal motivational principles more readily overlooked in works that stress sheer imagery or "sensibility.")

The courting of Gretchen, we take it, translates the "courtly" motive into sexual equivalents. Paradoxically, there is thus a sense in which this seduction is more of an "allegory" than are the "supernatural" or "preternatural" episodes. For the reader does not take those as "real," but as "symbolical"; whereas the courtship of Gretchen is quite realistically rendered, even Mephistopheles' producing of the fatal jewels not being presented as a particularly "magical" happening. Yet what is this constant attempt to see behind or beyond the sheer seduction as such, if not a dramatist's way of reversing the motives, by looking for what we might call the "underlying forms" of this courtship? And in the light of these, the courting of Gretchen becomes like a kind of "case history."

One might look for "characteristics" in the narrowest sense. For instance, in the midst of a fantastic episode, there is even a quatrain about a "northern artist" contemplating a journey to Italy. Knowing the importance of Goethe's Italian journey as a stage in his development, and that it interrupted his relations with Charlotte, we might dig for the most particularized kind of biographical connections. But whereas there are not grounds for ruling out such minute portraiture (and especially in the case of a writer so autobiographical as Goethe), we are contending that inquiries into the "fourth office" should begin much farther afield.

Thus, as regards the notion that "man errs so long as he strives," the usual way of interpreting such a statement might be to think of "erring" as a mere undesirable risk, the generalized description of an "occupational hazard" to which those who strive are exposed. But another way of approaching the Faustian duality would be to think of the two words as but different terms for the same act, observed from different angles. If a person were wholly adequate he would not err; nor, if he were wholly adequate, would he have to strive. And we are thus suggesting that the inadequacy connoted by either of the terms is *categorical,* or "original." That is, it is intrinsic to the social order as such; and in this sense it is "inherited" by all mankind, being "prior" to any individual lapse into "actual sin." These remarks are offered not as a dialectical exercise in the Hegelian "reconciling of opposites," but to explain why we think that motives of "guilt" are inherent in social hierarchy as such. For if this were true, then we should be proved correct in our search for the *social* motives inherent in *poetic* "catharsis." Signs of such "original sin" might then be looked for in every work, both as a statement about poetic symbolism in general and as a way of suggesting something important to look for in any particular poet's strategy of expression.

"Categorical guilt," in this *political* or *sociological* sense (the need to "strive and/or err" in that scramble or *Strudel* wherein pushing is indistinguishable from being pushed), would not necessarily be taken as an alternative to "original sin" in the strictly *theological* sense. But the secular nature of secular poetry should justify us in expecting that, *at the very least,* secular poetry should mirror (or be the sign of) categorical guilt *in the merely political or sociological sense.* A secular poet might not have grace enough to understand original sin in the theological sense; but he might nonetheless exemplify the sociological variant without the slightest conscious effort. In any case, Goethe is at least talking about a *worldly* mode of striving—for that is what Faust explicitly chooses.

Such concerns naturally come to a head in problems of the negative, since the negative itself comes to a head in the perfection of the Decalogical (the thou-shalt-not's proper to a given order of property). Such motives are variously perverted and disguised, though great works such as this afford us the "missing links" connecting clear and direct manifestations with unclear and perverted ones.

An easily observable departure, in the present work, is in Faust's resounding set of itemized curses, which ends significantly on his cursing of patience above all else (*Und Fluch vor allen der Geduld!*) "Patience" sums up the attitude of social control, not as imposed *from without* or *from above,* but as a kind of self-legislation, the free imposing of law by the lawgiver upon the lawgiver. (We are talking here along Kantian lines.) In a similar vein, Faust said he didn't care whether there were

Over and Under in the other world. Here is in principle the rejection of order, a rejection got by rejecting the principle of "mortification," or "renunciation" (*Entbehren*), that goes with any given order. Here is par excellence a *ministerial* value, though dramatized perversely, in Faust's curse (that prepared the way for Mephistopheles' appearance).

Later, musing in a romantic forest cavern, and turbulently nay-ridden as regards his designs on Gretchen, Faust likens himself to a cataract plunging down the mountain side, while Gretchen is as in a little Alpine hut standing quietly near by. His *im*patience is here expressed in terms imagistically positive, a thought that makes clear the ways whereby natural scenery can be endowed with motives of the social order, in this case even figuring a "fall." The correspondence may be even closer yet, as Faust further wishes that he could be like the stream in another respect, since the stream leaves the hut unharmed and expends its powers rather in tearing at its own rocks. (This kind of reflexive action would, as it were, get a semblance of self-control through a semblance of self-abuse, a motive that seems to flicker about the edges of the student scene in Auerbach's cellar, which ends when the bewitched youths awaken to find that the devil has set them all to pulling one another's *noses!*)

But regardless of how broadly or narrowly one conceives of the ways in which a work is the signature of personal (sociopolitical) motives, as soon as we begin looking for key terms, and for interrelations among them, we are turned in the direction of the "second order," as expanded in the omitted, earlier part of this discussion (and described there as the internal spinning of terms, from the standpoint of their intrinsic resources and obligations) .

Thus the striving-soaring-living-weaving nexus is found, within this structure, to tie in with the philosophy of "Becoming." (In a song of Christ's resurrection it is called "delight in becoming": *Werdelust.*) But "becoming" itself, in being analyzable as moments between the limits of before and after, lends itself well to dramatization in terms of the youth-age relationship (the turbulent waterfall would obviously be on the youthful side of such a slope). And while watching lest the youth-age alignment itself be conceived in too naturalistic or biological a sense (while being on guard, that is, lest we overlook the social motivations implicit both in these terms and in the closely related sexual ones), we do have here central moments to do with the work as viewed in its internality.

V. The Heroine as Perfect Sacrificial Victim

When discussing a character from the standpoint of its formal perfection, we are obviously concerned with its "persuasiveness" as a symbol for arousing our sympathies or antipathies. Such a concern with the effectiveness of a character-recipe bears upon the "fourth office" insofar as we ask what social judgments are exploited in the endowing of the character with specific traits. The first seventeen chapters of Aristotle's *Rhetoric*, Book II, set down the main principles to be followed in such character drawing, though there are many remote or perverse ways whereby these principles can be complicated to the point where it seems that, in notable respects, almost the opposite policies are being followed, in writers given to "post-Christian" paradoxes.

But the mention of rhetoric in this connection suggests also that such considerations involve us in the poetic equivalent of the "third office," a work's capacity to "move" the audience. We say "poetic equivalent" because the use of these principles for poetic purposes is quite different from their rhetorical application, which is directed toward practical results outside the work, whereas the rewards of poetic application are intrinsic to their functioning within the work itself. To say as much is to indicate how such a concern with a character recipe involves us in the "second office," either in the narrowly Ciceronian sense of the entertaining or the wider sense of the self-consistent (self-developing). The "first office" (to inform) figures here, insofar as the poet uses "signs" for the traits he would have the reader attribute to the given character. (Under certain conditions, for instance, the doing of a kindly act would be a sign that the character is kindly; under other conditions, it would be a sign that the character is a hypocrite; and so forth.)

First of all, plotwise, there is Gretchen's guileless devotion to Faust. She must be the ideal victim, both in the sense that she is deemed admirable when "sinning," and in the sense that her victimage seems "logical" (at least in terms of "poetic justice"). She is very young; the sign of her youthfulness is dramatically "rendered" when we see her playing hide-and-seek with the great man. At that stage of the development (the "becoming"), he was still seeking what she still kept in hiding. The childish game was interrupted by Mephistopheles, in the dramatic interest of more protracted titillation for the audience. (He had previously pronounced the formula, observing that pleasure is increased by delay and slow preparation; there he had stated as a matter of psychology what the dramatist in this interruption embodies as a principle of form.)

Here are some traits that Faust identifies with her (indirectly, by associating them with her room): holiness through which sweet twilight weaves; quietude; order; peacefulness; a plenteousness in poverty; a blessedness in "this prison." He then imagines her piously kissing a grandfather's hand, says that the spirit of plenty and order has taught her like a mother, that she is a natural-born angel, that her divine image was made by pure and holy weaving (the two references to weaving might remind us that later she will sit at the spinning wheel, singing of her fatal love). Though he was drawn here by thoughts of pleasure, he now feels himself dissolving into a *Liebestraum*.

In another connection, roundabout, he attributes to her a simplicity and innocence that do not know their own holy worth, and a meekness and lowliness that are the highest gifts of lovingly bountiful Nature. He is talking to her about herself, but she is so much a case in point that she misses the point.

Such terms, as it were, provide the "sloganizing" for her character. Another kind of indirect portraiture results from her placement in a whole list of female *personae*, whose various ways of contrasting with her are in effect comments upon her, or illuminations of her, helping to differentiate her from other species of a genus. They are, in brief review: Gretchen's friend, Martha, so sexually designing that Mephistopheles, who must appear to be courting her (as a device for diverting her attention while Faust courts Gretchen), complains that she could hold even the devil himself to his word. (Gretchen is no such schemer.) Lieschen, who gossips with Gretchen by the well and talks unfeelingly about another girl involved in sexual scandal. Lieschen does not know that she is forcing Gretchen to realize how her own conduct will be interpreted by the villagers. (Gretchen is not thus unfeeling, though she admits ruefully to herself that once she would have been.) Bärbelchen, not a character in the play, but the subject of Lieschen's gossip. According to Lieschen, she had got into trouble acting the grand lady (by her *Vornehmtun*) and deserved all she got when her lover abandoned her to disgrace. (We shall return to her when on the subject of the jewels, involving Gretchen's kind of *Vornehmtun*.) Various other incidental figures, whose different ways of contrasting with Gretchen are obvious: the old prostitute, on the defensive but proud of her skill as a professional; a vague throng of marriageable young ladies, sexually unappeased and inquisitive, but primarily interested in making standard marriages; old crones of the Witches' Kitchen.

As for Gretchen herself: First of all, we must believe that she possesses all the virtues of malleability generously attributed to her by the man who would mold her. If his yearning for sexual domination is a cameo, it is dramatically matched by the intaglio of Gretchen's generous disposition. His designs adding up to guile, she is reciprocally a delightful vessel of guilelessness. Only Mephistopheles affronts her sympathetic tendencies. His presence, she says with naïve suggestiveness, makes her "close up inside" (*Und seine Gegenwart schnürt mir das Innre zu*); and he even troubles her so much that for emphasis she uses a double negative, avowing that he has "no sympathy with nothing" (*Man sicht, dass er an nichts keinen Anteil nimmt*).

But, above all, we would stress Gretchen's reception of the fatal jewels. Modestly undressing, unawares, before Faust and Mephistopheles, having sung to herself of the King of Thule who was loyal to a goblet (that seems to have stood ambiguously for motives both maternal and erotic), when she finds the jewels she says that such things as these could be worn on a high feast day by a lady of the nobility (an *Edelfrau*).

She also asks herself: "To whom might this splendor belong?" (*Wem mag die Herrlichkeit gehören.*) As we have said before, we would stress the literal meaning of this word as "lordliness." Beginning as an epithet applied to the Lord's Creation, in the "Prologue," the term has turned up at many strategic moments in the text. At one end, there is Faust addressing God as "great lordly Spirit," at a time when, in profound remorse, he is pleading for Gretchen to be saved. At the other end there is Mephistopheles applying the word to Walpurgis Night. Here Gretchen applies it to the fatal jewels, which had suggested to her the attraction of nobility, though none would say that she was putting on airs as Bärbelchen had done.

Musing about Faust, Gretchen is sure that he is of noble birth (*aus einem edlen Haus*). That would explain, she thinks, why he had been so self-assured (*keck*) when first accosting her on the street. Later she confides to Faust that she had been worried lest something immodest or improper in her manner (*Was freches, Unänsthndiges*) had led him on. Such guilelessness prompts Faust to call her an "angel," a "heavenly vision." And she does indeed look up to him with exactly such simple loyalty as the three angels of the Prologue manifest toward their Lord.

Bärbelchen, who had put on airs, paid for her *Vornehmtun* with scandal. Gretchen is involved in a similar scandal—and there is the analogy of *Vornehmtun* in her relation to the jewels. But to say as much is to be reminded that her *perfection* as a victim for Faust's act was her undoing.

Perhaps we should mention two other traits. She had been like a mother to her younger, ailing sister, now dead. (A full analysis would certainly trace the "breast" theme through this work.) And she gives Faust a good description of her lower middle-class respectability, as with her references to the modest property left by her father and situated near the edge of town.

In sum, our point is this: While trying to characterize Gretchen as a *person,* we do so not in the interests of character portraiture as such but with reference to problems in the diplomacy of poetic symbolization. For instance, as a figure designed to arouse our sympathies, this child who later drowns her own illegitimate child is seen to have been a virgin-mother to her sister. This girl who dies in disgrace is seen to be intrinsically endowed with such spiritual inheritance as goes ideally with middle-class respectability, and extrinsically endowed with the ideal property requirements of such a status. When asking how "scandal" figures in such motivation, we confront subtler considerations of property and propriety, which move us into broader considerations of negativity—involving respects, for instance, in which the purely physiological facts of deflowering and extramarital impregnation can be poetically identified in relation to signs for social control (somewhat as when Mephistopheles, observing Gretchen's naive attempts to reclaim Faust for religion, grumbles that girls catechize men because they feel that, if a man complies on this point, he'll yield to them in other matters).

But the reference to flowers brings up another mainly "internal" consideration: Goethe's use of the "flower" image, with its more immediate radiations.

VI. THE "FLOWER" IMAGE, AND RAMIFICATIONS

As regards the internalities of the story, we note the dramatic irony that Gretchen herself plucked the petals of a flower when in search of a sign that Faust loved her. The test "came out right," so far as its signifying of an intense attachment was concerned. But with regard to the specifically Goethean terminology (*Röslein, Röslein, Röslein rot*), she was off to a bad start. Similarly, later Lies*chen* tells Gret*chen* that Bärbelchen has lost her little flower, her Blüm*chen*. And before Gretchen, in unconscious shamelessness, had despoiled a flower by way of poetic prognosis, the devil himself had twitted Faust for talking pruriently of her as though her honor and her favors were flowers to be plucked.

When Faust enters the prison, intending to rescue her, and she mistakes him for her executioner, she tells him that her "friend," who once was near, is now far off. Then, impressionistically, she sums up: "The wreath lies torn, the flowers are scattered." (Nor should we overlook the *functioning perversity* of this scene, the principle of negativity concealed in the dramatic irony whereby Gretchen's mistaking of Faust for her executioner is "substantially" true, even while being *literally* a sign of her madness.)

Here is an instance of further radiations in the flower theme: In the "Prologue in the Theatre" the poet, after talk of the surging and crushing that draws us against our wills into the *Strudel*, offers an alternative ideal: "No," he says; "Lead me rather to some quiet corner in Heaven, where for the poet there blooms but pure delight, where love and friendship [[. . .]] ," etc. Recalling that Gretchen was Faust's "angel," we might also note that she repeatedly addresses him as "friend." It is questionable how far such correlations should be traced, particularly when the terms are so ordinary; but in any case it is literal fact that the word for "love" here is abbreviated (*Lieb'*)—and it was similarly abbreviated in the punning formula of the students' song (about illegitimate pregnancy, *Lieb' im Leibe*), which poetically foretold the course of the Faustian seduction.

A bit later, after the director has said that, since it's hard to satisfy an audience, one should instead aim to mystify them, the poet remarks that a poet scatters the blooms of spring in the path of his beloved, whereat the jester (the *lustige Person* who, by our interpretation, is analogous to the Mephistopheles of the "Prologue in Heaven"? tells him to engage in the business of poetry as one carries on a love affair.

He also tells the poet that "the most beautiful bloom of youth" will gather at his play. This elicits from the poet a gorgeous set piece, a nostalgic cry for the return of the early days, when he was still in the stage of unfolding, of becoming (*im Werden*), the Goethean fatality of defloration thus being interwoven with a key term in the German philosophy of Development (while the next line talks of *Liebe,* with *schwebt* to rhyme with *lebt*). The poet refers to a bud that, in the youthful days, promised wonders, and to the picking (literally "breaking") of endless flowers that richly filled the valleys. Then he had both the drive for truth and the delight in falsity (*den Drang nach Wahrheit und die Lust am Trug*). And he yearns for the return of the days when he experienced his impulses uncontrollably (*ungebändigt*).

The flower theme (*read:* the "deflowering" theme) obviously fits well with the theme of Faust's magically regained youth. But by approaching the youth-age alignment as we have, we hope to have provided the means of making clear how "politically" or "sociologically" tinged this biological imagery is. We are trying to suggest that, once a social order (with its "pyramidal" logic) has attained its scrupulous analogues in modes of "self-control" or "mortification," then imagery of youth can stand for general principles of *resistance,* however roundabout, symbolizing political or social motives not intrinsic to the biological condition as such.

In this sense, we believe, Gretchen's seduction becomes an imaginal substitute for the principle of riot (and of precisely such riot as a court minister, *né* romantic poet, would basically distrust if it were expressed politically rather than in terms of a sexual analogue). Poor Gretchen was, indeed, the sacrificial vessel of the negativistic principle, itself not essentially "sexual" or "biological" at all, but shaped by the thou-shalt-not's of governmental order. Age being the time when, physiologically, one must "rein in," the dream of youth regained can stand correspondingly for outbreak.

Incidentally, while such tendencies toward "riot" (in the sociopolitical sense) can be transferred to *sexual* terms, Faust's killing of Gretchen's brother points toward a subterfuge more often deemed "respectable" today: the imagining of violence in terms of physical brutality and murder. Here in the background of Goethe's play is an element that later came to the foreground, perhaps in keeping with the cult of the kill that overhangs the modern scene in general. But be that as it may, when the transference of sexual terms has been completed in the "flower" image, then seductive defloration (with its peculiar kind of "violation") can fit well with the conditions of *becoming* that are also, in principle, *identifiable* with upheaval in general.

In sum, once social tensions (themselves compounded of both permanent and changing elements) have been translated into terms of a given "myth," the myth then brings up resources of its own. These resources are then capable of purely internal development within their own terms, though the use of such resources will reflect the personal bias of the user. That is, the dialectic is "in principle" absolute, being limited only by the scope of language as such; but in practice it is conditioned by the limitations of the particular practitioner.

We might here mention a pamphlet, *Love and Death* (by G. Legman). It is an attack upon the kind of murder mystery which has become a characteristic of our culture to a disturbing degree. With a certain slapdash brilliancy, and with some of the excessiveness "natural" to the pamphlet as a literary genre, the author undertakes to show how the imagery of physical violence serves as a legally and socially approved substitute for "indecent" thoughts of sexual violation. But we would want to go a step farther off, contending that the sexual fantasies themselves are a displacement of political motives.

Political, social ("hierarchal" or "pyramidal") motives would thus be present not just in imaginings of sexual "glamour" but in one's views of "nature" generally. Since a child begins his experience with natural images and personal relations, the social motives implicit in these "immediate" experiences are at first glimpsed but as vague forms beyond a fog, like premonitions of some "higher" reality. (Recall, for instance, how Wordsworth experienced the overtowering mountain when he had stolen the boat, a moralistic fear being translated into terms of a natural image sublimely threatening, hanging over him like a judgment, and even rising higher as he retreated.) In so far as one's perceptions of a "natural hierarchy" or "order" are an imaginative response to the morality of a given social order, there is a respect in which poetic "nature" is but the *incipient* manifestation of *society*. And in this sense, whatever might be the differences or even contrasts between "rural" and "urban" motives, there would be a sense in which Goethe, the "youthful" romantic poet, had already contained such potencies as attained fulfillment in Goethe the elderly court minister.

Such relations as the step from possibility to actuality, from hope to fulfillment, from *Werden to Gewordensein,* from sprout to seed, from emotion to intellect, from poetry to criticism, from "community" to "society," from plan to organization, from "culture" to "civilization," from "spring" to "fall," from internality to externality, can be dramatized quite fittingly in terms of the development from youth to age. Add to this the fantasy of an illicit sexual defloration, and you have

plenty of incentives to get things reversed, thinking of the phantasma-
goria in *Faust* as unreal and of the love story as real; whereas the phan-
tasmagoria comes nearest to disclosing the social motives that shape
the love story, causing it to be the allegory in this work, while the "supernatural" and "preternatural" scenes bring us (within the sources of
this medium) nearer to the "literal truth."

VII. Walpurgis Night

Faust has said, "No" to the thou-shalt-not's. He has *essentially* vio-
lated the sanctities of private property (beginning with the time when
he furtively entered Gretchen's bedroom and piously spied upon her
privacy). He has been "sexually radical." And the result is a pandemonium: all hell breaks loose. The wild night could, with justice, be
interpreted at least in all these various ways:

It could symbolize the aftermath of the sexual violation, the general spirit of perversity (*Widerspruch*) that was unleashed by the completing of this plan, as though the seduction had been a preparation
for something to come next. Or it could be the symbolic or "mythic
description" of the sexual violation itself. (That is, whereas the literal act of copulation could not be represented, it could be acceptably
translated into "imaginal equivalents.") Or it could be the kind of political subterfuge we have already mentioned, an imagery whereby the
principle of revolutionary overthrow could be expressed, but in a safer
form, a form that turned the imagination away from explicitly political considerations.

(There is the possibility that once political motives have become
publicly transformed into their sexual analogues the psyche can spontaneously dream its politics in sexual terms. If anti-authoritarian motives which could not be confessed directly without embarrassment or
risk were translated into terms of sexual "sins of the flesh to which we
all are prone," then the psyche might cleanse itself by the confessing
of untowardnesses not politically suspect. And this writer's admiration
for the resourcefulness of the psyche is great enough to make him feel
sure that such kinds of consciousness and/or conscience can be developed on a grand scale, particularly when mankind has had centuries
upon centuries during which to perfect itself in such subterfuges. This
shift in the psyche began to take place, we would imagine, about the

time when the pagan custom of "sacred prostitution" began to be con-demned as fornication, a praying to false gods.)

There is also a figuring of the topsy-turvy here, in the most literal sense. Things are upside down, as if the riotous flight were really a descent. Thus recall the passage in the *Strudel* of Walpurgis Night (the Dream intermezzo) where the Versatile (*die Gewandten*) announce that, in their merry state, if they can't go on their feet, they'll go on their heads (*Auf den Füssen geht's nicht mehr, / Drum gehn wir auf den Köpfen*). It is also worth noting that they call themselves an army *von lustigen Geschöpfen*—and one of the three speakers of the "Prologue in the Theatre" is the jester, or *lustige Person,* whose analogies with Me-phistopheles we have already mentioned

A further indication of the same sort is that the Walpurgis Night episode has several "dirty" passages. Formally (as regards internal con-sistency, an aspect of the "second office") this fact helps accentuate the close linkage between the Walpurgis Night section and the ear-lier drunken student riot of Auerbach's cellar, which also is "dirty." Musically, the riot theme of Walpurgis night is *incipiently* present, or announced, in the episode of Auerbach's cellar. This episode of the students precedes Faust's seduction of Gretchen (thus containing it "in germ," as sloganized in the refrain *Lieb' im Leibe,* concerning the girl extramaritally pregnant); and the witches' revels follow the seduction (thus "summing it up" in the various ways we are now considering).

We should also recall that the perversity is sloganized in sheer mathematical design in another episode that is quite like these in style: the scene in the Witches' Kitchen, also prior to the seduction. Here is where the witches' version of the multiplication table is given, in mud-dled counting from one to ten with vague additions and subtractions, all of which adds up to nothing (*Und Neun ist Eins, / Und Zehn ist keins. / Das ist das Hexen-Einmal-Eins*). In this scene Mephistopheles makes the first glancing reference to Walpurgis Night.

As regards the "sociality" of this episode in particular, and of the work in general: It is notable that, unless we overlooked the lines, no-body discusses the possibility of Faust's marrying Gretchen in the first place, though she would certainly have jumped at the offer. We take this to mean that the great man wanted not Gretchen, but what her sacrifice stood for: namely, riot, as revealed in the episode of Walpurgis Night. Here the incipiently perverse scruples of the poet (who ranged from romantic pre-minister to ministerial post-romantic) lead him to imagine the perfect revelry. And it, in turn, is announced in the student drinking scene, with its call: "Long live freedom! Long live wine!" (*Es lebe die Freiheit! Es lebe der Wein!*) And when thinking of that scene we should not fail to recall also, from the standpoint of the *Strudel*, Mephistopheles' rousing song of the flea who was made a minister, to the great embarrassment of the other courtiers, since they didn't dare scratch themselves (whereat the students exultantly join in the final refrain proclaiming their right to kill fleas).

There is a section in the work itself where such "hierarchal" motives as we are here considering are explicitly considered, though to an excessive degree made possible by the conditions of the drama. We have in mind an early, preparatory scene ("Before the Gate") where we are afforded a quick survey of classes and their motives. Here are such representative figures as a student praising beer, tobacco, and a well dressed girl; solid citizens praising the comforts of peace; girl-conscious soldiers; respectable girls angling for marriage; lower-class girls, who are thought more susceptible to sexual advances; the old whore, whom we have already mentioned with respect.

Faust says that all the citizenry are celebrating the Rerisen Christ, since they themselves on this day have risen from all sorts of wretched places: hovels, shops, mills, factories, and the like. This drastic analogy is drawn by a man who is about to mortgage his immortal soul. So far as this text is concerned, when trying to discern the social coordinates of poetic "beauty," with its corresponding kinds of "catharsis," we would start from the observation that the opening "Prologue in Heaven" is not concerned with such esoteric lore of Heaven as, say, a Swedenborg might have dealt with.

A moderate instance appears in Faust's opening monologue, and specifically in connection with the term *Strudel* (here the whirlpool of time, *Zeitenstrudel*). The steps are these: First there was imagination expanding in bold flight to infinity; but now we are content with trifles, as one joy after another is shattered in time's whirlpool. Now Care nests deep within the heart, causing hidden pains, restlessly disturbing rest and pleasure [[. . .]] and so forth. The next step is particularly pointed to our purposes. This temporal Care, we are told, lies concealed behind ever changing masks, such as house and court, woman and child, water, fire, knife, poison, so that one trembles before all things that never strike and must weep constantly for things one never lost. To our way of thinking, this is a figurative way of say-

ing that the particulars of life itself have become infused with the spirit
of the *Strudel,* the pyramidal guilt or anguish. (We might remember it
when looking for possible social motives in the *Angst* which Heidegger
attributes to wholly metaphysical causes.)

Long as this has been, we have omitted very many of the correlations we noted when making our superficial index of the terminology
in this work. But perhaps we should mention one other primary problem of signatures: the historical or developmental problem, the "vatic"
dimension of a work, in metaphorically foretelling things that we can
only know literally after the event. Unquestionably such unfoldings
occur, since conditions wholly here now were emergently present in
the past. The problem is in an embarrassment of riches: the resources
of generalization and specification are such that, in critical *vaticinium
post eventum,* a critic is impoverished indeed if he can't show how any
given author anticipated the future, particularly if the critic can make
up his casuistry as he goes along, and if he never has to worry about fitting all his casuistries together by schematizing their underlying principles. (The critic usually solves the problem rhetorically by clamor-
ously despising schematizers, and thus frightening his reader into not
daring to do otherwise.)

Broadly: Once you discern in Goethe the idealistic philosophy of
the becoming (tied to his key word, *Geist*) you are on the way to finding that he anticipated Hegel and thereby anticipated both communism and Nazism. That's easy. But what of the *particulars,* then? When
Gretchen, accosted by her seducer on the street, first refuses to be *led
by him* (she will go home *ungeleitet*), we are helped to be modest in
hindsight prognosis here by the fact that the word for street in this text
is *Strasse.* Otherwise, when the becoming has been reduced to sex and
flower, and the internal conditions call for a meeting on the street,
we might be tempted to say that Gretchen's first intuition had been
correct when she rejected what was, in sexual disguise, the political
seductiveness of a *Gauleiter!*

VIII. Concluding Comments

Intrinsic to symbol-using as such there is the "principle of perfection,"
the delight in carrying out terministic possibilities "to their logical
conclusion," in so far as such possibilities are perceived. This "entelechial" motive is the poetic equivalent of what, in the moral realm, is

called "justice." It is equatable with both necessity and freedom in the sense that the consistent rounding out of a terminology is the very opposite of frustration. Necessary movement toward perfect symmetry is thus free.[2]

Extrinsically, the practical limitations of a given social order and of the given poet variously burden or complicate the search for perfect form in this purely technical sense. Diversities in their modes of life make people mysteries to one another. Discordant material interests produce "tensions" that complicate the ability to decide even in sheer theory what perfect justice would be, or what perfect poetic justice would be. Various kinds of partial advantage are rightly or wrongly deemed available, and personal "strategies" are developed in response to these partial purposes.

Insofar as such "strategies" are "imitated" for their own sake, the extrinsic motivations are brought back within the orbit of the intrinsic, where resources natural to poetic mediums often allow for degrees of frankness not otherwise possible. Simplest example: the playwright can dramatically attribute to a "fool" or a "villain" some attitude which he might not otherwise be able to voice. And thereby at least he could get it said (thus satisfying a primary requisite of symbolic resourcefulness). The dialogue form offers the same diplomatic possibility in purely ideational matters. The lyric and the monologue-like essay are usually more confined in this regard. Satire is, of course, a risky form

---

[2] However, a "principle of perfection," or "entelechial" motive, should by no means be thought of simply as a virtue to be saluted with delight. As exemplified in specialized disciplines, it can make for very ill-omened conditions. Apparently it can set the boldest scientific imaginations to dreams of artificial satellites, the "conquest of outer space," and similar "Faustian" grandiosities, while the humbler promises of applied science as a benefit to mankind are still ludicrously far from being redeemed. In its "aestheticism," its sheerly formalistic aim to carry the resources of a given medium to their ultimate conclusion, it can make for a variant of the perversely Gidean *acte gratuit,* but in a guise that fits only too well with the current "global" goads to victimage. Such unappeasability would seem to result when this purely speculative or technical adventurousness is combined with ambitions set by the pyramidal motives of the Strudel inevitable to even rudimentary kinds of political order, and drastically more so in the case of our present complex administrative problems. There is, of course, another kind of perfection conceivable: the perfection that a humanistic ideal of education might aim at. Yet at best, we sometimes fear, such an ideal would be but faintly compensatory.

(a rhetorical danger to which, perhaps, we are partially indebted for the splendid fantasy of *Gulliver's Travels,* since its high percentage of universal satire helped in principle to protect the author's references to local personalities and issues).[3]

"Dramatistically," we would develop a view of language that permits us to watch always for the "social pageantry" of a given work, while always watching closely its purely internal developments. In this connection we look not only for "key words" and their bearings upon one another, but even for *puns* on those words. For though puns are grandest when they "make sense," the simple joy with which audiences often greet even sheerly nonsensical puns would seem to indicate that, within the limitations of the situation, such a response is mainly to a sheer internality of language as such. (We admit, however, that a sly pornographic suggestion in the offing helps intensify the explosiveness of the "yak.")

Puns, as so conceived, cover a wider area than is usually attributed to them. The punning of a good poet is complicated enough to make one dizzy, if one tries to see *clearly* all the possibilities that flutter vaguely about the blurred edges of his vision. And, methodologically, it is hard to make sure just how far this punning goes (since a given poet's puns are not necessarily identical with the puns that an appreciative reader may himself hear as the "overtones"). But we believe that

---

[3] In the London *Times Literary Supplement* of August 29, 1952, there is a relevant article, "The Soviet Dilemma," discussing the difficulties that beset recent Russian drama when certain theorists in authority decided that drama depicting contemporary situations within Russia should not depict conflict, "negative" characters, and the like, since the "new type of humanity" arising in the Soviet system had outgrown such conditions. Interestingly enough, this doctrine was later deposed by higher authorities. And there was always available, of course, the drama of conflict and negativism as regards the treatment of relations to foreign capitalism. Not having been able to follow the controversy at first hand, we do not know what all was touched upon. But motives can emerge in paradoxical ways, where art is concerned. In the theater of Corneille and Racine, for instance, the motives of the French Revolution emerged mainly in sexual terms. The principle of "control" being royal and masculine, the principle of "riot" was expressed in terms of feminine sensibility and passion. And Euripides seems often to have used feminine characters (such as Medea, and as Agave in the *Bacchae*) to stand for "submerged" principles of revolt in the political order.

a technique of indexing key words can help make more specific exactly how a terminology works in the idiom or dialect of a given author.

For instance, let us cite one purely terministic development we noted in *Faust* solely as a result of our indexing. (An ideally perfect memory, endowed with ideal accuracy of perception, plus ideal ability to recall the "annunciation" of a theme which had emerged at a stage in the development before its "future" was wholly graspable, might have been able to note this correspondence without the aid of indexing.) When Faust is making his bargain with Mephistopheles, he puts the matter thus: Let the devil enchain him, if ever he says to some moment of experience, "Tarry! Thou art so lovely." The words in German are, *Verweile doch! du bist so schön.* Surely, thereafter, each time the word for "lovely" or "beautiful" (*schön*) was uttered by Faust with regard to Gretchen, the Ideally Remembering Reader would have renewed the vibrancy of that passage.

But such an ideal reader would go further. In that line, the word for "tarry" is *verweile.* And, much later, it comes to fruition thus: When the seduction is near its tragic end, and Faust has furtively come into the prison where Gretchen is being held, he urges her to hurry and escape with him. In her pathetic confusion she answers, "Oh, wait! / I am so glad to wait, where you are waiting." In the light of our earlier entry, *this is a pun.* In German it reads: *O weile! / Weil' ich doch so gern, wo du weilest. Verweile* has become *weil'* and *weilest.* Yet we are not through. Faust answers, "Hurry! If you do not hurry, we shall pay dearly." But the words for "hurry" here are *eile* and *eilest.* Thus have we gone impetuously from *verweile* to *weile* to *eile,* a Faustian progression indeed. The impetuous Faust, we might say, cuts Gretchen short. And we might note further that the abbreviated verb form weil' sounds like the word for "because," weil. And we have a theory that a deflectively causal word, at such a revealing moment in the text, is well worth dwelling upon. For we dare have hopes that, once the necessary intermediate steps have been supplied, such a perturbation might be interpretable as the "natural sign" of some characteristic motivational kink in the Goethean tangle of motives.

Just what kind of ownership does figure in Faust's *Liebestraum* (the "exalted" aspect of his designs on Gretchen)? Clearly, Faust wants to possess her not just as a body, but as a person endowed with a whole catalogue of modest virtues. But he wants to possess her bodily too, even though (or because?) the conditions of his bodily possession will act as a mockery of these very virtues which he appraises resignation-ally in his initial stage of exaltation.

He would personally possess the personal virtues of a Gretchen, but at one remove, for he shows no desire to be himself endowed with these virtues. They are presumably feminine. He wants to possess them, we might say, aesthetically, by sheer *sympathetic appreciation* of them, in an appreciation that would not be confined to nonacquisitive forms of admiration. He wants to own the virtues by owning their owner (a treasure outside himself, yet brought within his dominion—not by compulsion, but by persuasion).

His ownership "necessarily" involves a despoiling, the transforma-tion of Gretchen into a victim. (Indeed, as we have said, the virtues themselves add up to precisely such guilelessness as make her suscep-tible to victimage.) In saying that the despoiling is *necessary,* we have in mind the fact that this is the story of an act that was, in its essential origins, a *seduction,* a *conspiracy,* involving the *Lust am Trug* that we previously saw associated with the motives of youth in flower.

Also, there may be the motive of the explorer, the inventor, the pro-moter, the empire-builder, the discoverer of virgin soil, the man who fells virgin forests, the man who sails into new Keatsian seas. (By our interpretation, in Coleridge's "Ancient Mariner" the stage of drought or total depression begins immediately after the motives of sexual de-floration have been indicated, the steps being: (1) "like God's own head, the glorious Sun uprist [. . .]"; (2) "We were the first that ever burst / Into that silent sea [. . .]"; (3) "Down dropt the breeze, the sails dropt down [. . .]"; (4) "the bloody Sun, no bigger than the Moon"—this second manifestation being the sun that fixed the boat at noon, a time that is at many places in Coleridge's verse, as in balladry gener-ally, linked with the moment of marriage.)

Frankly, we don't know what all this adds up to. (Perhaps only to *keins,* like the *Hexen-Einmal-Eins?*) But we do believe that when in quest of basic human symbolism one should risk even many blind and pointless tentatives, in the attempt to understand what ideal types of human victimage there may be, and how they are related to whatever system of property and' propriety, public and private, goes with any given social order. For human relations are dogged at every turn by victimage, and the freedom with which poetry can concern itself with these matters prompts us to inspect poetic symbolizations above all for their ability to express all variants of victimage.

At the very least, surely, Gretchen is a variant of beauty in distress, whatever range of motives that role may cover. More specifically, she is a variant of the wronged and forsaken maiden, another figure dear to balladry (and there are many ballad-like accents in the verse most immediately connected with her and her plight).

What *is* the "curative" function in such victimage? When considering Burns's lovely lyric, "Oh, wert thou in the cauld blast [. . .] I'd shelter thee, I'd shelter thee," one glimpses the possibilities of a man who, sensitive, unpretentious, and put-upon, turns not to self-pity but to kindly thoughts of someone still worse off, a beauty whom he imagines in dire misfortune, in order that he, himself so unfortunate, might nonetheless imagine himself coming to her aid. Then lo! we find: After he has thus imagined himself Goethe's Faust, aiding her he next imagines that, in their happy amative union, they would be no less than royal, for she wad be his queen, wad be his queen.

Faust is frightfully torn by pity for Gretchen after he sees the drastic extent to which poetic justice has victimized her. But Goethe's vastly brainier project apparently involves him in a higher degree of self-consciousness than is found in Burns's lyric. We might put it thus: Where Burns begins by imagining the beauty already in a condition of distress, Goethe has gone a step farther back and imagined a character who, in his lust for a kind of power, himself brings upon his lady precisely the condition for which he will pity her. Indeed, prophesying after the event, we would say that in his original furtive penetration into her bedchamber Faust was so deeply moved by the "personality" of the room because this personality already contained the fate that he would impose upon it because, for "hierarchal" reasons, he needed to.

The desire for "power," as so translated into the terms of a sexual-personal "myth," is not absolute, we feel sure. It must be relative, involving subtleties of superiority and inferiority, with reflections going back and forth between these states, somewhat as when we see, on the sunless portion of a crescent moon, the solar light which reached it roundabout, by first lighting up the Earth, then being relayed to a portion of the moon hidden from the sun, and then coming back again to us, reflected from the moon. Which is probably to say, in effect, that we should consider the power motives as "lunatic," even while recognizing how conditions compel them into intricate being.

Probably we should note also that seductionism, as dramatically defined in this work, has a homosexual aspect, too (along with the sadistic aspect, seen lurking behind its pity). For it reveals a resistance to the "norms" of heterosexual union, at least as defined by the ortho-doxies of that particular society. Internal analysis seems to indicate that the scene of student revelry is *incipiently* the episode of Walpurgis Night. So among the "Faustian" strands might be that of homosexual-ity; though we should remember first that it is *radically modified* by the many other strands that go to make up the total weave and, second, that, from the standpoint of the "hierarchal psychosis," no "sexual" motive is deemed "primary," in so far as the sheer "biology" of sexual courtship is modified by *social* norms (that is, by *administrative* or *po-litical* courtship).

However, poetic "catharsis" is not by any means confined to *victimage*. Croce, in his *Aesthetics,* identifies catharsis with expression in general—and there is certainly a sense in which, for a typically symbol-using animal, there would be a kind of "cleansing" got by the sheer fact of "getting something said." More subtly, there are modes of catharsis internal to the work, respects in which it "purifies" itself, and not merely through the "pity, terror, and similar emotions" which Aristotle associates specifically with catharsis in tragedy. Returning to our earlier point about "perfection," we might end this discussion by indicating how the "entelechial" principle operates in a certain kind of poetry which does not deal with "victimage" in the clear ways of trag-edy, though attenuations of the sacrificial principle can be glimpsed here. This closing example is intended to indicate both how *external* reference would be involved in the hypothetical work and how a purely *internal* purification would take place, though here in the more Pla-tonist form of a "revelation." Thus:

1) The "principle of perfection" could not be said to operate in any immediate purpose, as when a person reaches for something that he intends to eat.

2) But a kind of "ultimate projecting" is possible. For instance, when reaching for food, one may be said to do so, not just as a hungering organism, but as a *zoon politikon.*

3) Thus, one might not just "reach." One might "steal't the food, or "take what is rightfully one's own," or "be graspingly overea-

ger," or "manifest good breeding," or "in one's zest, laughingly throw all proprieties to the wind and make a dive for it," etc.

4) Here would be a motive, in terms of "action," that would "transcend" the motive of sheer motion (the purely physiological processes involved in an organism's use of its hand as an instrument for helping to satisfy purely physiological need).

5) Now consider an example of this sort: A storywriter of the "sensitive" school builds a story about some "mysterious moment" of childhood, some realistically described incident that is somehow felt to symbolize a "deeper meaning."

6) This would be the Joycean use of "epiphany," the discovering or unveiling of a moment that stands for much more than its sheer materiality.

7) Imagine such a story as so constructed that the sheer motion of reaching for food had, flickering about its edges, some such motive as is "dogmatically" symbolized in Eve's taking of the apple. (Here is an example we recently noted of such a "food-sex channel of affinity"; In the mathematical center of D'Annunzio's *Triomphe de la Mort,* just before the chapter headed "New Life," consider the "suggestive" connotations with which the girl's biting into the bread is surrounded. Beads of moisture about the mark of the bite are observed as pointedly as though one were witnessing a lewd kind of annunciation.)

8) Next, think of our hypothetical story as expressing a motive which was felt by its author to be the "ultimate" addition to such reaching (not in its nature as sheerly physical, but as personal).

9) Next, think of such a reaching as being similarly motivated even in moments not thus touched with "revelation" (though the "transcendent" motive would here figure remotely and faintly).

10) The "ordinary" material act could thus always be felt as vaguely "striving" toward the "perfection" signalized at the moment of the "revelation." And this would be the "entelechial" motive, the fulfillment or realization of its particular nature, its sociality.

11) This sociality, or ideality, transcending the sheer physicality or materiality of the act could then be interpreted as the "principle of perfection" in the act (a "perfection" that could be interpreted supernaturally or sociologically or both, according to the preferences of the interpreter).

12) A design much like that of the Kantian *als ob* would be implicit here, if one looked upon each everyday motion of reaching *as though* it contained some measure of an ultimate reaching—whereat the everyday reaching would be viewed piously, as an act infused with spirit, rather than as "nothing but" the materially motivated behavior.

In sum, a catharsis purely internal to a poetic medium as such takes place when the cycle of a work's inner consistency is revealed or finished. Such emergence and completion being got in terms suited to the specific natures of the various literary genres, they will differ in accordance with the genres. As regards the "tragic pleasure," the completion is largely contrived in terms of "pity, fear, and the like emotions" that go with the imitation of a "perfect" sacrifice. But the story that, like many of Joyce's early pieces in *Dubliners,* is built about an "epiphany" makes for a different kind of purification: it involves a kind of Platonist transcendence whereby a "symbolic" motive is discerned in purely material things or situations.

While both such kinds of "perfection" are discussible in terms of a work's inner consistency, they also involve tensions extrinsic to the work and set by the "personality" of the social order. An "entelechial principle" in the social order (what we have called the "hierarchal psychosis") thus coincides with the purely linguistic kind, the need of symbolic systems as such to move "freely" toward the "necessity" of ideal consistency.

We believe that, as contrasted with the purely physiological motives of organisms that are not typically symbol-using, the motives of human beings are fatally pervaded by such dualism in the drive toward wholeness.

Or, at least, such is the case with art under the conditions of empire, with what we might call the "poetry of statecraft" (most clearly exemplified in works like Aeschylus's *Oresteia,* Virgil's *Aeneid,* Shakespeare's *Coriolanus* or *Julius Caesar,* Corneille's *Cinna,* Goethe's *Faust,* but discernible in even tiny, "playful," "nonpolitical" forms, once we have the rules for "anticipating" the transformations proper to the various artistic species).

The revelation or fulfillment in "moments" suggests the possibility of a reverse situation whereby even trivial acts can be remotely the exemplars of "perfect" acts, as though duration were but a departure, or temporary exile, from the culminative moment. (For instance, all details of the study preparatory to some particular professional career are, in a sense, variously "infused" with the spirit of the overall aim.)

We believe that the analysis of poetic forms, when approached from this attitude, points to the essential motives both of poetry in particular and of human relations in general. Such an approach would by no means deny the role of material factors in the shaping of human relations; but it would seek to analyze the modes of "magic" by which material elements become inspirited, when the quests for truth, goodness, and power (the useful or expedient) are translated into the corresponding quest for beauty.

Index

Printed in the United States
64965LVS00005B/115

9 781932 559347